Excellence in Fundraising in Canada

Volume Two

THE DEFINITIVE RESOURCE
FOR CANADIAN FUNDRAISERS

TORONTO

EDITED BY GUY MALLABONE

Excellence in Fundraising in Canada - Volume Two

Copyright © 2014 Civil Sector Press, a Division of The Hilborn Group Ltd.

All rights reserved. No part of this publication may be reproduced, stored in any material form (including photocopying or storing it in any medium by electronic means and whether or not transiently or incidentally to some other use of this publication) without the written permission of the copyright holder except in accordance with the provisions of the Copyright Act. Applications for the copy- right holder's written permission to reproduce any part of this publication should be addressed to the publisher.

Warning: The doing of an unauthorized act in relation to a copyrighted work may result in both a civil claim for damages and criminal prosecution.

IMPORTANT:

The following materials are intended as general reference tools for understanding the underlying principles, techniques and conventions of philanthropic fundraising in Canada. The opinions expressed herein are solely those of the authors. To ensure the currency of the information presented, readers are strongly encouraged to solicit the assistance of appropriate professionals.

Further, any examples or sample forms presented are intended only as illustrations. The authors, publishers and their agents assume no responsibility for errors or omissions or for damages arising from the use of published information or opinions.

Library and Archives Canada Cataloguing in Publication

Excellence in fundraising in Canada : the definitive resource for Canadian fundraisers / edited by Guy Mallabone.

Includes indexes. Description based on volume 2. ISBN 978-1-927375-23-5 (v. 2 : pbk.)

1. Fund raising--Canada. I. Mallabone, Guy, 1957-, editor

HV41.9.C3E93 2014   361.7068'10971   C2014-907086-1

Excellence in Fundraising in Canada – Volume Two

Published by Civil Sector Press Box 86, Station C, Toronto, Ontario, M6J 3M7 Canada

Telephone: 416-345-9403
Fax: 416-345-8010
www.charityinfo.ca
http://hilborn-civilsectorpress.com

ACKNOWLEDGEMENTS

Editor
Guy Mallabone

Managing Editor
Lisa MacDonald

Cover art and book design
John VanDuzer, WISHART.NET

Production
Alan Tang

Publisher
Jim Hilborn

GUY MALLABONE

Guy Mallabone, MA, CFRE, is veteran fundraising professional with 35 years' experience as a development officer working in the Arts & Culture, Social Services, and post-secondary educational sectors. Born in Calgary, Alberta he earned his Bachelor of Commerce degree at the University of Calgary and his Master of Arts in Philanthropy and Development, at St. Mary's University in Minnesota.

Mallabone is an internationally recognized subject matter expert in the practice of fundraising and non-profit management, and currently serves as the President and CEO of *Global Philanthropic Inc. (Canada)*, an international full-service fundraising consultancy.

He has served the Association of Fundraising Professionals as a founding chapter President and international board member, and remains active in support of the professional as a mentor, coach, and presenter. He has served as a member of the International board for the CFRE Certification program, and currently chairs *Canada Advancing Philanthropy*, the national advocacy group responsible for successfully launching Canada's first Master's degree program in fundraising at Carleton University.

Guy is a frequent speaker at professional conferences locally, nationally, and internationally. He is a professor at the University of Bologna, Italy, Master's degree program in fund development, and has authored many articles, a book titled *The Fundraising Audit Handbook*, and is co-author of the largest study on donor motivations and barriers completed in Canada.

In 1999, he was selected as the fundraising professional of the year by AFP's Edmonton & Area Chapter, and again by AFP's Calgary Chapter in 2011. In 2009, Guy was recognized by Alberta Venture Magazine as one of Alberta's *Fifty Most Influential Citizens*, and by the Calgary Herald newspaper as one of the city's *Twenty Most Compelling Citizens*.

PREFACE

In order to understand what it means to raise money successfully, students and practitioners, volunteers and staff, must develop both a foundation of basic fundraising skills and an understanding of how to apply those skills within the context of other related fundraising initiatives. Volume One of *Excellence in Fundraising in Canada* focused on providing many of the "inside-the-pyramid" skills needed to operate a successful integrated fundraising program in Canada. Volume Two builds on these fundamentals, but also looks beyond the traditional pyramid to include topics such as diversity, international fundraising, fundraising metrics, and gaming; subjects that may be less familiar to some fundraising professionals.

read more…

The original idea for this book came from two great anthologies in fundraising. The first, *Achieving Excellence in Fundraising* has been a major success and taught us about the Rosso model in fundraising. A second edition, published by Jossey-Bass and edited by Eugene R. Temple, also became an outstanding resource for this profession. The second anthology, *The NonProfit Handbook in Fundraising*, published by AFP/Wiley and edited by Jim Greenfield, was equally groundbreaking in its contribution to the growth and professionalization of those working in the charitable sector. In both cases, dozens of scholars and expert fundraisers participated in the writing of the books; resulting in a true collaboration of thought, experiences and ideas, which in turn allowed many front-line practitioners to learn about best practice and how to put ideas into action.

We are confident that *Excellence in Fundraising in Canada, Volume Two*, will further extend the uniquely Canadian perspective that *Excellence in Fundraising in Canada, Volume One* brought to the existing body of fundraising knowledge. This book includes contributions from 18 Canadian fundraising professionals, all leaders in their field. Each author in Volume Two (different from those in Volume One) has contributed knowledge gained in Canada's non-profit sector - primarily through hands-on experience. In addition, many have also engaged in broader research, contributing in other ways to our understanding of what it means to work in fundraising in this country.

I had three main goals in producing this book:

Encourage best practice. This book is the result of tapping the best minds in our country on key topics of importance to fundraisers. It is important to teach our students, reinforce professional development in our practitioners, and remind ourselves that the techniques identified in this book have consistently shown results superior to those achieved through other means, and therefore can be used as a benchmark. *Excellence in Fundraising in Canada* places a clear emphasis on skill-based learning and best practice, as seen through a practitioner's lens.

Share the Canadian experience. Each author was asked to define best practice within their chapter, from a Canadian perspective and to provide a Canadian voice to the subject matter. Whenever possible, we have identified Canadian heroes, included Canadian examples and referenced Canadian expertise.

Provide an introduction to key fundraising concepts. This book provides the reader with a solid introduction to each topic presented. It's not designed to provide an in-depth exploration of all that could be written on the topic, but rather an excellent overview of key themes, allowing the reader to become adequately familiar with the subject matter. At the end of each chapter, the author has provided additional references for further exploration.

Excellence in Fundraising in Canada, Volume Two, has the integrity of an integrated work, yet builds on the platform established by Volume One. Each chapter addresses and contributes to an important fund development concept. As in Volume One, this book doesn't have to be read in sequential order. The reader can pick and choose from specific chapters that they wish to access.

Excellence in Fundraising in Canada, Volume Two, is a natural companion to Volume One, serving as a must-have resource for any new professional or those in mid-career who are looking to expand their skillset on a journey of continuous improvement.

In conclusion, *Excellence in Fundraising in Canada, Volume Two* is a useful tool for today's Canadian fundraising professional. It's written by Canadians, for Canadians and is packed with practical and applicable information.

E.H. Guy Mallabone
Calgary, Alberta
September, 2014

DR. ERIC P. NEWELL, O.C., AOE, FCAE

Excellence in Fundraising in Canada, Volume Two will serve as an important handbook in the non-profit sector in Canada by bolstering the capacity of fundraisers through application of the lessons learned in this book. In this way, they can help strengthen the sector by raising the resources and funding for critical programs and mission delivery.

Particularly in Canada, it has long been recognized that a robust and resilient non-profit sector is critical to strong and healthy communities and is a vital component of our nation's economy. Canada's non-profit sector is the second largest in the world and, according to Statistics Canada, tops $100 billion in annual economic activity. We have over 170,000 non-profit organizations employing more than two million people.

After several decades working with many non-profit organizations, I have found the single largest barrier to them realizing their potential is the difficulty attracting and retaining sustainable funding. It is certainly not for lack of effort, but many such organizations lack the experience and expertise to implement a highly effective and efficient ongoing advancement and fundraising program. In addition, the challenge is not getting easier. The Canadian Council of Chief Executives which comprises the CEO's of Canada's top 150 corporations determined that the annual average number of serious donation requests for each these companies exceeded 4,000. That means about 20 requests per business day and even though virtually all are in support of worthy causes, only about 10% are successful. More than ever before, success in the non-profit sector will depend on the capacity and effectiveness of staff charged with fund development and advancement.

As with corporations, individual philanthropists target their charitable investments and often, particularly for large gifts, the choice is deeply personal. In my own life I believe strongly that education is the great equalizer of opportunity. Accordingly many of the philanthropic gifts made by my wife and me provide for scholarships and bursaries largely oriented to the less fortunate members of society. We have placed a strong emphasis on creating educational and economic opportunities for Aboriginal youth designed to be a "hand up," not a "hand out." In building on this belief I founded *CAREERS: The Next Generation*, a non-profit Foundation, in 1997. Since then, CAREERS has helped guide over 500,000 high school students along the path to rewarding careers. This is extremely motivating because we are changing lives for a better future. Good fundraisers recognize the need to understand such passions and driving forces of potential philanthropists and then to develop the opportunities for them to "invest in their dreams."

Excellence in Fundraising in Canada, Volume Two, edited by Guy Mallabone, an outstanding professional with an extensive fundraising and advancement background, features the contributions from 18 leading Canadian fundraising professionals. While not ignoring the vast experience gained in philanthropy and fund development in the United States, the authors bring a uniquely Canadian perspective to this body of knowledge.

Volume Two, in particular, is designed as a helpful handbook broken down into logical chapters defining a total development program. The style is not academic prose, but rather compelling human stories providing useful strategies and tactics. Every fundraiser will want to have it as a ready reference.

Dr. Eric P. Newell
Edmonton, Alberta
September, 2014

Dr. Eric Newell, O.C., AOE, FCAE

Dr. Eric Newell is a retired Alberta business executive with a stellar history of corporate leadership and achievement, as well as an exemplary record of service to industry and community. His career has taken him to Imperial Oil Limited and Esso Petroleum Canada, but he is perhaps best known for his tenure at Syncrude Canada Ltd. where he served for 14 years as CEO (1989-2003) and for 9 years as Chairman (1994-2003).

Dr. Newell plays an active role promoting and creating opportunities for the wider community and is well-known for his successful and ongoing efforts to strengthen partnerships between education and business, and for championing corporate social responsibility. He served on the University of Alberta Board of Governors (1996-2002), before becoming the 18th Chancellor of the University (2004-2008). Among his numerous awards are four honorary degrees and he was appointed an Officer of the Order of Canada in 2000 and was inducted into the Alberta Order of Excellence in 2004.

TABLE OF CONTENTS

PREFACE
Guy Mallabone, CFRE

FOREWORD
Dr. Eric P. Newell
7

Chapter 1
A History of Philanthropy in Canada
Patricia Hardy, ACFRE
13

Chapter 2
Human Resources in Fundraising
Tim McConnell
29

Chapter 3
Fundraising in a Small Shop
Ligia Peña, CFRE
53

Chapter 4
Measuring Performance
Karen Van Sacker
83

Chapter 5
Organizational Culture
Kelly Morris and Andrea Morris
109

Chapter 6
Diversity in Fundraising
Krishan Mehta and Deborah Greenfield, CFRE
121

Chapter 7
Advocacy and Fundraising
Christopher F. Holz
135

Chapter 8
Telefundraising
Dan Abraham
153

Chapter 9
International Fundraising
Cathy Daminato
169

Chapter 10
Charitable Gaming
Ted Garrard
185

Chapter 11
Sponsorship
Brent Barootes
197

Chapter 12
Fundraising Creative
John VanDuzer
215

Chapter 13
Communication and Major Gifts
Anne (Coyle) Melanson, CFRE
229

Chapter 14
Fundraising and Social Media
James Howe
243

Chapter 15
Philanthropic Naming
Vincent E Duckworth, CFRE
259

Chapter 16
Entrepreneurial Fundraising
Kathryn Babcock, CFRE
277

Chapter 17
Grantwriting
Rob Peacock, CFRE
291

Chapter 18
Charity in Business
John Baker and John Pepin
305

CHAPTER 1

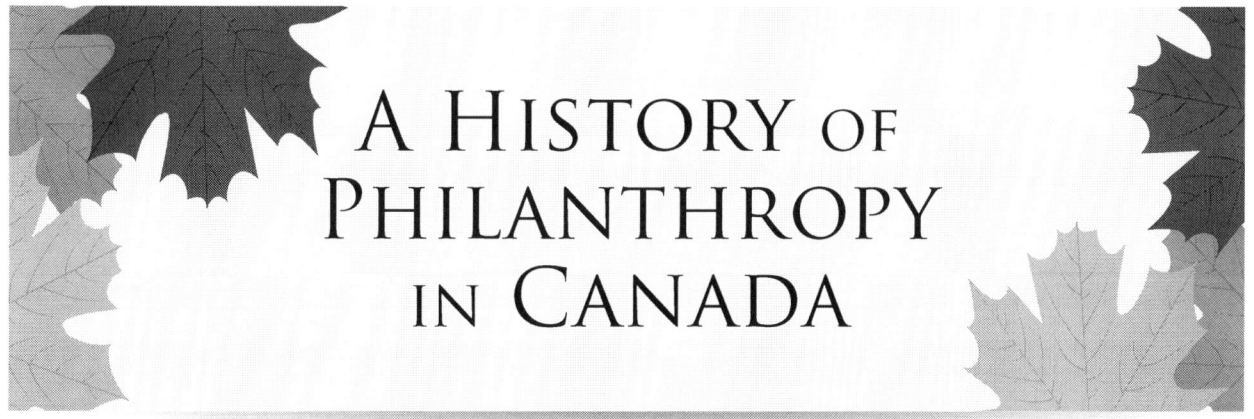

A History of Philanthropy in Canada

PATRICIA HARDY, MA, ACFRE

If you were launching a fundraising program in Canada today, do you believe that you would do the same things if you were working in the United States? As Canadian fundraisers, we often do not give this much thought; however, examining differences in fundraising practices offers insight into fundraising and its unique history in Canada.

read more…

Until recently, there has been scant original research about Canadian fundraising practices. That's all changing now. We're beginning to see Canadian studies of prospect identification techniques using Canadian demographics and psychographics, the economic contribution of Canadian voluntary organizations, and the use of Canadian government household statistics in market research to develop proposals for public policy change.

There are no comprehensive books about the history of philanthropy in Canada; however, there are two important pieces of work that are valuable for this subject. Samuel Martin's, *Essential Grace and Poverty*, and *Poorhouses and Private Philanthropy*, written by the Senior Scribes of Nova Scotia. Martin's book focused on government funding of the health, education, social service, culture and religious sectors and on how fundraising activities attempted to fill the gap when there was a shortage of government funding. The Senior Scribes focused on the early history of social welfare in Nova Scotia.

Martin's and the Senior Scribes contribution to the body of knowledge about philanthropy in Canada is significant because their scholarship examined the interplay of relationships between governments, churches and private philanthropy in the humanistic perspective. This institutional triad of government, church and private giving marked the unique genesis and evolution of a Canadian philanthropy already ensconced in a societal consciousness of social advance in comparison to our American neighbours. According to Bremner, in the United States philanthropy "has been one of the principle methods of social advance,"[1] while in Canada, social advance was rooted in those complex relationships between governments, churches and the community.

In particular, from the earliest days, Canadians have relied on their government to provide a social safety net, whereas the more individualistic tradition of the United States stimulated a philosophy of voluntary action for the public good.

While Canadians adopted many fundraising traditions from the United States of America, the two countries enjoy different political and economic histories. The basis for political order in the US has been built, in many ways, on an ethos of "life, liberty and the pursuit of happiness" whereas the Canadian approach has focused on "peace, order, and good government." Neither approach warrants greater merit than the other; however the evolution of distinctive political cultures has directly influenced unique philanthropic histories on both sides of the border.

For Canada, the diversification of philanthropy is as old a reality as philanthropy itself, but we are only now coming to understand and address the relationships between the philanthropic ideal and our culturally diverse reality.

Canada's population is spread across a huge landmass, mainly within one hundred kilometers of the US border. The north is sparsely populated, primarily by First Nations and Inuit people, while the rural Prairies are still largely a mix of early European settlers. Vancouver on Canada's west coast experienced a huge influx of Asians in the years prior to Hong Kong returning to China while the United Nations called Toronto the most diverse city in the world. Depending on where you are in Canada you will have a different experience of diversity in people's origins and language.

Our culture, diversity and history of philanthropy in Canada deserves a separate telling that informs us, as professional fundraisers, about elements of our national culture, social development and different donor motivations.

DEFINING PHILANTHROPY

This chapter uses a very simple definition of philanthropy: philanthropy is the practice of voluntary giving and receiving.

Of course, there are many aspects to what could be called the "philanthropic urge" – the desire to contribute to provide benefits for a broader and different community beyond one's immediate family. For Christians, it can be an intensely personal commitment to following the example of Christ by healing the sick, feeding the poor and helping the needy. Other religions, too, call on adherents to care for the less able. For humanists, the "philanthropic urge" may be rooted in a secular desire to help others – be it kindness, neighbourliness or shared ambitions for one's clan or community.

---

1   Bremner, R.H. (1988). *American Philanthropy*. Chicago: The University of Chicago Press. p. 2.

In Canada, there tends to be a particular ambivalence towards the very idea of philanthropy. Canadians place a very high value on personal kindness. The tradition of "neighbours-helping-neighbours" is as Canadian as our harsh winters - from which cooperative practices may have evolved as a means to thrive in difficult climates. Despite a history of community orientation, there still remains a significant body of thought in Canada that is uncomfortable with the idea of philanthropy. Some argue that community reliance on philanthropy gives the wealthy inordinate power to shape society according to their personal beliefs. The most egalitarian among us are offended at seeing community institutions (from museum and art gallery wings, to treatment and research centers in hospitals, to major buildings on university campuses) bearing the names of rich donors.

Those on the political left are concerned that the practice of philanthropy "lets the government off the hook" by supporting services that government should be duty-bound to provide to all citizens. In fact, over the past several decades in Canada organizations that once focused primarily on mutual support and direct help for those in need (from churches to labour unions to ethnic organizations) have identified political and lobbying action intended to generate government spending on their causes as a key part of their "charitable" duty, dedicating resources to these political actions that might previously have been spent to provide direct services to those in need. This sort of "anti-philanthropy philanthropy" is not unique to Canada, but it pervades virtually every part of the Canadian philanthropic landscape.

The term philanthropy means different things to different people and the uses and meanings of the word have changed over time and will likely continue to change, but the "philanthropic urge" itself is manifested in one form or another in virtually all societies, including early Canadian Aboriginal societies.

EARLY ABORIGINAL INFLUENCE

The history of philanthropy in Canada can be traced back to the practices of indigenous peoples who lived here before European settlement.

First Nations traditions include the idea of reciprocity and the "honour of giving."[2] For example, noted Buffalo hunter and Métis leader Gabriel Dumont was an early philanthropist who always took a last run through the buffalo herd to shoot animals for those families who did not have anyone to hunt for them. Some of the earliest recorded instances of philanthropy included the vital assistance indigenous people provided to early explorers and settlers, many of whom would have died without the support of First Nations people.

There was often a ritual element to Aboriginal philanthropy. Potlatches were elaborate give-away feasts used for various purposes. They facilitated food exchanges between groups and were also mechanisms for people to rise in the social scale.[3] Many lodges and service clubs to this day also include ritual elements that celebrate the shared purpose of members and recognize and honor individual contributions.

THE FRENCH INFLUENCE

In the 1600's, early French colonies in Quebec struggled with disease and poverty. These problems were so widespread and public begging became such a nuisance that, in 1685, the Governor established the Bureau of the Poor. This bureau was a Christian charity responsible for identifying the "unfortunate and miserable poor" and doing three things; ensure no one starved, find useful work for those capable of working and put an end to the public annoyance created by beggars.[4] This does not sound very different than

---

2   Wells, R.A. (1998). *The Honor of Giving*. Indiana University Centre on Philanthropy.
3   Dickenson, Olive. (1992). *Canada's First Nations*. Toronto: McClelland & Stewart Inc. p. 67. Note: Interestingly, the Canadian Government outlawed the potlatch in 1885, in part because of their belief that potlatches were a detriment to the expansion of the nation's economy. The anti-potlatching law was never actually repealed through formal legislative action; rather it was merely deleted from the Canadian legal codes in 1951.
4   Martin, Samuel. (1985). *An Essential Grace: Funding Canada's Health Care, Education, Welfare, Religion and Culture*. Toronto: McClelland and Stewart. p.59.

the way many communities are dealing with homeless people begging on the streets today.

The Bureau for the Poor appointed two women in each town to go door to door to collect alms. They were instructed not to press people for donations but "to allow all to contribute according to their means and dictates of conscience."[5] If this also sounds familiar it is because today's best practices in fundraising solicitation also encourage us to do this.

The next one hundred and fifty years saw the evolution of a symbiotic relationship between government and the Church with the French Crown providing resources to sustain a modest level of health care, education and welfare for settlers, while the Catholic Church provided relief to the poor and established alms houses for the aged, crippled and orphaned. Of course, these developments co-existed with instances of individual altruism and the pioneer ethic of helping a neighbour that is so integral to our history.

There are clear echoes of that relationship between the French government and the Catholic Church in today's interactions between social services and the government. Today, many social services combine reliance on government support with private efforts to raise funds, as did the Catholic Church in 17th century Quebec. While channeling money from the French Crown, the Church urged financially self-sufficient pioneers to make their own parishes self-sufficient through personal donations.

This practice of the church providing relief to the poor continued after the Plains of Abraham battle in 1759 until the French relinquished all territorial claims to what would become Canada.

THE BRITISH INFLUENCE

Early British rule followed the British Colonial tradition where the government did not want to provide money but wanted settlers to become independent and take care of themselves. This marked an abrupt change from the French system in Quebec and by the early 1800's the colonial government adopted the French practice of subsidizing church welfare organizations on a regular basis. This practice further cemented the Canadian tradition of government funding for private organizations to meet social needs without the government assuming the burden of delivering services directly.

Another key element of the British tradition – systematic measures to encourage charitable giving – also became part of the emerging Canadian tradition. With its roots in medieval times, Christian ideals, Roman precedents, and the Common Law, government permitted charitable donors to entrust property known as endowments usually to the church or other public authorities for charitable purposes. These endowments were part of a complex set of activities involving the Crown, noble families, the church, municipal bodies, guilds and other public entities through which poverty, dependency, and other needs were attended to. This British tradition subsequently had a great deal of influence on future Canadian practice.

Initially most charitable activity in Canada took the form of self-help and mutual help organizations focusing on members of the same family, ethnic group or religion. People in all parts of what was to become Nova Scotia began to set up their own self-help groups. In 1786, the Charitable Irish Society of Halifax was established with eighty-eight members at a meeting of merchants, fishermen, barristers, surgeons, justices, innkeepers, gentlemen and tobaccaneers, held in the Golden Ball Tavern.[6] The Society was founded to aid Irish Nationals "who shall be reduced by sickness, old age, shipwreck or other misfortune."[7]

The original parameters for service were changed in 1795 to include all suffering people, as well as financial aid for education.[8] At the same time, the Saint George's Society was organized in Halifax to provide assistance to needy persons of English or Welsh origins.[9] By the 1920's, the Charitable Irish Society began providing students with scholarships to Dalhousie University and later to Saint Mary's.[10]

During the early and mid -1800's numerous societies and organizations were established to help the needy. In addition to the groups for people of Irish,

---

5   ibid.

6   Nova Scotia Historical Review. (1986). The charter membership of the charitable Irish society 6 (1) p. 8.
7   Harvey, R.P. (1986). "*Black beans, banners and banquets: the Charitable Irish Society of Halifax at Two Hundred.*" Nova Scotia Historical Review. p.17.
8   ibid.
9   Senior Scribes of Nova Scotia. (1996). *Poverty, poor houses and private philanthropy*. Halifax: Queen's Printer, Communications Nova Scotia. p.38.
10 Nova Scotia Historical Review. (1986). The charter membership of the charitable Irish society 6 (1) p. 8 -15.

English and Welsh origins there were organizations that helped debtors in jail, and benevolent societies for almost every ethnic group and interest, as well as church-related missions and social welfare organizations. Each wave of immigration saw new charitable organizations started to help their particular group. Trade unions and fraternal societies offered protection for their members against financial loss resulting from unemployment, sickness, accident and death at a time when Government relief was sparse and inconsistent.

As Canadian society and our sense of community matured, we have seen increasing patterns of philanthropy that reach beyond particular affinity groups to address the needs of the community as a whole.

CANADIAN DEFINITION OF CHARITY: ELIZABETHAN POOR LAW

Following on English precedent, Canadian governments have provided a range of encouragements for charitable giving, including favourable tax treatment for charitable donations. These measures have their historical foundations in the Statute of Charitable Uses of 1601, also known as the Elizabethan Poor Law and the English Poor Law, passed by the British Government in 1601,[11] permitting the creation of charitable trusts and endowments to support schools, poor relief and general civic purposes.

The Statute of Charitable Uses of 1601 provided for collection of public funds and marked the beginning of government involvement in philanthropy/charity. The Statute sought to rationalize the administration of private charities: to specify the purposes for which funds could be devoted to charity, to ensure such funds were applied to the uses specified by donors, and to place the private charity under the supervision of the State. This statute was applied by the British to Canada's laws and even today is the basis for Canada's definition of charity.

Mid to late 1800's

This period saw the continued proliferation of organizations established to help particular segments of society, along with the emergence of large "legacy" philanthropic contributions and the genesis of provincial government support for hospitals.

Fur trader and merchant James McGill left £10,000 and his forty-six acre Montreal property to a provincial commission for the purposes of endowing McGill University. His family attempted for eight years to stop the donation but it went ahead in 1821. Historian, Michael Bliss says, McGill University "emerged as the first important creation of Canadian merchant philanthropy."[12]

Everywhere in Canada, this period saw a proliferation of charitable organizations and increasing government efforts to meet social needs. In 1820, the Halifax Poor Man's Friend Society, which provided food, clothing and fuel for the destitute and found work for the able bodied, was founded by a committee of prominent Methodist merchants. The Halifax Methodist Female Benevolent Society helped clothe the poor with garments of their own making.

In Montreal, the General Hospital was started by the Sisters of Charity in 1747, and by 1821 concerned citizens launched a fundraising campaign following the failure of appeals for financing to government and the governor-general. The new Board of Directors continued fundraising efforts and began construction of a new hospital building by mid-year. Donors to the campaign included John Richardson, Samuel Gerrard and John Molson.[13]

In 1830 the first provincial operating grant made to a hospital happened in what was then known as Upper Canada (the current Toronto region), to the York General Hospital. The £100 donation became an annual allotment[14] and marked the beginning of provincial government support for hospitals.

Concerned about poverty and people who were not working, two hundred and fifty people attended an 1836, public meeting held in Upper Canada. This meeting resulted in the introduction of the House of Industry Act that established public workhouses.[15]

In 1839, Charles Fredrick Allison purchased a building site in Sackville, New Brunswick to be used

---

11 Senior Scribes of Nova Scotia. (1996). *Poverty, poor houses and private philanthropy*. Halifax: Queen's Printer, Communications Nova Scotia. p.15.

12 Bliss, Michael. (1987) *Northern Enterprise*. Toronto: McClelland and Stewart Inc. p. 126.

13 Martin, Samuel. (1985). *An Essential Grace: Funding Canada's Health Care, Education, Welfare, Religion and Culture*. Toronto: McClelland and Stewart. p. 62 and 63.

14 ibid.

15 Smandych, R.C. (1991) *Upper Canada considerations about rejecting the English Poor Law, 1817-1837*. Winnipeg: University of Manitoba. p. 42.

for the establishment of a school that became Mount Allison College in 1858. Allison made a ten-year donation to the school of £100 per annum.[16]

Support for the treatment of physical and mental illness was also a concern and in 1841, Hugh Bell, a Methodist and the mayor of Halifax, gave his first year's salary to the creation of an asylum for the mentally ill.[17]

Orphaned children and unwed mothers had always been a concern and in 1849, at the invitation of the Archbishop of Halifax, The Sisters of Charity, a Catholic religious order, traveled from New York to Halifax to establish a facility for the care of orphaned Roman Catholic children. After two years, the Home of the Guardian Angel was caring for one hundred and twenty five children as well as providing refuge for unwed mothers.[18]

Religious orders were very important to early Canadian society as Sisters travelled far and wide to care for orphans and unwed mothers and in many cases they began hospitals and schools that are still operating today. In 1844, the Grey Nuns from the Sisters of Charity at the Hospital General in Montreal ventured to St. Boniface, Manitoba, on the Red River in today's downtown Winnipeg, and in 1845 the sisters undertook the work of teaching in Bytown (today's Ottawa) and in 1849 opened an orphanage in Québec City.

The Sisters of Misericordia also originated in Québec and in 1898 three sisters travelled to Winnipeg to establish an orphanage and home for unwed mothers. Their work evolved into a hospital and a school of nursing. Sisters in these orders were good fundraisers who managed to find local revenue to carry on their work. The number of women entering religious orders declined over the years and most of the organizations begun by charitable orders have now been taken over by governments while maintaining affiliated charitable foundations to raise philanthropic dollars to supplement government services.

Social gospel

The mid-1800's saw the rise of the Social Gospel Movement, which in Canada caused a shift in focus from individualism to collective well-being.

This philosophy of collective well-being forms the basis of Canada's present day social service network, including its universal health care system. This period also saw an elevation of public esteem for altruism, stimulating a flow of large philanthropic gifts to establish concert halls, theaters, schools, universities and hospitals – often bearing the name of the generous donors of the gifts, although this was less common in Canada than in the U.S. Canadian Social Gospellers tended to donate their money to their churches, which then allocated funds as they saw fit for the good of the community. The Social Gospel Movement was instrumental in shaping both the Canadian public's understanding of social problems and it's penchant for social reform.

In 1914, Social Gospellers and other reformers met in Ottawa at the First National Council on Social Welfare. Here we see the emergence of the "political action as philanthropy" theme in Canadian philanthropy. Discussions at these meetings concerned health care and education and many Canadian hospitals and schools were legacies of the strong support given during this period. Other results of the Social Gospel in Canada movement were declarations by all major denominations, which drew attention to systemic injustice in the country's economy and also proposed remedies. The eight-hour workday, living wages, old age pensions, labor safety, public arbitration, and public ownership of utilities were all legacies of the Social Gospel Movement in Canada.[19]

World War I breathed new life into the Social Gospel Movement. Social Gospel and subsequent reform movements in Canada spawned numerous charitable organizations. Business and labour groups decided to end the proliferation of fundraising campaigns and in 1918 the Community Chest (the pre-cursor to the United Way) held Canada's first federated fundraising effort for community services in Toronto.[20]

---

16 Rawlyk, G.A. Editor. (1990). *The Canadian Protestant Experience: 1790 to 1990*. Burlington: Welch Publishing Company. p. 231.
17 Scobie, C.H.H. and Grant, J.W. Editors. (1992). *The Contribution of Methodism to Atlantic Canada*. Montreal and Kingston: McGill. p. 99.
18 Ibid p. 40.

19 Clarke, B. (1996). *English Speaking Canada from 1854*. Murphy & Perin. *A Concise history of Christianity in Canada*. Toronto: Oxford University Press. p.334.
20 Martin, Samuel. (1985). *An Essential Grace: Funding Canada's Health Care, Education, Welfare, Religion and Culture*. Toronto: McClelland and Stewart. p. 69.

PHILANTHROPY IN THE 19TH AND 20TH CENTURIES

In 1869, Timothy Eaton opened a dry-good and haberdashery business at Yonge and Queen Street in Toronto, Ontario. Eaton's business would become Canada's largest department store with prominent buildings in every city. The company then established the Eaton Foundation that dispensed the family's charitable donations.[21] In 1910, Timothy Eaton's' son John, donated $360,000 to build and equip the Toronto General Hospital's Timothy Eaton surgical wing.[22]

In the 1870's, Hart Massey used a considerable amount of the fortune that he had amassed through his farm machinery business to build Methodist churches in Ontario. In some cases he also used his wealth to advance his own views. Examples of this were his $100 donation to the Police Benevolent society as thanks for police protection received during confrontations with Knights of Labor union organizers, and his large gift in 1888 to Victoria University in Cobourg because he did not want it to merge with the University of Toronto. He also contributed $60,000 to complete the building of Fred Victor Mission for the homeless in downtown Toronto.[23] Finally, in 1918, Massey philanthropy led to the creation of Canada's first private family foundation, The Massey Foundation, established with the residuals of the estate of Hart Massey to allow his children to control a vehicle "of permanent usefulness."[24]

This period in Canadian philanthropic development also saw great advances in individual philanthropy to cultural organizations, some examples include:

- Massey Hall, the famous concert hall in Toronto was built with a donation of $152,000 from Hart Massey in remembrance of his eldest son who died suddenly in the prime of his life.[25]

- The Andrew Carnegie Foundation contributed $US 2,559,660 to establish libraries in Canada.[26]

- The Winnipeg Art Gallery established in 1912 when a group of Winnipeg businessmen, recognizing "the civilizing effects of art," each contributed $200 and rented two rooms in the old Federal Building at the corner of Main and Water Streets, to become the first civic art gallery in Canada.[27]

- In 1913 the Royal Victoria Theater (a national historic site) opened in Victoria, British Columbia thanks to a contribution from Simon Leiser.[28]

PHILANTHROPIC RESPONSE TO DISASTER

Canadians have always prided themselves on their response to disaster. One early example of this followed the 1917 Halifax Harbor explosion where a munitions ship exploded three weeks before Christmas, killing 1,600 people instantly[29] and leaving thousands maimed and homeless.

The worldwide relief effort raised $30,000,000.00. Within 48 hours of the event, the Free Press and Winnipeg Tribune announced the formation of separate Halifax relief funds. Reminding readers the calamity affected the entire country, the Winnipeg Free Press opened its columns for donations "to facilitate sending to the sufferers in Halifax the assistance of which they stand in such dire and pressing need."[30] Nine days after the explosion, the Free Press announced the relief fund had raised $34,182.19 "from all parts of the country," including Saskatchewan, New Brunswick, Grand Forks, N.D., and 25 Manitoba communities.[31]

The First World War provided more opportunities for partnership between government, private organizations and individuals. In 1917, Parliament passed the War Charities Act, which allowed charities to register

---

21 ibid p. 9.
22 McQueen, R. (1998). *The Eatons: The Rise and Fall of Canada's Royal Family.* Toronto: Stoddard Publishing Co. Ltd. p.1.
23 Collins, P. (1977). *Hart Massey.* Don Mills: Fitzhenry & Whiteside Limited. p. 29 and 33, 34 and 48.
24 Martin, Samuel. (1985). *An Essential Grace: Funding Canada's Health Care, Education, Welfare, Religion and Culture.* Toronto: McClelland and Stewart. p. 263.
25 Collins, P. (1977). *Hart Massey.* Don Mills: Fitzhenry & Whiteside Limited. p. 29.
26 Rochester. M.K. (1996). "American philanthropy abroad: library program support from the Carnegie corporation." Libraries and Culture, 31 (2) p. 350.
27 History|Winnipeg Art Gallery Web Site. http://wag.ca/about/facts/history
28 Leonoff, 1995, p. 233).
29 Dupuis, Michael, Winnipeg Free Press, Reprinted Dec 12, 2012, Wikipedia, http://www.winnipegfreepress.com/opinion/fyi/shock-waves-181651901.html
30 Ibid.
31 Ibid.

as official War Charities and to raise money for the "relief of suffering or distress."³² Interestingly, another result of the war was the 1917 introduction of Canadian Income Tax, which included charitable donation calculations.³³

ORGANIZATION OF PHILANTHROPY

By the early 1920's, the proliferation of charitable organizations and appeals for donations began to lead to diminishing returns. This period saw the emergence of partnerships between business and labour union leaders formed to establish federated campaigns such as the Community Chest, which later became the United Way. On January 19, 1925 the Halifax Community Chest was organized with the backing of the Halifax Board of Trade. The first financial campaign was launched in May 1925 and raised $55,000.00.³⁴ By 1958 eighty-two community funds including Community Chests and federations reported making donations to thirty-three national agencies.³⁵

The first community foundation in Canada, The Winnipeg Foundation, was established in 1921 in Winnipeg, Manitoba when successful Winnipeg banker, William Forbes Alloway wrote a cheque for $100,000. Alloway saw the creation of the Foundation as a way for him to give back to his community. The second gift made to the Foundation was "an anonymous donation of three $5 gold coins, symbolic of the Foundation's spirit – that any gift, no matter the size, can make a difference in the community."³⁶

The exploding number of charities

The 1930's were known for the Great Depression and came to be known as the Dirty Thirties by many. It was also a time when churches of all denominations conducted huge relief campaigns. While successful in alleviating the harsh realities facing many in society, the motivations behind the poor relief were sometimes questioned as a tool to address the rising fear of communism and not just to address the needs in society. The following quote by J.D. Belshaw, illustrates this concern: "…the attendant fears of Bolshevism and shrinking congregations, and not simply a desire to issue charity in anonymity, were powerful motive forces within the administration of church relief to Vancouver's unemployed."³⁷

In 1931 the Catholic Archbishop of Vancouver, William Mark Duke, introduced the American concept of Catholic Charities to Vancouver. This umbrella organization canvassed for donations and administered funds to various Catholic groups. It merged with the interdenominational Vancouver Welfare Federation but the merger lasted just one year and it was not until 1940 that a union with Protestant and Jewish causes was renewed.³⁸ By 1967 Canadian Catholic Charities were involved in 158 social action projects including family services, community development, mental and physical health, housing and prisoners.³⁹

In 1934 Canada's second community foundation, the Vancouver Foundation was established.⁴⁰ In the same year there was a police raid on a house in Vancouver, which was owned by Reverend Roddan's United Church that ended a particular source of funding. The house had been rented to a group of prostitutes.⁴¹

In 1936 The Federal government published the Quinquennil Census: Charitable and Benevolent Institutions in Canada. This provided "a fairly complete picture of the work carried on by institutions and welfare agencies organized primarily for the care of dependent adults and children in need of care or protection or both."⁴²

Demand for the type of services provided by the charitable sector grew steadily after the end of the Second World War. The generation that had survived both the Depression and the war made some drastic changes in Canadian society in the postwar period. Re-

---

32   Canada, *Acts of Parliament*. (1917). p. 349.
33   Dominigue, R.P. (1996). *The Charity Industry and Its tax treatment*. Ottawa: National Library. p. 5.
34   Senior Scribes of Nova Scotia. (1996). *Poverty, poor houses and private philanthropy*. Halifax: Queen's Printer, Communications Nova Scotia. p. 65.
35   Canadian Welfare Council, (1959). *Allocations to national organizations*. Ottawa: Community Funds & Councils Division: The Canadian Welfare Council. p. 1-23.
36   About Us|History, The Winnipeg Foundation. http://www.wpgfdn.org/aboutus-history.php

37   Belshaw, J.D. (1987) *Two Christian denominations and the administration of relief to Vancouver's unemployed, 1929-1939*. British Journal of Canadian Studies, 2 (2). p. 300.
38   ibid p. 294.
39   Catholic Charities Council of Canada. (1967) *The Bulletin*, 5 (3) p. 19.
40   Martin, Samuel. (1985). *An Essential Grace: Funding Canada's Health Care, Education, Welfare, Religion and Culture*. Toronto: McClelland and Stewart. p.264.
41   Belshaw, J.D. (1987) *Two Christian denominations and the administration of relief to Vancouver's unemployed, 1929-1939*. British Journal of Canadian Studies, 2 (2). p. 293.
42   Dominion Bureau of Statistics. (1936). *Quinquennil census: charitable and benevolent institutions in Canada*. Ottawa: Kings Printer. p. 6.

sponding to public demand, the government began to assume more responsibility for health, education and welfare, traditionally areas of interest to philanthropy. Canadians valued these new services, supported them with taxes, and came to consider them an important part of Canadian society.

In his 1985 book, *Essential Grace*, Samuel A. Martin looked at the financing of health, educational, welfare, and cultural services over the period of 1946 to 1969. He found that throughout this period funding had come from government, corporations, foundations and individuals, but that significant shifts had occurred in the relative importance of these contributors. Canadians, in spite of average increases in wealth, were donating less to humanistic service. Corporations had also decreased their share. Thus, although overall spending on humanistic service had increased substantially, there was far less individual and corporate participation. In fact, governments accounted for 90% of spending on humanistic services in 1969 as compared with 76% in 1946.[43]

Martin noted that in 1985 there were 60 degree-granting institutes in Canada, 47,000 registered charities of which 50% were social welfare organizations, 100 theaters, 34 orchestras, 16 dance companies, six opera companies, 150 large art galleries, museums, planetariums and public archives.[44] Virtually all of them were responding to changes in government support with increased individual fundraising efforts.

The number of Canadian charities rose from 909 in 1936 to 39,965 in 1980, a more than forty-fold increase in less than fifty years.

After years of steady increases in government funding for social services, the last decades of the 20th Century saw increased pressure on public finances and the rates of public spending grew more slowly or even, in some cases, declined. While many hospitals were started by religious organizations and then taken over by municipalities and provinces, Canadian universities began as government institutions. Despite this, many large universities began fundraising early in their history. McGill University has launched a development campaign every year since the end of World War II and by 1981 raised $13 million in annual gifts and became the richest university in Canada with an endowment of $150 million. Provincial funding for universities steadily decreased during the 1980's and this decrease seriously taxed the financial health of many institutions.

In the mid 1970's the financial crunch for hospitals began to build due to cutbacks in government and they began to look for ways to generate revenue from the private sector. Health organizations had not been part of the United Way and the larger charities began developing their own fundraising machines in the mid 70's.

In 1980, Terry Fox, who had lost one leg to cancer, began his Trans-Canada Run for Hope on April 17 and raised $23 million for cancer research by the time of his death on June 28, 1980. The Terry Fox Foundation was formed after his death and continues to raise millions of dollars through runs each year.

Private family foundations emerge

The Massey Foundation had been established in 1917 but it was not until 1937 that John Wilson McConnell, a Montreal industrialist, established the second family foundation, The McConnell Foundation. In the 1940's the Atkinson, Morrow, McLean, Ivey and Laidlaw family foundations were established and in 1946 the Atkinson Foundation gave its first grant to the Toronto Hospital for Sick Children.[45]

During the 1950's a number of major foundations were established. These included foundations started by millionaires, McLaughlin, Bickell, Bronfman, Greenshields, Lawson, Eaton, Molson, Woodward and Muttart.[46]

Non-Canadians also began to contribute to Canadian philanthropy in significant ways. In 1950 the Donner Canadian Foundation was established by William H. Donner (a US citizen), through the provision of a sizable endowment when he died in 1953.[47] The Donner family chose Canada's centennial year, 1967, to "embark on a course of professional grant making that has contributed well over $100 million to more than 1,000 projects across Canada and around the world."[48]

---

43 Martin, Samuel. (1985). *An Essential Grace: Funding Canada's Health Care, Education, Welfare, Religion and Culture.* Toronto: McClelland and Stewart. P. 14-16.
44 ibid.
45 Martin, Samuel. (1985). *An Essential Grace: Funding Canada's Health Care, Education, Welfare, Religion and Culture.* Toronto: McClelland and Stewart. p. 263-265.
46 ibid. p. 265.
47 ibid. p. 266.
48 Donner Canadian Foundation Web Site, http://www.donnerfoundation.org/

Throughout the 1960's eighteen major foundations were incorporated, including the Windsor, Beaverbrook, Eldee, Dunn, Tanenebaum and Bombardier foundations. Le Fondation Levesque was established by Jean-Louis Levesque to celebrate his 50th birthday.[49]

The Devonian Group (Harvie Family of Alberta) and the Van Dusen, Loblea and Kahanoff family foundations were established during the 1970's.

In 1974, a group of thirty-eight foundations formed the Association of Canadian Foundations (ACF) whose chief interests were the legal and taxation issues affecting foundations. In 1981 they launched a successful lobby campaign to protest new federal tax policy for charitable foundations and the Finance Minister agreed to remove the requirement that foundations declare the full amount of capital gains as income, subject to the disbursement rules.[50]

The Agora Foundation was established in 1979 to provide support to the charitable sector by assisting in the development of organizations and projects designed to advance philanthropy in Canada. The Laidlaw Foundation provided an initial grant of $50,000 to the Agora Foundation so it could undertake the planning and development phase of what became The Canadian Centre for Philanthropy.

The Atkinson Foundation published *A Call to Alms: The New Face of Charities in Canada* by Andre Picard 1997. Picard's work investigated the impact of government cutbacks on Canada's voluntary sector and was a seminal work.

GOVERNMENT INVOLVEMENT IN PHILANTHROPY

Government has always played a role in Canadian philanthropy. The following are key dates in the history of government involvement:

- **1951**. The Government of Alberta began the regulation of charitable fundraising through the Public Contributions Act.[51]
- **1966**. The Minister of National Revenue requested that charities begin to file returns on their activities and also register with the ministry so that the tax receipts they issued could be checked.
- **1969**. The Charities Committee of the Canadian Bar Association (CBA), Wills and Trusts Section, was established to gather information about Canadian philanthropy. The Committee had been established by CBA members who had developed an interest in charity through their work with Wills and Trusts. The first task the Committee set itself was to gather information on both operating charities and foundations and to examine the laws that controlled them.
- **1971**. The Charities Committee sponsored a study of foundations by Victor Peters and Frank Zaid. Peters and Zaid met with some success but, in the end, they managed to obtain detailed information on only 19 foundations. The same year, the Committee drafted a resolution asking that the Department of National Revenue make available to the public a list of the names and addresses of charitable organizations. This resolution was passed by the CBA at its Annual Meeting in September 1971 but was rejected by the Minister of National Revenue.
- **1976**. Revenue Canada enacted new guidelines for charitable organizations that required to them disburse 80% of gifts received on charitable activities. Foundations would be required to disburse 90% of their income. By 1977, charities were required to spend a minimum amount on charitable activities and to file public information returns known as T3010's. These information returns were public and available to anyone who wanted to gather information about the sector.
- **1988**. The Federal government introduced new provisions that governed the tax treatment of charitable donations. The standard $100 deduction was replaced with a two-tiered non-refundable federal tax credit, which provided a 17% credit for the first $250 donated and 29% for any donations exceeding that amount.
- **1996**. The Federal government raised the annual ceiling for charitable donations to 50% of net income or 100% in the case of bequests. Where

---

49 Martin, Samuel. (1985). *An Essential Grace: Funding Canada's Health Care, Education, Welfare, Religion and Culture.* Toronto: McClelland and Stewart. p. 267 & 268.
50 Ibid. p. 271- 273.
51 McCormick, P. (1995) *Regulation of charities in Alberta: summary report.* Toronto: Canadian Centre for Philanthropy. p. 3.

appreciated capital property was donated, the 50% ceiling was further increased by 50% of the resulting taxable gain.

- **2006**. The Federal Government eliminated the capital gains tax on gifts of listed securities.

- **2009**. The Canada Revenue Agency released a revised and final version of its Policy on Fundraising. This new version was quite different in tone and substance from the original draft and incorporated many suggestions raised by AFP (Association of Fundraising Executives) and a coalition composed of Imagine Canada (formerly the Canadian Centre for Philanthropy), Health Charities Coalition of Canada and numerous other organizations.

- **2009**. In response to requests by AFP chapters and members in Canada, the Minister of Canadian Heritage declared November 15, as National Philanthropy Day in Canada. The declaration made Canada the first country in the world to permanently establish National Philanthropy Day as an official annual celebration.

PROFESSIONAL FUNDRAISERS

As demand for services increased, so did the need for training and professionalism, particularly in the area of fundraising. The National Society for Fundraising Executives (NSFRE), had been chartered in New York in 1960 and in 1970 the Ontario Chapter (now Greater Toronto Chapter) became NSFRE's first chapter outside the United States.

The first Canadian fundraising conference was held in 1978 and sponsored by Oyez Limited. More than 170 people from across Canada attended to hear sessions from Samuel Martin on the decline of giving, and Allan Arlett and Art Bond on foundations. The following year, conference speakers included financial analyst Arthur Drache on federal legislation affecting charities, and more sessions with detailed instruction on fundraising.

The NSFRE began its Certified Fund Raising Executive (CFRE) program in 1980 and awarded its first CFRE credential to Canadians in 1981. The International CFRE credential is now an independent organization providing professional fundraising certification throughout the world. The following year NSFRE's annual conference was held for the first time outside of the United States in Toronto and the name was changed to the International Conference on Fund Raising. Present at the conference were professional fundraisers from the United States, Canada, Mexico, England, Ireland, France and Australia. The conference was a huge success, attracting 800 people, a record at the time.

A Code of Ethical Principles was developed by NSFRE and adopted by the Toronto chapter in November 1991. In 1995 the NSFRE Canadian Task Force was established and in 1998 the first fully Canadian CFRE exam was offered. By 1999, NSFRE chapters and membership in Canada were expanding rapidly, and Canadian members pointed out that the word "national" in NSFRE's name was inaccurate. They pushed to change the name to reflect the organization's increasingly international scope. After study by a task force and significant member input, the board and Delegate Assembly changed the organization's name to the Association of Fundraising Professionals (AFP).

The Advanced Certified Fundraising Executive (ACFRE) credentials were first awarded in 1993 but it was not until 2000 that the first Canadian achieved ACFRE certification.

In 2003 the First International Summit on Fundraising was held in Toronto, Canada, with 23 representatives from 19 countries. In 2005, Leslie Weir and Pat Hardy were the two Canadian fundraisers presenting at the first First Hemispheric Congress–Latin America organized by AFP and held in Mexico City, Mexico.

CONCLUSION

What modern fundraising refers to as "philanthropy" has, by one name or another, evolved along with the other parts of the Canadian experience, from Aboriginal traditions of mutual help and support to the relatively spontaneous (and anonymous) phenomenon of "crowd funding" through social media that's emerging today.

As philanthropy has evolved in Canada, there have been historic shifts – from a time when philanthropy was often seen as something only wealthy people did to a more modern view of community-wide giving as an important and positive aspect of our society.

Along the way, there have been some distinctive and repeating patterns to that evolution. Successive waves of new Canadians have moved from patterns of help and support centered on the family and the ethnic or religious community to donating more of their time, energy or wealth towards the achievement of shared broader community goals. These changes have also been accompanied by institutional shifts, as the vehicle for philanthropic giving has moved from the Church to more secular organizations.

Designing fundraising programs to operate in our specific Canadian environments is still more an art than a science. And like the early Impressionist painters, a fundraiser should strive to see beyond the "what's there now" to a more dynamic, personal and less systematic view.

In Manitoba, an impressionistic view can be had by looking at the names of the donors and sponsors of the main high-profile charitable and cultural organizations. The transition is striking – from English, Irish and Scots predominating in early years to Germanic and then Icelanders. Also, Manitoba's Mennonite and Jewish Communities donate all out of proportion to their numbers. Recently, other group names began to appear – including South American and Asian names as growing diasporas sought refuge and built significant communities in the province. So, the ethnic evolution of philanthropy continues in Manitoba. New communities are immediately responsive to their own members' needs. These donors often move from that to efforts for community-wide improvement, both out of altruism and out of a desire to have their group assume its "rightful role."

Like Manitoba, each province in Canada has its own parallel philanthropic history. As fundraisers, you'll want to develop your own impressionistic view of *your* community. Look at the names on your donor lists. Which groups are less represented? Which are new?

Look at your community. Which groups do you think are most likely to appear on those donor lists in greater numbers going forward? How do they relate to your fundraising goals?

If your cause is new, which newer groups might be your logical targets? Are the potential philanthropists among the groups your cause serves? Are you engaging young people in your efforts? Who are they? Can you engage their parents at the same time?

Is there a large population you can engage more effectively by positioning your cause as part of an effort to pressure government to aid in solving the problem to complement/replace voluntary efforts?

What other fundraising ideas occur to you as you look at your impressionistic view of your philanthropic environment?

The Real Conclusion: Canadian philanthropy is the creative art of connecting willing donors and worthy causes.

While Canadians adopted many fundraising traditions from the United States of America, the two countries enjoy different political and economic histories. With our "Multicultural" approach as opposed to the U.S. "Melting Pot," new groups in Canada evolve their way into the mainstream more slowly than south of the border, and retain their sense of particular identity longer.

Ultimately, however, your fundraising success will depend on your ability to connect with your community, and your impressionistic view is probably your best guide.

In Canada, the government will continue to play a more central and activist role in meeting social needs than in the U.S. and charitable organizations will continue to consider political action a key strategy to meet needs. Faced with tightened public finances, however, we will almost certainly see increased private fundraising activities, too. With more fundraising programs and increased competition for the charitable dollar, there will also be increased pressure on organizations to enhance their "value proposition" – their answer to the question "Why should I give my money to you instead of someone else?"

While Canadian research about fundraising and donors is somewhat limited, fundraisers need to use existing research, along with new psychographic software and other digital and web-based tools to further nurture relationships. In organizations where fundraisers have little time or resources for relationship fundraising, they need to learn to make a case to their organizations on the importance of increased investment in these practices. Board members and funders need to understand the importance of investing in relationships if they want their organizations to have a sustainable future.

Charitable organizations will be under continued pressure to raise more money by diversifying their donor base. In 2006, Canada's Census indicated 16.2% of our population was visible minorities. Statistics Canada is projecting that by 2031, 30% of the population could belong to a visible minority.

In Diane Francis' book *Who Owns Canada Now*, she notes that in 1986 only 5 of our country's 32 richest people (16%) were immigrants. But in 2007, 28 (37%) of Canada's 75 billionaires came from other countries. In addition, the list of names from *Who Owns Canada Now* reads like the global diaspora that Canada has become.

The future of philanthropy in Canada will no doubt continue to reflect the diversity and symbiotic relationships between individuals and government that we have seen since Canada became a country. And as it all evolves, we'll rely on our "impressionistic view" of our real fundraising environments.

ADDITIONAL RESOURCES

Books

- ADAMS, M. (1997). *Sex in the snow: Canadian social values at the end of the millennium.* Toronto: Penguin Books of Canada.

- BLISS, MICHAEL. (1987) *Northern Enterprise.* Toronto: McClelland and Stewart Inc.

- CLARKE, B. (1996). *English Speaking Canada* from 1854. Murphy & Perin.

- COLLINS, P. (1977). *Hart Massey.* Don Mills: Fitzhenry & Whiteside Limited.

- DICKENSON, OLIVE, (1992) *Canada's First Nations.* Toronto: McClelland & Stewart Inc.

- FRANCIS, DIANE. (2006) *Who owns Canada now: old money, new money and the future of Canadian business.* Toronto: Harper Collins Canada.

- HARVEY, R.P. (1986). *Black beans, banners and banquets: the Charitable Irish Society of Halifax at Two Hundred.* Nova Scotia Historical Review.

- MARTIN, SAMUEL. (1985). *An Essential Grace: Funding Canada's Health Care, Education, Welfare, Religion and Culture.* Toronto: McClelland and Stewart.

- MCQUEEN, R. (1998). *The Eatons: The Rise and Fall of Canada's Royal Family.* Toronto: Stoddard Publishing Co. Ltd.

- MURPHY, T. AND PERIN, R. (1996). *A Concise History of Christianity in Canada.* Toronto: Oxford University Press.

- PICARD, A. (1997). *A call to alms: the new face of charities in Canada.* Toronto: The Atkinson Charitable Foundation.

- RALSTON SAUL, JOHN. (2008). *A fair country: telling truths about Canada.* Toronto: Penguin Canada.

- SENIOR SCRIBES OF NOVA SCOTIA. (1996). *Poverty, poor houses and private philanthropy.* Halifax: Queen's Printer, Communications Nova Scotia

- WELLS, R.A. (1998). *The Honor of Giving.* Indiana University Centre on Philanthropy.

URLs
- WWW.CHARITYFOCUS.CA
- WWW.ENVIRONICS.CA
- IMAGINE CANADA WWW.IMAGINECANADA.CA.
- HTTP://WWW.METISRESOURCECENTRE.MB.CA/
- HTTP://WWW.STATCAN.GC.CA (Statistics Canada 2006 and 2010 Census.)

ABOUT THE AUTHOR

Patricia Hardy MA, ACFRE
President, The Tunnelwood Group

Patricia Hardy has practiced fundraising since 1982. She was the first Canadian to achieve professional certification as an Advanced Certified Fundraising Executive (ACFRE), and is one of the few Canadians holding a Masters degree in Philanthropy and Development. A recognized leader in the profession, Pat was honored by the Association of Fundraising Professionals, Manitoba Chapter with the establishment of the, Patricia Hardy Scholarship for Advancement. Pat was also a contributing author to the first Canadian fundraising textbook, "Excellence in Fundraising in Canada."

CHAPTER 2

HUMAN RESOURCES IN FUNDRAISING

TIM McCONNELL, MPA, SPHR, CMC

Fundraisers are people whose job it is to seek financial support for a charity or institution. They raise funds and collect money for a beneficiary or cause. They solicit and gather voluntary donations of money. Fundraisers include any employee working in the fundraising/development department of an organization and are vitally important for most non-profit organizations.

read more…

Fundraising is a profession. It includes professional practitioners with career aspirations dedicated to skill mastery and knowledge sharing with colleagues. It also meets the five standard criteria defining a profession, as established by Lilya Wagner, in her book *Careers in Fundraising*:

- An established body of knowledge
- Educational standards
- Continuing research
- Standards of professional practice
- Self-regulation [1]

The profession of fundraising is maturing. We are seeing:

- Increased professionalism, as witnessed by the proliferation of courses and training programs (from event management courses to Master's degrees in Philanthropy).
- An increasing body of knowledge, research and literature.
- Growing demand for accountability by non-profit organizations.
- Increases in philanthropic giving.
- Increasing use of technology in fundraising.[2]

This chapter addresses the "care and feeding" of fundraisers. That is, the challenges and activities involved in the recruitment, compensation, (performance) management, training, career development and retention of that unique individual, the professional fundraiser.

Aspects of Human Resources (HR) in fundraising to be covered in this chapter include: HR strategy; HR planning; staffing; compensation; performance management; training and career development; retention; and succession planning.

HR STRATEGY

A strategy is a plan - a road map to get you from where you are now to where you want to go in the future. An HR Strategy (HRS) is a concrete plan created to align the HR function to the organization's primary business strategy – in this case fundraising.

An HR Strategy should be the key human resources document in your organization, a statement about the strategic role of HR. The primary objective is to translate business strategies into HR priorities. It allows you to proactively plan, implement, manage and communicate an ongoing integrated approach to HR – specifically designed for fundraisers.

Useful purposes for an HR strategy include:

i.) Ensuring the organization has the human capacity and capability to support its fundraising goals and objectives.

ii.) Defining how to best align the skills and competencies of the resources available.

iii.) Defining your approach to the effective recruitment, selection, retention and management of fundraisers.

iv.) Ensuring fundraisers with the right skills and competencies are in the right jobs, in the right locations, at the right time.

v.) Creating an appropriate work environment that is in compliance with legislation and is sensitive to both management's and employees' needs.

vi.) Enabling staff to work in a role that is interesting and challenging, in an environment that is healthy, safe, inclusive and respectful; where they can learn, grow and progress in their career.

vii.) Recognizing the inter-dependencies of a variety of HR elements within an overall HR conceptual model.

viii.) Providing a structure for the various HR management disciplines and functions.

ix.) Fostering a culture which reflects organizational values.

---

1 Wagner, Lilya. (2002). *Careers in Fundraising.* John Wiley & Sons, Inc., New York.
2 Ibid.

ELEMENTS OF AN INTEGRATED HR STRATEGY

Your strategic business plan for fundraising and development is always at the top. The HR Strategy exists primarily to implement the business plan.

There are three circles within the diagram (Figure 2.1). The core, or inner circle, lists the foundational items in any HR program. The middle circle shows the six major steps in the employee life cycle. The outer circle outlines the main supporting programs in HR management.

The diagram is "bookended" by two vital HR functions; your HR Policies and Procedures and Measurement.

The model is (or should be) integrated. Every element is interconnected. Changes to any single HR function can and will impact other HR functions.

HR PLANNING

HR Planning is a process to identify your fundraising workforce needs for the future. As part of your HR Strategy, it involves the specific design and implementation of plans and programs to ensure that the right number of individuals with the right skills are available at the right time and place to meet operational needs. It guides decision-making and drives the HR strategy.

Guiding principles of HR Planning are to:

- Determine the types of functions, skills and number of fundraising positions required in your organization.

- Identify the gap between the demand and supply for employees.

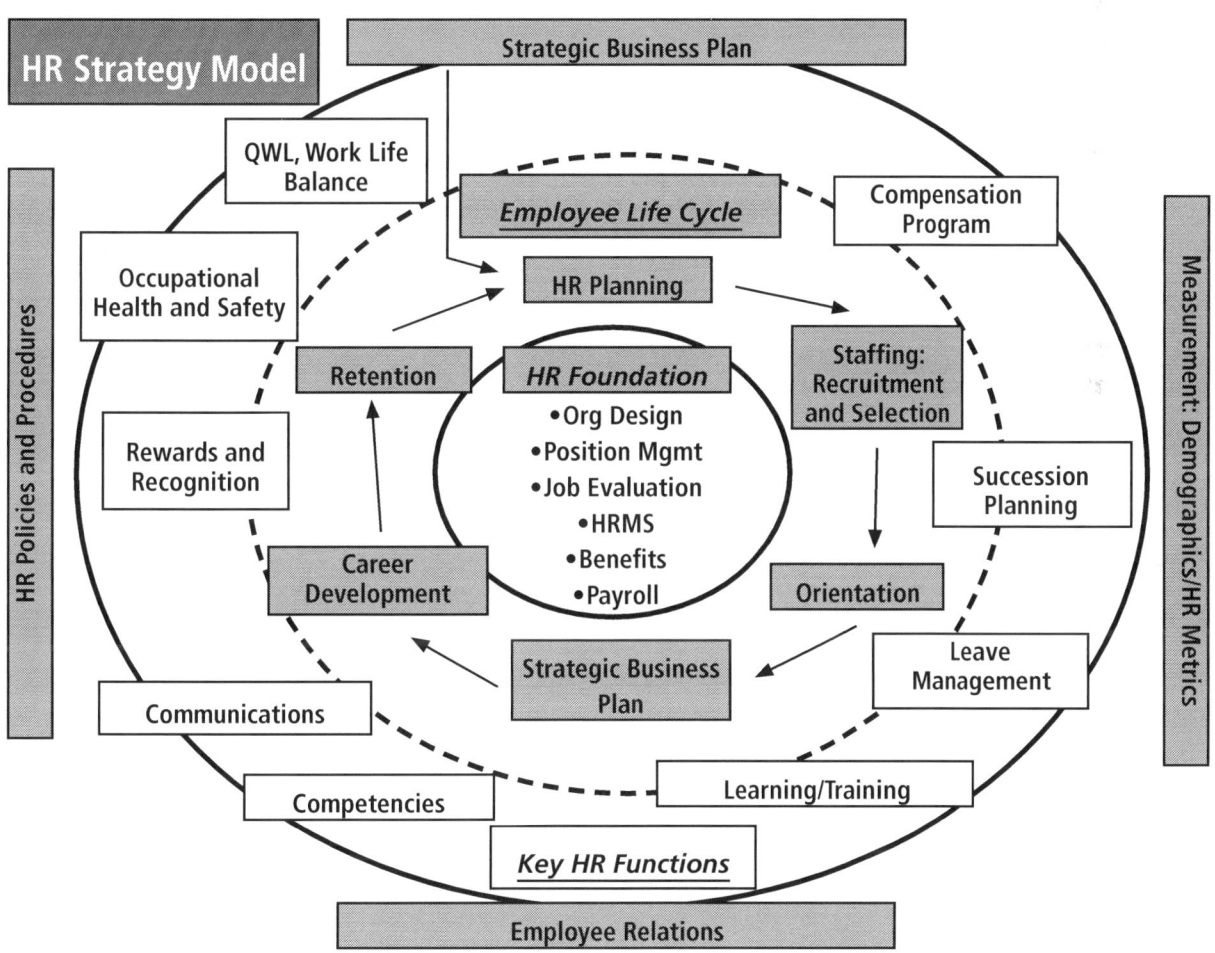

Figure 2.1

- Consider short, medium, and long-term needs.
- Determine the best way to address the gap (i.e. workforce numbers, job roles and skills).
- Align organizational requirements with financial and human resources planning.
- Align resources with program requirements on a continual basis.

It is important that HR Planning is not a one-time exercise or a fixed plan that never changes. For HR Planning to be successful it must be integrated with other planning processes such as reducing labour costs, limiting skills shortages, improving career management, and enhancing learning.

Your HR Strategy and HR Plan for fundraisers should be reviewed and approved by your Board of Directors. It is important they be involved in this process.

Figure 2.2 provides a sample list of fundraising job titles by level and potential career path. Titles are important in fundraising organizations. Some organizations apply "job title inflation" so that donors perceive they are dealing with senior fundraisers.

JOBS IN FUNDRAISING

The first step in HR Planning in fundraising organizations is to determine work requirements and jobs. Consider "what does a fundraiser do (besides the obvious, asking people for money)?" Roles, tasks and general areas of concentration include:

- Prospect and donor research.
- Data and records management.
- Relationship management; building and maintaining relationships within the organization and externally.
- Direct mail – producing and distributing written materials to a targeted audience.
- Special events – organizing functions which raise funds.
- Major donor solicitation – working with people who have the capacity to make large gifts to the organization. This includes identifying and qualifying major gift donors, cultivating them and asking for the gift.
- Planned giving – a technical area involving tax structures, benefits and implications.[3]

---

3   Ibid.

Level	Title	Area
Entry Level	Volunteer	Every area
	Administrative Assistant	Philanthropy
	Assistant	Researcher
		Foundations
		Donation Administration
	Administrator	Gift Processing and Data
	Researcher	Prospects
	Coordinator	Philanthropy
		Special Events & Sponsorships
		Campaign
		Fundraising
		Development
		Annual Giving
Mid-Level	Associate	Planned Gifts
	Officer	Development / Annual Fund
		Campaign
		Communications
		Development / Corporate Partnerships
		Special Projects
		Gifts, Major / Planned Gifts
		Corporate Development / Resource Development
		Special Occasions Program
Senior Level	Relationship Specialist	Philanthropy
	Specialist	Fundraising
		Prospect Research
	Fundraiser	Fundraising
	Senior Officer	Development
Management	Manager	Development
		Records
		Planned Giving / Legacy Giving
		Fundraising
		Research and Grants
		Direct Marketing
		Data Base & Direct Mail Program
		Events / Special Events
		Communications
	Senior Manager	Philanthropy
		Events & Community Engagement
	Director	Major and Planned Gifts
		Special Events
		Annual Fund / Annual Giving
		Donor Relations
		Philanthropic Planning
		Community & Corporate Engagement
		Development
		Communications & Annual Giving

Figure 2.2 (continues)

Level	Title	Area
Senior Management	Senior Director	Philanthropy
	Vice-President	Capital Campaign & Development
		Advancement
		Development
		Donor Relations & Communications
		Corporate Engagement
		Annual Giving Programs
		Major Gifts
		Philanthropy
		Philanthropy & Community Engagement
		Corporate Partnerships
	Chief Development Officer	Development
	President / CEO	Foundation

Figure 2.2 (continued)

Job Description: Director of Development

Figure 2.3, provides a representative sample of a Job description for Director of Development, provided courtesy of the HR Council.[4]

STAFFING

Once you have planned which jobs and how many are required, you need to write a job posting, and then find qualified applicants to fill your positions.

Staffing is the process of identifying, attracting, and assessing qualified job applicants for your fundraising positions. It includes two separate components, recruitment and selection. Guiding principles are to:

- Recruit personnel based on a resource model which includes a mix of internal job postings and external, hiring from multiple sources.
- Treat candidates in a fair, consistent and transparent manner.
- Follow legally defensible recruitment and selection processes.

"Organizations are churning through Development Directors. Why? Because they are not hiring well. They don't understand what fundraising is, and what it requires."[5]

Skills, attributes and characteristics of fundraisers

There are many qualities and credentials that are key attributes of a successful fundraising professional. These include:

- Professional competence and technical skill;
- Ability and motivation to learn;
- Human relations skills;
- Creativity;
- Leadership;
- Being a team player;
- Ability to command respect and self-confidence;
- Positive outlook and vision;
- Honesty and integrity;
- Adaptability, flexibility and perseverance; and
- Having the courage to fail.[6]

How do you find applicants with these attributes? Sources for recruiting fundraisers can include:

- Internal promotions (a function of the size of your organization);
- Employee referral programs;
- On-campus recruiting;
- Employment agencies (both traditional agencies and specialty recruiters);

---

4 The HR Council. http://hrcouncil.ca/hr-toolkit/right-people-job-descriptions-director-development.cfm (Ottawa, 2014)
5 McManus, Andrea. (2014). The Development Group. Calgary.
6 Wagner, Lilya. (2002). *Careers in Fundraising*. John Wiley & Sons, Inc., New York.

Purpose: The Director of Development creates and oversees the implementation of a strategic approach to fundraising including major gifts, corporate donations, grant solicitation, and in-kind resources.

Primary Duties and Responsibilities

1. *Plan fund development activities*

   - Collaborate with the Board of Directors and Executive Director to create a fund development plan which increases revenues to support the strategic direction of the organization
   - Implement the fund development plans in accordance with ethical fundraising principles
   - Monitor and evaluate all fundraising activities to ensure that the fundraising goals are achieved
   - Monitor trends in the community or region and adapt fundraising strategies as necessary

2. *Organize fund development activities*

   - Develop and manage timelines for various fundraising activities to ensure strategic plans and critical fundraising processes are carried out in a timely manner
   - Develop policies and procedures for the development department which reflect ethical fundraising practices
   - Prepare and submit grant applications as outlined in the fund development plan to generate funds for the organization
   - Oversee the planning and execution of special fundraising events as specified in the fund development plan to generate funds for the organization
   - Identify and develop corporate, community and individual prospects for the organization's fundraising priorities
   - Oversee the administration of a donor mailing list and database which respects the privacy and confidentiality of donor information
   - Coordinate in-kind donations and make decisions regarding the issuing of receipts

3. *Staff fund development activities*

   - Recruit, interview, and select well-qualified fund development staff
   - Engage volunteers for special fund development projects using established volunteer management practices

4. *Manage fund development budget*

   - Develop and gain approval for an annual income and expenditure budget for the fund development program
   - Prepare regular reports on progress, budgets, receipts and expenditure related to fundraising and the management of the fund development activities
   - Monitor expenses and analyze budget reports on fund development and recommend changes

5. *Promote the organization*

   - Foster an understanding of philanthropy within the organization
   - Develop a comprehensive communication plan to promote the organization to its donors and maximize public awareness of the fundraising activities of the organization
   - Coordinate the design, printing and distribution of marketing and communication materials for development efforts
   - Build relationships with community stakeholders to advance the mission and fundraising goals of the organization

Figure 2.3

Qualifications

Education: University degree
A certificate in Fundraising Management is an asset
Professional designation: Certified Fund Raising Executive (CFRE) designation is an asset

Knowledge, skills and abilities

- Knowledge of fundraising management
- Knowledge of federal and provincial legislation affecting charities
- Knowledge of special events planning and management
- Knowledge of the management of volunteer resources
- Knowledge of the *Canadian Centre for Philanthropy's* Ethical Fundraising and Financial Accountability Code

Proficiency in the use of computer for: Fundraising software, Word processing, Databases, Spreadsheets, E-mail, Internet

Personal characteristics

- Creativity/Innovation: Develop new and unique ways to improve the finances of the organization and to create new opportunities.
- Behave ethically: Understand ethical behaviour and business practices and ensure own behaviour and the behaviour of others are consistent with these standards and aligns with the values of the organization.
- Build Relationships: Establish and maintain positive working relationships with others, both internally and externally, to achieve the goals of the organization.
- Communicate effectively: Speak, listen and write in a clear, thorough and timely manner using appropriate and effective communication tools and techniques.
- Focus on donor needs: Anticipate, understand, and respond to the needs of donors to meet or exceed their expectations within the organizational parameters.
- Foster teamwork: Work cooperatively and effectively with others to set goals, resolve problems, and make decisions that enhance organizational effectiveness.
- Lead: Positively influence others to achieve results in the best interest of the organization.
- Make decisions: Assess situations to determine the importance, urgency and risks, and make clear decisions which are timely and in the best interests of the organization.
- Organize: Set priorities, develop a work schedule, monitor progress towards goals, and track details, data, information and activities.
- Plan: Determine strategies to move the organization forward, set goals, create and implement actions plans, and evaluate the process and results.
- Solve problems: Assess problem situations to identify causes, gather and process relevant information, generate solutions, and make recommendations and/or resolve the problem.

Experience: 8 to 10 years of fundraising experience

Figure 2.3 (cont.)

> **HR PLANNING CASE STUDY:
> THE OTTAWA HOSPITAL FOUNDATION**
>
> The Ottawa Hospital Foundation is a prime example of a professional, well-planned, well-structured and well-managed fundraising organization. They raise over $20 million a year and treat fundraising as a business.
>
> Their organizational model includes a Board of Directors representative of and well-connected in the community and a strong volunteer base. From an HR Planning perspective, the Foundation offers the following set of 16 positions representing the full range of fundraising functions from entry level to senior management:
>
> - President and CEO.
> - Vice-Presidents of: Donor Relations and Communications, Annual Giving Programs, Philanthropy, and Corporate Partnerships.
> - Directors of: Philanthropy, Corporate Partnerships, Special Events, and Finance and Administration.
> - Manager of Planned Giving.
> - Coordinator, Philanthropy (x2)
> - Development Officers (x4)
>
> Demographically, most staff are mid-career. The Foundation's HR challenges include turnover at the junior levels, competitive salary rates, and broadening career development so that junior staff can grow out of the entry level special events roles. While they promote from within where possible, the Foundation also fills vacancies externally – including bringing in transferable skills from other (non-fundraising) professions.

Some organizations interviewed for this chapter (see *Acknowledgements*) reported a sufficient number of qualified applicants for their mid-level fundraising positions. Others reported a lack of qualified applicants, especially at mid-to-senior levels. In the latter case, some organizations are being proactive and flexible by hiring from outside the field, bringing in candidates with transferable skills from other professions. For example, sales representatives or business account managers who have strong relationship management skills contacts in the community. The view is that the technical aspects of fundraising can be trained. In these cases, sought after attributes included: Business skills, strong communications skills (e.g. persistency, storytelling), client relationship skills, high self-esteem, organization skills, and questions asked during the interview.

Once you have received job applications and shortlisted those who meet all or most of your requirements, you need to conduct an interview in order to assess the candidate's personality, knowledge and skills as well as the veracity of their CV. While some have doubts about the accuracy of interviews as a selection mechanism, they are still extensively used. A favourite tool of HR professionals is behavioural-based interviewing, which focus directly on past experiences.

Figure 2.4, created by Penelope Burke,[7] provides a list of suggested fundraising-specific interview questions.

Reference checking

Once you have a preferred candidate, you should always check references to confirm the details of their CV and past work experience.

Figure 2.5, created by Penelope Burke,[8] provides a list of suggested fundraising-specific reference questions.

Sources for recruiting fundraisers conttinued:

- Executive search firms (headhunters);
- Newspapers;
- Recruitment websites (job search engines, job boards, professional Associations);
- Networking events;
- Social media (LinkedIn, Facebook etc.)

---

7   Burke, Penelope. (2013). *Donor Centered Leadership*. Cygnus Applied Research, Chicago / Hamilton.
8   Ibid.

Suggested Fundraising-specific Interview Questions	
Area	Question
Experience	Describe your fundraising experience.
	Share an example of a campaign that you personally conducted.
	What is the largest gift amount that you have ever requested?
	How many gifts did you secure last year from individual donors?
Achievements	What were your fundraising goals last year?
	Describe your performance against those goals.
	What was your goal last year for the number of donor contacts per month?
	How often did you meet or exceed that goal?
	How has fundraising revenue increases under your direction?
	What techniques have you successfully deployed to secure visits with reluctant prospects?
	For the largest gift you personally secured last year, what were the steps you went through?
	What were the barriers or difficulties you had to overcome to secure this gift?
	What has been your proudest fundraising achievement in the last five years?
Disappointments	Describe your least successful campaign.
	What have you learned from that disappointment?
	How have you put what you learned into action?
	What problems did you encounter in meeting your fundraising goal last year?
	What steps did you take to overcome these?

Figure 2.4

Suggested Fundraising-specific Reference Questions
Would you hire this person again…into the same job?
Did the candidate meet your specific targets and questions?
Can you verify the accuracy of information in the candidate's resume, specifically fundraising goals achievements, educational qualifications etc.?
How would you rank the candidate with other fundraisers who have worked with you (in terms of overall performance)?
Could you have achieved the same level of success in your fundraising operation without this person?
How does this candidate handle poor results?
Why did you not attempt to retain this individual on staff?
Can you describe how the candidate functions while under pressure?
How would you advise we manage the candidate for best results if we hire him/her?
What was this candidate's most significant contribution to your organization?
What feedback have you had from donors about the candidate?

Figure 2.5

Compensation

Once you've hired your fundraisers you have to pay them. Compensation is the remuneration received by an employee in return for their services. It includes both the direct and indirect rewards that a fundraiser is provided with in return for their contribution. Compensation includes the way salary is administered and involves determining how much an employee gets paid and how this process is managed over time.

This includes ensuring that all three aspects of equity are attained (internal, external, and employee).

Internal Equity: The extent to which compensation programs apply uniformly across all employees, both horizontally and vertically. Internal Equity is determined by job evaluation and involves the relative ranking of positions within the organization.

External Equity: The extent to which a compensation program compares to competitors in the same labour market.

Employee Equity: The extent to which employees in the same position or job grade are paid relative to each other. This includes how an employee progresses through a salary range and is rewarded based on their individual performance.

Components of a compensation system include:

i.) Job analysis: Determines the job description, knowledge, skills, and abilities required to effectively perform the work.

ii.) Job description: A list of duties, responsibilities, reporting relationships and working conditions of a job.

iii.) Job evaluation: The process of determining the worth of a position to the organization. Jobs must be evaluated based on skill, responsibility, effort, and working conditions in order to comply with Pay Equity legislation. Based on the results of the evaluation, jobs are allocated into job grades. Each job grade has a corresponding salary range (Internal Equity).

iv.) Salary ranges: Consist of a salary minimum, midpoint, and maximum based on the organization's compensation strategy and a pay policy line derived from the external market (External Equity).

v.) Pay structure: Includes job grades/levels and salary ranges (Internal Equity).

vi.) Salary administration policies: Determine how employee salaries increase over time (Employee Equity).

Salary Source	Boland Survey of Not for Profit Sector Salaries		The Resource Corporation - Development Sector Compensation Survey	
Position	Job Match Title	Median Salary - Ontario	Job Match Title	Median Salary - All Canada
Fundraiser	Fund Development Associate	$50,394	Development/ Fundraising Office	$53,900
	Fund Development Specialist	$75,525		
Director of Development	Top Fund Development Executive	$115,608	Development/ Fundraising Manager	$79,605

Notes:
Boland Survey of Not for Profit Sector Salaries - Ontario (Peter T. Boland & Associates, Alberta, 2013)
The Resource Corporation (Toronto, 2013)

Figure 2.6

vii.) Fundraiser salary data.

viii.) The conduct of salary surveys is both a science and an art. The science lies in the rigour of proper statistical methodology and the accuracy of quantitative analysis. The art exists in aspects such as:

ix.) Labour market determination – identifying those hiring organizations against whom you compete in each geographic market.

- Sourcing – obtaining salary data from the comparable organizations.
- Job Matching – Ensuring that the level, tasks and responsibilities of your Manager of Fundraising position (for example) are equivalent to the Manager of Fundraising position in the comparable organizations or third party salary survey (just because the titles are the same does not mean it is the same job).
- Pay Policy Position – Using the average or median of the external salary survey data to then determine where you wish to pay relative to the competition. That is; do you wish to lead the market (pay more), match the market, or lag (pay less than) the market?

That said, we offer the following representative pieces of data from published salary surveys (for illustrative purposes only). The two surveys (Figure 2.6 and Figure 2.7) were conducted by independent third party professional compensation consultants – with the data provided directly by the HR departments of employer organizations.

These survey data sets were obtained from the internet and are presented for general information purposes only. The data is provided primarily by individual employees.

Job Title	Average Salary (2013)
Foundations Assistant	$29,256
Fundraising Coordinator	$36,000
Development Coordinator	$43,512
Fundraising Manager	$61,500
Fundraiser	$69,000

Figure 2.7

SalaryExplorer.com, a broad international web-based salary survey organization, reports the preceding salary comparison data for Canadian Fundraising and Non-Profit organizations.

Charity	Total Revenue	Total Salary	Pay as % of Revenue	Top Salary Range	Full Time Staff	Part Time Staff
United Way Ottawa	$34,577,954	$5,084,825	14.7%	$200 - $250K	89	35
CHEO Foundation	$25,440,895	$2,626,182	10.3%	$250 - $300K	27	15
Ottawa Hospital Foundation	$21,370,710	$2,964,865	13.9%	$200 - $250K	35	3
University of Ottawa Heart Institute Foundation	$14,214,632	$1,321,249	9.3%	$200 - $250K	16	4
Queensway-Carleton Hospital Foundation	$8,644,721	$988,459	11.4%	$200 - $250K	12	2
Ottawa Regional Cancer Foundation	$5,193,496	$2,022,165	38.9%	$160 - $200K	26	4
Ottawa Mission Foundation	$5,997,934	$527,185	8.8%	$80 - $120K	7	2
Ottawa Senators Foundation	$3,671,264	$613,620	16.7%	$120 - $160K	7	9

Figure 2.8

The Association of Fundraising Professionals (AFP) – Calgary provides this information:[9] Chief Development Officers in Canada earn an average of $101,146.

In Canada, CFRE's reported average salaries of more than $16,500 higher than the average for respondents with no certification.

There were positive correlations between average compensation and the size of an organization's budget and amount of fund's raised, as well individuals' age, level of education and years of professional experience.

In addition, the Ottawa Citizen[10] reports the following salary data obtained from the Canada Revenue Agency for 2012 / 2013.

9 Association of Fundraising Professionals – Calgary. http://afpcalgary.afpnet.org/International/RepResdetail.cfm?ItemNumber=17412
10 *The Ottawa Citizen*. (June 23, 2014, Ottawa).

Compensation challenges in fundraising

With respect to internal and external equity, a challenge for fundraiser salaries is "who is the relevant comparator?" There are two different approaches:

Fundraising / Development departments in many organizations are often viewed as regular employees by corporate HR. Their relevant comparator is therefore internal, that is, other positions in the same organization. Internal equity is achieved because all positions in the organization are ranked by level of responsibility via a Job Evaluation / Classification review, assigned a Job Grade, and paid fairly based on tenure and experience within the corresponding salary range. External equity is achieved when the organization surveys and pays competitively with similar organizations in that geographic location. The challenge arises when/if the rates of pay for the fundraisers are not comparable to (i.e. less than) fundraisers in other Development departments in the same city. This then creates flight risk and recruitment challenges.

Some organizations respond to these challenges by offering non-quantitative prerequisites to their fundraisers. These include:

- Working from home (where feasible)
- Flexible hours
- Additional vacation time
- Lieu time for overtime worked
- Reimbursement of professional membership dues
- Training and development opportunities including "stretch" assignments, "acting" opportunities and cross-training

MENTORING AND COACHING

The approach above is sometimes addressed by de-linking fundraiser salaries from the internal compensation program and tying them directly to competitive rates for other fundraisers outside of the organization. This addresses external equity but creates internal equity issues within the organization. Many Foundations follow this approach, for example, since they are often separate entities from their hospital or university.

Incentive pay is the other major challenge for fundraisers. There are many similarities between fundraisers and sales professionals. Both occupations require prospecting, database management, customer/donor engagement and persuasive skills. Most sales people are incentivized. Some receive a direct commission; others are part of a sales compensation program and/or receive bonuses.

It can be argued that, for performance management and rewards and recognition purposes, fundraisers receive incentive pay for successful results. However, it is viewed as unethical to provide fundraisers with a percentage bonus tied to the amount of dollars raised through fundraising. That is, bring in a $10,000 donation and personally receive 10% of that as a bonus. Specifically, the AFP Code of Ethics states:

"Members shall not accept compensation or enter into a contract that is based on a percentage of contributions; nor shall members accept finder's fees or contingent fees. Members may accept performance-based compensation, such as bonuses, provided such bonuses are in accord with prevailing practices within the members' own organizations and are not based on a percentage of contributions." (Association of Fundraising Professionals Canada) [11]

Development departments – those that offer incentive pay – follow these guidelines by not tying bonuses to individual donations, or even to overall financial results, but to broader and more general performance evaluation objectives such as "exceeds expectations." This is addressed in more detail in the following section.

PERFORMANCE MANAGEMENT

Performance management is all about feedback. It involves the processes used to rate, appraise, and reward fundraiser performance. It involves three key factors:
1. Guiding and teaching fundraisers to do what it takes to meet organizational goals.
2. Providing a continuous cycle of setting expectations, observing performance, coaching, training and giving feedback.
3. Strong communication.

Benefits of performance management for the organization include improved productivity and results. If it is done correctly, the benefits for fundraisers include increased morale, pride in the job, greater self-responsibility and longer job tenure.

"Everyone needs and deserves to hear about the contribution they are making as well as what changes they should be making. For high performing talent, performance review is even more critical as this type of employee demands a clear roadmap and sense of future path in order to stay engaged and connected."
- Paula Roberts, Executive Vice President, Plan Canada [12]

---

11 Association of Fundraising Professionals Canada. (2007). *Code of Ethical Principles*. Sections 21 and 22. Toronto.
12 Roberts, Paula, Plan Canada. Quoted in Spears, Marnie A., *"The Retention Issue."* Philanthropic Trends Quarterly, KCI Ketchum Canada Inc., Issue 3, Toronto, 2013.

The guiding principles of performance management are to:

- Provide feedback; every employee likes to know "how they are doing."
- Ensure expectations are relevant, attainable but challenging, realistic, specific to the requirements of the job, and aligned with organizational, project and personal goals.
- Address poor performance.
- Regularly discuss and manage employee performance in an open, fair and professional manner.
- Support and reinforce high performance work and contribute to the achievement of plans.
- Most fundraising organizations conduct performance reviews of their staff. Most of these are annual. The steps in an annual performance management cycle are straightforward:
    - Review the job description (roles and responsibilities).
    - Set performance standards, goals and expectations (both organization-wide and job-specific). These should be specific, measurable, achievable, realistic and time-framed. (SMART!)
    - Communicate these to the employee and mutually discuss.
    - Observe performance.
    - Provide coaching and training as appropriate.
    - Provide informal feedback regularly throughout the year.
    - Provide formal performance feedback in a documented manner.

Ideally, the performance appraisal discussion is an exciting opportunity to summarize feedback (which is provided regularly), provide motivation and set goals. As opposed to the dreaded HR-mandated form-filling exercise focused on mistakes. With respect to performance evaluation criteria, research in fundraising has findings as shown in Figure 2.9.

Additional detailed information can be found on fundraising metrics in Karen Van Sacker's Chapter on *Measuring Performance*.

There is debate about whether or not these are the correct criteria. For example: Is gross revenue a reliable indicator of success? If you face high costs in the attainment of that revenue, then net revenue is probably more appropriate.

Is the number of active donors an appropriate measure? What about increasing the average gift value of existing donors?

In addition to the measures identified above, other goals that can be used to measure major gift performance include:

- Number of "moves" completed annually.
- Number of "asks" completed annually.
- Close rate (gifts versus asks).
- Contact reports submitted in a timely manner.

TRAINING / CAREER DEVELOPMENT

Training and development involves improving current and future performance by increasing an employee's skill and knowledge. The guiding principles of training and development are to:

- Provide multiple avenues for learning – e.g. conferences, job enrichment, job rotation, and job enlargement – in addition to formal training, as appropriate;
- Provide an environment of continuous learning to renew employees and to support career development;
- Reinforce the use of new knowledge and skills on the job; and
- Motivate employees to develop and utilize their full potential.

Performance Evaluation Measures Favored by CEO's, Directors and Managers [13]			
Criteria	CEOs Assessing Directors of Development	Directors of Development Assessing Fundraising Managers	Fundraising Managers Assessing Non-Management Staff
Increase in # of active donors	58%	62%	51%
Gross revenue raised	58%	60%	52%
Improvement in donor retention	53%	47%	57%
Net revenue raised	45%	26%	21%
Reduction in cost per dollar raised	40%	25%	18%
Improvement in average gift value among retained donors	37%	37%	19%

Figure 2.9

FORMAL EDUCATION

It is also possible to receive post-secondary formal education in fundraising and development. At the college level, certificate and diploma programs include (for example):

- Fundraising Management - Algonquin College, British Columbia Institute of Technology
- Fundraising – Vanier College
- Fundraising and Volunteer Management – Humber College
- Fundraising Development – Mohawk College
- Fundraising and Resource Development - Georgian College
- Events Management – Bow Valley College

At the university level, programs offered in Canada include:

- Certificate in Fundraising Management – Ryerson University
- Event Management Certificate – Mount Royal University
- Canada's first Master's degree in Philanthropy and Non-Profit Leadership, launched at Carleton University in the summer of 2013.

PROFESSIONAL ASSOCIATIONS / DESIGNATIONS

There are numerous professional organizations which provide support to fundraising professionals.

The *Association of Fundraising Professionals* (AFP) is the largest in Canada. They are an international professional association of individual fundraisers and fundraising executives that advances philanthropy. The AFP fosters the development and growth of fundraising professionals, works to advance philanthropy and volunteerism, and promotes high ethical standards in the fundraising profession.

There is also:

- CAGP (Canadian Association of Gift Planners) – particularly useful for planned giving professionals.
- AHP (Association of Health Care Professionals) – particularly useful for fundraisers working in hospitals.

---
13 Burke, Penelope. (2013). *Donor Centered Leadership.* Cygnus Applied Research, Chicago / Hamilton

- CCAE (Canadian Council for Advancement of Education) – particularly useful for Canadian college and university fundraisers.
- CASE (Council for Advancement and Support of Education) – useful for university and college fundraisers.
- APRA Canada (Association of Professional Researchers for Advancement) - representing researchers, front-line fundraisers and other professionals with an interest in the field of advancement research.
- APC (Association of Philanthropic Counsel) - supporting independent philanthropic consulting firm owners and consultants in fundraising organizations.

Areas of support provided by these associations include: knowledge centres, fundraising conferences, educational courses and webinars.

CODES OF ETHICS

The CFRE (Certified Fund Raising Executive) is the professional designation for fundraisers. This greatly enhances the credibility of fundraising as a distinct profession. It is administered by CFRE International. Initial certification requires candidates to document information in four categories: Education, Professional Practice, Professional Performance, and Volunteer Service.

The application works on a point system. Candidates must document a minimum number of points in each of the four categories in order to be approved to take the CFRE exam. The examination is intended to assess candidates' mastery of the body of knowledge required to perform fundraising tasks – based on current practices. It consists of 200 multiple choice questions. Successful candidates must re-certify every three years. (CFRE International)[14]

CFRE-related exam preparatory courses cover the following topics:

- Philanthropy
- Donor research
- Marketing and communications
- Solicitation programs
- Relationship management
- Securing gifts
- Volunteers
- Management
- Accountability

RETENTION

Retention is an organization's ability to retain its staff. Employee turnover is a persistent and expensive problem for Fundraising / Development departments; each separation results in lost time and productivity and leads to significant training and recruiting costs.

UnderDeveloped, a recent study of challenges facing non-profit fundraising, found that:

"Many Development Director positions have been vacant for months. 50% of Development Directors anticipate leaving their current jobs in two years or less. 40% don't plan on even staying in the Development field for their entire career."[15]

Retention can be a major challenge due to the high mobility of labour and the shortage of qualified candidates for skilled positions. An organization's ability to achieve its business mandate is highly dependent on the performance of your employees.

"Staff retention is important for donor relationships and for fundraising revenue. Vacancies equal interrupted relationships and lost revenue."[16]

Unanticipated changes in the employee resource pool can have devastating business impacts including: service cutbacks, disrupted projects, overruns on schedules and budgets, quality issues, and loss of corporate memory.

---

14 CFRE International (2013). Alexandria, Virginia.

15 Bell, Jeanne and Maria Cornelius. (2013). *UnderDeveloped – A National Study of Challenges Facing Nonprofit Fundraising*. CompassPoint / Haas Jr. Fund, Oakland CA.
16 Battisti, Sylvie and Tara George. *Hiring and Retaining Great Fundraisers*. (Presentation. KCI Ketchum Canada Inc., Toronto, 2014)

"In a field where building relationships is key, and where practitioners acknowledge that doing so takes time, finding and holding on to good fundraisers is as integral to profit as finding and holding on to good donors."[17]

The following are top reasons why fundraisers leave an organization.
1. Disengagement with the organization (and the Board)
2. Compensation
3. Lack of growth opportunities (especially in smaller organizations)
4. Dissatisfaction with co-workers
5. "Retention Getters"

So how do you get people to stay? The ability to retain fundraisers so that they can provide an effective contribution to your organization's success is an outcome of your HR practices. But what works, and what doesn't work?

More money is not always the answer. In any case, most Fundraising/Development departments these days have few extra dollars. Non-monetary HR practices that can be employed to increase commitment and decrease turnover include:

- Non-monetary recognition of performance (try saying "thank you")
- Empowerment (increased responsibility for work and decision making)
- Fairness (equitable rules and procedures)
- Employee development (job rotation, mentoring, training)
- Work-life policies (flextime, flexible leave practices)
- Information sharing (communicate, communicate, communicate)

For most fundraising professionals, a significant portion of their motivation is derived from the satisfaction of successful donor results, the recognition they receive from their managers for a job well done, and the feeling that they are truly an important part of the organization. Where other facets of HR are equal (i.e. positions, goals, compensation, office etc.) those organizations that focus on recognition and talent development often find this to be a competitive advantage in recruiting and retaining fundraisers.

Training is too often seen as a perk when it should be viewed as an essential investment in the intellectual capital of the organization. Training, coaching, developmental assignments and job rotation programs send a clear message that management is seeking to establish a long-term relationship with employees. Managers must help employees shape and direct their careers, so they can gain experience within the organization rather than outside it. Your ability to do this however, is a function of your size.

SUCCESSION PLANNING

What do you do when a key fundraiser announces they are leaving? Are you prepared? It's a bit late for retention activities, so do you jump immediately into recruiting mode? No, look within your organization first.

Succession planning is the flexible, long-term, developmental view of future staffing. It is not just for management, it can apply to all of your fundraising positions.

There is a difference between individual "replacement" planning and broader "succession" planning. Replacement planning concentrates on immediate needs and a "snapshot" assessment of the availability of qualified candidates for key management vacancies.

"Grooming your replacement" is no longer an adequate solution to a succession policy. Succession planning is concerned with longer term needs and the cultivation of a supply of qualified talent to meet those needs. The challenge is not to merely replace fundraisers as they leave the organization, but to develop staff "in advance" to meet anticipated future requirements. A key aspect of overall HR planning is having a systematic process for defining future skill requirements, identifying candidates and matching this demand to supply.

A primary challenge for organizations is to develop broadly experienced and seasoned fundraisers in a way that is simple, practical, meaningful and fair. This will allow you to focus on a talent pool, rather than on

---

17 Burke, Penelope. (2013). *Donor Centered Leadership.* Cygnus Applied Research, Chicago / Hamilton.

individual backups for key positions. It also allows for greater flexibility in preparing succession plans across departmental/functional lines.

Succession planning involves a more intensive management review of job requirements, changing organizational needs, candidate information, appraisal information, and the specific developmental interests and choices of the candidates. It also calls for more systematic planning for the broadening of individuals' career potential.

Organizations need to consider their succession planning needs, create an awareness of this as a priority among directors and managers, and introduce new ways of thinking on this subject. Specifically:

- Adopt a corporate philosophy of short- and long-term fundraiser development.
- Identify a Director-level corporate "champion" for succession planning (not the Director of HR).
- Develop a succession planning strategy statement.
- Overcome the resistance from line managers that all of this is "too much work" and that it is easier/ faster just to recruit an external candidate.
- Incorporate fundraiser development into the broader training/learning program regime.
- Systematically identify a series/program of developmental assignments and incorporate this into business and workforce planning.
- Establish an annual fundraiser succession planning and review process - also called "depth reviews"
    □ Present an analysis of the fundraiser talent supply and planned development activities
    □ Rank your fundraisers by potential (low to high), both short- and long-term
    □ Identify high-potential succession candidates
    □ Examine short-term replacement availability for key positions
    □ Prepare long-term development plans for succession candidates
    □ Develop guidelines for a uniform approach to performance appraisals and the assessment of career development needs
    □ Implement the required training and development programs
- Review the process every year.

CONCLUSION

In this chapter we have provided an overview of the major disciplines within Human Resources management and how to apply these concepts to the field of fundraising. Fundraising is a specialized function and a unique profession in our society. It requires not only a certain skill set but a certain aptitude. As such, charitable organizations face multiple challenges in recruiting fundraisers; including rewarding, motivating, training, developing and retaining them.

This chapter has provided a "tool kit" for successfully addressing these challenges. The bottom line? Pay attention – none of this happens by itself. The rest is up to you.

TIPS!

When building an HR strategy for your charitable organization, consider the following best practice tips:

- Plan ahead. What are your fundraising requirements? What types and levels of fundraising positions do you need to accomplish your goals? How many positions do you need? (How many can you *afford* might be a better question.) Write this out in an HR strategy and an HR plan.

- Use job descriptions. These are not bureaucratic and inflexible contrivances of the HR department. They are very useful tools. A concise job description is useful in HR planning and budgeting. It can be used for job postings, interview guides, new employee orientation, training, career development, compensation and performance management.

- Don't hire the wrong people. It can be very tempting to hire the closest (seemingly) qualified person at hand when your campaign deadline is approaching and you need a body fast. This decision will come back to haunt you. Take the time to carefully and properly recruit, interview and select the best candidate for your fundraising position and your organization.

- Get rid of the wrong people. Managers hate to fire employees, especially fundraisers. They often debate, ponder, worry, procrastinate and agonize over it. Staff watch in bewilderment as the poor performer drags the team down, waiting for management to "do something." Follow the correct practices and procedures for performance management and discipline. It that does not work, make the decision and terminate the employee in a respectful, professional and legal manner.

- Spell out the rules of engagement. An Employee Handbook is another useful tool and not a contrivance of the HR department. Yes, you can be flexible. But clearly outlining the office policies, procedures and expectations for fundraisers drives consistency.

- Pay your fundraisers appropriately. This requires knowledge of what is appropriate. Have a compensation policy and program and follow it. Ensure that you have internal equity (as described earlier). Ensure that you know your relevant labour market (e.g. other positions within your institution or the market for fundraising positions in your community).

- Engage your fundraisers. Are your staff "happy campers?" Do you know? If morale is low, productivity suffers and your donors are unhappy.

- Recognize your fundraisers. Provide positive feedback. When a fundraiser does a good job, acknowledge it and say "thank you." The intrinsic motivation created by those two little words is astonishing.

ACKNOWLEDGEMENTS

I would like to thank the following individuals who generously provided their time, expertise and wisdom as interviewees for this book.

Brian Bowman. Director, Alumni Development, SAIT Polytechnic (Calgary)

Kathy Bedard. Director of HR Consulting, McConnell HR Consulting Inc. (Ottawa)

Lisa Green. Vice-President, Capital Campaign & Development, St. Boniface Hospital Foundation (Winnipeg)

Tim Kluke. President and CEO, The Ottawa Hospital Foundation (Ottawa)

Jeff Lucier. (Former) Director of Human Resources and Organization Development, United Way Centraide Ottawa (Ottawa)

Andrea McManus. President, The Development Group (Calgary)

Joyanne Mitchell. Development & Alumni Relations Manager, Lethbridge College (Lethbridge)

ADDITIONAL RESOURCES

- ASSOCIATION OF FUNDRAISING PROFESSIONALS. "Code of Ethical Principles." Toronto, 2007. Sections 21 and 22.

- BELL, JEANNE AND MARIA CORNELIUS. (2013). *UnderDeveloped - A National Study of Challenges Facing Nonprofit Fundraising*. Oakland: CompassPoint / Haas Jr. Fund.

- BURKE, PENELOPE. (2013). *Donor Centered Leadership*. Chicago / Hamilton: Cygnus Applied Research.

- CARBONE, ROBERT F. (1998). *Fundraising as a Profession: Clearinghouse for Research on Fund Raising*. Maryland: The University of Maryland College Park.

- CFRE: CERTIFIED FUND RAISING EXECUTIVE. *www.cfre.org*. 2013. 2014.

- CHARITY INFO. *www.charityinfo.ca/categories/fundraising-careers*. 2014.

- CHARITY VILLAGE. *www.charityvillage.com*. 2014.

- DURONIO, MARGARET A. AND EUGENE R. TEMPEL. (1997). *Fundraisers: Their Careers, Stories, Concerns, and Accomplishments*. San Francisco: Jossey-Bass Publishers.

- GEORGE, TARA AND SYLVIE BATTISTI. "*Hiring and Retaining Great Fundraisers*." *Convene Canada*. Ottawa: Association for Healthcare Philanthropy, 1 May 2014. Presentation.

- IDEALIST. *www.idealist.org*. 2014.

- LYSAKOWSKI, LINDA AND NORMAN OLSHANSKY ACFRE. *You and Your Nonprofit: Practical Advice and Tips from the Charity Channel Professional Community*. CharityChannel LLC, 2011.

- MAAS, INEKE. "Resources That Make You Generous: Effects of Social and Human Resources on Charitable Giving." *Social Forces* (2009): 87 (4).

- McConnell, Tim. (2012). *The NPO Dilemma: HR and Organizational Challenges in Non-Profit Organizations.* New York: Data Motion Publishing.

- Philanthropic Trends Quarterly. "Retention Issue." *Trends Quarterly* Third Issue (2013): 7.

- Pynes, Joan E. (2008). *Human Resources Management for Public and Nonprofit Organizations: A Strategic Approach.* San Francisco: John Wiley & Sons.

- Sargeant, Adrian and Elaine Jay. (2010). *Fundraising Management: Analysis, Planning and Practice.* London: Routledge.

- Wagner, Lilya. (2002). *Careers in Fundraising.* New York: John Wiley & Sons.

- Weinstein, Stanley. (2009). *The Complete Guide to Fundraising Management.* Third Edition. New Jersey: John Wiley & Sons.

- Young, Lilly Cohen and Dennis R. (1989). *Careers for Dreamers and Doers: A Guide to Management Careers in the Nonprofit Sector.* New York: The Foundation Center.

ABOUT THE AUTHOR

Tim McConnell, MPA, SPHR, CMC Managing Partner of McConnell HR Consulting Inc.

Tim is a Senior HR Strategist with over 25 years' experience in Human Resources management, both as a Director of HR and as a senior HR consultant. Tim provides advice and guidance on HR Strategy, Compensation, and Organization Design to clients in the public, private and not-for-profit sectors.

Tim holds a Diplôme d'études collégiales (DEC) from Vanier College, a B.A. in Political Science and Economics from McGill University, and a Master's degree in Public Administration from Carleton University. He has earned professional designations in HR in both Canada (CHRP) and the United States (SPHR). He is a Certified Management Consultant (CMC) and recently earned the Human Capital Strategist (HCS) certification from the Human Capital Institute (HCI) in Washington, D.C.

Tim was an adjunct professor in the Advanced Program in HR Management at the Rotman School of Management, University of Toronto from 2002 to 2008. He is also a former Sessional Lecturer at Carleton University, teaching HR Management in the graduate School of Public Administration from 1993 to 1997.

He is a seasoned public speaker and the published author of several articles on HR management, Succession Planning, Compensation and Organization Design. Tim's book, The NPO Dilemma – HR and Organizational Challenges in Non-Profit Organizations, was published in New York in 2012.

Tim is a past-President of the Ottawa Human Resources Professionals Association (OHRPA) and a past-President of the Human Resources Professionals Association of Ontario (HRPAO). He was a member of the Board of Directors of the Boys and Girls Club of Ottawa and Chair of the HR Committee from 2008 to 2011.

CHAPTER 3

FUNDRAISING IN A SMALL SHOP

LIGIA PEÑA, CFRE

"I need to raise $1.5 million for my small shop," said one fundraiser to his friend who works at a big hospital foundation. "Oh that's easy, just ask one of your top donors!" he answered.

Therein lies one of the biggest differences between fundraising in a small and a big shop. Fundraising in a small non-profit is a particular beast with its own set of challenges such as limited resources and cultural differences. But at the same time it has several advantages over larger shops.

read more…

It's difficult to gauge exactly how many small non-profits and registered charities operate in Canada. There is great debate on how to define a small shop. Should the definition be based on the number of individuals responsible for fundraising? The operational budget of the organization? The fundraising revenue or the total number of salaried employees? Or should it be a combination of these or other factors?

There is presently little consensus around the definition of what constitutes a small shop for fundraising. For the sake of this chapter, we will define a small shop as *a non-profit or registered charity with no more than one full-time or part-time professional dedicated to the fundraising function.*

There are 170,000 non-profits and registered charities in Canada. Small organizations comprise three-quarters of the Canadian non-profits and employ approximately 168,000 people.[1] This translates into over 127,500 "small" charitable and non-profit organizations in Canada.

However, the top 1% of non-profits and registered charities take home 60% of the revenue.[2] On the surface, this doesn't bode well for small shop fundraisers who struggle on a daily basis to raise the necessary funds to run a shelter for battered women, a dance company for emerging artists, a school for autistic children or an immigrant defence agency.

Working as a fundraiser in a small non-profit is no easy task. In the best of cases, it is a balancing act between senior management's expectations, fundraising capacity and resource management. In the worst cases, there is no culture of philanthropy, the wrong person is responsible for fundraising, and/or the fundraising professional isn't supported by the board of directors or management. However, with proper planning and support, small shops can raise impressive sums of money and deliver their mission.

This chapter has two primary audiences in mind, the fundraising professional working in the small organization and senior management of that small organization. The two must work hand-in-hand. If small shops are to succeed in their fundraising, senior management must understand the challenges and intricacies that raising funds in their organization must contend with.

---

1   HR Council for the Nonprofit Sector. (2010). Compensation of Full-Time Employees in Small Charities in Canada. http://www.hrcouncil.ca/documents/LMI_smallcharities_2010.pdf Retrieved January 2013.
2   Imagine Canada findings on the Canadian nonprofit sector: http://www.imaginecanada.ca/node/32.

THE DNA OF A SMALL SHOP

Small non-profits have a different DNA than their larger counterparts. The differences are most notable in the management approach, human resources, financial resources, capacity building, networks and access to technology.

Large organizations tend to have greater access to financial resources, networks, volunteers, and visibility. But, they aren't as nimble and change can be challenging. Multiple levels of management can slow down the decision-making process and be a detriment to fundraising efforts.

Conversely, small non-profits benefit from significant advantages that allow them considerable freedom and that can be the envy of large organizations.

Advantages of small shop fundraising
- Lateral management style
- Fewer (if any) silos
- Collaborative work environment
- Flexible and cohesive
- Less bureaucracy
- Greater team integration
- Very "roll up your sleeves" approach
- Easier to make decisions (less management layers)
- Greater access to Board members and senior management
- Quick to respond to opportunities
- Greater sense of belonging
- More ability to set direction
- Closer connection to the mission and case
- Often times led by visionary founders who are still present

Despite the advantages, however, small non-profits display less attractive attributes that inevitably pose challenges to fundraising, and often times weaken the organization's capacity to raise money and to succeed.

Disadvantages of small shop fundraising

- Little to no risk tolerance therefore no innovation
- Reactive rather than being proactive
- Board members and senior management may have less tolerance or appreciation for the ongoing need to invest time and money to building a loyal donor base
- Organizational self-esteem issue (we're too small thinking)
- Higher risk of burnout by the professional
- High staff turnover
- There are less people to brainstorm with
- Unrealistic expectations
- Lack of human and financial resources to meet fundraising expectations
- Board members may not see the value of hiring a fundraising professional
- Fewer people to help with strategy and planning
- More difficulty prioritizing work or strategies that maximize efficiency

---

TIP!

Burnout is an issue in any work environment but small shop fundraisers are at greater risk. To learn more about why fundraisers leave their jobs and how to reduce the high turnover, read Penelope Burk's book **Donor Centered Leadership** (2013).

OBSTACLES AND GROWTH

In his article, "*5 Critical Obstacles To Resourcing Small Non-profits,*"[3] Eric Fellman, President of Ascent Group cites obstacles he has observed among American organizations. These obstacles are also prevalent in the Canadian context:

Obstacle #1: Focus on survival, not growth

Smaller organizations focus on making payroll or keeping a specific project or program running for the current fiscal year. This creates a "crisis fundraising" culture within the organization and while this works well in the short-term, over time donors will grow tired and will eventually stop responding.

To survive, the organization must grow. To grow, the organization must think beyond the current financial needs and think bigger by focusing on inspiring donors to give bigger gifts and think differently by demonstrating its impact in the community.

Obstacle #2: Lack of focus

Smaller non-profits are typically led by visionary individuals whose passion dominates their waking (and sleeping) hours. What excites this kind of leader the most is the next opportunity to serve, and his or her passionate pursuits tend to drive the entire organization. Unfortunately, organizations like this can easily fall into the trap of pursuing every opportunity that comes along, which then leads to a diffusion of focus and diluted impact.

Obstacle #3: Failure to manage opportunity due to urgency

Often professionals in small non-profits will focus on the urgent matters instead of the important things that need to be done to raise money, such as reporting to past funders or setting up meetings with major donors. Not allowing procrastination is important. Professionals fail to seize opportunities at hand by not prioritizing properly and by focusing on the seemingly "urgent" tasks.

Obstacle #4: Telling "Our Story" instead of listening to donor interests

One of the most misunderstood phrases in fundraising is *donor appeal*. This term is mistakenly understood to be the message the organization *thinks* it needs to develop in order to "appeal" to the donor, thereby unlocking the necessary donations to accomplish its

---

3   Eric Fellman. "*5 Critical Obstacles To Resourcing Small Nonprofits.*" Retrieved from http://landing.pursuant7.com/article/0214_5_obstacles/article.php?email=1&spMailingID=8028518&spUserID=MzcyMzk2MjQ1ODgS1&spJobID=122014166&spReportId=MTIyMDE0MTY2S0

mission. All donor communications need to start with the donor in mind, providing the message or information he or she wants to hear—not what *we think* they want to hear. While being donor centric is an issue for organizations of all sizes, it's particularly challenging for smaller organizations.

Foundation representatives are constantly commenting on how many requests they get for funding where it was obvious the writer spent no time studying their giving patterns and request processes.

Before asking, "What should we say?" organizations should employ due diligence to find out not only what has resonated with donors in the past, but also what they are seeking from the organization. Having worked with numerous organizations and their representatives, I have come to focus on two key questions that should be asked of every donor: "How did you come to know about our organization?" and "What motivates you to support us?"

Obstacle #5: Lack of a simple, yet complete development plan

A great majority of small non-profits do not have a written development plan. Yet that plan is the key to carrying out the activities that will prepare the soil for organizational growth.

Some local government agencies or community foundations will partially fund organizations that wish to hire a consultant to prepare a development plan. Alternatively, there are plenty of samples online or on the Association of Fundraising Professionals website. (A sample development plan is provided later in this chapter).

Fellman continues his article[4] by sharing three steps on the path to growth:

1. *Start by thinking outside-in, not inside out.*
   This is not "think outside the box" advice, although that can be good too. This means you should identify your key audiences—donors, users, the beneficiaries of your services—and start a program of regularly listening to them.
2. *Be creative in staffing with volunteers and others.*
   Younger generations increasingly want to become involved with the causes they support. Interns and people re-entering the job market need a first job experience. Visit or call your local university's student, local government employment offices or volunteer bureau to enquire about posting volunteer opportunities.
3. *Focus on strategic actions that empower your strategic plan.*
   Most planning (strategic and otherwise) falters in the execution. At the end of every planning session, you need to set forth actions with a timetable and a person responsible for completing each one. These don't have to be complicated.

HIRING THE RIGHT SMALL SHOP FUNDRAISER

Admittedly, working in a small non-profit is not for everyone. The particular challenges that fundraising professionals must surmount in small shops can be difficult and exhausting. As such, to succeed in such an environment, the professional must be:

- Resourceful
- A fundraising generalist
- Entrepreneurial
- Collaborative and able to lead volunteers
- A self-starter
- Capable of wearing different hats and juggling differing projects at the same time
- Flexible
- Creative

The list is not exhaustive but it paints a picture of the profile senior management should be looking when recruiting for a fundraising professional. A recommendation I often make to small shops that are recruiting is to be as honest as possible about the reality of the challenge that awaits the fundraiser. This can be done in many ways: by including a brief "about us" section on the job posting, by talking about it during the telephone pre-interview (if this is done), or at the interview. There are two important reasons for this:

(a) the person who is doing the hiring can gauge the interviewee's reaction which will provide clues if there is a personality fit with the organization, and

---

4   Ibid.

(b) no one likes to accept a job offer only to realize on day one that the organization or the job is nothing like what was advertised.

Lastly, outlining the direct and indirect reporting relationship is important to clarify from day one. This avoids confusion and misunderstanding. But more importantly, it sets an environment of trust and understanding of where the small shop fundraiser stands within the organization and where he/she can turn to for help and support.

BOARD INVOLVEMENT IN FUNDRAISING

Regardless of the size of the organization, board members are an integral part of fundraising. This is particularly true in small shops where they may be involved in the delivery of the programs and services or be responsible for running the daily operations of the organization.

The relationship between board members and fundraising professionals can sometimes be difficult with both sides having conflicting visions of how fundraising should be conducted. But more often, the discomfort lies in the notion of what fundraising actually is.

A common misconception among small shop board members is that fundraising is just about "asking" for money. Yet we know as fundraising professionals that it is not the case. We need to teach board members that fundraising is not just about money, it's not even just about asking. Fundraising is about the *relationships* we develop with donors so that they are inspired to realize their dreams through our organizations. Fundraising is about telling the story of those who benefit from our organizations. Bringing board members to understand this is what will change how their support the organization's fundraising efforts.

In the context of small shop fundraising, what is the role of the board? Gail Perry, MBA, CFRE says that the number one role of a board member is to advocate for the non-profit.[5] Beyond a board's fiduciary and governance roles, the board should advocate for the non-profit which in turn will provide the organization with opportunities to raise donors and funds.

Inspired by Gail's list of the 10 fundraising responsibilities of every board member,[6] here is how small shop fundraisers can engage their board members to contribute to the organization's fundraising efforts:

1. Make a proud, personal annual gift.
   Board members must make a meaningful gift that is within their financial means. This demonstrates their commitment to the organization thereby "leading by example." By the same token, the small shop fundraiser must also coordinate with the Executive Director how board members will be asked. One should never assume a board member will donate simply because they serve on the board. Every individual deserves to be invited to contribute to your organization so make the ask respectful, personal and impactful.

2. Communicate your organization's fundraising program strategies.
   Fundraising is not a given for everyone. In fact, most people are immensely uncomfortable with the idea of asking for money. Small organizations sometimes don't have access to highly connected individuals who are used to fundraising. As the professional, you must make time to educate board members on various fundraising approaches and strategies and to take the fear out of fundraising. They will feel empowered and more comfortable which in turn will help the organization raise more funds.

3. Engage board members on other aspects of fundraising that isn't "asking."
   One of the advantages of working in a small shop is having easier access to board members. Make the time to sit with every board member, get to know them personally, understand their strengths and weaknesses and what expertise can be utilized for fundraising functions. Here are some tasks you can give your board members to get them more engaged in fundraising:

---

5 Perry, Gail. (2007). Fired-Up Fundraising, Turn Board Passion in Action. p.10.

6 Perry, Gail. "*10 Fundraising Responsibilities of Every Board Member.*" Retrieved from http://www.gailperry.com/2013/11/fundraising-responsibilities-every-board-member/

a) *Make thank you calls*
Some board members will breathe a sigh of relief! Provide the board member with a brief sample text to follow that includes at least one key question: "*What motivated your gift?*" and then ask the board member to report back on the experience and how donors answered the question. A non-profit who had a board member making thank you calls found out that a donor had left a bequest in her Will to the non-profit. This information allowed the organization to thank her again and continue stewarding her according to the type of gift she had pledged.

b) *Communicate with donors by sharing stories and impact.*
Through the thank you calls, board members can share stories about your programs.

c) *Help identify prospective donors and open the door with introductions.*
Small shops often have difficulty acquiring new donors. Board members can play an integral role in identifying prospective donors and opening doors to new networks. Talk to your board members and understand the breadth of their individual networks.

d) *Help cultivate donors.*
Make it easy and fun for board members. Ask board members to host tours, cocktails or a party. After implementing site visits with board members in my organization, I immediately noticed their engagement and enthusiasm towards fundraising go through the roof. Try it!

e) *When/if appropriate, ask for contributions.*
If a board member is keen and comfortable asking for donations, provide training and put her to task. Tag-team and set up appointments with donors.

4. Support and encourage all fundraising activities.
Board members need to be generally supportive of all fundraising activities. To make it even easier, identify the board members who are true allies to fundraising efforts and engage them. You may not win over every board member but remember that enthusiasm is contagious. With time, this enthusiasm will infect other board members.

5. Help develop the fundraising plan.
Through continuous engagement and education, board members can contribute to the development of the fundraising plan. Nothing engages small shop volunteers more than to be part of the planning and the implementation of a plan. It may not be for every board member but those who will want to take part will feel a greater sense of involvement, commitment and satisfaction towards their volunteer experience.

6. Ensure that fundraising has adequate resources and support.
This is the biggest challenge facing small shops across the country. However, it has been demonstrated time and again that an organization that invests in, and staffs its fundraising operation adequately, raises more money. When fundraising is consistently staffed and funded, you have long-term success. (Read the case study from the Regina Humane Society later in this chapter to see how investing in fundraising has increased their fundraising revenue by 59%).

7. Attend public events and bring prospects and friends.
Small shops are notorious for holding lots of events so make sure your board members attends them. Let them know which are the "must attend" and which are "optional."

As a small shop fundraiser, you play the role of motivator, educator, and task master. When board members have a clear idea of what you need from them, they can give it to you. If you expect them to know instinctively, nothing will get done and the organization will not reach fundraising success.

There are some success stories of board members supporting fundraising efforts in a way that changes the course of an organization. An engaged and motivated board is one that can elevate an organization's profile and fundraising success. However, this does not happen without leadership, perseverance and planning.

CASE STUDY: SUCCESSFUL BOARD PARTNERS

In June of 2013, I accepted the role of Director of Development at a small shop. After a bad experience at a previous organization, I began my new job with a little trepidation but a lot of hope that this time around it would be better. I spent the first two months meeting individually with board members to gauge their passion towards the organization, as well as their interests and abilities to support fundraising efforts. As I got to know them better, I devised a plan to leverage the board's skills, availabilities, interests and strengths in a way that motivated them and in turn, helped advance the fundraising program.

The board member that was a partner in a law firm reviewed the board policies I wrote; the one who self-identified as a planned giving advocate helped me develop our legacy program; the one who was the most connected among a category of donors made asks and those who were door-openers joined me in site visits. Everyone was tasked with varying jobs that supported our fundraising efforts. At the end of my first fiscal year, we had raised 56% more than the previous year, raised our profile among donors, and acquired new donors but more importantly, every board member was proud and excited about their/our successes. Perhaps the greatest outcome for me as a professional was that it made me enjoy my work even more which motivated me to push further to achieve greater success.

While this situation is not the norm in the non-profit sector (although it should be) small shop fundraisers sometimes forget that part of their role is to find ways to collaborate with board members to reach fundraising goals. It is not easy. Board members and senior management sometimes create obstacles, but we must find a way to navigate around those obstacles in order to serve our organizations. And when you have successfully engaged your board to support fundraising efforts, all the other pieces will fall into place.

SMALL SHOP PLANNING FOR FUNDRAISING SUCCESS

"If you don't know where you are going, you will wind up somewhere else" - Yogi Berra

Success in fundraising requires thought, preparation and planning. This is even more true in small shops, but I can already hear all you small shop friends say ... *"but I don't have time to stop and plan, I need to meet our goal or else."* Imagine if you made the time to plan and then you would know exactly where to put your best effort and how to track the advancement of your development plan?

The following are key components to focus on in developing the foundation of your small shop fundraising:

The small shop development plan

After conducting an informal poll among my colleagues, 95% of small non-profits I surveyed did not have a written development plan. This figure is astounding considering that without a plan, the organization is accepting a process of blindly swinging at opportunities, hoping to knock something down.

Effective planning requires vision and leadership. It means setting direction for the future by answering the following questions:

- Who are we?
- What distinguishes us from our competition?
- What do we want to accomplish?
- How will we reach our goals?
- How do we hold ourselves accountable?[7]

With limited resources and time, it's even more important for the small shop fundraiser to have a strong development plan that identifies both financial and non-financial goals and the strategies to reach those goals. What the plan will enable the small shop fundraiser to do is to focus, through the year, on the strategies that ensure goals are met and limit, or avoid, spontaneous ideas that can derail the fundraising efforts.

---

7 Seiler, Timothy. (2003). "The Total Development Plan." Achieving Excellence in Fundraising, p. 60.

Your small shop development plan will help the organization to:

- Foster an internal culture of philanthropy
- Identify potential funding sources
- Develop relationships with prospects and donors
- Position itself
- Maximize resources through careful planning and implementation
- Organize fundraising activities
- Evaluate and improve development activities

The development plan can be as simple or as elaborate as you want it to be. The key is to know who the organization's constituents are and setting SMART goals for each constituent category. Keeping in mind that philanthropy is about building relationships, it is advisable to set financial and non-financial goals that will help advance the fundraising program and enable the organization to reach various goals.

At a minimum, the small shop development plan should include strategies for:

1. Direct mail and electronic solicitations
2. Staff and board member campaign
3. Major gifts
4. Foundation and corporate grants
5. Stewardship and donor cultivation

> **TIP!**
>
> **Set SMART Goals**
>
> **S**pecific
>
> **M**easurable
>
> **A**chievable
>
> **R**ealistic
>
> **T**ime-related

The following **Sample Development Plan** is an exerpt from the *AFP First Course in Fundraising* (©Association of Fundraising Professionals), and provides an excellent example of a fund development plan.

SAMPLE ANNUAL FUND DEVELOPMENT PLAN

ABC LITERACY CENTER, INC.

FY 2009 FUND DEVELOPMENT PLAN

INTRODUCTION

The purpose of developing an annual giving development plan is to help the staff and board set realistic income goals with respect to the annual budgeting process. The plan also outlines the strategic steps required to reach those goals, as well as board and staff responsibilities in accomplishing the plan.

This proposed FY plan identifies targeted financial goals necessary to support the FY operating budget being recommended by the Finance and Executive Committees as of (date). The plan will be revised and updated on an as-needed basis in conjunction with revisions to the operating budget.

I. FINANCIAL GOALS

PROJECTED FY OPERATING BUDGET: $618,118.00

Income Categories	FY 2008 Income Actual	FY 2009 Income Projections	% of Total 2009 Income
Government	$385,972.00*	$380,851.00	62%
Foundations	37,003.00	27,000.00	4%
Individuals/Family Trusts	62,033.00	53,000.00	9%
Service Organizations	2,045.00	2,000.00	.3%
Federated Campaigns (ST, CFC, United Way)	89,692.00	107,000.00	17%
Special Events	32,155.00	32,000.00	5%
Other (Unsolicited Income)	17,955.00*	3,000.00	.5%
Interest Income	1,800.00	2,500.00	.4%
1998 Excess Revenues		10,767.00	1.8%
TOTAL INCOME	$628,655.00	$618,118.00	100%

(including approximately $13,000 in one-time gifts)

SAMPLE ANNUAL FUND DEVELOPMENT PLAN (CONT.)

II. STRATEGIC GOALS (non-monetary goals impacting success of plan)

- 100% giving by ABC, Inc. board, executive director, and key staff (92% giving was achieved in previous FY).

- 100% participation by board in some fundraising task, including cultivation of donors (65% participation was achieved in previous FY).

- Enhanced communications re: fund development within the board and with prospects, including regular presentations at board meetings by fund development chair.

- Develop plan for ongoing recruitment/training of fundraising volunteers. Recruit a minimum of ten non-board volunteers to work in fund development.

- Develop new prospects for both personal solicitation campaign and direct mail solicitation; cultivate family foundations/trusts.

- Strengthen donor cultivation program and board and staff understanding of the purpose and process of cultivation.

- Actively involve ABC, Inc. staff and students in special events and fundraising activities. (e.g., In previous FY <u>students</u> helped with several direct mails, supported phonathon, walk, yearbook campaign, and student recognition evening; <u>staff</u> coordinated the concert, participated in walk, contributed graphic design work for direct mail and publications, and received an Achievement Award for their increased participation in the last United Way campaign.)

- Strengthen coordination between the public relations and fund development committees to further support fundraising efforts.

- Maintain systems for ongoing monitoring/evaluation of progress in all areas of fund development.

SAMPLE ANNUAL FUND DEVELOPMENT PLAN (CONT.)

III. SOLICITATION STRATEGIES

A. PERSONAL SOLICITATION CAMPAIGN

<u>Board Solicitation</u> (Chairs: President, Fund Development Chair)

Time Frame: September-December, 2008

# of Prospects: 26

Goal: 100% giving; $7,000 (Amount raised in previous FY: $7,800)

Method: Personal solicitation. Request amounts based on donor history (one-time annual giving in lieu of multiple direct mail solicitations; these individuals will, however, get notice of special events.)

Solicitors: *President and Fund Development Chair*

<u>Individual Solicitation</u> (Chair(s): Name(s), with 12 team solicitors)

Time Frame: September-December, 2008

# of Prospects: 50-75 top individual donors, Advisory Board, family trusts/foundations

Goal: $30,000; 60% renewals, 15% gift upgrades ($28,500 received/pledged for FY 2008)

Method: Personal solicitation by board and non-board volunteers (one-time annual giving in lieu of multiple solicitations.)

Solicitors: (names)

SAMPLE ANNUAL FUND DEVELOPMENT PLAN (CONT.)

B. SPECIAL EVENTS

1. Walk for Literacy
(Walk Chair: Name) (Phonathon Co-Chairs: Names)

Time Frame:	October 2, 2008
# of Walkers:	100
Goal:	$16,000 gross/$14,800 net (FY 2003 Walk grossed $16,100)
Method:	Mailing: 2,500 pieces; phonathon 2 weeks later to recruit walkers, pledgers, donations; news articles and other promotional publicity; other personal recruitment by board, staff, students.

2. Student Recognition Evening
(Chair(s): to be named)

Time Frame:	April-June, 1999
# of Prospects:	650 individuals (previous attendees/invitees, new)
Goal:	$3,500 gross/$0 net; 350 guests, volunteers, and students ($4,000 raised by 2008 Recognition Evening.)
Method:	Invitation mailed; follow-up phone calls, face-to-face soliciting; newsletter announcement.

3. Yearbook/Ad Campaign
(Chair(s): Name(s))

Time Frame:	December, 2008 – May, 2009
# of Prospects:	75 corporate sponsors; 100 businesses; 35 individuals/other
Goal:	$10,500 gross/$8,000 net; 60% renewal ads, 15% upgrades, 10% new (over $12,000 gross raised in 2008 campaign)
Method:	Mailing; follow-up phone calls and personal soliciting.
Solicitors:	Board, staff, volunteers, college interns, students.

SAMPLE ANNUAL FUND DEVELOPMENT PLAN (CONT.)

4. Benefit Concert
(Chair(s): Name(s))

- **Time Frame:** March 25, 2009
- **Attendance Goal:** 350
- **Goal:** $2,000 gross/$1,500 net (concert raised $2,000 in 3/08)
- **Method:** Mailings, radio and TV PR., flyers, posters, newsletters, and newspaper coverage
- **Solicitors:** staff, volunteers, other?

C. DIRECT MAIL

1. Direct Mail

- **Time Frame:** December, 2008
- **# of Prospects:** 2,500 (1,000 new)
- **# of Donors:** 200
- **Goal:** $8,000; 60% renewal, 15% gift upgrades, 5% new donors ($8,000 raised in most recent Holiday Drive)
- **Method:** Mailing with remit enclosure; follow-up articles in newsletter; holiday mailing possibly signed by individual students from each class. Follow-up mailing to major donors in previous campaign who have not renewed their gift.

SAMPLE ANNUAL FUND DEVELOPMENT PLAN (CONT.)

2. Direct Mail

Time Frame: April-May, 2009

# of Prospects: 3,000 (1,000 new)

# of Donors: 200

Goal: $ 8,000; 60% renewal, 15% gift upgrades, 5% new donors ($6,000 raised in 2008 Friends Drive)

Method: Mailing with remit enclosure; follow-up articles in newsletter; and follow-up letter within one month to non-respondents (if staff resources permit). Mailing possibly signed by selected board members and students. Follow-up mailing to major donors in previous campaign who have not renewed their gift.

D. GOVERNMENT AND FOUNDATION GRANTS

Time Frame: On-going throughout the year

# of Reports: 165

# of New Prospects: at least 10

Goal: $365,528: 9 government applications; $30,000: 15 foundation proposals; $65,000

Method: Finance Director and relevant program staff prepare grant applications.

SAMPLE ANNUAL FUND DEVELOPMENT PLAN (CONT.)

IV. CULTIVATION STRATEGIES (MAKING "FRIENDS")

The purpose of cultivation is:

A) To add prospects to our donor base and develop them to become active supporters and regular donors; and

B) To improve relationships with current board members, donors, volunteers, and other friends of ABC, Inc., to build a greater understanding of how they can help our agency achieve its mission.

Donor and volunteer recognition are critical to the cultivation process. Cultivation needs to be discussed regularly at board meetings to encourage each board member to become part of the cultivation process.

OPEN HOUSES:

This is a responsibility of the P.R. Committee; chair(s) to be named through that committee.

Time: Twice per year - December, 2008 (Donor Recognition), April, 2009 (Volunteer Recognition).

Goal: Appreciation evenings at ABC, Inc. for donors and volunteers; opportunity to see facilities, meet staff and students; recruitment of potential volunteers; and cultivation of potential donors.

Method: Special mailings with invitations; newsletter articles; public announcements; personal invitations by board.

Responsible: Board, staff, students, other volunteers.

COMMUNICATIONS

Holiday Card: Holiday greeting card to 300 friends and major donors (this is not a solicitation).

Newsletter: 6x per year. Sent to agency mailing list (3,500+) provides regular updates on agency programs, student writings, activities, and special events. Mailing list includes funders, donors, volunteers, home-based students, elected officials, other agency executives, and service providers.

Annual Report: Annually to coincide with July 1 fiscal year. Mailing in September. This is a major communications tool sent to government and private funding sources, large donors, agency executives, and public officials, and is submitted with most proposals and requests to large donor prospects.

SAMPLE ANNUAL FUND DEVELOPMENT PLAN (CONT.)

Student Yearbook: Another major communications tool featuring student writings. Distributed at annual Recognition Evening and mailed to major corporate sponsors of event and major ad-takers, major funding sources as well as new prospects.

Other Publicity/Public Relations: A separate public relations plan will be developed by P.R. Committee to help reinforce cultivation efforts of this Fund Development Plan. A close communications linkage between the Fund Development and P.R. Committees needs to be maintained to adequately support the objectives of the Fund Development Plan.

Our P.R. plan may include such strategies as:

- Radio and TV PSAs
- TV coverage of special events
- Newspaper and magazine articles
- Articles in ABC, Inc. and other agency newsletters
- Community Bulletin Board announcements to publicize events
- Radio and TV interviews
- Displays in public buildings
- Brochures
- Bookmarks
- Posters/Flyers
- Video and/or slide show presentation
- Speakers Bureau (board and staff volunteers)
- Publicity/outreach to private and government workplaces to encourage participation in federated campaigns (posters, brochures, etc.)

SAMPLE ANNUAL FUND DEVELOPMENT PLAN (CONT.)

V. ASSISTING THE FUND DEVELOPMENT PLAN AND PROCESS

- The Fund Development Committee will meet 6 times a year to review the progress of the plan and, with fund development staff, will identify problems and solutions.

- Development staff and committee chair will discuss development issues on a regular basis.

- Committee chair and development staff will monitor sub-committee chairs; committee chair will follow-up re: problems.

- Development Committee will discuss fund development plan and progress at monthly board meetings.

- Development staff will provide financial and statistical data with which to help evaluate progress of the plan.

VI. FUND DEVELOPMENT CALENDAR FY 2009

July	Preparation of Annual Report
	Review results of June Recognition Dinner
August	Annual Report mailed with cover letter
	Plan P.R. for United Way, government employee Campaigns
	Send letters to government and CFC Donors
September	Mailing/phonathon/other publicity for Literacy Walk
	Personal solicitation of board members (Sept.-Nov.)
	United Way employee campaign at ABC, Inc.
October	Literacy Walk
	Follow-up re: walk pledges
	Personal campaign with large donors (Sept.-Dec.)
	Direct Mail #1 planned
November	Discuss cultivation strategies (On-going)
	Evaluate results of Literacy Walk

SAMPLE ANNUAL FUND DEVELOPMENT PLAN (CONT.)

November (cont.)	Prepare holiday mailing/mailing lists
	P.R. Committee will plan Open House
	Evaluate previous ad campaign for yearbook and plan 2009 campaign
December	Direct Mail #1
	Holiday Open House
	Advance solicitation for corporate sponsors of yearbook
	Review progress of personal annual campaign
January	Review results of Direct Mail #1
	Review progress of ad campaign
	Review results of personal campaign
	Plan benefit concert
February	Review progress of ad campaign
	Continue discussions of cultivation strategies
	Review plans for Volunteer Recognition Evening
	Review plans for Student Recognition Evening
	Review plans for benefit concert
March	Finalize plans for Direct Mail #2
	Update progress on ad campaign
	Review results of Federated Campaigns (United Way, ST, CFC)
	Benefit concert (See February)

SAMPLE ANNUAL FUND DEVELOPMENT PLAN (CONT.)

April   Volunteer Recognition Evening

Process Direct Mail #2

Review results of benefit concert

Update Progress re: ad book campaign

Update Progress re: Recognition Evening

Begin FY 2010 fund development planning process

May   Complete ad campaign

Review progress re: Direct Mail #2

Update Progress re: Recognition Evening

Mailing for Recognition Dinner

Begin planning for 5th Annual Literacy Walk

June   Recognition Evening

Review results of ad campaign and dinner ticket sales

Update results of Direct Mail #2

Full board to approve FY 2000 Fund Development Plan

THE CASE FOR SUPPORT

Developing and articulating the organization's Case for Support is vital for a small shop's fundraising efforts. Non-profits know they require financial support to deliver their mission. The Case makes that argument to constituents – it is the rationale that explains what the organization aims to achieve.

Unfortunately, the majority of small shops do not have a written Case for Support. While it will not prevent organizations from raising funds, having a Case for Support can facilitate the process of developing appeals and grant proposals for the fundraising professional. Taking the time to write the Case will save both time and energy when you write appeal letters or grant proposals.

To get started, gather the following resources: mission statement, organizational goals and objectives, description of programs and services, finances, governance structure, staffing, facilities and service delivery, planning and evaluation and history of the organization. Armed with these documents and working in collaboration with colleagues, board members and some key long-time donors, the writing can begin.

The case should answer the following questions:

- What is the problem or social need the organization is addressing?
- What services and programs are offered to address this problem?
- Why is addressing this problem important?
- What is the organization's market for these services?
- What are the staff's competencies to deliver these programs and services?
- What are the organization's plans for the future?
- Who should support the organization?

Don't worry about the Case being perfect – it is intended to be an internal document that will change as the organization evolves. Periodical review of the Case will ensure that it remains current and up-to-date. Finally, don't forget to include photos and testimonials of your service recipients to demonstrate your organization's impact. The essence of fundraising success is a fully articulated Case for Support that sets bold goals for the organization and enthusiastically inspires donors to be involved.

An excellent overview of creating a case-for-support was produced by Pearl Veenema, in Chapter 3 of *Excellence in Fundraising in Canada, Volume 1*.[8]

The database

I remember my first consulting client. It was a very small grassroots mental health organization that had hired me to "get them organized." When we started talking about their donor database, the office administrator showed me a stack of lined, three-hole punch sheets with names and donation amounts handwritten in pencil on them.

Fundraising is, by nature, driven by data. Without a proper database, fundraising will become an even greater challenge. Many small shops begin with a basic list in Excel or Access but eventually grow out of it when fundraising activities grow and become more strategic. Admittedly, a proper donor database can be a very expensive investment for a small shop but the solutions they offer will enable the small shop fundraiser to be more efficient and to raise more funds in the long run. As such, senior management should look at a donor database as a revenue generating investment/tool as opposed to an expense line on a balance sheet.

Here are some of the pros and cons of having a "from a box" donor database:

Pros	Cons
Quick and complete view of all donor interactions	Only track donations but not interactions
Preset reports	Reports must be done manually
Ability to send e-appeals from the database	No connection between email blast solution and database
Capacity to upload donations into accounting software	Donation report must be manually uploaded to accounting software

---

8   Veenema, Pearl. (2011) "Chapter 3: Case for Support." *Excellence in Fundraising in Canada*. Civil Sector Press.

Pros	Cons
• Most databases are now hosted "in the cloud" enabling access from anywhere • Ease to track pledges, monthly donations and grants • Moves management capacity • Donations made online will automatically upload to the database • Quick processing of donations • Tech support	• Usually available on local server and not as easily accessible from outside of the office • Expensive one-time cost and recurring annual support/maintenance fee

Figure 3.1

Of course, this list is not exhaustive but it presents a snapshot of the solutions a donor database can bring to the small shop fundraiser.

In selecting a database for your organization you need to consider the state of your current fundraising program, where you see your program in the next 5-10 years and your budget. You may not need to purchase the most elaborate software available. Perhaps it'll be better to start with a simpler database and wait until the needs of the organization warrants upgrading to a more robust tool. There are several starter solutions offered by TechSoup Canada, but also ask organizations similar to yours what tool they use. To help in your decision-making process, read "Finding the Perfect Fundraising Database in an Imperfect World" by Robert Weiner.[9]

---

9   Weiner, Robert. *Finding the Perfect Fundraising Database in an Imperfect World*. http://www.rlweiner.com/grf/grf_finding_perfect_database.pdf

ADAPTING SMALL SHOP FUNDRAISING STRATEGIES

Scaling is essential when working in a small shop where everything relating to fundraising rests on the shoulders of one, maybe two, professionals. We already determined that having a development plan ensures that the few resources available are directed at the strategies that will yield the biggest return.

Individual giving

When your organization is fairly young and it doesn't have many donors, how do you build that list? This is the most common question I hear from small shop fundraisers. The truth is, building a loyal list of supporters is time-consuming and will not yield results immediately but with consistent efforts it will pay off.

Consider the following tactics for acquiring names of prospective donors:

- Have a signup sheet at every event. Gather every name possible. Offer a door prize as an incentive.
- Ask your current donors to refer your organization to their friends. People like to ask their friends to be part of something they believe in.
- Use your website to collect email and contact information. Make this a prominent feature and prioritize the collection of names.
- Leverage social media platforms to engage with the public (more of that in the next section).
- Organize a crowdfunding campaign to gain new supporters using online tools like *indiegogo*.
- Engage your board in brainstorming names.
- Recruit volunteers to engage in donor identification and qualification activities.
- Consider renting lists of donors from likeminded organizations.
- Consider exchanging your list of donors with a list of donors from another likeminded organization.

Make building your donor list (prospect identification) a fun activity that is based on key communication messaging found in your Case for Support. But don't wait to have an extensive donor list to start soliciting donors through mail or online. No matter how small your list is, start exercising your solicitation muscles and ask for gifts. Thank and steward your donors, then ask again, and again, and again.

After a donor has donated three to four times, invite the donor to join your monthly giving program. Boast about the advantages of becoming a monthly donor and the impact their gift will make. Every opportunity to give, that you offer offline must also be made available online. Your web presence must be similar to your mail offer - thereby reinforcing your key messaging.

The advantage small shop fundraisers have is that they can get to know their supporters very quickly and have meaningful conversations about the impact of the donations. The key to your success will be those short but meaningful conversations you will have with the donor when you call to say thank you. As the relationship develops, you will be able to invite donors to give more often and at higher amounts. Before you know it, you will have a robust donor list to steward and solicit.

Major Gifts
Through careful stewardship and cultivation, individuals will start self-identifying themselves as major donors. But first, let's define what a major gift is in the context of a small non-profit.

People often wrongly assume that a major gift must be in the hundreds of thousands of dollars. In fact, nothing could be farther from the truth. The term "major gift" is relative, meaning that it is whatever amount is considered significant in comparison to all other gifts to your organization. For one organization a major gift will be $500 and for another, it may be $15,000. Whatever the amount you chose, know that this can change if you notice an upwards trends among your major donors.

Individual major gifts are the lifeline of your development plan. Individuals account for 85% of all major gifts to non-profits (foundations and corporations account for the rest). The difficulty is making the case to the board for investing in these constituents. After all, they want to make sure the organization meets its budget. When faced with push back, take the opportunity to educate senior management and board members about the importance of building relationships in order to access unrestricted donations for the organization.

By repeating this over and over again, and by continuing to steward these individuals, you will not only build strong relationships with your donors, but they will be inclined to invite others to join and to advocate for the organization.

Foundation and Corporate Major Gifts
Foundations and corporations have become more and more strategic in their giving habits. Indeed, their ways of approaching philanthropy are very similar. Both are looking to meet specific needs: whether to continue the wishes of the founders of the foundation or to meet a certain business interest. There has been a surge of corporate foundations being established to respond to the ever-increasing requests for financial support.

As a small shop fundraiser, you cannot neglect to include corporations and foundations in your development plan. Now that you have your Case for Support written and the funding priorities have been identified, here are few steps to follow:

1. *Do your prospect research.*
   Careful prospect research will help you to streamline your grantwriting and ensure you approach the best funding partners. Armed with your list of prospects, create a "grantwriting calendar" so you know when every proposal is due over the next year.

2. *Ensure you match the right prospect with the right project/program.*
   Carefully read the funder's philanthropic interest and make a connection with your project/program throughout the proposal.

3. *Call to introduce the organization.*
   If possible, call the funder to introduce yourself and your organization. Clarify any funding questions you may have and invite them for a site visit. Many funders will not take calls or refuse a visit but sometimes, small family foundations or community foundations will accept. It doesn't hurt to try, provided the guidelines indicates that they accept calls.

4. *Ask for the right amount.*
   Foundation ABC may have supported your local university's library to the tune of $2million but that doesn't mean it'll support your resource centre at 100%. Be realistic. Look at their donation history and identify

organizations they supported that are similar to your size. Gauge your ask accordingly and continue identifying other prospects to cover the rest of your project/program budget.

5. *Follow the funder's guidelines.*
   Nothing ensures a quick rejection like not following the funder's guidelines to the letter. Do not attempt to divert from their instructions and ensure you only send what they ask for.

6. *Thank you.*
   If the answer was negative, call to obtain feedback on your proposal then thank the prospect for considering your proposal. If the answer was positive, call immediately to say thanks and send a letter within 24 hours. If the acceptance letter does not make a mention of it, mark your calendar with a follow-up to send a report on the funded project/program.

Here are some additional tips to remember as you write your grant proposals:

Mistakes too many applicants make:	Ways to help assure repeat funding:
1. Talking mainly about problems, not solutions.	1. Get your reports in on time.
2. Describing specific problems with general solutions.	2. Provide all the information that is requested.
3. Prolific use of buzzwords and jargon.	3. Put the funder on your mailing list.
4. Budgets that don't add up.	4. Send a thank you note.
5. Parroting the funder's guidelines without linking them to the work.	5. Show that you did what you said you would do.
	6. Explain why you didn't do what you said you would do.

Figure 3.2

One final note on prospect research. There are many online tools to help you in your research. Databases like Fundtracker, Big Online and Grant Connect can help you with your research and show you funders' granting priorities and donation history. This will make the small shop fundraiser's job so much easier than having to search the Web.

Access to these databanks can be quite costly and your organization may not have the funds to pay for this. However, the investment will be quickly recuperated with as little as 2-3 successful proposals. Enquire about small non-profit pricing or extended payment plans. Most services usually understand the reality of small shops.

SPECIAL EVENTS

How often have board members or senior management decided to organize a last minute event because they knew they weren't going to raise enough money through other means?

Special events have always been the "go-to" fundraising activity of small shops. Inexperienced board members revert to special events because they don't understand how fundraising works and how other strategies yield higher return on investment. Despite repeating the low ROI of events over and over, it is the professional's responsibility to change the culture and to move away from events by taking the time to educate decision-makers and propose alternatives.

However, not all events are a terrible idea. Events are a good strategy to adopt when the goal is not primarily to raise money and are a particularly good idea for small shops to assign in:

- Acquiring new donors: "friend"-raising
- Raising the organization's public image
- Recognizing and thanking donors or volunteers
- Launching a signature event that will be repeated every year

To alleviate the workload that events create, recruiting trustworthy and hardworking volunteers is fundamental. Setting goals, assigning tasks and deadlines as well as creating a budget will make planning events much easier. Special events can also allow organizations to evaluate potential new board members by tasking them with jobs.

A WORD ABOUT LEGACY GIVING

Legacy giving, or planned giving, as it is more commonly known, is the holy grail of the fundraising program. Small non-profits shy away from legacy giving because it is still viewed as too complicated and filled with legal jargon. Nothing could be farther from the truth.

Small shops can easily start establishing a legacy giving program by talking about bequests in newsletters, on the organization's website and on donation coupons. In fact, 90% of legacy gifts are through bequests. As baby boomers age, there will be a huge wealth transfer and non-profits who have taken the time to cultivate their donors and offer this type of donating option will surely reap the benefits.

Here are some simple steps to establish your small shop legacy program:

1. Track the number of "expectancies." (a promise by a donor to make a gift to a non-profit at some future date) However, that promise may be revoked at any time prior to the donor's death. In other words, the charity is expecting to receive the gift at some future date, but ultimately it may not receive it if the donor changes his or her mind.[10]
2. Visit your favourite non-profits' websites and look at what they're doing on legacy giving - imitation is the greatest form of flattery!
3. Call your donors to thank them for their gifts and pay attention to cues or information that may tell you they are potential legacy donors.
4. Include a "Did You Know" column in your newsletter and briefly inform donors the impact of leaving a legacy to the organization through a bequest in their Will.
5. Provide simple and easy to find bequest language on your website with the name and telephone number of a contact person.
6. Develop a special legacy giving appeal to be sent via mail. Make sure your copy is in large font (13 - 14 serifs fonts like Times New Roman, Georgia, or Garamond, etc.).
7. Follow up with potential donors by visiting them and talking about the type of legacy they want to leave in the world.

Such a program is a long-term investment. It can take from 5 to 10 years before the organization sees any results but when it does, it can have a significant impact. In the meantime, find a mentor, become a member of the Canadian Association of Gift Planners and learn what you can about legacy giving.

CASE STUDY: REGINA HUMANE SOCIETY

Karen Dackiw, CFRE is Director of Development at the Regina Humane Society. She has been working at the animal rescue for five years. The organization has two fundraisers: herself and an events coordinator. During her tenure, the team has increased fundraising revenue by 59% and they now raise close to $1.5 million a year. Here is how the team did it:

- Completed a full development review of all activities including a cost analysis. This had never been done before and guided the strategy going forward.

- Adopted a narrative approach for all of the fundraising and communication materials. The focus shifted to telling the story of one animal at a time, knowing that most people cannot understand what it means to help 4,500 animals every year. Most people can relate to, and feel for these animals one-on-one. For instance, the calendar was changed to feature twelve animals that had been adopted over the past year. Each month shows a before and after photo with a story about the animal. Donations to the calendar appeal doubled in one year alone.

- Stopped doing ineffective fundraising events that were a time and money drain for the organization. There was pushback on some of these choices but the team persevered.

- Added resources to grow fundraising events that were under-performing but showed potential.

---

10 Tempel, Eugene R., Timothy L. Seiler and Eva E. Aldrich. (2010). *Achieving Excellence in Fundraising*, John Wiley & Sons. Page 102.

- Direct mail materials were redone and follow-up appeals were added to all direct mail pieces to recover lost donors.

- Small special events were cut and the focus shifted towards having a fewer, larger signature events.

- A holiday catalogue was created. (It is now their largest fundraiser!)

- Established an animal adoption sponsorship program which brought in new donors.

- The organization cut a large telemarketing program that was commission-based and not donor-centered.

- Donors are now called to ask to join the monthly donor program or to make a year-end donation if they haven't already done so.

- Focusing on monthly giving was a huge piece of the fundraising program's growth. A pre-authorized withdrawal plan was created and sign up forms were added to every mail piece, newsletter, etc. This program has grown by 250% over the last eight years.

- Personalized donor stewardship activities were increased and hand-written cards were sent as often as possible.

- Management invested in fundraising staff by paying for memberships to the Association of Fundraising Professionals, to attend conferences, and to take educational courses.

- A positive and results-focused communications strategy was adopted. Previous materials and communications were depressing and accusatory to people. Materials and social media were refocused on positive messaging and how people can get involved.

- The board was instrumental in developing a strategic plan with measurable benchmarks. They were supportive and active in the fundraising activities.

CASE STUDY: TEN OAKS PROJECT

Holly Wagg and Julia Alarie co-founded the Ten Oaks Project, an Ottawa-based organization that engages and connects children and youth from LGBTQ communities through programs and activities rooted in play. The organization was found in 2004 and had very modest beginnings. Ten Oaks has one and a half salaried staff and the rest of the work is volunteer-driven.

From the beginning, it was decided that the organization would build support using digital media. Focusing only on online tools, the burgeoning organization built its constituents' base through email solicitations. This was done by engaging the board to approach their networks and act as ambassadors for the organization.

The organization also decided on organizing one signature event per year. From humble beginnings, the event raised $4,500 in the first year. Ten years later, the event raises $45,000. Major gifts from individuals are a main focus of the organization's fundraising plan as are grants and third-party events.

Communications is the cornerstone of this organization's efforts. This includes a robust website, an electronic newsletter, email appeals, an engagement strategy for alumni and having volunteers call donors to thank them or to convert them into monthly donors.

TIPS FOR THE SMALL SHOP

Here is a list of tips to consider implementing right away to help maximize your small shop effectiveness:

1. *Create a development plan so that you are raising funds for the next fiscal year.* This will avoid the incessant madness of trying to scramble constantly to come up with ways to meet budget needs.
2. *Establish a monthly giving program as soon as possible.* After a donor has made a minimum of

three one-time gifts, invite them to join your monthly giving program. Focus on how the recurrent gifts will have impact - not on how easy and cheap it is to give monthly.
3. *Encourage pledging over time.* When soliciting major gifts from individuals, foundations or corporations, explore the possibility of multi-year commitments.
4. *Stagger your multi-year major gifts.* This way they don't all begin and end at the same time.
5. *Steward and cultivate your multi-year donors.* Try and provide as much stewardship to these donors, as you would for your annual donors.
6. *Organize thank-a-thons.* Do this with board members, staff, volunteers or event recipients of your organization's programs and services.
7. *Focus more energy on donor stewardship and cultivation* A good rule-of-thumb is to provide more time on stewardship and cultivation, than on special events. When you show a donor love, the gifts will come in. Consider this story of a former small shop fundraiser who had received a $5,000 donation for her organization (a major gift for the small hospital). Upon doing some research, she learns that the donor is a high-ranking executive at a big tech company in Ontario. As it turns out, one of the board members had gone to school with the donor and agreed to call him to thank him for the donation. He learned the donor's mother had had surgery at the hospital and they were both very grateful for the excellent care she had received. After a few months of cultivation, the donor decided to make an even bigger donation –this time, a donation of stocks in the amount of $279,000.
8. *Be realistic and don't expect to do everything at once.* Set long-term goals (no longer than three years), then break these down into yearly objectives and then again by quarterly objectives. This will prevent you from feeling overwhelmed with the magnitude of the work and will provide management with a tool for which to evaluate the progress of the fundraising program.
9. *Plan for growth by involving board members in the budget planning process.* Often times board members get excited when fundraising revenue increases but may not understand that it has a direct impact in the workload of the staff. To ensure the organization continues to have fundraising success, it may have to increase human resources.
10. *Find mentors who will support the fundraising professional.* This will give the fundraiser a place to bounce ideas, receive feedback, provide advice, be inspired and motivated. Use social media to find other fundraisers. There are many on Twitter who are very active and who share a myriad of information FOR FREE! Look at the *Additional Resources* section for a list of fundraisers on Twitter.
11. *Make professional development a priority.* A professional that is constantly learning will inevitably manage a successful fundraising program. Provide a budget for a membership to any fundraising professional association as well as for attending local and national conferences. Some professional associations offer payment by instalments for the membership dues as well as bursaries to attend conferences.
12. *Put a lot of effort into training and educating board members.* Consider inviting another locally respected fundraising professional to offer a workshop. If you don't know any, contact your local fundraising professional association chapter for recommendations. Often, they will agree to give a workshop for free.
13. *Work toward creating an integrated program.* Slowly and consistently integrate all the elements that make fundraising successful: such as communications, cultivation, and offering donors different ways to give and get involved. Slow and steady, is more sustainable than giving immense bursts of energy on one thing - it can be confusing for the donor and is simply not sustainable.
14. *Invest in a good database.* Resist the urge to build a custom database when you can get something out of a box already created specifically for non-profits.
15. *Focus on the fundraisers well-being: physically and emotionally.* The burn-out rate among

small shop fundraisers is very high. A sick fundraiser is not working at 100% capacity. Creating a work-life balance is fundamental to avoid exhaustion or worse, resignation from the professional.
16. *Create a list of planned giving prospects and expectancies.* You can't manage what you can't measure. This will give you a baseline to measure and cultivate those relationships.
17. *Focus on a good quality communications.* Include testimonials and good stories.
18. *Don't be a stranger.* Pick up the phone every day and call to thank a donor.
19. *Seek sponsors.* Look for a funder to cover the cost of fundraising expenses such as a new donor database.
20. *Have a good website.* This will allow you to capture visitors' contact information and email. There are so many free or cheap website templates available, there is no reason why every non-profits shouldn't have a website.
21. *Running out of steam and you need timely help?* Get a summer intern from your local university or college. The federal government also offers many programs that will cover the cost of hiring a summer intern. Inquire at your local employment office.
22. *Consider exchanging your donor list.* List exchange or rental is an excellent way to build your organization's donor list.
23. *Focus on the bigger potential.* Look to the programs that will yield bigger and better results rather than what is easy and simple. There are no quick fixes in fundraising!
24. *Get the tough tasks out of the way first.* Look at focusing time on those tasks that you dislike the most or that require more of your attention, early in the morning. Although I enjoy calling donors, I leave it to the end of the day so I can finish my day on a high note.
25. *Review your weekly checklist.* Finally, at the end of every week, make a mental list of all your accomplishments. This will prevent you from beating yourself up because you didn't get through your entire to-do list and will remind you of how much you're getting done.

CONCLUSION

To survive as a fundraiser in a small shop you have to be strategic, organized, patient, flexible and focused. You need to be a warrior. The many testimonials and case studies demonstrate that small shops are resilient and successful. The work is not always easy but the rewards far outweigh the challenges. By putting in place the many strategies outlined in this chapter, slowly and steadily, fundraising excellence will be achieved for the small shop fundraiser.

ADDITIONAL RESOURCES

- EISENSTEIN, AMY. MPA, ACFRE, (2014). *Major Gifts for Small Shops: How to Leverage Your Annual Fund in Only Five Hours per Week.* California, USA: CharityChannel Press.

- EISENSTEIN, AMY. MPA, ACFRE, (2010). *50 Asks in 50 Weeks: A Guide to Better Fundraising for Your Small Development Shop.* California, USA: CharityChannel Press.

- GREENFIELD, JAMES M. (1996). *Fund-Raising Cost Effectiveness A Self-Assessment Workbook.* USA, John Wiley & Sons.

- KLEIN, KIM. 5TH EDITION, (2007). *Fundraising for Social Change. California*, USA: Jossey-Bass.

- MALLABONE, GUY. ED., (2012). *Excellence in Fundraising in Canada.* Toronto: Hilborn.

- MALLABONE, GUY, AND BALMER, KEN. *The Fundraising Audit Handbook.* http://www.canadianfundraiser.com/Bookroom/productDescription.asp?crypt=DXpwDhYdd2t9f2seeHduBAMUfxgdFXhwdH92cwUQdXZ9eWYDFmULBg4

- PERRY, GAIL. (2007). *Fired-Up Fundraising Turn Board Passion into Action.* Hoboken, N.J.: Wiley.

- TEMPEL, EUGENE R., ED., (2003). *Hank Rosso's Achieving Excellence in Fund Raising.* San Francisco: Jossey-Bass.

Fundraisers on Twitter:

This list is not exhaustive but you can start following these fundraisers who make Twitter a vibrant and free professional development tool. Look at who they follow and add more to your list of fundraisers on Twitter. It's an easy and free way to learn and exchange on topics relating to the non-profit sector and on fundraising.

Canadian-based Fundraisers	US-based Fundraisers
Andrea McManus, CFRE @TDGAndrea	#fundchat @fundchat
Barth Gillan @barthg	Alice Ferris, ACFRE @aliceferris
Daniella Mailing @daniellamailing	Dan Blakemore, CFRE @dan_blakemore
Good Works @_goodworks_	Dave Tinker, CFRE @davethecfre
Guy Mallabonne, CFRE @AskMuscle	Gail Perry, CFRE @gailperrync
Holly Wagg, CFRE @hollywagg	Jim Anderson, CFRE @GoalBustersJim
Jeff Gignac @jeffgignac and @JMGSolutions	John Dawe, CFRE @johndawe
Karen Dackiw, CFRE @karendackiw	Josh Hirsch @joshhirsch1
Kelly Morris @kellyannmorris	Laura Amerman, CFRE @leamerman
Leah Eustace, ACFRE @leaheustace	Lisa Chmiola, CFRE @houdatlisa
Ligia Peña, CFRE @ligiafpena	Sandy Rees @sandyrees
Liz Rejman, CFRE @erejman	Shannon Doolittle @shannondoolittle
Michelle Vinokurov @michellevinokurov	
Sam Loucks Laprade, CFRE @GryphonReport	
Scott Fortnum, ACFRE @scottfortnum	
Tania Little, CFRE @tanialittle	

ABOUT THE AUTHOR

Ligia Peña, CFRE

Ligia is the Director of Development at the MOSD Foundation (Montreal Oral School for the Deaf) since 2013. For the past 13 years, she has been working with a wide range of organizations; from mental health, environmental education, at-risk youths to international NGOs. Working on all aspects of fundraising, communications and management, her true passion has always been to empower small non-profits to be strong, resilient and sustainable so they may realize their important mission.

In recent years, Ligia has been presenting on the topic of planned giving for small shops and ethics in fundraising.

Ligia is very active in the Canadian non-profit sector by serving on several committees at the Association of Fundraising Professionals. She also serves on the Board of Directors of Girls Action Foundation.

CHAPTER 4

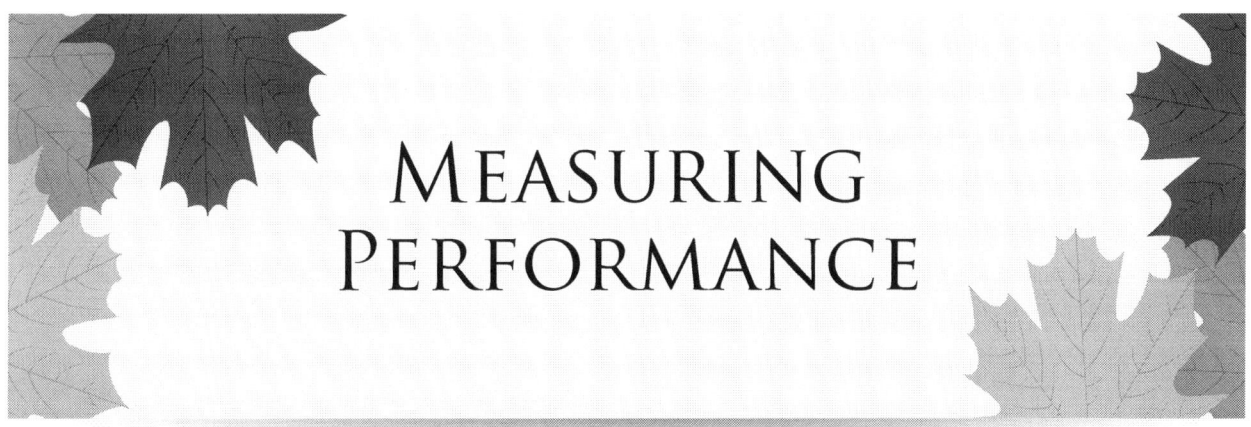

MEASURING PERFORMANCE

KAREN VAN SACKER, MBA, MAICD

As I considered this topic of measurement and performance, I thought back on the multitude of not-for-profits of all shapes and sizes that I've worked with and for over the years and how measurement is used (or not) to inform strategy and inspire action. It is an area of management that we all acknowledge intellectually as pivotal, but often place in the "too hard" box to be dealt with during a quiet time that never quite arrives.

read more…

The challenge often is how to sift through the masses of data that we deal with every day, to extract those key measures that paint a clear picture of our reality and allow each member of the team, from the board director through to the person who takes RSVPs for event programs, to initiate positive actions that attract increased levels of private investment to our organizations.

Without the clear picture that metrics and measurement can bring into focus, planning and target-setting is based on wetting your finger to test the wind, with day-to-day activities that run their course without the benefit of a clear sight line to chart and monitor progress.

The questions therefore are, "how can the sound analysis of data inform, motivate and guide behavior?" and "what are the essential metrics that can be readily distilled and used as markers to guide the way forward?" Where is the balance between financial and non-financial performance metrics that will keep people focused on the road ahead?

This chapter will present a cross section of metrics as useful tools for measuring, assessing, monitoring and benchmarking performance. These will cut across governance, management and program operations, and when applied appropriately, inform planning and facilitate personal and organizational excellence.

THE KIS PRINCIPLE: KEEP IT SIMPLE!

Let's be honest: metrics and measurement is not the most scintillating topic, especially for those among us who don't have a "math brain." To make sense of it all, I've interspersed the chapter with illustrations, case studies and tips for applying concepts. I hope each reader will find useful ideas.

However, the most important take-away it the KIS Principle: Keep it simple! Pick those metrics and measures that make sense for you and your organization based on where you're at... and sometimes that may mean getting the organization to the point of collecting the right data for measuring performance.

WHAT IS THE END GAME?

As my colleague and instigator of this book, Guy Mallabone, is fond of saying: "money drives mission." Therefore, metrics must perform a decision-making function that allows us as professionals to deliver increased levels of funding to organizational priorities. The first step is to determine the decisions you wish to inform and audience/s who will be using them.

Some questions to consider include:

- How will these measures be used?
- Who are the users?
- What actions or changes do we want these metrics to drive?
- How will I source and report on these metrics on an ongoing basis?

SEVEN PRINCIPLE USES OF METRICS AND PERFORMANCE MEASUREMENT:

1. Investment decisions that grow your capacity to raise more money.

2. Individual performance management and tracking that ensures each member of the team is focused on and achieving personal and organizational goals.

3. Program performance metrics that allow managers to assess, evaluate and improve outcomes as part of a best practice continuous improvement cycle.

4. Data capture for more targeted, high-impact program outcomes.

5. Issues identification and problem-solving whether program or people focused.

6. Improving organizational efficiencies; and, most importantly,

7. Measuring and reporting on donor impact.

Figure 4.1

Language and tools are as important as the picture they paint. The principles we apply to negotiating high impact philanthropy should be applied in equal measure to business decision-making: know your audience and use the strategies and tactics that solicit the decision and lead to the actions you seek.

MEASURING FINANCIAL PERFORMANCE

The purpose of financial performance measurement is to bring a hard-edge to evaluation that ensures we, as fundraising professionals, are strategically pursuing fundraising excellence and maximizing mission impact.

However, senior executive and board members oftentimes will make the statement that our metrics don't reflect the real cost of fundraising (e.g. inclusive of staff and overheads). As fundraising professionals and nonprofit leaders, we must develop sound practices that use metrics at multiple levels, to evaluate specific fundraising programs and also to assess organizational effectiveness. Our ultimate goal is to make the best use of scarce resources, both in terms of people and programs, to deliver on our mission.

Two common measures of financial performance are "return on investment" and, in the fundraising profession, "cost per dollar raised." Both are ratios used to assess the cost-benefit of a given revenue generating venture.

1. Return on Investment (ROI)

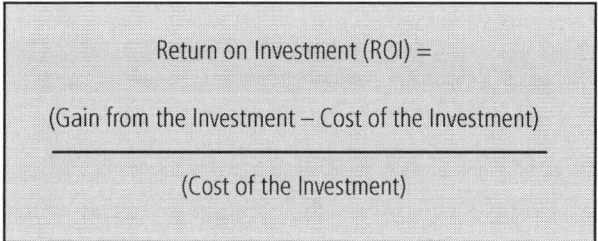

Figure 4.2

This measurement is considered the mainstay of the business world and a measure your board members will understand. It is an indicator of the quality of a given investment, depicting how many times over your original investment (in a major gift officer for example) delivers results. *Figure 4.3* provides a visual representation of Return on Investment.

Using ROI and margins to benchmark overall performance against peer organizations is easily and rapidly accomplished by analyzing annual reports drawn from competitor web sites. Comparisons should be taken with a grain of salt as many variables will be at play. However, if you are looking to facilitate a major cultural shift towards a higher performing complement of fundraising programs, peer benchmarking is a must.

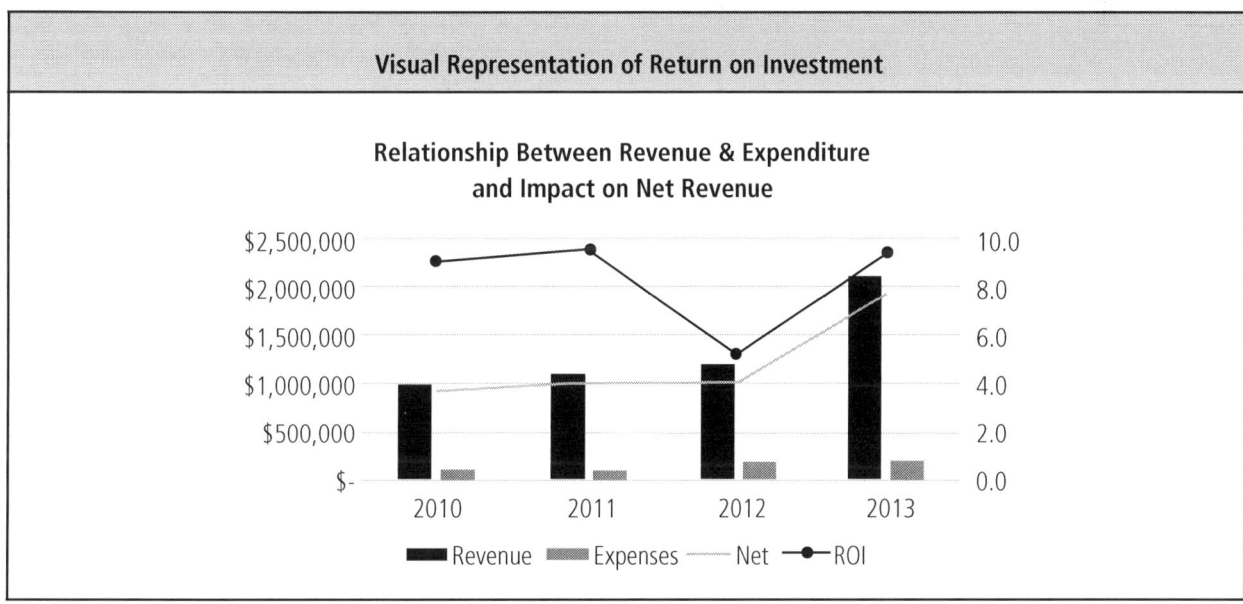

Figure 4.3

Look to those organizations who you wish to emulate and use a strategic and detailed comparative analysis to present the case.

There are two primary reason to consider using the ROI measure:

A) Firstly, most of our board members would be popping the champagne for a business that delivers returns exceeding 0.75 (75%) let alone 2.0 (200%). Yes, our goal remains creating better communities, but support the emotional case for investment with the rational one, and use the tools at your fingertips to back a winning proposal to your board and sophisticated donors.

B) Secondly, ROI focuses a discussion on donor impact: "$0.75 of every gift advances our mission."

2. Cost-Per-Dollar-Raised

$$\text{Cost Per Dollar Raised (CPDR)} = \frac{\text{Program Cost}}{\text{Total Program Revenues}}$$

Figure 4.4

Cost per Dollar Raised is a traditional measure of fundraising effectiveness. It's widely used across the fundraising profession and sometimes considered industry jargon but is a readily available yardstick and can be used to great effectiveness with donors. It is the flip side of ROI, presented from the negative perspective (cost) rather than the positive (impact).

What statement is more compelling?

- "$0.80 of every dollar raised improves… healthcare in our community, feeds a child, funds new artworks, etc."

or

- "We only spend $0.20 of your gift to fund our operations."

When evaluating CPRD vs ROI, it's valuable to consider how we evaluate fundraising in charitable causes in general. Dan Pallotta, activist and fundraiser calls out the double standard that drives our broken relationship to charities. Too many nonprofits, he says, are *rewarded for how little they spend — not for what they get done*. Instead of equating frugality with morality, he asks us to start rewarding charities for their big goals and big accomplishments (even if that comes with big expenses). In this bold talk, he says: "Let's change the way we think about changing the world."

The following excerpt comes from Dan Pallotta's TED Talk 2013 (March 2013), entitled, *The Way we Think about Charity is Dead Wrong.*[1] Give it a read and challenge your perception about which of these two measures you prefer to use.

"So we've all been taught that charities should spend as little as possible on overhead things like fundraising under the theory that, well, the less money you spend on fundraising, the more money there is available for the cause. Well, that's true if it's a depressing world in which this pie cannot be made any bigger. But if it's a logical world in which investment in fundraising actually raises more funds and makes the pie bigger, then we have it precisely backwards, and we should be investing more money, not less, in fundraising, because fundraising is the one thing that has the potential to multiply the amount of money available for the cause that we care about so deeply."

I'll give you two examples. We launched the AIDSRides with an initial investment of $50,000 dollars in risk capital. Within nine years, we had multiplied that 1,982 times into $108 million dollars after all expenses for AIDS services. We launched the breast cancer three-days with an initial investment of $350,000 dollars in risk capital. Within just five years, we had multiplied that 554 times into $194 million dollars after all expenses for breast cancer research. Now, if you were a philanthropist really interested in breast cancer, what would make more sense: go out and find the most innovative researcher in the world and give her $350,000 dollars for research, or give her fundraising department the $350,000 dollars to multiply it into $194 million dollars for breast cancer research?

---

1   http://www.ted.com/talks/dan_pallotta_the_way_we_think_about_charity_is_dead_wrong

2002 was our most successful year ever. We netted for breast cancer alone, that year alone, $71 million dollars after all expenses. And then we went out of business, suddenly and traumatically.

Why? Well, the short story is, our sponsor split on us. They wanted to distance themselves from us because we were being crucified in the media for investing 40% of the gross in recruitment and customer service and the magic of the experience and there is no accounting terminology to describe that kind of investment in growth and in the future, other than this demonic label of overhead. So on one day, all 350 of our great employees lost their jobs because they were labeled overhead. Our sponsor went and tried the events on their own. The overhead went up. Net income for breast cancer research went down by 84%, or $60 million dollars in one year.

This is what happens when we confuse morality with frugality. We've all been taught that the bake sale with 5% overhead is morally superior to the professional fundraising enterprise with 40% overhead, but we're missing the most important piece of information, which is, what is the actual size of these pies? Who cares if the bake sale only has five percent overhead if it's tiny? What if the bake sale only netted 71 dollars for charity because it made no investment in its scale and the professional fundraising enterprise netted $71 million dollars because it did? Now which pie would we prefer, and which pie do we think people who are hungry would prefer?

Our generation does not want its epitaph to read, "We kept charity overhead low." We want it to read that we changed the world, and that part of the way we did that was by changing the way we think about these things. So the next time you're looking at a charity, don't ask about the rate of their overhead. Ask about the scale of their dreams, their Apple-, Google-, Amazon-scale dreams, how they measure their progress toward those dreams, and what resources they need to make them come true regardless of what the overhead is. Who cares what the overhead is if these problems are actually getting solved? If we can have that kind of generosity,

a generosity of thought, then the nonprofit sector can play a massive role in changing the world for all those citizens most desperately in need of it to change."

Other useful tools for analyzing financial performance are *"profitability indicator ratios"* or *"profit margins analysis."* In the for-profit sector, the objective of margin analysis is to detect consistency or positive/negative trends in an organization's revenues and operations. Positive profit margin analysis translates into positive investment quality.[2]

From a not-for-profit (NFP) perspective, profit margins analysis allows NFP leaders (executives and boards) to understand the revenue and cost drivers of each fundraising program, track overall organizational performance, benchmark against peer organizations in the sector, and allocate resources for maximum impact.

The two ratios most useful to the NFP sector are: *gross margins* and *net margins*. However, ratios can also be used to monitor and compare the levels of investment applied to cost centres and overheads, as well as the impact of new investment when comparing current year results to those of a previous year.

From a management perspective, margins clarify the relationship between income and expenditure and can be adapted and put to practical use across many contexts.

3. Gross Margins

$$\text{Gross Margins} = \frac{\text{Total Fundraising Revenue} - \text{Direct Fundraising Costs}}{\text{Total Fundraising Revenue}}$$

Figure 4.5

Gross margins and cost-per-dollar-raised are useful for comparing programs to each other and assessing portfolio balance. For example, a portfolio of fundraising programs weighted towards those with low margins (high cost per dollar raised) may drive down overall returns. See Figure 4.6 for a visual representation of Margins.

---

2   *Profitability Indicator Ratios: Profit Margin Analysis*; Richard Loth; http://www.investopedia.com/university/ratios/profitability-indicator/ratio1.asp

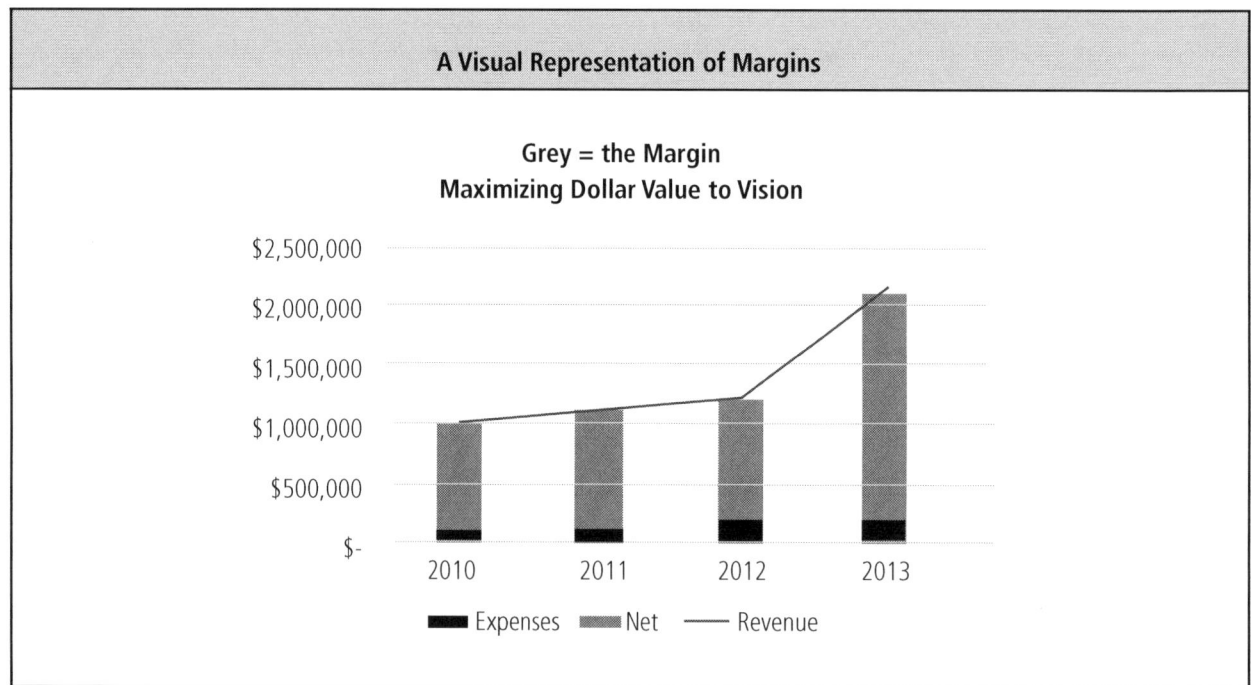

Figure 4.6

Margins are also widely used for benchmarking: against previous years' performance, programs against those of peer institutions and/or mission impact.

4. Net Margins

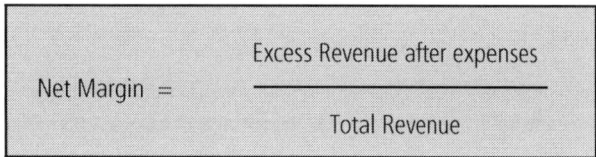

Figure 4.7

Expressed as a percentage of net revenue (or excess of revenue after expenses) against total income, net profit margins measure how much an organization retains from total revenues to contribute to mission (mission impact) and growing its fundraising capacity. Net margins are the measure we use to tell the story of donor impact. Board members with business backgrounds would be highly attuned to the use of margins for tracking and monitoring performance.

CASE STUDY 1: ANALYZING ORGANIZATIONAL PERFORMANCE, VGH+UBC HOSPITAL FOUNDATION

VGH and UBC Hospital Foundation has a proud track record of attracting high impact philanthropy to Vancouver Coastal health's top tertiary teaching, patient care and research hospitals on British Columbia's Lower Mainland.

One of the ways that VGH and UBC Hospital Foundation ensures excellence in health care is by making the best use of every dollar raised. In 2012-13 the Foundation's cost per dollar raised was 19 cents (excluding lottery revenue and related expenses), significantly lower than the industry average of 31 cents. The financial highlights below, drawn from their 2013 audited financial statement are an affirmation of the Foundation's strong performance.

But what additional information can a thorough analysis of the financial statements using indicator ratios tell us about VGH and UBC Hospital Foundation that could inform strategy and plans over the short, medium and long term? The table following the financial highlights presents an analysis of margins and returns for specific programs and overall performance.

Table A: VGH & UBC Hospitals Foundation Financial Highlights 2013

Revenue		2013	Δ	2012
	Philanthropic	$ 32,197,871	10.9%	$ 29,031,165
	Events	2,301,900	-2.9%	2,370,562
	Investment and Other Income	7,925,468	-29.7%	11,267,588
		42,425,239	-0.6%	42,669,315
	Lottery Ticket Sales	19,016,697	17.5%	16,187,077
Gross Revenue		**61,441,936**	**4.4%**	**58,856,392**
Expenses				
	Direct Fundraising	5,300,719	30.7%	4,055,757
	Events	499,910	-18.2%	611,276
	Management and Administration	2,220,234	2.8%	2,159,975
		8,020,863	17.5%	6,827,008
	Lottery (includes prizes)	15,139,752	14.2%	13,253,982
Total Expenditure		**23,160,615**	**15.3%**	**20,080,990**
Excess of Revenue over Expenses Before Grants		**38,281,321**	**-1.3%**	**38,775,402**
Funds Granted for				
	Equipment	8,374,327	-35.9%	13,062,131
	Education, Research and Patient Care	14,107,698	-6.1%	15,026,950
		22,482,025	-20.0%	28,089,081
Excess of Revenue over Expenses		**15,799,296**	**47.8%**	**10,686,321**
Fund Balances Beginning of Year		133,656,760	9.5%	122,039,736
Change in Fair Value of Investements		4,400,916	373%	930,703
Fund Balances End of Year		**$ 153,856,972**	**15.1%**	**$ 133,656,760**
Fund Balances Beginning of Year		133,656,760	9.5%	122,039,736
Change in Fair Value of Investements		4,400,916	372.9%	930,703
Fund Balances End of Year		**$ 153,856,972**	**15.1%**	**$ 133,656,760**
Analysing Overall Returns				
ROI (excluding lottery)		429%		525%
Cost per dollar raised (excluding lottery)		$ 0.19		0.16

CASE STUDY 1: Analyzing Organizational Performance, VGH+UBC Hospital Foundation (cont.)

Program Analysis (2013):

Understanding program costs and revenue drivers is essential for fundraising leaders. The analysis in Table B and C shows returns broadly under the headings of philanthropic, event and lottery income. Within philanthropic programs, each program leader should be using these basic formulae to assess program performance (1) across the fundraising portfolio, (2) across years, and (3) benchmarking against peer institutions.

Table B: Analysis of Net Revenues by Source

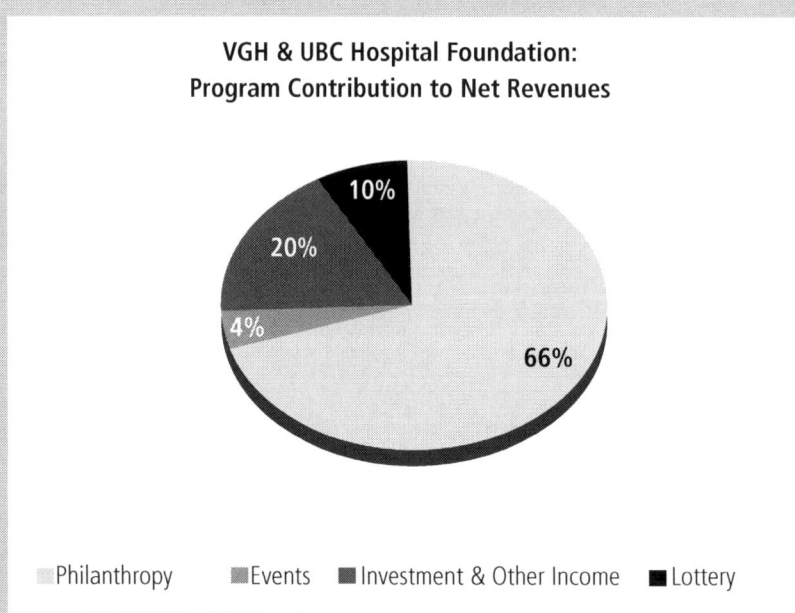

Table C: Analysis of program returns and margins

	Philanthropic	Events	Lottery
ROI	507%	360%	26%
Cost Per $ Raised	$ 0.16	$ 0.22	$ 0.80
Gross Margins	84%	78%	20%

CASE STUDY 1: Analyzing Organizational Performance, VGH+UBC Hospital Foundation (cont.)

Calculating the Marginal Return on New Investment:

This analysis is a bit trickier but essentially assesses the ROI of new investment. Based on the financial statements (see Table D), we can see that the Foundation board approved new investment in fundraising programs ($1,244,962), which delivered an additional $3,166,706 to hospital programs, for a marginal return on investment of 154% (or cost per dollar raised of $0.39).

The same set of formulae can be used to assess the impact of new investment into the lottery. We can see that a more significant investment ($1,885,770), delivered a positive ($2,829,620) but lesser return of 50%.

Finally, we can see that in reducing investment in event programs, the Foundation had a positive impact on the bottom line! An 18.2% reduction in event expenditure ($111,366) only reduced revenues by $68,662 thus a positive marginal impact of $42,704 or marginal return of 38%.

Table D: Analysis of Marginal Return on New Investment

Fundraising Programs	Revenues	Expenses
2013	$32,197,871	$5,300,719
Less: 2012	$29,031,165	$4,055,757
Change	**$3,166,706**	**$1,244,962**
Marginal Impact	$1,921,744	
Net Marginal ROI	154%	
Cost per $ Raised	$ 0.39	

Lottery	Revenues	Expenses
2013	$19,016,697	$15,139,752
Less: 2012	$16,187,077	$13,253,982
Change	**$2,829,620**	**$1,885,770**
Marginal Impact	$943,850	
Net Marginal ROI	50%	
Cost per $ Raised	$ 0.67	

Events	Revenues	Expenses
2013	$ 2,301,900	$ 499,910
Less: 2012	$ 2,370,562	$ 611,276
Change	**$ (68,662)**	**$ (111,366)**
Marginal Impact	$ 42,704	
Net Marginal ROI	38%	
Cost per Dollar Raised	N/A	

> **CASE STUDY 1: Analyzing Organizational Performance, VGH+UBC Hospital Foundation (cont.)**
>
> Of course, all three investment decisions delivered positive outcomes for the Foundation. However, as a leader, we should now be assessing whether or not each investment decision was the right one, and asking all program staff to think creatively about how to continue to grow impact.
>
> **Drawing conclusions from measuring performance:**
>
> I) While the fair market value of the investment portfolio has increased dramatically by 372.9%, investment income had dropped significantly (-29.7%) impacting the Foundation's bottom line and, without knowing the detail, its grant making ability to the Hospital (-20.0%). The strategic imperative would be identifying and pursuing strategies that counterbalance the unpredictability of the investment markets.
>
> II) From a forward-looking perspective, we as leaders should be assessing opportunities to again increase investment in those program areas that offer the greatest potential. As identified above (Table D), increased investments in fundraising and lottery totalling $3.1 million produced almost $6 million in new revenue.
>
> III) Analysis highlights that all programs are not equal. Investment returns in philanthropic programs are 507% compared to lotteries at 26% (Table C). On one hand, as so eloquently stated by Dan Palotta, "If investment in fundraising actually raises more funds and makes the pie bigger, why should it matter?" On the other, within the philanthropic programs portfolio, leaders will be delving deeper into program detail to assess fresh opportunities for further enlarging the pie.
>
> IV) While ROI on the lottery is low, a marginal contribution equal to 10% of revenues (Table B) make the business case for the lottery a worthwhile endeavour.
>
> V) Shifting budget out of low performing programs (events) can deliver positive returns. The opportunity cost of NOT shifting funds away from poor performers represents a waste of valuable resources.
>
> VI) From a donor reporting perspective, presenting lottery separately from philanthropic impact makes sense because it draws a clear line between gaming revenues and philanthropically driven revenue streams. Clearly, a focused effort on philanthropic income is more cost effective (delivering returns of over 500% as compared to 26% for lotteries) it represents 66% of net revenues and therefore delivers the greatest value back to VGH and UBC Hospitals.
>
> This last statement also delivers a powerful statement to the board of the role of volunteer leaders and of the importance of growing major gift capability.
>
> Finally, in addition to program performance, the financial statements portray a picture of sound financial management, with only 3.6% of total revenues allocated to management and overhead costs (Table A, "management and administration costs"). The message of effective management, the case for building fundraising capability, and donor impact can be used in equal measure by boards, managers, fundraising staff and donors to inform decision-making and take positive action.

DONOR IMPACT REPORTING ON ENDOWMENT PERFORMANCE

One of the major questions arising from an analysis of the VGH and UBC Hospitals Foundation financial highlights centres on that of investment management and donor impact reporting on endowment performance.

While working at The University of Queensland (Australia) I often heard donors argue that they could achieve a better return on investment than the University, making the case for endowment appear flawed and lacking urgency. And that may well be true given the lack of restrictions the individual investor enjoys over the not-for-profit (although the charitable sector enjoys tax free status thus "after tax" comparisons are essential).

Nevertheless, we hear wonderful stories of how successful business leaders are transforming the NFP sector through their generosity. The incredible partnership between Canada's Michael deGroote and McMaster University is one such example. This is achieved when visionary leadership and good governance go hand in hand. Thus, transparent and regular reporting to current and prospective donors both in terms of endowment performance and donor impact help make the case for endowment and should be a vital component of your donor communications plan.

Investment performance calculations are not a subject that we as fundraising professionals have to perform; that is the role of our investment experts. However, we should be constantly on the lookout for examples of good endowment reporting.

One such example can be found on the McMaster University website (www.mcmaster.ca/impact/endowment). The Annual Endowment Report 2012-13 details growth over 10 years, unrestricted versus restricted, mission impact of investment income (how funds are disbursed to the University), and FAQs backed by data-driven performance measures to make a complex subject more easily understood while demonstrating good governance.

The Council for Advancement and Support of Education (www.case.org) also has an excellent selection of sample materials for endowment performance reporting.

EXAMPLE - COMPUTING ROI, MARGINS AND COST PER DOLLAR RAISED

Q1: What is the ROI on a $100,000 investment inclusive of salary and operating costs that generates an income of $1 million? Cost per dollar raised? Gross margin?

Response:
- **ROI** = ($1 million - $100,000)/$100,000 = 900% (a return of 9 times the original investment
- **Cost per $ raised** = $100,000/$1 million = $0.10 (for every $1 raised, we spend $0.10)
- **Gross Margin** = ($1 million - $100,000)/$1 million = 90%

Q2: The ABC Foundation raised $32,460,000. Direct fundraising costs amounted to $7,250,325, support programs and services totalled $1,630,263 and the Foundation fixed costs and overheads $650,250. What are gross revenues? The gross margins? Net revenues? Net margins? Cost per dollar raised? How can you express margins allocated to support programs and services, and to Foundation operations? What is the overall return on investment?

Response:
- **Gross Revenue** = $32,460,000 - $7,250,325 = $25,209,675
- **Gross Margins** = $25,209,675 / $32,460,000 = 77.7%
- **Net Revenue** = $25,209,675 - $1,630,263 - $950,250 = $21,629,162
- **Net Margins** = $22,929,162 / $32,460,000 = 69.7%
- **Cost per dollar raised** = ($7,250,325 + $2,630,263 + $650,250) / $32,460,000 = $0.29
- **Overheads** = $650,000/$32,460,000 = 2% of budget
- **Support Programs & Services** = $1,630,263 / $32,460,000 = 5% of budget
- **ROI** = ($32,460,000 - $10,530,913)/ $10,530,913 = 2.09 times

PREDICTING FUTURE INCOME

In the fundraising profession and in NFP management, understanding and using "averages" can be useful tool for projecting revenue and identifying trends. Such tools include "rolling averages" and "compound averages." We understand concepts such as compound interest when applied to a mortgage or investment portfolio, but few people understand how to use these tools or apply them to an NFP context.

1. Rolling Average

    Rolling averages smooth out the bumps that could occur due to a one-off, larger-than-life gift, a sudden economic downturn, or a natural disaster that diverts community support for a given period. Used over multiple years, they help identify trends which could present opportunity, or negatively impact your organization if unaddressed.

    Typically, bequest programs use rolling averages for predicting future income. However, other factors such as known bequest expectancies also inform budget estimates.

    The formulae for calculating rolling averages generally use an "average straight line growth" method, which only considers the benchmark used as the point of departure. To use the example of a savings account, interest is only calculated on the original deposit, and new deposits, not on the interest earned.

2. Compound growth

    Compound growth rates use a complex financial formulae that recognizes that the investments of previous years build on each other. To use the example of a savings account, compound interest is the interest on the interest that will make a deposit grow faster. Thus compound growth, is growth that builds on the growth of the year before.

    Average and compound growth rates can also be used to understand the long-term impact of investment decisions - for example, the upward revenue swing resulting from investment in capital or comprehensive campaign that drops off once goals are achieved. Critically, using averages as an analytical tool can provide strategic insight and a longer term view about where the organization is or should be heading.

Figure 4.8[3] shows how to use averages in an NFP context.

FORMULA FOR CALCULATING AVERAGE GROWTH RATES

Where "n" = number of years, and "i" = growth rate

$$\text{Rolling average} = \frac{(\text{funds raised yr1} + \text{yr2} + \text{yr3})}{3}$$

$$\text{Straight line growth rate} = \frac{(\text{funds raised Yr}^n - \text{funds raised yr1}) \times 100}{(\text{funds raised yr 1})}{n}$$

Compound growth:

- When the future is unknown:
  Future Income = $(\text{Past Income})(1+i)^n$

- When the growth rate is unknown:
  $i = (\sqrt[n]{\text{future income}/\text{past income}}) - 1$

* these formulae can be applied using any calculator.

Figure 4.8

---

[3] *Calculating averages.* University of Oregon. http://pages.uoregon.edu/rgp/PPPM613/class8a.htm.

CASE STUDY 2: CALCULATING AVERAGE GROWTH RATES

The ABC Society is heading into strategic planning and wants to predict revenues for the following three to five years. Below is a table of funds raised over a six-year period. The following exercises walk through the use of each of the above formulae.

Sample Results (ABC Society)

Year	2008	2009	2010	2011	2012	2013
Funds Raised	$2,000,000	$3,050,000	3,000,000	$3,025,000	$3,250,000	$3,500,000
Change		$1,050,000	($50,000)	$25,000	$225,000	$250,000
Rate		52.5%	(1.6%)	0.8%	7.4%	7.7%

Based on the data provided above, we can calculate the following growth rates:

A) Predict income in 2011, 2012, 2013 and 2014 using rolling averages.

- 2011 = (2008+2009+2010)/3 = ($2,000,000+$3,050,000+$3,000,000)/3 =$2,683,333
- 2012 = (2009+2010+2011)/3 = ($3,050,500+$3,000,000+$3,025,000)/3 = $3,025,000
- 2013 = (2010+2011+2012)/3 = ($3,000,000+$3,025,000+3,250,000)/3 = $3,091,667
- 2014 = (2011+2012+2013)/3 = ($3,025,000+3,250,000+3,500,000)/3 = $3,258,333

B) Calculate the straight line growth rate to project 2014 income

"n" = 6 years; 2013 = $3,500,000; 2008 = $2,000,000

= (($3,500,000-$2,000,000)/$2,000,000) X 100 / 6
= ($1,500,000/$2,000,000) X 100 / 6 = 12.5%

Projected revenue in 2014 = 2013 + 12.5% = $3,500,000 X 1.125 = $3,937,500

C) Find the compound growth rate to project income in 2014, 2015 & 2016

Future income = 2013 = $3,500,000;
Past income = 2008 = $2,000,000
"n" = 6; "i" is unknown

Based on the formulae: future income = (past income) $(1 + i)^6$
However, as "i" is unknown, the formulae using the square root must first be applied: i = ($\sqrt[n]{\text{future income/past income}}$) - 1

$$i = (\sqrt[6]{\$3,500,000/\$2,000,000}) - 1$$
$$= (\sqrt[6]{\$1,500,000}) - 1$$
$$= 10.7 - 1 = 9.7\%$$

> **CASE STUDY 2: CALCULATING AVERAGE GROWTH RATES (CONT.)**
>
> Now that the growth rate in known, revenue predications can be made for 2014, 2015 and 2016.
>
> 2014 = 2013 + 9.7% = ($3,500,000)(1.097) = $3,839,500
> 2015 = 2014 + 9.7% = ($3,839,500)(1.097) = $4,211,931
> 2016 = 2015 + 9.7% = ($4,211,931)(1.097) = $4,620,488

A word of caution against relying solely on financial indicators to assess performance: financial statements are a photograph in time of what was banked (funds received, in our industry jargon).

Financial statements, for example, don't tell us anything about the pledge portfolio or associated cash flow projections, or how "cost centres" drive donor cultivation and future revenue potential, or about the impact of time on major gifts and planned giving. This underscores the importance of taking a long-term view of ROI and of the role of non-financial metrics in tracking, measuring and forecasting performance.

The following sections present metrics that can be uses alongside financials, in more practical ways, to help staff and volunteers stay the course and deliver more to mission.

MAXIMIZING THE IMPACT OF YOUR TEAM

Too often, I hear fundraising professionals try to sweep the question of fully costing fundraising programs, that is to include "all fixed and variable costs when computing the amount of money it takes to produce and distribute one unit of output."[4] Why? The premise is often that these budget expenditures are indirect and overheads, and therefore shouldn't be included in ROI analysis (or cost per dollar raised).

However, when it comes to improving organizational effectiveness and increasing mission impact, having the courage to delve into the detail and challenge the status quo is the only way forward. Assessing the full costs of any program or facet of your fundraising operation enables management to truly understand the cost drivers, and the real return of the fundraising operation to the organization.

So what to include in full costing analysis? In the example of an annual fund program, in addition to the cost of preparing and producing a mail package, consider the salary costs associated with preparing copy, coordinating appeals, gift processing and donor relations. Does this mean that you cut your program because the real costs are frightening? Of course not! But the findings may spur you to find greater efficiencies including automation and process analysis, or to quantify the impact of the annual fund on your major donor program.

In considering a full costing analysis, practitioners should consider *"Activity Based Costing,"* which means matching costs to the activities that consume resources.[5] In our organizations, the broad categories of activities include:

- Revenue centres – each fundraising program including social enterprise.

- Cost centres (non-revenue generating) including gift processing, governance, finance and administration, donor relations, communications and marketing.

A review of how staff allocate their time, while detailed and requiring goodwill on the part of leadership, is not complicated. Nor does it have to be 100% accurate. An open and consultative process for capturing data on how staff allocate their time to the specific activities combined with financial ratios can be an eye-opening experience.

Some of the organizational performance questions that can be answered through activity based costing include:

- Are fundraising staff over burdened with administrative duties?

---

4 Full Costing. www.Investopedia.com

5 Activity Based Costing. www.businessdictionary.com

- How much time do our major gifts staff actually engage with current and prospective donors?
- Are staff overly focused on low-return programs (ROI less than 2.5)?
- Are those smaller programs delivering significant, let alone positive returns?
- Are some staff wearing too many hats and does this compromise quality and impact?
- How can we reorganize our work to be more strategic and higher impact?
- Can busy work be outsourced so staff can be more strategic?
- What are our "real" cost centres and what is acceptable as a cost of doing business?
- Do we have capacity to grow within our existing complement of staff?

While at the University of Queensland (Australia), the Office of University Advancement underwent this analysis for campaign budget modelling. My role as Director, Campaign and Fundraising comprised developing the University's prospect management framework (policy and performance management guideline) as well as partnering with senior management to achieve campaign readiness.

Working with the Director, Advancement Services, the analysis required sitting down with each prospect manager to truly understand how each person allocated their time within the prospect management framework (from leadership annual giving to principal gifts and including the amount of time prospect managers allocated to non-fundraising activities). The results were quite astonishing. Of 29 people with prospect management duties (including myself as a member of the advancement executive), we discovered that over 8 FTEs (full-time equivalents) were allocated to non-fundraising duties! In an environment where internal staff and committee meetings can be voracious consumers of precious time, we were able to arm ourselves for purposeful discussion with academic leadership to help a team of highly experienced fundraising professionals – a precious resource of the University – become more externally focused.

CASE STUDY 3: THE TAPESTRY FOUNDATION FOR HEALTH CARE

When Tapestry Foundation for Health Care Chief Executive, Ann Adams, was considering opportunities to grow her organization, she turned to performance metrics and financial analysis to better understand how to position her team for greater success.

Her goals were: (1) improve fundraising program outcomes and impact, (2) understand the cost drivers behind managing a portfolio of revenue generating programs supporting multiple legal entities, and (3) assess the Foundation's business model to position it better for growth.

Tapestry Foundation was created from the amalgamation of healthcare foundations serving Vancouver-based Providence Health Care's six community hospitals, hospices and residential care facilities. This decision created opportunity and critical mass for small facilities to join together and begin harnessing their fundraising potential. Tapestry Foundation now serves eight sites with other organizations seeking the Foundation's expertise. This is driving Ann and her board to seek better systems for assessing existing programs and opportunities arising.

Further, with unrestricted income increasingly difficult to source for core operations, the impetus was to understand the real costs of site and program management, inclusive of salaries.

The process involved an in-depth analysis of the current business model and the allocation of costs to Foundation activities, revenue and non-revenue generating. Using the principles of activity based costing, ROI analysis and cost per dollar raised, Ann Adams was able to:

- Assess the actual ROI for each revenue centre and each of the eight sites;

- Quantify the fixed and variable costs per site;

- Determine the ROI for each of the eight sites;

- Identify opportunities for increasing fundraising performance and impact; and

- Understand the cost drivers that need to be addressed to improve operational efficiencies.

One of the principal outcomes was the development of a new business model to take to her board, and a decision-making framework for testing scenarios for growth.

How did she tackle the situation at the outset?

CASE STUDY 3: The Tapestry Foundation for Health Care (cont.)

Step 1: Understanding how staff allocate their time

The first step entailed interviewing each member of staff to understand how they allocated their time (as a percentage) within the three main areas of the Foundation's activities:

1. revenue generating programs (philanthropy, events and social enterprise);

2. support programs and services (marketing & communications, donor relations, gift processing); and

3. overheads (governance, finance and administration).

Step 2: Allocating revenues and expenditures to activity centres

Using the principles of activity based costing, the next step required charting revenues and expenditures against each activity. Tapestry Foundation quantified the cost impact of such activities as data preparation and gift processing, internal handling of mail coordination, preparation of direct response letters, research and writing the communications materials, and allocated it to the relevant activity.

Step 3: Detailed financial analysis of operations

Tapestry Foundation was thus able to determine the marginal contribution of each revenue centre (each annual appeal, major gifts, events, gaming, social enterprise, etc), and the marginal cost of non-revenue generating centres to the bottom line.

Questions arising from such analysis were many and varied including:

- What is the case for investment for growing major gifts capacity?

- How can better direct mail donor segmentation improve returns?

- Would outsourcing aspects of direct mail give better strategic focus and growth opportunities to good staff?

- How can roles and responsibilities be better distributed to allow staff to achieve greater focus on strategic activity and therefore improve outcomes?

- What is the best cost-benefit ratio for a duo-purpose program such as the donor newsletter (donor stewardship and gift solicitation)?

- What existing resources can be reallocated for greater impact?

- What new resources are required to support growth and arising opportunities?

- If the sector average is $0.31 cost per dollar raised, what is the right balance for a small healthcare foundation and how should it realign its fundraising portfolio to close the gap on the industry average?

CASE STUDY 3: The Tapestry Foundation for Health Care (cont.)

Step 4: Undertaking a cost-benefit analysis by site

Once Tapestry Foundation's CEO had a clear picture of programs and operations, she was able to proceed with a site by site analysis. This was more complex. Questions were asked about:

1. the allocation of funds raised per revenue centre to each site;

2. the allocation of staff time on a per site basis;

3. how to allocate the cost of non-revenue generating centres (e.g. marketing and communications) to each site; and

4. assessing the value of fixed costs that the foundation incurred before any funds were raised at all (e.g. board governance and reporting) and allocating those costs to sites.

This step allowed Tapestry to conduct ROI analysis on a per site basis and assess a "management cost" cost per site.

Step 5: Redefining the business model

The final step meant drawing on the analysis to improve the Foundation's business model.

Questions arising from such analysis are equally varied including:

- How do we scale for growth?

- How do we budget and fund our costs now and in the future?

- What are the characteristics of a "model site" or a "model program" and how can they be replicated to new and/or existing sites?

- What is the "start-up cost" for bringing a new site on stream?

- What does the business and budget model look like for site planning?

- What is the correlation between fundraising success and site leadership engagement?

- How can the Foundation's business model help foster greater site ownership of outcomes (costs and benefits)?

- How do we use this intelligence to engage site leadership more actively in the fundraising process?

This final step created a framework for assessing arising opportunities: new fundraising programs, site expansion and a numbers-based decision-making framework for evaluating and negotiating with new sites.

While the answers and decision impacts are still to be determined, the information provided by undertaking a thorough analysis will inform and support organizational development and cultural change.

PROGRAM METRICS

Program metrics are where non-financial metrics come into their own. In fact, as predictors of income they will play the more important role.

Identifying and tracking performance metrics for individual programs (and individual staff) can seem overwhelming. Three basic measures are useful starting points:
1. *Industry benchmarks* per program (Canadian)
2. *Lead indicators* – those metrics that when tracked ensure that you're heading in the right direction and are staying the course
3. *Lag indicators* – backwards looking metrics that tell you where you have been and if you are tracking in the right direction

The following table provides a snapshot of metrics for the gamut of fund development programs. Once you have decided which ones are critical for your organization to track, setting up data capture systems and reports will translate into regular monthly, quarterly and annual monitoring mechanisms.

Some organizations still do not distinguish between "funds raised" and "funds received." However, in focusing on the former, fundraising professionals will compound their investment in long-term relationships into long-term revenue growth. By converting annual donors to major, regular and planned giving donors you can shift your focus away from the "constant ask" on onto long-term relationship building.

"Funds raised" means also including in your "counting," commitments that cannot be banked (e.g. pledges, agreements, regular gifts, gifts in kind, etc.). "Funds received" is cash and marketable assets received, and which are recorded on your balance sheet; those which are recorded in your financial statements.

It should be noted that CASE does not allow non-philanthropic commitments to be counted in "funds raised." However, the NFP sector is more complex and multifaceted than philanthropy. Thus a nuanced approach is required.

Figure 4.10 provides metrics for monitoring, tracking and forecasting funds raised and funds received.

Program	Benchmark (cost per dollar raised)	Lead Indicators	Lag Indicators
Major Gifts	• $0.10 - $0.15 • 1:3 close rate on proposals to qualified prospects	• # qualified prospects • # assigned prospects • # moves / month • Close rate • Default rate	• # & value of proposals pending • $ pledge (raised) • $ and in-kind received (new) • $ received (prior year pledge installments)
Planned Giving	• < $0.10	• Bequest expectancies • Demographics of bequest expectancies • % gifts from known bequestors • # qualified prospects in bequest pipeline • # assigned qualified prospects	• # & value of bequests in probate • # & value of bequests received

Program	Benchmark (cost per dollar raised)	Lead Indicators	Lag Indicators
Major Gifts	• $0.10 - $0.15 • 1:3 close rate on proposals to qualified prospects	• # qualified prospects • # assigned prospects • # moves / month • Close rate • Default rate	• # & value of proposals pending • $ pledge (raised) • $ and in-kind received (new) • $ received (prior year pledge installments)
Planned Giving	• < $0.10	• Bequest expectancies • Demographics of bequest expectancies • % gifts from known bequestors • # qualified prospects in bequest pipeline • # assigned qualified prospects	• # & value of bequests in probate • # & value of bequests received
Regular Giving	• $0.10 - $0.15	• # prospects • Contact rates • Close rates • Default rate	• Value of portfolio • $ pledged • $ received
Direct Mail renewal / Donor Clubs	• $0.20 to $0.25 per $1.00 raised	• # current donors • Average gift • # of gifts • Attrition rate • Sybunt/Lybunt renewal rates	• Response rate per appeal • $ raised • $ and in-kind received • # donors • # gifts
Direct Mail acquisition	• $1.25 to $1.50 per $1.00 raised	• Quality of list	• Response rates
Membership Programs	• $0.20 to $0.30 per $1.00 raised	• Attrition rates • Acquisition rates • Renewal rates	• Appeal response rates • # members • Value of fees generated

Budget Forecasting	Lead Indicators	Lag Indicators
Annual cash flow targets (funds received) = payment on commitments plus cash and in-kind goals for each program	Add together: • Value of pledge expectancies • value of regular donors • bequests in probate • Aggregate of lead indicators for each programs • aspirational growth targets Minus: • default rate on pledge expectancies and regular donors	Gifts "banked" in fiscal year including: • Monthly / quarterly reports with variation (+/-) against budget • payments on previous years' pledges and agreements • new cash received • value of in-kind (property) gifts received • value of bequests received (property and cash)
Annual target for funds raised (new money)	• Aggregate of goal for each program • Sector / organizational benchmark	• New commitments in fiscal year plus new gifts of cash and property: • Monthly / quarterly reports with variation (+/-)

Figure 4.10: Metrics for budget forecasting

Non-financial metrics that could also be considered include:

- # volunteers and volunteer growth
- # of subscribers to newsletters and other publications (print and electronic)
- Website analytics
- Number of volunteers and staff leaders participating in the cultivation and solicitation of major and planned donors
- Data capture (e.g. editing and enhancing database records including contact reports) in a timely manner
- Attendance and data capture from non-paying events

SETTING, MONITORING AND MEASURING INDIVIDUAL PERFORMANCE

Building and supporting a team of volunteer and staff leaders is one of the most important objectives of the development leader. The complexity of human resource management is not to be underestimated, comprising direct reports, staff of other departments within the organization, and volunteers.

The ultimate objective in setting, monitoring and reporting on performance targets is creating a supportive team environment where success is celebrated, where everyone can learn from the good, the bad and the ugly, and where each individual feels motivated and supported in the achievement of organizational and personal goals.

Managing individual performance is always tricky. A good rule of thumb is to celebrate success publicly, and areas needing improvement privately.

The main game in dealing with poor performance is to use metrics constructively as a signal, and to use private conversation to unpack the situation and identify the real barriers to positive outcomes. Questions to consider in major gift performance management are:

- Is it fear of the phone for discovery calling?
- Is it the call to action?
- Is someone great at the "ask," but stumbles on negotiation and follow up? Or the reverse?
- Too much talking and not enough listening?
- Are staff and volunteer leaders being used appropriately? Are they trained? Have they briefed properly in advance?

A discussion in a non-threatening environment to role-play, develop scripts and analyze post call can help. Think about how you can pair a junior fundraising professional up with a senior practitioner to "show and tell," or talk through scenarios and scripts. Take the pressure off a new CEO or board member by focusing on their story, rather than the ask.

SHARED GOALS

In addition to applying the above metrics to set and monitor annual performance targets for each member of the team, great leaders also use team metrics to promote, measure and celebrate collaboration. Shared goals might include:

- # referrals to other programs (e.g. donors, volunteer prospects, memberships, ticket buyers)
- Timely submission of contact reports in the database to assist with collaborative communication sharing
- Cross-promotion of other programs (e.g. ensuring major gift donors and prospects are invited and encouraged to attend events and contribute to the annual fund; annual fund referrals to the major gifts and planned giving teams)
- Staff participation across program teams whether in planning and/or execution (e.g. strategy, ideas generation, hosting, event set-up and take down)
- Consistent public recognition of team achievements
- Shared goals and targets supporting cross-unit collaboration
- Financial rewards

In implementing and rewarding shared goals, it is important to be able to track and report on team effort effectively and transparently.

REPORT CARDS

Given that "money drives mission" and "together we're better," using a subset of high level metrics can be useful tools for tracking, measuring and reporting on organizational performance, and for building an internal culture of support for the Development Office.

There are two types of report cards that should be developed:

1. Governance reporting

Generally, the CEO would prepare the report to the Board presenting the previous period's results, projections for the next period and any matters that require highlighting (positive and negative).

The report card to the board should be simple and policy-focused. The goal is to ensure "heads in and hands out' at the board table. Such high level indicators should include:

- Funds raised (new money including new cash gifts and pledges)
- Funds received (new cash plus pledge installments)
- Progress against annual targets (expressed as a %) including value and # of gifts
- # and value of proposals pending (i.e. outstanding asks)
- # and value of bequest expectancies and gifts in probate
- Highlight of outstanding achievements including individual program outcomes
- Indicator of any issues arising (trends, risk and/or events documented)
- Decision/s required including gift acceptance and namings that requires board approval

2. Unit reporting

Universities, colleges, schools, health care and service agencies, many of which will be tracking results from multiple sites: in all cases, success requires the collaboration of team leaders who don't report to the

Chief Development Officer but who have a vested interest in fundraising success.

The development of shared goals set by the CEO or documented in a "service agreement" set performance expectations that guide and focus the team effort.

Some institutions use a "unit-based performance framework" to create a report card inclusive of the development office objectives, as well as the institution's wider revenue objectives. Indicators can include the number and value of philanthropic gifts as well as constituency engagement outcomes, benchmarked against annual targets. As organization's move towards implementing their fundraising programs, the report card can be enhanced with more targeted metrics, which could include such measures as program staff involvement and the use of volunteer leaders.

CONCLUSION

Measuring performance can be an incredibly complex undertaking. The key for success is to allocate quality time in the establishment phase to determine the metrics that are most critical to your organization, at the macro organizational level, and at the micro level, by program and for each staff person. As these metrics will become your benchmarks across multiple years, it is important to allow proper consideration in building them with your leadership team and ideally with involvement from an experienced board member.

Each metric adopted needs to be easily trackable, supported by standardized reports, with every team member held responsible for capturing and recording progress (two possible metrics unto themselves).

As stated at the outset, metrics and measurement are designed to guide and motivate positive behaviors. Those behaviours, supported by strong leadership and a team commitment to achieving results as a collaborative effort will drive personal excellence and organizational achievement.

One last thought about metrics and measurement: keep it simple and remember that your team is made up of people. Use your metrics to inspire and motivate.

ADDITIONAL RESOURCES

Books/Articles

- CASE Reporting Standards and Management Guidelines, Edition 4. (2009).

- Collins, Mary Ellen. (2014). "The Great Debate." Advancing Philanthropy, Spring. Association of Fundraising Professionals.

- Hewitt, Les. (Retrieved July, 2014)."How well do your visual performance metrics rate against these criteria? How to turbo charge your continuous improvement culture." LinkedIn. https://www.linkedin.com/today/post/article/20140630101939-20021064-how-to-turbo-charge-your-continuous-improvement-culture?_mSplash=1

- Saul, Jason. (2004). Benchmarking for Non Profits. Fieldstone Alliance.

- Willmer, Wesley K. (2008). Advancing Small Colleges, A Benchmarking Survey Update. CASE.

URLs

- www.apfnet.org - Hot Topics: Fundraising Costs. AFP Resource Centre.

- http://www.case.org/Samples_Research_and_Tools/Samples.html) - Endowment reports. Council for Advancement and Support of Education.

- www.imaginecanada.ca - Sector Source. Research about Giving, Research about Volunteering, Trends in Individual Donations (1984-2010).

- www.investopedia.com - Formula, definitions, examples of financial analysis concepts.

ABOUT THE AUTHOR

**Karen Van Sacker, MBA, MAICD
Vice President & Senior Consultant
Global Philanthropic Canada**

Karen Van Sacker is an accomplished fundraising executive with over 30 years as a non-profit leader. She began her career in sport management in 1984 at the national level quickly moving into the fundraising profession. Ms Van Sacker has specific expertise working with executive leaders and boards, and strength in organizational development.

Karen returned to Canada in September 2013 following 11 years in Australia to open Global Philanthropic's Vancouver office. She served 8 years in the Australian university sector, most recently as Director of Fundraising and Campaign for The University of Queensland where she was responsible for campaign readiness, principal gifts and international advancement strategy, including the negotiation of 8-figure gifts as a member of an integrated team.

She serves on UBC's Thunderbird Athletics Council, was a board member of the Byron Bay Writers Festival and Secretary to The University of Queensland in America. She has served the profession as a chapter executive and on conference committees.

Karen completed her BA at University of British Columbia, a post-graduate certificate at L'Université Laval, a MBA from Concordia University and the Australian Company Directors' program. She is bilingual in French and English.

Her analytical skills are brought to bear in this chapter on Performance Management and Metrics, which aims to draw on personal experience and live case studies..

CHAPTER 5

ORGANIZATIONAL CULTURE

KELLY MORRIS, BSC AND ANDREA MORRIS, BA

Osmosis: an ability to learn and understand things gradually without much effort.

Throughout the pages of this book, we discover the essentials of best-practice fundraising. We learn (or relearn) the basics of a comprehensive fund development program to help us raise money to meet our missions. No doubt, if a charity followed the majority of advice in this book, it would be a pretty successful fundraising organization.

The culture of an organization is not normally part of a "nuts and bolts" course on building a fundraising program. So if that's the case, why do we need a whole chapter about culture? Because "culture is king."

read more…

The culture of your organization is fundamental to the foundation of success of the rest of the program. It is difficult to deliberately establish, and even more challenging to change once it is in place. If the culture of your organization is working against you, it might mean that you could implement all of the standards outlined in these chapters and still fail at fundraising. However, this need not be the case.

If we breakdown the topic of organizational culture and understand why it is important, we can then identify the most critical elements of a healthy, productive fundraising culture, and learn how to diagnose and fix some of the most common challenges faced by charities in Canada.

WHAT IS ORGANIZATIONAL CULTURE?

"Organizational culture is the behavior of humans who are part of an organization and the meanings that the people attach to their actions. Culture includes the organization values, visions, norms, working language, systems, symbols, beliefs and habits. It is also the pattern of such collective behaviors and assumptions that are taught to new organizational members as a way of perceiving, and even thinking and feeling. Organizational culture affects the way people and groups interact with each other, with clients, and with stakeholders."[1]

In other words, "culture becomes the 'residual' explanation for whatever is happening that cannot be explained by other means."[2]

With such a broad and comprehensive topic, we are refining the scope of the discussion to focus on the *critical elements* of organizational culture that create conditions for fundraising success.

If you are in a mature organization that has put all of the nuts and bolts of a fundraising program in place, and yet you know that the whole organization could be performing better, looking at the culture of the organization could be a revealing exercise.

If you are at the early stages of developing a fundraising program, focus on building a strong culture right away so that there is no "re-engineering" project required to fix the culture in the future.

WHO IS RESPONSIBLE FOR FUNDRAISING AND STEWARDSHIP AT YOUR CHARITY?

The typical answer is usually "the fundraising/development staff" or "the executive director." Some might say that it is members of the board of directors or some set of volunteers who are responsible. Of course these things are all true. However, fundraising is the responsibility of *everyone* in the organization in some way.

In 2013, the Governor General of Canada, His Excellency David Johnston, presented to the first cohort of graduates from Carleton University's new Masters of Philanthropy and Nonprofit Leadership and spoke candidly about his work in the industry, specifically in higher education. He described how his team worked diligently to create substantial change in the context of external relations at the University of Waterloo and described how "friend raising" and the establishment of collaborative networks was everyone's job in the organization. Through the team's efforts, they brought about very positive change in the culture of the institution. A video of his speech can be found at https://www.youtube.com/watch?v=CKvv7a1LEik.

At our university, we often say that the parking attendants and the student services staff are key to our fundraising success. You can imagine the blank stares that come from these seemingly outrageous statements.

However, let's think about this. Donors to the university tend to visit campus periodically, therefore use the parking facilities. Until recently with the use of automated systems, the parking attendants were often the first to greet our guests. Also, many of our donors are alumni, which means their whole university experience impacts their philanthropic feelings toward the university in the future. Parking attendants and student services are some of our front-line, externally facing representatives. How they treat the community matters to our reputation, which in turn, affects our fundraising success.

Who is on the front line at your charity?

---

1 Source: http://en.wikipedia.org/wiki/Organizational_culture
2 Grant, Michael, and Shamonda. (2013). *Hope, Culture and Innovation: The Secret Sauce*. Ottawa: The Conference Board of Canada.

Do they know that they play an important role in reputation management?

We are not suggesting that everyone in the organization know what our cost-per-dollar-raised ratio should be, nor do they need to know which of the people they are serving is a donor. What is important however, is that they know that our ability to achieve our goals and execute on our mission depends on people they meet, many who make decisions to give us their own money, with no expectation of return, simply because they believe that what we do is critical to society.

That said, the board, the executive and management of your charity must have a more sophisticated understanding of the role of philanthropy in your organization's success. And it must be communicated, unapologetically at every turn.

In *Excellence in Fundraising in Canada, Volume One*, Andrea McManus wrote a chapter on Governance and Boards and stated that one of the "real conundrums in fundraising – that is – the involvement, engagement and interaction with boards of charitable organizations."[3] While Boards are the guardians of the mission and hold fiduciary responsibility for its health, there is still some mystery around the engagement piece and the expectation of fundraising by them and for the organization.

Having spent time around many charitable organizations and fundraising consultants over the years, we often hear queries from leaders (both staff and volunteers) looking to establish or enhance a development program. Too often, the expectation is that they will hire a fundraiser (sometimes at too low a level in the organization) and that new person will take care of the development program. Recently, we asked a freshly minted CEO of a major charitable organization how he planned on handling the fundraising for the operation. He answered, "Oh, I'll just hire it out." This is an organization that raises several million dollars in gifts and sponsorships annually. There was a pause before responding, then we said: "Well, that might work the first time your donor is asked for a significant gift. But if there is no stewardship capacity in the shop and no ongoing cultivation of your new donors, you will not get a second gift from that donor. And it is awfully expensive to find new donors." In a subsequent conversation, we heard that he is rethinking his overall plan for fundraising.

The key point to make here is: while there is expertise available through consultants and professional in-house staff, fundraising and donor stewardship cannot be farmed out. This mistaken notion persists in the largest and (what appear to be) the most effective fundraising organizations. Without the understanding that everyone in the organization has a role to play in the philanthropic process, many opportunities to engage donors are missed, or worse, relationships are broken due to an interaction that had nothing to do with a formal fundraising process.

One might ask, why, if philanthropy is so critical to an organization's success, does the responsibility for it get passed around like a hot potato? The reasons are probably some variation of the following:

- Asking people to give money away is considered to be uncomfortable.
- Most people don't know how to do it well.

The good news is that the above challenges can be solved with an education process that is appropriate for your organization in order to develop skills and understand the philanthropic process. With the demand for more private funding, opportunities for learning are readily available.

All staff involved in fundraising should be active members of a professional association such as Association of Fundraising Professionals, Association of Healthcare Philanthropy or a group specific to their industry, such as the Canadian Council for the Advancement of Education. These serve the need for professional development and offer the added benefit of networking and exposure to best practices. Board members and other volunteers can also participate in the program offerings such as one day courses, "lunch & learns" and conferences.

That said, to ensure that all volunteers receive the same information and develop the skills needed to move a particular organization along, we recommend a tailored training program with mandatory participation by volunteers and senior staff. A professional fundraising consultant can work with you to assess the best program for your needs. They can either deliver the program themselves, or connect you with the right resources. This education must be an ongoing part of board development and executive development.

After regular exposure to the theory and practice of philanthropy, the discomfort that many feel about be-

---

3   MacManus, Andrea. (2011). *Excellence in Fundraising in Canada*, Chapter 6.

ing involved in fundraising will go away. When we are really successful, all volunteers and professional staff will see themselves as contributors to the philanthropic goals of the charity, whether fundraising is in their job description or not. That's pretty magical.

WHY ARE WE RAISING MONEY?

The answers to this question need to be visionary in nature (i.e. describe a future state where your charity's work will impact the world for the better) yet crisp and specific enough that potential donors in your community will know how they can help. The closer you are to the centre of the philanthropic function for your charity, the more specific and detailed you need to to be about the opportunities for giving and the benefits to community as a result of the gift. We often call this the "so what?" factor.

We are doing this fundraising campaign so.... what?" So what will happen in the future? So what will be the impact? How many people in your organization, both staff and volunteers can articulate answers to these questions? This is a significant test of your philanthropic culture. The degree to which you are able to give a thorough and correct answer to this question, the stronger your culture will be.

Before charities embark on any campaign activity or new fundraising initiative they need to prepare a *Case for Support*. (See *Excellence in Fundraising in Canada, Volume One - Chapter* 3.) The Case for Support is usually described as the document that tells a potential donor what you are raising money for, and why. Its messages are often used for brochures, websites and other communications materials for your campaign. There is no question that developing a case is important for your external audiences. A well thought out Case for Support can provide answers to the "so-what?" question.

That said, the process of developing the case can help you assess and improve your philanthropic culture if you do three important things:
1. Engage a variety of stakeholders.
2. Listen to their feedback.
3. Address gaps in understanding and/or shortcomings in commitment that might prevent your charity from being successful in its campaign.

You could also add number four and make sure the items discovered are put into action.

This is one time when the "journey" is worth more than the "outcome." The journey of developing a Case for Support will encourage dialogue and discussion within your organization, and create a strong sense of ownership of the result, and thereby contribute to a stronger culture.

The process of creating a strong Case for Support will help you understand everyone's perceptions about such broad questions as:

- What is the impact of our charity?
- What are the priorities for donor dollars that will make the greatest difference to our community?
- Will people be prepared to give to those priorities?
- Do our stakeholders (including executive and staff and volunteers) believe we can fulfill the promises we are making to our donors through this campaign?

Overall, the building of the Case for Support will test the awareness, understanding and commitment of people who will "make or break" your fundraising efforts. Answers to these questions that sound like "I don't know" or "I'm not sure we can achieve that" are opportunities to probe and find out how the organization can improve its efforts and strengthen the culture of philanthropy.

Most importantly, acting on the good advice you get by asking these questions will do a great deal to bring your stakeholders closer to your mission, and in the process, build a stronger culture.

CONNECTING DONORS TO CHARITABLE ACTIVITY

Last year, we sat down with a friend of the university who is known for his leadership in the charitable sector. He is a volunteer on prominent charitable boards, has been chair of major campaigns and made fairly significant major gifts to his favorite charities. This man knows the inner workings of fundraising operations better than most in Canada.

Yet, with all of this experience, he was child-like in explaining the story of a recent visit to his own alma mater in the United States. The university invited him to spend the day on campus where he sat in on a class at the business school. The professor then asked him to take a small group of students to a break-out session to work through a business case, where he was able to contribute his significant experience to help the students learn. After class, the dean of the school toured him through the new building, pointing out the impact of philanthropy.

The visit ended with a dinner on campus with other donors, and an overnight stay in one of the dorm rooms set aside for visitors. He described this experience to us with glee, and made the point that we in Canada can learn from this attentive approach to donor stewardship. He knew that the point of his visit was to cultivate him toward his next gift. He understands that there was a major gift officer assigned to his "file" to make sure he had this experience. He was still thrilled. This is a prime example of how a "culture of philanthropy" adds value to all stakeholders.

The question for us then becomes, what are you doing to plug your donors into your charity? Not every charity has the resources of a major U.S. business school to plan custom stewardship activities for each donor. However, every charity has a product, and usually has a location where it does business. How can you bring your donors closer to you? Can you seek their advice and counsel on an ongoing basis?

In 2011, Guy Mallabone spoke about his *Fundamental Fundraising Truth*, stating that, "people give their money to things in their life that they are closest to."[4] He made the case that if you believe in this fundamental truth then your primary fundraising responsibility is to bring people closer to your organization. There is a lot of talk about treating donors as investors in a business. This is a good mindset for a charity with all of its funders. Not only is this experiential engagement good for the relationship with the donor, it is good for the culture of the organization. Engaging donors in your activities is key to developing a culture of philanthropy, because it reminds those we serve (such as students) and those who lead our charities (such as faculty and executives) that donors help to make our efforts possible.

> **TOP 10 INDICATORS OF PHILANTHROPIC CULTURE**[5]
>
> 1. Your board and leadership can both pronounce and spell the word philanthropy.
>
> 2. When someone calls to make a donation the receptionist knows what to do.
>
> 3. Accountability is a word your organization lives by, not pays lip service to.
>
> 4. You recognized that your primary role is not fundraising – it is building the philanthropic culture in your organization so that philanthropic relationships can survive and thrive.
>
> 5. Your organizational leadership understands and acknowledges the difference between philanthropy, development and fundraising.
>
> 6. You have a Statement of Philanthropic Values. Engage everyone to do this.
>
> 7. Development is a core function that is long term, strategic and responsive to community needs.
>
> 8. Fundraising is everyone's job. Everyone has a role to play – ambassador, enthusiastic communicator, connector, cultivator, solicitor and steward.
>
> 9. 100% of your Board makes a philanthropic gift to your organization based on their ability to give. Your board will then demonstrate its ownership of fundraising.
>
> 10. Donors are viewed as stakeholders in your organization. They are investors who care about what you do.

Let's think creatively on how we can engage with our donors to bring them close to our organization. Work with your team and ask yourselves:

- What kind of experience do our donors want?
- What kind of experience do they deserve?

---

4   Mallabone, E.H. Guy. (2011). Excellence in Fundraising in Canada, *Volume One*, Chapter 9.

5   McManus, Andrea. (2011). *The Fundraising Beat*, The Development Group.

Many donors would not want us to go to much trouble or expense to please them. So the effort should be relative to the gift level or gift potential. If we cannot do it in person, how can we use technology to actively engage our donor community? How can we ignite their passion and give them a feeling of investment and ownership? The strategy should be specific to your charity, but there are hundreds of good examples to follow. Make this a part of your fundraising strategy – ask your staff and the people served by your organization – how would they like to connect to people who reach into their pockets and give money to their effort no expectation of return? You'll be amazed at the ideas.

HOW DOES THE ORGANIZATION KNOW IT HAS BEEN SUCCESSFUL AT FUNDRAISING?

It is often said that fundraising is both an art and a science. Philanthropy is by nature a human activity, motivated by people's commitment to a cause and a desire to make a piece of the world a better place. To achieve success in fundraising, there must be an emotional connection between the donor and the organization, and programs and strategies outlined in these chapters give us to the tools to create that personal connection in a way that attracts donations.

Dr. Donald B. Calne, a neurologist at the University of British Columbia, says, "the essential difference-between emotion and reason is that emotion leads to action while reason leads to conclusions."[6]

At regular intervals, however, charities must analyze and evaluate the scientific side of their fundraising efforts to understand whether the programs and people involved are achieving the desired results. The level of commitment to this evaluation is another test of the organization's culture of philanthropy.

This is not a course on evaluation of fundraising programs. There are several tools out there to audit your organization and evaluate programs and staff.

The point is to ensure that there is regular, objective evaluation of the efforts and outcomes around fundraising that will help the organization improve its programs, provide feedback to staff and volunteers and either reinforce success or give constructive criticism as necessary.

Much like the process of developing a Case for Support that can have an impact on the charity's culture and teach us what we can do to ensure success, a regular evaluation, or assessment of campaign program results, can articulate what is working and what is not.

Too often, fundraising is evaluated by too narrow a point of view without taking into account factors that contribute to success or failure. To be valuable, the evaluation must be broad based and have multiple viewpoints, so that the board and executive (and then staff) get the full picture of performance.

To strengthen the culture of philanthropy within your organization, we recommend regular evaluations of both staff and programs using standard tools – tools that the organization believes will give them the information they need from both internal and external audiences. Professional fundraising staff must be aware of and agree to the evaluation tools so that there are no surprises at any point in the process.

We like the comprehensive tool called, *The Fundraising Audit Handbook* by Guy Mallabone and Ken Balmer.[7] The advice and templates in this package provide a thorough and multi-faceted approach to analyzing your strengths, weaknesses, fundraising performance and culture.

A lack of commitment to evaluation and feedback is common. It is also understandable given the pressure under which non-profits work – there are always too few resources to do all we want to do - and it seems appropriate at times to keep doing the good work rather than stopping to evaluate. This is the trap that we get into if there is not a strong commitment to evaluation all the way up to the senior levels including the board of directors.

It is also important to benchmark our performance against our peers and participate in professional development societies that allow us to learn from our colleagues from other organizations. External reviewers can often play a role in ensuring we are using appropriate tools and strategies to evaluate our programs.

---

6   Calne, Donald B., http://en.wikipedia.org/wiki/Donald_Calne

7   Mallabone, E.H. Guy and Balmer, Ken. (2010). *The Fundraising Audit Handbook*, Civil Sector Press.

What are the risks to building a culture without evaluation? To name a few:

- Too much investment in fundraising programs that no longer lead to "good enough" results
- Communications strategies and/or messages that are outdated or no longer effective
- Donor fatigue or dissatisfaction
- Underperforming staff are allowed to continue to represent us
- Weak leadership, unchecked, leading to the departure of dissatisfied staff
- Fewer resources available to be applied to our missions

If evaluation is not a priority for the executive and the board, it tells you a lot about the organization's commitment to a culture of philanthropy. If evaluation is rigorous, regular and effective, we can consistently improve our fundraising strategies and activities, correct our course as necessary and demonstrate to both our internal community and our donors that we are committed to excellent stewardship of precious philanthropic resources.

WHAT DO YOUR STAFF AND VOLUNTEER FUNDRAISING TEAM MEMBERS HAVE TO SAY ABOUT THEIR EXPERIENCE WITH FUNDRAISING AND YOUR ORGANIZATION?

At the outset, we defined organizational culture as being the behavior of humans who are part of an organization and the meanings that the people attach to their actions.

There is no more simple a test of a successful philanthropic culture than to gather candid feedback from the individuals who are part of your organization and talk to them about their efforts to attract gifts from donors in a very competitive environment.

Fundraising staff and volunteers think about culture every day, whether they know it or not. They experience it when they talk to donors. They have it played back to them in conversations and actions from members of the community. If they feel the wind at their back in their efforts to raise money, that's a sign of a good culture. If they feel that they have appropriate resources (time, tools, skills, ideas, leadership) to be effective, this is a great thing. Staff and volunteers are excellent barometers and ambassadors to the community. They exist at the interesting and unique intersection in the organization with one foot inside the organization and one foot outside the organization.

If volunteers are satisfied and engaged with your organization, others in the community will know about it. They recruit others. They share your Case for Support. They commit to you over time and become great relationship managers, thereby extending your reach well beyond the potential of paid staff alone.

The satisfaction of both staff and volunteers gives an excellent perspective of the health of an organization's culture. If your staff and volunteers aspire to rise in the ranks of your organization rather than be successful and take their precious skills elsewhere, you are doing something right. Unfortunately, this is not the case often enough.

"The nonprofit sector has typically framed the problem of the revolving door as a staffing issue: We just can't find good development directors, and when we do make a hire, they don't perform well or they leave too soon!"[8]

Fundraising staff, volunteers and non-profit leaders who are successful fundraisers are a very hot commodity. In contrast, charities have little flexibility and resources to offer the kinds of perks that might attract or help to retain the best people. Also, professional fundraising is a relatively new field, which means there are too few experienced leaders available to mentor and educate a new generation. What is left then to ensure a healthy talent pool for our charities? The most important thing is to find ways to sustain a healthy culture, and that includes giving your employees and volunteers the resources they need.

When we talk to young colleagues about what is most important to them as they build their careers in philanthropy (either professional or volunteer) what we most often hear is that they want to be a part of a team with the highest standards of practice. They want to learn and get the opportunities to work on

---

8   Bell, Jeanne & Cornelius, Marla. *Underdeveloped: A National Study of Challenges Facing Nonprofit Fundraising.* http://www.compasspoint.org/sites/default/files/images/UnderDeveloped_CompassPoint_HaasJrFund_January%202013.pdf. This excerpt is reprinted, with permission from CompassPoint Nonprofit Services.

important campaigns in a professional environment. There are other motivators, of course: they want to make a good living, feel that they are having an impact on a cause they care deeply about and they want to be part of a positive environment. People who choose employment in non-profits are usually committed citizens who are willing to make some sacrifices for the greater good. However, more and more, the culture of the organization is the motivator for talented people to come *and* go from organizations.

We know that the human elements of our organizations can make or break our success and ability to deliver to the mission. Yet so few people are putting the necessary conditions in place to keep fundraising staff satisfied, and engaged with the community. Author and fundraising researcher, Penelope Burk recently released a book dedicated to the topic titled, *Donor Centred Leadership, What it takes to Build a High Performance Fundraising Team*. In it, she reveals the results of studies about human resource issues affecting the health of organizations. Among the great pieces of advice throughout, Penelope shares the key characteristics of the best chief executives: In short, they are:

- goal oriented
- strategic in their approach to fulfilling the mission
- respectful and supportive of fundraisers professional judgment
- aware of the importance of the role they play as CEOs in making fundraising successful
- supportive of fundraising when dealing with the board
- skilled at interacting with donors and asking them for gifts

Penelope's research highlights what we believe are the most important resources we have as we build our organizations – our people. Without the ability to compensate staff and volunteers the way that our for-profit friends can, we are left with no choice but to offer the most attractive culture possible. And as demographics shift and we attract more millennials into our sphere, we need to be prepared to listen to fresh ideas and new approaches to our efforts. In short, we need to be prepared to invest in the people who represent us, and that means time, education, commitment to a positive working environment, and as Penelope's summary points out, we need to *lead by example*.

To bring about change in the culture of your organization vis-à-vis its working environment, deliberately initiate a discussion and keep the following points in mind:

- Find a way to ensure candor, even if it means anonymous surveys.
- Find out what thrills people in your organization and reinforce those experiences. Celebrate strengths and successes.
- Find out what your people think about the expectations set out for them. Do they have what they need to be successful? If not, why not?
- How can you attract new people to your organization and retain them if there are fundamental flaws in your culture?
- Find out what the flaws are and address them to the extent you can as quickly as possible.
- Ask: What are they saying about us?

CANADIAN CULTURE: IS IT WORKING AGAINST US? IS IT CHANGING?

It is tough to answer these questions without making sweeping generalizations about a whole country and its more than 80,000 charities. However, when looking at the statistics, it is easy to understand why it is challenging for our organizations to focus on private philanthropy.

In a report tabled by Imagine Canada, *The Canadian Non-Profit and Voluntary Sector, in Comparative Perspective* we learn that:

"Canadian nonprofit and voluntary organizations receive more revenue from government than do those in other countries. Government funding is particularly prominent in the fields of health, education, and social services reflecting the special form that the welfare state has taken in Canada and echoing what is found in a number of European countries. Government support also plays a prominent role in the funding of civic and advocacy organizations. Fee income dominates in the remaining fields. Philan-

thropy accounts for nine percent of total nonprofit and voluntary organization income..."⁹

With less than 10% of our funding coming from philanthropy, it is no wonder the fundraising effort can be relegated to the sideline. However, the same report also goes on to say that charities report significant issues that affect *"their future vitality... which can be attributed to the challenges they have had adjusting to changes arising from the substantial retrenchment of the Canadian state that occurred in the 1990's."*¹⁰

A CALL TO ACTION

In order to survive and thrive, Canadian charities need to strengthen their commitment to building an organizational culture that encourages and strengthens private philanthropy as a source of revenue. This will be particularly challenging for older generations of both donors and leaders who came of age during a time when governments were relied upon more heavily.

The younger generation of volunteers, donors and leaders gives us reason to hope for our collective "culture of philanthropy." The millennial generation is an entrepreneurial bunch, especially when it comes to their charitable efforts and they have come into the professional world with less reliance on government agency to solve the financial challenges that our charities face. We believe that, armed with knowledge and some experience around the fundamentals of non-profit leadership and fundraising, the next generation will come into their own and do things differently by design and necessity, and a more philanthropy culture will emerge naturally, as a result.

ADDITIONAL RESOURCES

Books and Reports

▶ BELL, JEAN AND MARLA CORNELIUS. (2012). *Underdeveloped, A National Study of Challenges Facing Nonprofit Fundraising.* Compass Point Nonprofit Services and Evelun & Walter Haas Jr. Fund. CompassPoint Nonprofit Services, 500 12th Street, Suite 320, Oakland, CA, 94607. http://www.compasspoint.org

▶ BURK, PENELOPE. (2013). *Donor Centred Leadership, What it takes to Build a High- Performance Fundraising Team*, Cygnus Applied Research.

▶ GRANT, MICHAEL, AND HOPE SHAMONDA. (2013). *Culture and Innovation: The Secret Sauce. Ottawa:* The Conference Board of Canada.

▶ HALL, MICHAEL, ET AL. *The Canadian Nonprofit and Volunteer Sector in Comparative Perspective, 2005* http://sectorsource.ca/sites/default/files/resources/files/jhu_report_en.pdf

▶ MALLABONE, E.H. GUY. (2011). *Excellence in Fundraising in Canada, Volume One.* Civil Sector Press, The Hilborn Group.

---

9 *The Canadian Nonprofit and Volunteer Sector in Comparative Perspective* http://sectorsource.ca/sites/default/files/resources/files/jhu_report_en.pdf

10 Ibid.

ABOUT THE AUTHORS

Andrea Morris, BA

Andrea Morris is a Senior Director in the Office of Advancement at the University of Alberta where she has worked in major gifts and leadership positions since 2000. She currently leads the faculty-based advancement programs and oversees the Office of Corporate and Foundation Relations. Andrea holds a Bachelor of Arts degree in Communications from the University of Ottawa. She is based in Calgary, Alberta.

Kelly Morris, BSc

Kelly Morris is an Associate Director of Development, Leadership Annual Giving at the University of Calgary and has had the privilege of working with a great team since 2013. Previously working as development consultant, Kelly had the opportunity to work with all types of charitable organizations to help build capacity and advance their causes. Prior to working in the nonprofit industry, Kelly worked in Melbourne, Australia in the digital media world honing her skills in account management and client service.

Kelly holds a Bachelor of Social Sciences in Sociology and Public Policy and Public Management from the University of Ottawa. She is based in Calgary, Alberta.

It is also worth mentioning that Andrea and Kelly grew up in a household where their mother, Bonnie Morris was a pioneer of fundraising in Canada. She recently retired after a 40-year career in executive roles with the United Way of Ottawa, the University of Ottawa and the United Way of Canada. Needless to say, fundraising and philanthropy has long been a topic at the Morris family dinner table.

CHAPTER 6

DIVERSITY IN FUNDRAISING

KRISHAN MEHTA, MA AND
DEBORAH GREENFIELD, MKTG CERT, CFRE

With more than 200 ethnic groups spread across Canada, charities are beginning to ask questions about how diversity is influencing our fundraising efforts. We must remember, however, that "diversity" refers to a wide range of social and cultural categories, including race, age, gender, sexual orientation, nationality, religion, income level, language and disability.

read more…

This chapter asks readers to appreciate the value of building an inclusive organization. Why? For us, it is not only the right thing to do, but there are also tremendous financial and social dividends for charities that are open to working with emerging donor groups.

Drawing on key terms, empirical research and best practices in the field, this chapter provides several useful tips for building a diverse and inclusive fundraising shop.

INTRODUCING DIVERSITY AND INCLUSION

While diversity and inclusion have been mainstay topics in the charitable sector for several decades; globalization, immigration, recent advances in communications, and national policy decisions have informed new curiosities about different cultural approaches to philanthropy and how best we can build long-lasting and trusting relationships with emerging donor groups.

Celebrated scholar Benedict Anderson coined the term "imagined community"[1] to describe how certain values and ideas bind people together, sometimes from coast to coast. In Canada, multiculturalism and diversity are often called out as important features of our national identity – our imagined community. And as we continue to welcome immigrants and affirm the rights of minoritized groups, other countries are looking to Canada to learn about social inclusion and equity.

But making sense of diversity and inclusion can be difficult – especially for fundraisers and social profit leaders – for a few reasons.

1. The topic requires deep reflection about who you are, what your organization does and where new opportunities exist. Does your charity serve a distinct population? Are you located in a rural or urban setting? Do your volunteers and donors have diverse skills, backgrounds and interests? Are diversity and inclusion part of your organization's DNA? These are just some of the questions that fundraisers and volunteers are asking in an effort to achieve success and build inclusively-minded organizations.

2. There is no formula that guarantees a gift from a "diverse" donor. While there are distinct cultural cues that may inform the giving interests and habits of emerging groups, we must remember that giving is a deeply personal act, and any attempt to apply individual strategies to a wider group of donors will inevitably yield great frustration – on both sides of the table. Giving is also context-driven, which means that we must pay attention to the donor's personal interests and needs, which may or may not be informed by cultural background.

Figure 6.1[2]

3. Diversity is a tidy word for a very broad concept that has been ascribed to a wide range of communities. While we commonly use the word "diversity" to talk about race, class, age, ethnicity, gender, sexual orientation and ability, there are many other internal and organizational dimensions that fall under the diversity umbrella: location, income, employment status and so on.

Figure 6.1 provides a useful frame of reference for all of the ways diversity can be understood, even

---

1 Anderson, Benedict. (2006). *Imagined communities: Reflections on the origin and spread of nationalism.* Verso Books.

2 Gardenswartz, Lee, and Anita Rowe. (1998.)*Managing diversity: A complete desk reference and planning guide.* New York: McGraw-Hill.

though it is often several of these factors that make up one's personality and culture. Add to that all of the nuances related to family background, regional differences, intergenerational issues, and community politics – and there you have an exciting and endless journey of cultural discovery!

PREPARING FOR THE JOURNEY: CANADA'S POPULATION IS CHANGING

If this is such a complex and unwieldy topic, is there anything we can learn from all of the diversity initiatives out there? The simple and resounding answer is yes. There are a number of lessons from the field that can help you build an inclusive fundraising practice. However, before we get to the "how to," we would like to take a moment to review the most significant quantitative data points that help explain why inclusion should matter to all of us.

- According to a recent study conducted by BMO Harris Private Banking, almost half of Canada's wealthy are either immigrants or first generation Canadians, and one-third of high-net worth Canadians are women.[3]

- Another study by Protean Strategies shows that Canada's LGBT community possesses 22% more discretionary dollars than the average Canadian. The community's before-tax income amounts to about $98 billion or approximately 7.2% of the GDP.[4]

Let's also take a look at the broader demographic realities.

- Canada boasts the highest percentage of foreign-born citizens compared to the other G8 countries.[5]

- In 2012, Canada welcomed 257,515 newcomers, a record number for seven consecutive years.[6]

Clearly, immigration has created a society of mixed languages, cultures and religions. According to Statistics Canada:

- The majority of Canada's foreign-born populations live in the urban centres of Ontario, British Columbia, Quebec and Alberta.

- Over 200 ethnic origins were reported in the 2011 National Household Survey, and 13 of those had surpassed the one million population mark.

- More than 200 languages were reported in the 2011 Census of Population, either as a home language or mother tongue as well.

- 17.5 % of Canadians reported speaking at least two languages at home, compared to 14.2% in 2006.[7]

While there remain some gaps in our understanding of giving amongst several emerging donor groups, there has been a comprehensive analysis of philanthropy among immigrants.

- While immigrants tend to have lower household incomes, they are inclined to donate more than Canadian-born donors. For example, immigrants with annual household incomes of less than $40,000 gave an average of $404 to charitable and non-profit organizations, compared with $214 for their Canadian-born counterparts.[8]

- Data from previous surveys have consistently shown that, among immigrants, those who have been in Canada longer are more likely to donate, and the average annual amount they give is larger. The most recent results reconfirm this trend:

---

3 BMO Harris Private Banking. (2013.) *"BMO Harris Private Banking Changing Face of Wealth Study: Diversity Reigns Among High-Net Worth Canadians,"* Bank of Montreal. http://newsroom.bmo.com/press-releases/bmo-harris-private-banking-changing-face-of-wealth-tsx-bmo-201306130880233001

4 Alicia Androich. (2012). *"Welcome in the Gaybourhood: lessons from Marketing's first LGBT conference."* Marketing Magazine. http://www.marketingmag.ca/brands/welcome-in-the-gaybourhood-lessons-from-marketings-first-lgbt-conference-56185

5 Statistics Canada. (2013). *"Immigration and Ethnocultural Diversity in Canada, National Household Survey, 2011."* http://www12.statcan.gc.ca/nhs-enm/2011/as-sa/99-010-x/99-010-x2011001-eng.pdf

6 Andy Radia. (2013). *"Canada's immigration numbers peaking for seventh consecutive year: 2012 statistics."* Yahoo News. https://ca.news.yahoo.com/blogs/canada-politics/2012-immigration-statistics-released-canada-remains-one-most-235820655.html

7 Thomas, Derrick. (2012). *Giving and Volunteering Among Canada's Immigrants.* Statistics Canada, http://www.statcan.gc.ca/pub/11-008-x/2012001/article/11669-eng.htm

8 Ibid, 2012.

- In 2010, the likelihood of giving money to charitable or non-profit organizations was higher for long-term immigrants who had been in Canada for 30 years or more (90%), than for recent immigrants in Canada less than 10 years (79%).
- Also, long-term immigrant donors tended to give larger average annual donations.[9]

UNPACKING THE TERMINOLOGY: WHAT DO DIVERSITY AND INCLUSION MEAN?

As we continue to explore this topic, it is important to remember that *diversity* and *inclusion*, although related, mean different things. According to the Canadian Institute of Diversity and Inclusion, diversity speaks to the individual: "It is about the variety of unique dimensions, qualities, and characteristics we all possess."[10] Inclusion, on the other hand, is "about creating a culture that strives for equity and embraces, respects, accepts and values difference."[11] The Royal Bank of Canada puts it simply, stating that "diversity is the mix; inclusion is getting the mix to work well together."[12]

These distinctions are important because having a diverse group of volunteers and donors doesn't automatically lead to inclusion. It is the series of positive and productive *actionable* initiatives that move us from diversity to inclusion. It was once said that, "Diversity is like being invited to the prom. Inclusion is like being asked to dance." And more leaders are favouring a long-term inclusion strategy that focuses on *how* best to leverage diversity towards meeting the goals of the charity. Having a diverse donor and volunteer base simply isn't enough.

Different takes on giving

Charitable giving is a part of all societies, and these values can be found in sacred texts that are passed down from generation to generation. Hindus, for example, believe in the concept of *seva*, which means charitable "service." Within Indigenous traditions, philanthropy is a form of reciprocity, particularly giving back to nature and the environment. In Islam, charitable giving is called *zakat*, where individual wealth and access to resources inform how much one gives. Similarly, in Judaism, *tzedakah* refers to a religious obligation to give. In Buddhist traditions, giving is done without any expectation of return or recognition. Some African diaspora groups use the word *ubuntu* to describe acts of selflessness. While the nuances of giving within these and other communities can be found in many books and articles, what is important to understand is that giving is universal and still speaks to the Latin origins of the word *philanthropy*, meaning love for humankind.

In Canada, religion has a very significant impact on giving. One Canadian study conducted by Ida Berger showed higher giving amongst those who attended a religious service one or more times per week.[13] In religious institutions, worshippers are often exposed to a steady stream of messages that encourage "giving" of time and money as part of their religious commitment and altruism.

Practically speaking, giving behaviours aren't always rooted in faith-based teachings or centuries-old giving practices. For example, many youth are learning about philanthropy through the formal educational system, and a growing number are relying on social media channels, text message donation options, crowdsourcing platforms and group sharing sites to express their support for a cause. Other forms of giving are sometimes connected to a struggle for social justice, such as lesbian, gay, bisexual, transgender, and queer (LGBTQ) rights, access for people with disabilities or gender equity. While some may argue that each of these groups tend to favour specific giving tools and methods, as we all know *personal experiences* influence how people give – and in most cases this depends on how you are able to match their interests with your organization's mission.

We must remember that as cultures mix and future generations build their own giving traditions, current norms and practices are bound to change as well. Therefore, it is important to be open to embracing emerging trends and technologies as part of your

---

9   Ibid, 2012.
10 Canadian Institute of Diversity and Inclusion. (2014). *"D&I Defined."* http://www.cidi-icdi.ca/about/di-defined/
11 Ibid, 2014.
12 Royal Bank of Canada. (2014). *"What is Diversity and Inclusion?"* http://www.rbc.com/diversity/what-is-diversity.html

13 Berger, Ida E. (2006). *"The influence of religion on philanthropy in Canada."* Voluntas: International Journal of Voluntary and Nonprofit Organizations, 17.2: 110-127.

commitment to inclusion. Do you know what people are saying about your charity across the digital divide? Is that having an impact on how much you raise and from where you raise it? You bet it does. And this becomes pronounced as we look at diaspora groups, where traditional community (or family) bonds extend along the ether. Of course the tempo of giving from the diaspora increases during times of great crisis back home. For example, a charity called *Jusoor* was recently established in Toronto (with fundraising events in many global cities) to harness the giving capacity of Syrians living in Canada and beyond.

The major lesson here is that your charity should think and act globally, especially with all of the new and exciting ways you can create awareness outside of our traditional parameters or borders.

PRACTICAL TIPS FOR BUILDING AN INCLUSIVE CHARITY

Fostering a genuinely inclusive environment takes time, dedication and resources. In some cases this may involve a reevaluation of the traditional tools and approaches we often take for granted. In our review of those Canadian charities with a strong inclusion focus, we have distilled the most important features that will certainly help you build a meaningful inclusive fundraising practice.

1. *Everyone inside needs to believe in the power of inclusion – and it starts at the top.*

   The role of the charity leader in promoting diversity and inclusion cannot be overstated. No matter the size of your organization, the person at the top sets the tone of the organization. If the president, CEO or executive director prioritizes activities that advance inclusivity, then managers, staff, volunteers and donors will inevitably rally around this too. Many charity leaders have demonstrated their commitment to inclusion through the following initiatives:

   - Creating opportunities for inclusion training and professional development on a regular basis.

   - Acknowledging and celebrating holidays and cultural events.

   - Making a commitment to hire a diverse range of people with different skills, interests and backgrounds.

   - Inviting suggestions from colleagues about how to build greater participation from all staff.

   - Encouraging and supporting the development of social and affinity groups within the team.

   - Personally reaching out to donors and volunteers to learn about cultural similarities and differences.

   - Valuing different giving traditions, while making space to incorporate these practices into fundraising work.

> *Researchers at The Diversity Institute, Ryerson University showed that eight out of 13 charities (and four out of five foundations) had no visible minorities in senior management.*[14]

2. *Diversity on your board.*

   Board diversity remains one of the greatest challenges for charities. As noted earlier, an organization needs to start with a "mix" in order for the mix to work well together. But this must be meaningful; having diverse representation on your board without deep engagement opportunities doesn't work. According to a research report by DiverseCity, there are great benefits to having a diverse board, as noted in Figure 6.2:[15]

   Practically speaking, when it comes to diversifying your board, the same study cited several tips from another report on diversity and the non-profit sector:

   - Conduct a diversity audit of your board.

---

14 *DiverseCity Counts 2: A Snapshot of Diverse Leadership in the GTA: the Second Annual Research Report Measuring Diversity Among Leaders with a New Focus on the Media.* (2010). Diversity Institute in Management and Technology, Ryerson University.
15 *Insights on Diversity in Leadership.* (2013). The Diversity Institute, Toronto.

Reported benefits to diversity on boards

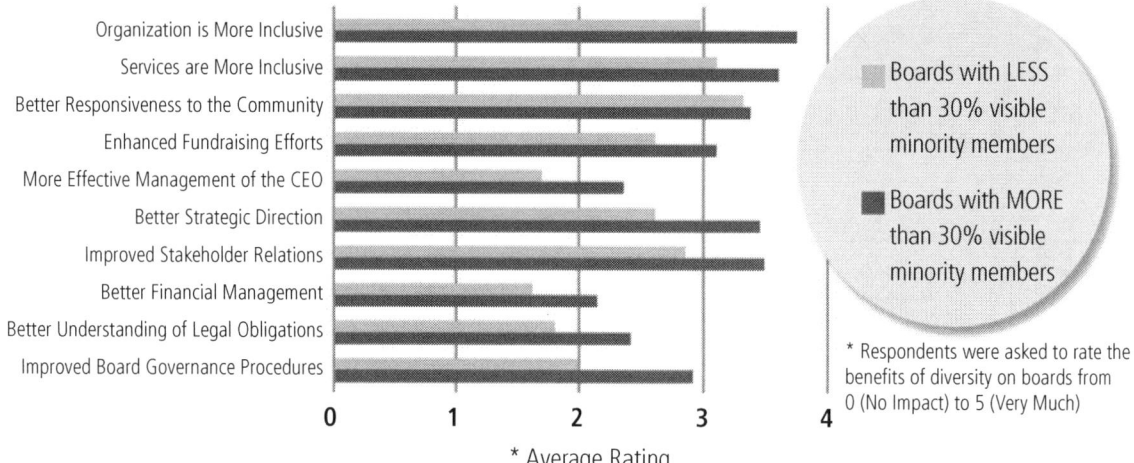

Figure 6.2

- Focus on the skills needed to meet the organization's strategic priorities.
- Set explicit goals in the selection process.
- Seek members with a variety of skills and expertise, based on differentiated life experiences.
- Encourage diverse board members to take on additional responsibilities as part of your engagement plan.
- Train all board members on diversity issues through orientation, mentoring and ongoing education on cultural competency building.
- Mainstream diversity in the organization's activities.
- Measure results of diversity by its impact.

3. *Help define what success means when it comes to inclusion.*

   When it comes to building an inclusive organization, there will always be new opportunities and lessons that will help enhance your fundraising practice. While there is no endgame when it comes to this topic, several charities have developed signposts to help them gauge their success and impact. Work with your colleagues and volunteers to determine which of these traits are realistically achievable for your organization:

- Our charity is led by a group of volunteers that have a wide range of skills, interests, cultural backgrounds and life experiences.
- Our charity's marketing materials reflect the community we serve and the donors we want to engage.
- We actively discuss issues of diversity and inclusion, and seek to build unconventional philanthropic relationships.
- Diversity and inclusion are part of our organization's core values.
- We seek input from our donors, volunteers, staff and other partners when it comes to inclusion.
- We support and participate in cultural events and initiatives that speak to the communities where we live and work.
- We recognize that diversity can sometimes be "hidden" (for example, you might not know if someone has a disability), so we always make an effort to create a bias-free and accessible working environment.

There are, of course, many other ways to define success, but we recommend that you start with three or four initiatives and then add more as you make progress. Remember to articulate these initiatives in writing and create regular reminders to review them with your colleagues.

4. *Build trust before asking for money.*
   We have seen far too many organizations alienate their "diverse" donors or volunteers by asking them to open a door into their community (or worse yet ask for a gift) without taking the time to build trust. Inviting someone to participate on your fundraising committee or board is just one step. Here are some other useful information for building greater trust and loyalty.

   a. *Expect a longer cultivation period:* For major gift prospects, be sure to allocate more time to get to know what their interests are, how connected they feel to the communities they belong to, and so on (especially if this is a new relationship). Don't be afraid to ask questions, particularly around some of the cultural approaches to giving that may be different from what you already know. This can be a tricky balancing act, however, because they might not have all the answers or be able to speak on behalf of their entire cultural group. We have learned the importance of learning about one's *perspective* and avoiding the "what-do-*your*-people-do" line of questioning.

   b. *The importance of the "all in" factor:* It is often said that an organization's most loyal donors are those who are involved and invested on all levels, at the governance table and on the ground. When it comes to inclusion, this is critical to building trust. Don't be afraid to talk about the challenges or opportunities that your organization faces. Ask for advice on how to approach these issues and, if appropriate, see if they can assist with a non-fundraising matter, like a policy document or special project. Showing that you value their insights – over their cultural background – always goes a long way.

   Finally, you must first show loyalty to get loyalty in return. Just as we seek the attention of our donors, they too are looking for gestures of dedication. While this may be true for donors of all backgrounds, making genuine, culturally-relevant moves to show your interest in building bridges within their communities certainly helps. As noted earlier, this can be done through participation in, and sponsorship of, activities that bring various communities together. You can also send e-cards to mark different occasions and holidays. We have seen a growing number of charities organize their own events at occasions such as Diwali, Hanukkah, International Women's Day, Black History Month, Eid, Pride, and so on. Mark these and other relevant events on your calendar and participate wherever there may be a critical mass or key donors and volunteers.

5. *Measure, measure, measure.*
   Use readily available statistics and facts to help make the case for broadening or focusing your prospect strategies. Many recent studies have underscored the growing diversity of the Canadian population, and these studies can help set the stage for making inclusion a priority within your organization. Some national charities draw on census data to do this. Here are just a few of the data points[16] that we find particularly compelling:

   - One out of five people was born outside of Canada, well above all of the G8 countries.
   - The three largest visible minority groups – South Asians, Chinese and Blacks – accounted for 61.3% of the visible minority population. They were followed by Filipinos, Latin Americans, Arabs, Southeast Asians, West Asians, Koreans and Japanese.
   - 72.8% of Canada's immigrant population reported a mother tongue other than English or French.

   There are many other quantitative studies available online and on government websites where you can drill down to find provincial and municipal demographic information as well.

   You can also draw on your own data to help make the case. Some charities have analyzed their databases to identify where there may be concentrations of donors living in ethnic

---

16   Statistics Canada. (2013). "Immigration and Ethnocultural Diversity in Canada, National Household Survey, 2011." http://www12.statcan.gc.ca/nhs-enm/2011/as-sa/99-010-x/99-010-x2011001-eng.cfm

enclaves. A company like Environics Analytics, which identifies consumer interests and giving behaviours based on residential address segmentation and last name affiliations, can help you better understand the level of diversity amongst your existing donor base.

Once you have a solid foundation, you can begin to chart your progress on a number of other fronts too: event participation, targeted communications, giving on scheduled direct mail solicitations, email campaigns, and so on.

6. *Revisit your outreach efforts, particularly your online marketing and communications.* How many times a day do you retrieve information online or use your mobile device to communicate? The reality is that an effective online and digital presence is absolutely critical to generating buzz about your cause. Simply put, the internet has made your organization a borderless, 24/7 operation, and social media and mobile communications are now mainstay features of our modern world.

In 2013, social network users around the world rose from 1.47 billion to 1.73 billion; and by 2017, it is estimated that over 2.5 billion people will be using one or more social media channel every day.[17] As a result, it is important to take stock of how well your marketing and communications materials are received by a diverse range of communities.

Here are the top four questions leaders of inclusively-minded charities have been grappling with when it comes to non-profit marketing via web and social media:

   i. Is your online presence accessible and barrier-free? Ask yourself: Can people with varying visual abilities adjust the size and font of the text on your site?

   ii. Does your website have multilingual translation capability? Helpful tip: you can apply Google Translate to your website to change your online text into hundreds of different languages.

   iii. Do the images you use reflect the people who may be visiting your site remotely? Will people see themselves in the pictures you display?

   iv. Can you use customized targeted online ads to appeal to the communities you want to engage? The competition in the online marketing world can be stiff, so consider leveraging YouTube, Facebook, Google ads and promoted tweets to get people to engage with your cause and drive traffic to your website and giving page.

Don't forget the vast opportunities that still exist through traditional media, especially with the growing number of ethno-cultural newspapers and magazines, television programs and radio stations in Canada. These are important media and some charities are using them to promote events, seek volunteers and ask for money.

---

17   eMarketer. (2013). *"Social Networking Reaches Nearly One in Four Around the World."* http://www.emarketer.com/Article/Social-Networking-Reaches-Nearly-One-Four-Around-World/1009976

CASE STUDY: EMBEDDING INCLUSION AT MARKHAM STOUFFVILLE HOSPITAL

At the Markham Stouffville Hospital (MSH) Foundation, diversity and inclusion has led to great fundraising success. The Foundation's vision is to inspire and earn support from every member of its community. According to Statistics Canada, visible minorities make up more than 70% of Markham's population, making it Canada's most diverse community. And its fundraising achievements would not be possible without the support of its immigrant populations.

Having recently completed the largest capital campaign in the hospital's history, several ethno-cultural groups contributed almost 10% of the funds raised:

- Canadians of Pakistani Origin ($2M)

- Great Wall (Chinese and East Asian) Fundraising Group ($1M)

- Sikh Community ($250,000)

- Tamil Community ($250,000)

- Macedonian Community ($100,000)

Through annual fundraising dinners, often organized in conjunction with a culturally significant occasion, these groups introduced MSH to hundreds of families and individuals. Additionally, these initiatives help raise awareness about Ontario's ever changing healthcare system for new Canadians.

MSH Foundation's philosophy for success is simple:

Relationships are Key ~ A Proud Heritage

- Build genuine relationships based on trust and respect.

- Ensure the leaders representing the community are well respected, connected and can influence others.

- Engage members of diverse communities in meaningful ways by inviting them to volunteer and including them in various events.

- Make a concerted effort to understand the values and motivations of different cultures and be aware of "diversity within diversity" factor.

- Show you care by actively participating in and attending their events and celebrations.

> ### CASE STUDY: EMBEDDING INCLUSION AT MARKHAM STOUFFVILLE HOSPITAL (CONT.)
>
> **Partnering for the Long Term ~ An Extraordinary Future**
>
> - Apply a cultural lens to everything you do and embed it throughout your business plan, instead of developing a separate "diversity strategy."
>
> - What does your organization do to support diversity? At MSH, services are available in different languages, Halal food is available to patients, and female physicians and medical staff care for Muslim women whenever possible. New birthing suites are large enough for multiple families and friends to witness birth in the Sikh tradition.
>
> - Consider media opportunities beyond the traditional channels by promoting and recognizing donations using ethno-cultural media.
>
> - Remember, the ultimate, long-term goal is to identify new major gift prospects.
>
> Now, more than ever before, hospitals rely on their foundations to drive innovation and enable growth. For ethno-cultural donors, supporting Markham Stouffville Hospital has been a source of great pride and provides a real sense of belonging. Giving back is an important way to participate in and contribute to Canadian society.
>
> Contributed by; Suzette Strong, M.A., CFRE
> CEO, Markham Stouffville Hospital Foundation

CONCLUSION

In the end, much of this work helps build your cultural intelligence. Making sense of the various approaches to diversity and inclusion may seem overwhelming at first, but countless fundraisers have benefitted from the new doors that have opened up for them. This chapter is meant to initiate a conversation and inspire reflection on the potential of growing your organization to reflect and include the changing face of Canada.

While there are many tips and best practices to draw from, time and time again we see that the most successful charities have made a deep and intentional commitment to inclusion. This begins with embedding it in your strategy and values, followed by getting everyone to see its potential through leadership, measurement, events, cultivation efforts, and marketing and communications. In all cases, it is the confluence of these areas that make inclusion work effectively.

We also believe that a focus on culture can help bring people of different backgrounds together. What do you have in common? What can you learn from one another? Even though some people don't identify as "diverse," everyone can rally around culture – whether it's based on race, religion, nationality, gender, sexual orientation, workplace interests, family structure, hobbies and so forth. Begin with issues that you have in common.

Finally, we have learned that there is no monolithic group within the broad diversity spectrum. For example, there is no single "South Asian community." Under this category there are thousands of racial, religious, cultural, regional and linguistic differences. And this can be said of every community group. The "diversity within diversity" factor is crucial to our understanding and appreciation of this complexity.

Remember: this is a journey with no final destination. However, if you make a commitment to inclusion, great social and financial dividends will be found along the way.

ADDITIONAL RESOURCES

Books, Articles and Reports

- Capek, Mary Ellen S., and Molly Mead. (2007.) *Effective philanthropy: Organizational success through deep diversity and gender equality.* MIT Press.

- Duschinsky, Jon. *Philanthropy in a Flat World: Inspiration Through Globalization.* (2009). Vol. 185. John Wiley & Sons.

- Dwyer, Rocky J. (2009). "Prepare for the impact of the multi-generational workforce!" *Transforming Government: People, Process and Policy* 3.2: 101-110.

- Fredette, Christopher. (2012.) *Leadership Diversity in the Nonprofit Sector: Baby Steps, Big Strides, and Bold Stances*, A DiverseCity Counts Research Project Report.

- Fredette, Christopher. (2006). *Creating Diverse Non-profit boards: engaging multiple dimensions of power.* Banff, Alberta: ASAC.

- Katsioloudes, Marios. (2012). *Global Strategic Planning.* Routledge.

- Klein, Kim. (2011). *Fundraising for social change.* Vol. 21. John Wiley & Sons.

- Pettey, Janice Gow. (2002). *Cultivating Diversity in Fundraising (AFP/Wiley Fund Development Series).* Vol. 194. John Wiley & Sons.

- Scott, Katherine, Kevin Selbee, and Paul B. Reed. (2006). *Making connections: Social and civic engagement among Canadian immigrants.* Kanata, ON: Canadian Council on Social Development.

- Shaw-Hardy, Sondra, Martha A. Taylor, and Buffy Beaudoin-Schwartz. (2010.) *Women and philanthropy: Boldly shaping a better world.* John Wiley & Sons.

- The Diversity Institute. (2010). *Diversity Counts 2 Report* Toronto: Diverse City, The Greater Toronto Lealdership Project. Ryerson University.

- Thomas, Derrick. (2012). *Giving and Volunteering Among Canada's Immigrants.* Statistics Canada.

- Wagner, Lilya, and J. Patrick Ryan. (2004). "Achieving diversity among fundraising professionals." *New Directions for Philanthropic Fundraising* 2004.43:63-70.

- Whitaker, Laura. (2014) *Nonprofit Organizations & Social Media Fundraising.*

URLs

- http://afpinclusivegiving.ca/
- http://www.cidi-icdi.ca/
- http://diversecitytoronto.ca/wp-content/uploads/Diversity-on-Non-Profit-Boards-Toolkit.pdf
- http://maytree.com/
- http://www12.statcan.gc.ca/nhs-enm/2011/as-sa/99-010-x/99-010-x2011001-eng.cfm
- http://lgbtgivingnetwork.org/
- http://southasianphilanthropy.org/
- http://kciphilanthropy.com/download_trends/pt-022011.pdf
- http://www.thephilanthropist.ca/index.php/phil/issue/view/96

ABOUT THE AUTHORS

Krishan Mehta, MA

Krishan is Executive Director, Campaign at Ryerson University. Previously, he has held a variety of fundraising, alumni and marketing roles at Seneca College and the University of Toronto. Krishan is also an instructor in Ryerson's fundraising management program and a PhD candidate at the University of Toronto where he is conducting research on the philanthropy of high net-worth immigrants in Canada. He serves as Vice President of Inclusion and Equity and President-Elect for the Association of Fundraising Professionals Greater Toronto Chapter and Co-Chair of the Inclusive Giving Project, a multi-year government-funded program that brings together donors, community leaders and non-profit managers to share their experiences of giving and fundraising within twelve diverse communities across Ontario.

Deborah Greenfield, Mktg Cert, CFRE

Deb has had an extensive career in fundraising, marketing and community relations. Currently, she is the Director of Development at the Ted Rogers School of Management, Ryerson University. Prior to this, she was Campaign Manager at Centennial College in Toronto and Director of Marketing and Development for the Grand Theatre in London. She has helped establish national planned giving programs and participated on a taskforce that developed and established Canada's first graduate program in philanthropy. Deb has also initiated and implemented institutional marketing and communications plans for local and international markets with a focus on the arts, retail, hospitality, education, health and media. She has been a guest lecturer and taught in university and college programs. Presently, Deb is pursuing an MBA part-time and volunteers with various community associations and municipal boards.

CHAPTER 7

Advocacy and Fundraising

CHRISTOPHER F. HOLZ, MA

Every day, political leaders and public servants make decisions that impact our lives – from the local decisions that improve the communities where we live, to establishing policies that have global significance. More often than not, these decisions are shaped, or informed, by advocacy efforts.

read more…

Politics, power, strategy…advocacy: this is not just the world of politicians, business interests, organized labour, and lobbyists. Canadian non-profit organizations, citizens groups, and charities have been at the forefront of policy-making in this country through their advocacy efforts, whether related to building a case to government for infrastructure funding, or imposing sanctions on a country for human rights violations.

Although the association may not be initially apparent, advocacy and fundraising have become increasingly connected in the non-profit world. Fundraisers that lead capital campaigns often use government relations to build the case for matching government funding support. Not-for-profit's (NFP) that provide front line services to the public often receive funding from government, thanks to fundraisers who manage government grant applications and reporting.

Whether you are a seasoned practitioner, or newly inheriting the responsibility of engaging government on behalf of your organization, this chapter provides a comprehensive overview of the art and science of government relations as it applies to the NFP sector. It provides a practical guide on how to create an effective government relations campaign using the process and tools in the lobbyist's toolbox, whether related to a fundraising objective, or any other broader challenge or opportunity. For the fundraising professional, it also provides an examination of how charitable organizations can integrate advocacy campaigns with fundraising to improve results.

This chapter is organized as follows:

I. **Overview**: provides a brief explanation of key concepts, including: a definition for advocacy; lobbyist registration requirements in Canada and the provinces; as well as Canada Revenue Agency limitations/restrictions on some activities undertaken by registered charities.

II. **Strategy:** this section provides an overview of how to create an effective government relations strategy for your not-for-profit organization. This process includes going through a comprehensive methodology to focus the issue, identify the objective, assess strengths and weaknesses, frame your arguments, choose your tools, and build your strategy.

III. **The lobbyist's tool box:** some of the various "tools" that lobbyists use (tools, tactics and techniques) are outlined here, and include an explanation of how they work, under what circumstances, their strengths and weaknesses, and when to use them.

IV. **Launch, measure and adjust:** This section will outline how campaigns are run, elements of successful campaigns, measuring impact, and adjustment/fine-tuning.

V. **Advocacy and fundraising**. This final section will illustrate how advocacy and fundraising are connected, and provide an examination of why charitable organizations can sometimes integrate advocacy campaigns with fundraising to improve results.

I. OVERVIEW

In this section, I will use the words "advocacy," "government relations," and "lobbying" interchangeably, but there are some subtle differences. Advocacy, in the context of government engagement, can be defined as the broad process whereby an individual or group aims to influence public policy through both direct communication (meetings, calls, correspondence with decision makers, etc.) and indirect means of communication (advertising, earned media, etc.). Government relations or lobbying is a form of advocacy with the intention of influencing decisions made by government officials (parliamentarians, political staff, public servants) through direct forms of communication.

WHAT ARE THE "ROOTS" OF LOBBYING?

There is a debate about where the term "lobbying" originates. One view is that the term was coined by U.S. President Ulysses S. Grant (1869-1877) to describe the "wheelers and dealers" that bought him drinks at the lobby bar of the Willard Hotel in Washington DC where he often enjoyed cigars and brandy. However, a lexicographer from the Oxford English Dictionary has demonstrated that the term in fact originates long before this period in the UK, referring to the efforts to engage Members of the House of Commons and House of Lords in the lobbies of Parliament, before and after parliamentary debates.

The role of advocacy in democracy

Advocacy is important to the health of any democracy, and lobbying is a legitimate activity. By engaging government, citizens and interest groups have an opportunity to at least inform public policy, and often to help shape decisions. Societies work best when people speak with one another. This is especially so for non-profits and charitable organizations that have been at the forefront of some of the major policies that have shaped this country and Canadian society.

Lobbying: Rules and registration requirements

In Canada, and in most provinces, lobbying is a regulated activity with requirements for registration and disclosure of lobbying activities. At the federal level, the Commissioner of Lobbying – an independent Officer of Parliament – has oversight of lobbying activity, administers the Lobbyists' Code of Conduct, and publishes the online registry where anyone can access information on current and historical activities undertaken by lobbyists and lobby groups. In most Canadian provinces, and some municipalities, a lobbying commissioner (or similar office) performs the same function, although the rules and requirements do vary considerably.

With respect to charitable organizations and non-profits at the federal-level, there is a multi-step process to determine whether it is a requirement for you or your organization to register as a lobbyist. The key question is the "significant part of duties" test. Like Ontario, the federal registration requirements provide an exemption for in-house lobbyists that spend less than 20 % of their time on lobbying activities, although there are differences in how this is calculated. The federal requirements are as follows:

> "The officer must file a return when one or more employees communicate with public office holders on behalf of the employer, and those duties constitute a significant part of the duties of one employee or would constitute a significant part of the duties of one employee if they were performed by only one employee."[1]

---

1 Office of the Commissioner of Lobbying. "*Advice and Interpretation: A Significant Part of Duties ("The 20% Rule")."* Accessed on May 2, 2014 at: http://www.ocl-cal.gc.ca/eic/site/012.nsf/eng/00115.html

---

LOBBYING REGISTRATION ACROSS CANADA

Ontario was the first province to introduce lobbyist registration requirements (in 1998), and since then most other jurisdictions in the country have followed suit. But the requirements vary considerably across provincial jurisdictions, and some municipalities.

In provinces such as Nova Scotia and Ontario, registration occurs essentially once, and provided that the registry is current and captures all current and projected lobbying activities, only periodic updates are required. For in-house lobbyists (organization), both provinces provide an exemption from registration. In-house lobbyists that spend less than 20% of their time undertaking lobbying activities during a three-month period are not required to register.

In addition to lobbyist registration requirements, Ontario passed legislation in 2010 called the Broader Public Sector Accountability Act (BPSAA) that curtailed the ability to hire lobbyists by certain "broader public sector" organizations, such as hydro entities, hospitals, school boards, universities and colleges, and other organizations that receive $10 million in government funding from the Province. These organizations may retain lobbyist services, but are prohibited from paying for these services with government funds, and must sign an attestation form indicating this. Nova Scotia passed similar legislation in 2011.

Alberta provides an exemption to organizations that spend less than 100 hours per year on activities deemed to be lobbying, as defined by Alberta's Lobbyists Registration Act.

The City of Toronto's lobby registration system is far more onerous in several respects: essentially each and every interaction must be registered on the online registry within three business days of the occurrence.

In 2013, the Government of Saskatchewan was the latest province to introduce legislation for the regulation of lobbying activities through the creation of a Conflict of Interest Commissioner.

Assuming government relations activities extend over a one-month period, the 20% threshold would be the equivalent of one full business day per week during a five-day work week. In Ontario and Nova Scotia, the measure is taken over a three-month period. As well, while the federal requirements include all prep time, travel time, and actual lobbying, Ontario only includes lobbying activities to determine the time spent.

Before you commence any advocacy related activities, it is important that you review the applicable registration requirements for the level of government you plan to engage. As each level of government has differing requirements, and these requirements are often changing, it is strongly recommended that you visit online the appropriate lobbyist registrar to acquaint yourself with the very latest requirements.

Canada Revenue Agency (CRA): permitted vs. prohibited advocacy activities

In addition to lobbying registration requirements, Canadian registered charities must comply with the *Income Tax Act*, which permits charitable and political activities (with certain limits), but prohibits partisan activities. The CRA requirements ONLY apply to Canadian registered charities, and not non-profit groups that do not have charitable tax status.

To be clear, a registered Canadian charity may take part in advocacy activities as a way of furthering its charitable purpose(s).[2] CRA provides guidance on activities that fall under three areas:

I. *Charitable activities*, as defined by CRA's policy statement, and through interpretations and case law. Many activities that would seem to be political in nature are deemed to be charitable activities by CRA, such as communicating with elected representatives or elected officials, some public awareness campaigns, publicly releasing representations made to government, presenting to a committee of Parliament, etc.[3]

II. *Political activities* (which are generally restricted to 10% of a charity's resources). Political activities are defined by CRA as political action, such as encouraging the public to contact elected officials to urge them to support/oppose a law, policy, regulation, etc. Political activities are permissible provided they are part of the charity's overall purpose. Making gifts to qualified donees intended for political purposes is also included in this definition, as a result of changes implemented in the 2012 federal budget. The Act requires that substantially all of a registered charity's resources must be devoted to charitable activities, which CRA deems to be 90% for most charities. (Smaller charities have some additional flexibility outlined in CRA's guidance). What this means in practice is that 10% of the charity's resources may be used for activities CRA deems to be "political activities," in addition to advocacy activities that are deemed to be "charitable."

III. *Partisan activities*. Partisan activities can be defined as the direct or indirect promotion or opposition of a political candidate or party, and is a prohibited activity for registered charities under the *Income Tax Act*.[4]

The CRA's *Policy Statement on Political Activities* provides useful examples and tests to illustrate the types of activities that are permitted as either charitable or political, and areas that would be deemed to be partisan and therefore forbidden.

It should be noted that a charity that intends to go beyond the limits permitted in the *Act* may do so by establishing a separate and distinct organization that is not a registered charity to carry out these activities. According to the CRA: "No limitations are placed on political activities of such a body; it has complete freedom within the law to support any cause it chooses. But the charity cannot fund that separate organization or make resources available to it for any other impermissible political activity."[5]

---

2 2012. *Policy Statement CPS-022, Political Activities*. Canada Revenue Agency. (Accessed March 14, 2014 at: http://www.cra-arc.gc.ca/chrts-gvng/chrts/plcy/cps/cps-022-eng.html)
3 Ibid., and see also: Imagine Canada (2013). "Sector source – Political Activities."
4 Imagine Canada. (2014). "The Narrative – Advocacy."
5 2012. *Policy Statement CPS-022, Political Activities*. Canada Revenue Agency. (Accessed March 14, 2014 at: http://www.cra-arc.gc.ca/chrts-gvng/chrts/plcy/cps/cps-022-eng.html)

II. STRATEGY

An issue has emerged that impacts your organization. An opportunity has developed, where your NFP can benefit. Your board has determined that there is a need to pursue an advocacy campaign to address a crisis in the sector. The government has declared that it is moving in a direction that threatens your organization. Whatever the cause, a decision has been made – or made for you – that requires the development of a government relations strategy and plan.

One of the great failures of some lobby groups is that not enough time is spent thinking through the issue and developing a strategy to guide the advocacy effort. While "strategy" is a candidate for the most overused term in business-speak, it is critical to developing a winning campaign and achieving advocacy objectives.

"Strategy is the art of creating power."[6] It is the development of a plan to achieve an objective, using limited resources. In a non-profit context, the concept of limited resources will be familiar – and that is why strategy is so very important.

The development of a strategy – whether you represent a non-profit group, or a multinational business enterprise – requires a step-by-step process of thinking through your issue from stem to stern, and developing a plan to guide your work. It is helpful to think of an hourglass, as the process starts wide, narrows to focus on a campaign goal and objectives, and then widens as you build the strategy and supporting tactics. The following points provide detail this process of thinking and planning.[7]

Information and research

Perhaps counter intuitively, step one is not setting the goal for the campaign, or developing the strategy that will guide your activities. Good strategies are based on firm information and knowledge. In a government relations context, that includes determining a number of things that you will inherently know, or will require further research of your organization, and the issue environment that is relevant. Gathering information and conducting research need not take weeks, but it is absolutely necessary in developing a firm grasp of what is in play.

Answering the following key questions will help to lay the foundation for your strategy:

- Which government decision-making process is relevant to this issue, and where are we currently in this process?
- Who are the relevant Ministers, political staff, public servants, etc.?
- What existing relationships do we have, and how strong/weak are these?
- How is our organization perceived by government decision-makers?
- What is the existing policy and how do we fit in it? Are there precedents?
- Is there legislation required or amended? What are the regulations and do they need to be changed?
- What are the big issues currently driving the government's attention? (Economic crisis, fiscal crisis, security crisis, internal political division, public opinion polling, election cycle, scandal, etc.)
- Are there campaign commitments from the parties that are relevant to this issue?
- Are there ministerial statements, speeches or commitments by government officials that are relevant?
- What are politicians saying about this issue, or similar issues?
- What may help motivate decision makers to support our cause? (arguments, policies, other groups, political considerations)
- What are other stakeholders saying about this issue, or similar issues?
- Does this issue have media coverage or public profile?
- Are there other jurisdictions that have implemented this policy? In Canada? In the U.S.? In other countries?

---

6   Freedman, Lawrence. (2013). *Strategy: A History* (New York: Oxford University Press).
7   For readers who are familiar with public relations theory, this is similar to the RACE process: research (fact finding), action (planning), communication (launching campaign) and evaluation.

If you can answer most of these questions, you will be in a good position to develop your strategy and the components of your campaign. In most cases, this information can be obtained through web searches, a scan of recent media, or you will inherently know the answer, but it is important to be as thorough as possible.

Analysis
Based on the information you have collected, and the issue you have identified, it is at this stage that the heavy lifting occurs. One of the most straightforward methods of analysis is the traditional SWOT method:[8] a structured process of evaluating **s**trengths, **w**eaknesses, **o**pportunities and **t**hreats by assessing relevant internal and external factors. The SWOT analysis has its challenges,[9] but it is a useful, structured form of analysis that allows the user to ask and answer questions that help give shape to a strategy (from the perspective of the organization).

The SWOT analysis uses a matrix to help visualize the relevant factors that emerge as you undertake the exercise. While a SWOT analysis can be conducted by one person, it is often better to work as a group to capture differing points of view that may be relevant.

The first part of a SWOT analysis is an examination of *internal* factors that will be relevant to the core issue at hand. Assessing "strengths" means an examination of specific internal factors that are relevant such as the following:

- A strong, existing funding relationship with the Ministry or federal department;
- Whether your organization has a high public profile and is considered an important stakeholder of government;
- Has the board and executive of your NFP determined that this issue is a priority and are willing to dedicate resources?

Strengths provide a potential competitive advantage to your organization.

"Weaknesses" refer to those internal factors of your organization that will limit or hinder your ability to achieve your goals. Examples could include:

- Limited public profile of your organization
- Limited time to dedicate to government relations activities
- The size of your organization

It is important to be realistic about what are truly strengths and weaknesses so that you can adequately address these. As well, while it is useful to be comprehensive, there is not much value in throwing in the kitchen sink while carrying out the analysis. Be judicious.

The next two areas refer to *external* factors that your organization will need to take advantage of, or address, in the development of a strategy.

"Opportunities" are external factors that create space for you to act that are related to your issue/objective. They are potential paths to success. Examples include:

- The media has published several stories on this issue
- The issue has the attention of the public
- The government has expressed willingness to explore options to fund/address the issue
- High profile individuals have expressed interest in the issue

At the opposite end, "threats" are external factors that will have a direct impact on your organization achieving your objective. These could include:

- A statement by a cabinet minister that funding is being reduced to address budget shortfalls.
- Media have undertaken an investigative report into the sector, and certain organizations have received some negative press.
- There are numerous other stakeholders that are active, and potential funding is limited.
- Stakeholders in your sector are divided and are working at cross-purposes.

At the end of the process, you will have identified a variety of factors in each quadrant – but not all of these have the same value or importance. Once an initial draft of a SWOT is completed, it is necessary

---

8   The technique is credited to Albert Humphrey, an American business and management consultant that created the process in the 1960's when working for the Stanford Research Institute.
9   One of the key challenges of SWOT analyses is that it suggests that all strengths and weaknesses are on the same footing/have the same impact, when this is not actually true. It also does not prioritize issues – this must be done separately.

to go through a prioritization process to give value to the items that truly will matter; and others that may be less relevant. You should rank in each quadrant the most important factors that have been identified, and consider options to capitalize on strength and opportunities, as well as measures to mitigate weakness and avoid/limit threats. In most cases, the information that will come out of this will be tactical ideas to take advantage of something, or to mitigate a threat or weakness, but in some cases the SWOT will help you identify the strategy to guide your work.

The information from research you gathered in step one, combined with the analysis you have undertaken in step two, should be enough for you to finalize the goal and objectives for your campaign and to construct a strategy to deliver the results you seek.

Goal and objectives

By analyzing the strengths and weaknesses of your organization, as well as opportunities and threats, you can then determine the goal of your campaign. Is it to obtain infrastructure funding from the Government of Canada? Is it to change legislation to permit a greater role for your NFP in the delivery of affordable housing? Every strategy must be guided by a succinct, clear goal that is specific and measureable. Your goal should be informed by the information gathering you have conducted, and the analysis you have performed. Is your goal achievable? Under what conditions? Goals set without context, information, or analysis are rarely realized.

There is a subtle difference between "goals" and "objectives." Campaign objectives are secondary to the goal of a campaign, but help to support and provide shape to the strategy. Supporting objectives could include things such as:

- Creating a broader public profile for your NFP (or ensuring that your organization stays below the radar);
- Engaging existing donors in the overall campaign activities to broaden and deepen your relationship;
- Maintaining your existing relationships with the government, while applying soft pressure; etc.

Objectives often take into account the resources you have in place, or the circumstances (environment) where you are operating that will have some impact on obtaining your goal.

Building the strategy

The analysis you undertake is going to give you useful information that will help shape your strategy and will include some key findings. In part, your analysis is going to help you answer the following 4-P's:

- **Process**: what is the relevant process for getting what we want? (i.e. Cabinet decision, legislature approval, regulatory change, etc. How long will this take?)
- **People**: who are the relevant decision-makers and influencers?
- **Policy**: what is the relevant policy framework for this issue? How does it fit in with the government's existing policies / commitments?
- **Politics**: what are the politics of this issue?

But the strategy has to be more than this – it needs to take into account the strengths and opportunities you identified, and deal with the weaknesses and avoid/minimize the threats you have been able to forecast. The following are some of the archetypal strategies that have been used for many government relations campaigns. While the list is by no means exhaustive, it will help you generate your own ideas, or think about your issue in a different way. Some of the more common examples include:

- Re-framing the issue into something that the government/public wants to solve: recast the issue as a health, environmental, economic development, public safety issue.
- Shaping the proposal to fit with the government's strategic directions / platform commitments (both in language and in substance): using the language of the government and its stated goals, recast your issue/objective in a way that makes it easier for government decision makers to say "yes."
- Building public pressure to force the government to act, by engaging the public, or media or stakeholders (or all). This approach can work if it is truly believed that you can motivate these groups to be vocal, and sustain their support /

coverage, and because alterative options would likely yield a worse outcome.

- Making the issue a sensitive local issue for a key decision maker. (i.e. Does the issue have the potential to become a local election issue?) This is relatively high-stakes, but can work under the correct circumstances.

III. THE LOBBYIST'S TOOL BOX

The tools (tactics and techniques) in the lobbyist's tool box can be incredibly effective at building the case for government to act, or increasing the pressure so that the government has no other choice but to act. But just as a sledgehammer is ineffective at addressing most small problems, and an Allen key has limited use for larger ones, the tools and techniques that lobbyists use to advance their strategic goals each have a strength and weakness, and need to be used cautiously to be consistent with your strategy, goal and campaign objectives.

This section covers some of the more common tools, tactics and techniques that we use in campaigns – how they work, their strengths and weaknesses, and examples of their effective use. I have categorized the items below into three categories:

Messages

Whatever campaign you undertake – whether direct engagement of government, or a broad-based campaign to engage the public – you will need to be guided by a series of key messages that will be reflected in everything you do. In addition to your strategic direction, the research and analysis you undertake will also help identify the key issues and messages that will be necessary for you to communicate with government, and other audiences.

There are numerous resources online that provide advice on the development of key messages, but generally your messages should cover these areas:

- Who you are (background on your organization)
- The issue and "ask" of government
- Arguments (and facts) to back your request
- What you are proposing as a next step with government

The message track should also include a series of key questions and answers, whether they be from government decision-makers, media, the public, donors, or whatever other group may take an interest in this issue and your campaign. Be tough: the harder the questions, the more prepared you will be. As a rule of thumb, your message track should be about nine messages maximum (two or three under each heading), although more complex issues may require more content. Be as judicious as you can – brevity is best.

The document is intended for internal use, but much of its content will be made public in one form or another. As your campaign unfolds, it is likely that you will find some messages are stronger or work better than others, so ensure that you manage "version control."

The purpose of the key message document and Q's & A's is to inform all other communications materials you will need to generate as part of your campaign. These could include:

- Introductory letters / emails requesting a meeting
- A policy brief – a 2-page document that provides a relatively high-level summary of the issue, arguments and proposed solution you are proposing to government
- A policy submission – a more robust document that delves into some detail about the issue, policy rationale for what it is you are asking, and research or facts to back up your points
- A presentation to government
- Materials that are to be used to build stakeholder / media / public awareness

Undertaking this work up front will reduce the amount of time necessary to develop these other materials.

Relationship building

The next set of tools, or really tactics, is related to building a better and deeper relationship with government. Relationship building should be an ongoing activity – not just when you want something from government, or when government is looking to take something away from your organization.

The following are legitimate, non-partisan ways that NGOs and charities can foster relationships with political decision makers, and public servants. Whether your charity is a frontline service provider, or you are lesser known to the public, *it should be the goal of every NFP and registered charity to have a relationship with the local representatives in your community (whether municipal, provincial or federal).*

In many cases, elected officials that represent your community will have constituency offices that provide a resource to community members on a range of matters: from navigating the government bureaucracy, to accessing local services in the community. If you are a frontline service provider, building this basic relationship with the constituency office can be very effective at broadening and deepening your relationship with your elected representatives. Similarly, if your organization is a front line service provider that receives funding from government, you should develop a working relationship with public servants that provide the annual funding grants.

The following are some additional informal ways in which NGOs can foster these relationships, provided that they are done in a non-partisan fashion:

- NFP events: when you have a public event, it may be appropriate to invite local elected representatives and/or public servants where you maintain an ongoing funding relationship.
- NFP news events: on a case-by-case basis, you may want to evaluate whether obtaining a quote from an elected representative(s) is appropriate, perhaps because your organization is celebrating an anniversary of providing services to the community, etc.
- Attending (relevant) government announcements / speeches: sometimes attending a government announcement, or a public speech by a key Minister, affords the opportunity to meet with decision makers and their political staff.
- Government consultations: while a formalized process, public consultations (by their nature) provide an opportunity to provide input into policy-making, as well as an opportunity to meet with public servants, and sometimes political decision makers.

As an ongoing activity, relationship building can help build your NGO's "capital" with government, and the more capital you have, the more you can spend when you need to. It is very important that as an NGO or registered charity you ensure that your outreach activities are non-partisan (see CRA guidelines provided earlier in the chapter).

While ongoing relationship-building is ideal, sometimes an issue emerges that requires that you build new relationships with decision makers that you do not already know. Your strategy will have identified several key political and public service leaders that are relevant to your campaign. The strategy will also outline the order of meetings so that you can quickly build momentum in your campaign.

The following are some helpful hints and reminders for preparing for these meetings, conducting them, and follow-up afterwards.

Before the meeting

- Develop a carefully crafted script, and determine who says what (if it is a group). Identify who is the "lead."
- Keep attendees to a small group (three maximum).
- Share some information in advance, as well as a draft agenda for the discussion (if appropriate).
- Develop materials:
  - Letters and emails (requesting meetings)
  - Briefing notes (leave behind material)
  - Presentation (if PowerPoint, keep it short, but it does not necessarily need to be a presentation)
  - Fact sheet on your organization
- Most importantly, BE PREPARED. Make sure you research the background of the elected person you are meeting, recent issues where they have been quoted in the media or in the legislature, so that you have as much information as you can about their headspace before the meeting begins.

During the meeting

- Arrive early – clearing security in some government buildings can take awhile, so be sure to leave sufficient time.
- Expect decision-makers to be a few minutes late.
- At the beginning, re-confirm the amount of time that the decision maker has available.
- What to say?
  - 20% of the time identifying who your group is, background and context related to your issue/objective
  - 50% is the ask (including your supporting arguments)
  - 30% identifying solutions and next steps
- Make decision-makers aware of:
  - Issues you have with policies, but also potential solutions. There is no point in just outlining concerns without some option(s) that could address them.
  - Actionable requests of government.
  - How your interests can help the government/decision maker achieve their own objectives, but be careful about not overstating this.
- Make sure to watch body language and adjust your presentation and responses accordingly. Take notes for follow-up purposes.

After the meeting

- Away from where you just met, you should review the meeting.
  - What worked? What should be adjusted?
  - What are the follow-up commitments, next steps, and who will follow-up?
- Send a note to thank the decision-maker for the meeting, and note the follow-up items.
- No meeting exists in isolation – working with government is an ongoing process.

In many cases, when you meet with an elected official, you will also be meeting with political staff. Political staff are the gatekeepers to decision-makers, and help to inform and shape decision-making. While meeting with a Minister is often ideal, more often than not you will be meeting with political staff and/or public servants instead. This is often the same as meeting with the Minister directly, so treat these meetings as you would if you were meeting with a Minister.

You will find that political staff are getting younger and younger – often in their mid-20's or early 30's. Do not be put off by the age of the person you are meeting – they are there for a reason which may not be clear to you, but is very clear to the Minister who put them there. Lastly, not all political staff and Ministers will be fully aware of your issue, or will have a deep knowledge of their Ministry (especially if they are relatively new to the portfolio). Be patient and provide broader context if you find the audience is not responding to your messages.

Strength-building

Whether you are a billion dollar enterprise, or the smallest charity in Canada, one thing that you may be surprised to have in common is that it is not always easy to get the attention of government. At its best, government relations is a constant activity of building and deepening your relationship with government so that when an issue, or opportunity emerges, you will have some infrastructure in place to be able to achieve your goals.

But more often than not, this isn't the case. The following *tools* are some of the more common "strength-building" techniques that help to create a chorus of voices to support/amplify the messages you are sharing with government. Used correctly, they can help build the case for government to act…or put pressure on government to step up.

A) **Stakeholdering and coalitions**

As a charity or NGO, you may be a lone voice with government…but to the extent that others share your views, or support your organization, you have an opportunity to create a chorus of support. The analysis you undertake when developing the strategy will have identified stakeholders – some that will share your views, and perhaps others that will not or will run contrary to what you are proposing. Building an alliance/coalition with other credible stakeholders (credible to you, and hopefully credible to government) will, at a minimum, amplify your voice and arguments.

In some cases, the stakeholders you partner with will have their own influence over decision makers – perhaps they are a local NGO that is supported by the local MP who happens to be the Finance Minister, or the group has a broad relationship with the media. Building a coalition allows for an aggregation of each NGO's network of relationships with decision makers, media, and other influencers.

For issues that will impact your sector overall or could impact several NGOs, a coordinated alliance/coalition is useful in dividing tasks and resources. But coalitions are only successful to the extent that there is a level of trust among the participants, a willingness to participate and dedicate resources, a common view on goals, objectives, and tactics, and a body that is tasked with making decisions relatively quickly. One of the weaknesses with coalitions is something called the "slowest boat" problem – where the group moves only as fast as the slowest member (usually on issues or concessions to government). Another challenge is a tendency for "group think" which is divorced from the reality of what is really happening.

In some cases, the issue or objective impacts only your organization, so a coalition is not necessary for stakeholdering purposes. In these situations, it is still very helpful to reach out to other groups that are potentially supportive of your cause and are willing to share their name, and perhaps a letter of support. In some cases, it may be appropriate to have these stakeholders participate in meetings with you. Where possible, it is advisable to reach out beyond the NGO sector to business groups or associations as this will help "broaden" your support.

The following case study is a recent campaign example of stakeholdering that helped an NGO achieve its government relations goals:

> **CASE STUDY: SHERIDAN COLLEGE INSTITUTE OF TECHNOLOGY AND ADVANCED LEARNING**
>
> What: Seeking $31.2 million from the provincial and federal governments for a new campus in Mississauga.
>
> Stakeholders: The College engaged several Mississauga stakeholders to build and broaden the case for government support, including the Mississauga Chamber of Commerce and corporate donors to the College (headquartered in Mississauga). Actions included letters of support, as well attendance at meetings with some key government decision makers.
>
> Outcome: The College received its funding which was the subject of a major announcement by all three levels of government in 2009.

B) Grassroots

When executed properly, grassroots tactics can be very effective in building public pressure on government. Some recent examples include:

- The decision to cancel a $1.2 billion power plant in Oakville, Ontario after significant opposition from local residents and businesses, following an extensive campaign.[10]
- Citizen opposition to the introduction of the HST in British Columbia, resulting in a referendum and ultimately the resignation of Premier Gordon Campbell.[11]

While these campaigns resulted in significant policy reversals from government and attracted provincial, and even national media, they were effective because grassroots members were very motivated to participate and had a personal link to the issue.

Components of a successful grassroots campaign include:

- A clear and measurable goal
- Simple and consistent messaging

---

10 Karen Howlett. "*Ontario pulls plug on gas-fired plant*" in The Globe and Mail. Published on October 7, 2010. See also www.campbellstrategies.com
11 Justine Hunter and Wendy Stueck. "*Campbell's stunning resignation leaves fate of HST up in the air.*" In The Globe and Mail. Published on November 3, 2010.

- A motivated and organized volunteer base that has a personal connection to the issue

One of the key challenges with grassroots efforts is the issue of recruitment and maintaining motivation, which is why this tactic does not always work in government relations campaigns. Focus on where support is likely to be strongest such as your core constituency group (membership, existing volunteer base, local area residents). With an initial basis of support, you can use other recruitment vehicles to grow your army such as:

- Word of mouth
- Social media networks like Facebook, Twitter and websites
- Local canvassing
- Existing donors
- Recruitment events
- Print opportunities like local newsletters and flyers
- Earned media / advertisements
- Lawn signs

Managing a grassroots campaign also has its challenges. To be effective, a Chair or Steering Committee needs to be established with clear responsibilities and good communication with the membership. Grassroots tactics need to be coordinated with the overall campaign, so maintaining this link and control is critically important.

Depending on the nature of your campaign, there may need to be training provided to grassroots members on campaign activities, especially if you intend to deploy your network in a meeting campaign with government decision makers. Creating a meeting guide (i.e. "How to meet with your MP"), as well as messaging and other materials, are helpful tools to keep your grassroots members engaged and delivering the messages that you need to have delivered. As well, if you intend to use your network this way, you will need to ensure you capture the feedback from these meetings so that you have the latest information on how things are unfolding. This can be done in a template email that identifies key questions so that grassroots members can provide as much information as possible.

Occasionally, grassroots tactics include membership participation in rallies, events or protests. This can sometimes be effective, but if - and only if - you are able to secure a sizable turnout. Rallies can also be effective in generating media coverage, if it is part of a larger communications strategy. If a rally is being used as a tactic, consider using visuals and "gimmicks" to illustrate the core message you are communicating to media and government.

Lastly, to sustain the interest of your grassroots members, you will need to provide them with campaign updates via calls, emails or meetings. Too much contact is unhelpful, but too little creates other problems. Email and social media are useful ways this can be done and will help reduce the amount of effort required by the organizers.

C) **Earned media**

Earned media can be an effective way of building awareness of government and the public on an issue, and to gradually build support. It is also an effective way to completely alienate government and wreck your campaign. If you are considering using an earned media campaign as part of your tactics, it is important that you balance your messaging so that you can create room for the government to bargain with you. Scorched earth campaigns will not work in the long run.

Media relations as a tactic can help a campaign achieve its objectives, but only if it can be sustained over a period of time. It is necessary to have ongoing news stories with developments along the way, rather than a one-shot announcement.

The first step in using this tactic is to develop a media plan to help introduce and sustain the story you want to communicate to government and the public, while ensuring that it can work with the other aspects of your campaign. Media relations also need to be "flexible" and take advantage of media opportunities, so that you can slow down if you are making progress in your direct discussions with government. Unless you have the internal capacity, you may wish to consider hiring a government relations or public relations professional, or retaining a GR and PR firm to assist.

An earned media campaign could include several tactics, such as:

- *An announcement / media studio event*: this is high stakes, so if you go this route you must ensure that what you have is newsworthy, well organized, and that the news event is brief.

- *News releases*: news is news, but not all news releases contain news. If you are going to be issuing news releases, be sure that there is enough content to warrant a release.

- *Issue monitoring*: sometimes other events occur that provide an opportunity for you to get coverage on your issue. Monitor the news cycle for these opportunities, and be prepared to take advantage of them when they occur.

- *Building and maintaining relationships with reporters*: a key measure of success will be your ability to engage with reporters, and maintain a relationship so that you can continue advancing stories as necessary, when there is a campaign milestone or development.

IV. LAUNCH, MEASURE AND ADJUST

With strategy in hand, you are ready to launch, but the best strategy in the world will not get you anywhere if you do not take the time to listen to what others are saying and evaluate how your campaign is progressing.

A big part of advocacy campaigns is listening to what others are saying – whether from government, stakeholders, the media, or the public. As your campaign progresses, it is important to set goals and measure performance: are the messages working / resonating? Are we achieving our grassroots recruitment goals? How is the dialogue with government progressing? The intention is not to second guess every meeting or activity, but there is a need to periodically review progress, and progress is rarely linear: you will find you advance three steps, and sometimes go back one or two. It's progress, not perfection.

Over the course of the campaign, you will hit some key milestones: perhaps a meeting with the Minister, or a rally you undertake that captures media coverage. Each milestone is an opportunity to evaluate progress, and make adjustments as necessary.

V. ADVOCACY AND FUNDRAISING

Advocacy and fundraising are similar in many respects. In the non-profit world, it can be helpful to think of "advocacy" as a form of fundraising – government fundraising – especially when related to capital campaigns or similar government funding initiatives. In some cases, advocacy campaigns can be leveraged to support fundraising campaigns, and vice-versa. By actively advocating for an idea, case, or cause, charitable organizations can increase exposure to potential donors and thereby increase potential contributions. However, there are other circumstances where advocacy and fundraising will *not* work well together, depending on the nature of the issue, tactics, or perceptions of donors and government decision-makers.

Fundamentally, advocacy can enhance a charitable organization's access to private philanthropic support (either through corporate donations or individual donations), as well as potential government grants. When advocacy is connected to fundraising, the potential for an increase in donor contributions can be the result. Advocacy uses messaging to target individuals and people already connected to the organization's mission. Not surprisingly: "people willing to advocate on behalf of a cause are frequently willing to support it by pulling out their wallets."[12]

Integrating advocacy with fundraising is a powerful way to accomplish an NFP's goals, and ultimately deliver its mission. It is a very effective way to identify and qualify new prospective donors, and create powerful engagement strategies to cement their support for the cause in the future.

According to IPM Advancement, the benefits of Non-profit Advocacy for Fundraising can include:[13]

Bringing awareness to an issue

Without non-profit advocacy campaigns, the public may never know about some important issues. According to an article in *The NonProfit Times*, a business publication for non-profit management, the Natural Resources Defense Council (NRDC) began an advocacy campaign to inform people of the Bush

---

12 Blackbaud. "*Connecting on-line advocacy with fundraising.*" https://www.blackbaud.com/files/resources/downloads/WhitePaper_ConnectingOnlineAdvocacyAndFundraising.pdf

13 IPM Advancement. "*How Non-Profit Advocacy Campaigns Impact Fundraising,*" http://www.ipmadvancement.com/wp-content/uploads/2013/04/ipm-whitepaper-advocacy-campaigns.pdf

administration's use of tax dollars to shoot wolves – an endangered species. The campaign brought in 73,000 new wolf activists. One year later, 31,000 of these activists took another action.

Some advocacy campaigns may create a great platform for fundraising because they make an issue public and attempt to place pressure on government. Sometimes the intention is not so much to engage government to motivate a change in policy, as it is to create a public issue for fundraising purposes.

Builds relationships
Advocacy campaigns are excellent vehicles for cultivating and deepening relationships. By collecting contact information, non-profit organizations grow their lists. Through issue education and regular communication, non-profits draw constituents into the organization and help make them feel part of the solution.

Keeps donors engaged
Advocacy campaigns encourage action to support a specific cause. In addition, research studies show when people take action on an issue, they are much more likely to donate to the cause. Some cases-in-point: the American Civil Liberties Union (ACLU) found engaging in two or more actions resulted in four times the likelihood of making a donation. The residents of Oakville at a grassroots level contributed their time but also their dollars to organize and fund a multifaceted campaign that included retaining two lobby firms, a public relations firm, legal counsel, consulting engineers, and others.

Increases visibility
Digital media enables non-profit advocacy organizations to reach large audiences quickly, easily and economically. In addition, online payment processing platforms securely and effortlessly connect advocacy campaigns with fundraising requests.

When looking to implement an advocacy campaign, consider these *four* ideas as ways to link fundraising to the advocacy strategy:[14]

i.) Link an issue to a timely news event

By linking an issue to a current news event, a charitable organization may draw more attention, and as a result, create more urgency.

---
14 Ibid.

This may lead to additional supporters stepping forward for the first time to make a donation, and help increase the size of the constituency base, the grassroots army, and potential funding contributors to the organization.

ii.) Link online advocacy with fundraising

The advocacy campaign should make use of a centralized website, e-mails and social media. A payment processing platform to accept donations must be easily accessible from any online venue.

iii.) Ongoing communication with donors

When advocating for a cause and connecting it to fundraising efforts, charitable organizations must keep the issue alive and current for their donors. By delivering multiple communications (e.g. focusing on topics of interest such as new items affecting the cause, or highlighting a famous person who supports the cause) over a pre-defined time period, a charitable organization can better engage people and help them feel more connected to the mission of the organization.

iv.) Use a two-step process including advocacy action and donation

Advocacy can encourage action, and fundraising can encourage donating. The goal of linking the two together is to have the constituent do both: take action, and make a donation.

There are many reasons to integrate advocacy with fundraising. The synergies achieved by this collaboration can help charitable organizations increase their prospect acquisition response rates, and allow creative ways to involve and engage constituents. The greater degree that we are able to engage with constituents, through actions like advocacy and acting on behalf of our organization, the greater the likelihood that they will make a donation to our cause.

A word of caution - there are some circumstances where advocacy and fundraising will not work well together. Some advocacy campaigns or tactics may generate criticism from individual or corporate donors, putting your fundraising goals at risk. For example, a charity that takes a very public position on a controversial issue may alienate existing or potential corporate donors. This may be a risk worth taking, but it should be noted. Similarly, fundraising campaigns that are linked to public advocacy campaigns may motivate government decision makers to cease engagement, if there is recognition that the true purpose of the campaign is not dialogue but fundraising.

Moreover, advocacy campaigns that are seen to potentially contravene the *Income Tax Act* may come under CRA scrutiny. In 2012, the CRA launched an $8 million special audit to determine if charities have been adhering to the CRA's requirements. Many in the charitable sector saw this as a political move by the federal Conservative Party in response to the advocacy activities undertaken by some environmental groups opposed to pipeline expansion and Alberta oil sands development.[15] According to a Canadian Broadcasting Corporation (CBC) news story in 2014, the CBC was able to confirm that the CRA is undertaking audits of a number of Canadian environmental charities including: The David Suzuki Foundation, Tides Canada, The Pembina Foundation, Environmental Defence, as well as Amnesty International Canada, a social justice organization.[16]

Fundamentally, advocacy and fundraising can work together very well to create a compelling movement that delivers government and fundraising objectives, but this needs to be carefully constructed. When in doubt, get the advice of a government relations professional or fundraising consultant.

CONCLUSION

Every day, non-profit groups and registered charities in Canada use advocacy to fulfill their charitable mandates, raise funds for capital projects or front-line services, and help inform government policy-making. Here are just a few examples of campaigns that have received attention here in Canada, or abroad, and their impact:

1. **Mothers Against Drunk Driving – Canada (MADD):** as a public safety organization, MADD has been at the forefront of promoting driver safety and cracking down on drinking and driving in Canada, which has led to legislative changes, operational measures to crack down on this illegal driving behavior, and a change in the public perception of this activity.

2. **Canadian Hemophilia Society:** Canadians who contracted HIV and Hepatitis C during the tainted blood catastrophe engaged in a legal and comprehensive government relations strategy to build the public case for support and action by the federal and provincial governments. After countless hours of hard work and sacrifice, grassroots, earned media and direct outreach activities, as well as using the Canadian Court system, these victims were able to reach settlements with government to provide compensation for the harm that was caused ($2.7 billion settlement).

3. **The Scarborough Hospital (TSH) (in Toronto):** the epicenter of the SARS-outbreak in North America, TSH had a significant capital and operating shortfall after battling SARS for several months. TSH worked hard to fight the virus, but also ensure that it had the funds to continue operations. After a short campaign of engaging government decision makers, TSH was successful in obtaining the necessary operating and capital funding to get the work done.

---

15 Paul Waldie (2012). "*New rules in budget 'create more fear' among politically active charities*" in The Globe and Mail, September 6, 2012. (Accessed via web on April 15, 2014 at: http://www.theglobeandmail.com/news/politics/new-rules-in-budget-create-more-fear-among-politically-active-charities/article4102573/).
16 Evan Solomon and Kristen Everson (2014). "*7 environmental charities face Canada Revenue Agency audits – Charities fear they may lose charitable status.*" Accessed on May 25, 2014 at: http://www.cbc.ca/news/politics/7-environmental-charities-face-canada-revenue-agency-audits-1.2526330).

Effective campaigns have some key characteristics that are common:

- *Strategy*: there is a core strategy that is guiding the work of the campaign team and members (see section 2).
- *Control*: there is a strong leadership structure that can manage what is happening in the field, or being communicated to government. It can start and stop activities to take advantage of opportunities, or address challenges. Most importantly, it can make decisions quickly.
- *Flexibility*: effective campaigns can adjust their tactics to take advantage of developments as they occur in real-time.
- *Speed*: it isn't necessary that things always happen quickly – more often than not you will find that government can move slowly – but when an opportunity or threat presents itself, speed is a key factor in successful campaigns.
- *Patience and persistence*: most campaigns are a balance between patience and persistence. Government decision-making can be slow, so it is important to be patient. As well, government engagement needs to be persistent without being annoying.

Fundraising can also be greatly and positively affected by advocacy campaigns. By actively advocating for an idea, a case or cause, charitable organizations can increase exposure to potential donors and thereby increase potential contributions. Advocacy makes sense for an organization's cause by bringing focus and action on an issue. But it is also a very effective way to help raise additional money by identifying and qualifying new prospective donors, and creating powerful engagement strategies to cement their support for the cause in the future.

In summary, non-profits and charitable organizations play an important role in policy-making in this country. That role becomes more powerful and effective when developing a strategy to guide your advocacy efforts, levering fundraising capacity along the way, and correctly using the tools that lobbyists use each and every day.

ADDITIONAL REFERENCES

Lobbyist Registration Requirements

Every level of government has its own lobbyist registration requirements, and they are often changing. It is strongly recommended that you visit the website of the appropriate lobbyist registrar to determine the latest applicable requirements for registration. A simple internet search will take you to the appropriate lobbyist registrar website for the level of government you intend to lobby.

Canada Revenue Agency Requirements

▶ Canada Revenue Agency. *Policy Statement CPS-022, Political Activities.* http://www.cra-arc.gc.ca/chrts-gvng/chrts/plcy/cps/cps-022-eng.html

▶ Carter, Terrance S. and Karen J. Cooper. *"Playing by the Rules: Political Activities fair fame for charities."* Charity Law Bulletin No. 286. http://www.carters.ca/pub/bulletin/charity/2012/chylb286.htm

▶ Imagine Canada. (2014). "Sector source – The Narrative - Advocacy." http://sectorsource.ca/sites/default/files/resources/files/narrative-issue-sheet-advocacy-en.pdf

How Cabinet decision-making works in Canada

▶ The Privy Council Office (2013). *Decision-making processes and central agencies in Canada: Federal, Provincial and Territorial Practices – Canada.* Accessible at: http://www.pco-bcp.gc.ca/index.asp?lang=eng&page=information&sub=publications&doc=aarchives/decision/canada-eng.htm

Additional reading

▶ Carney, William Wray. (2008). *In the News: The Practice of Media Relations in Canada.* 2nd edition. Calgary: The University of Alberta Press.

▶ Elson, Peter R. (2011). *High Ideals and Noble Intentions: Voluntary Sector-Government Relations in Canada.* Toronto: University of Toronto Press.

- Elson, Peter R. (2007). "A Short History of Voluntary Sector-Government Relations in Canada." *The Philanthropist*. Vol. 27, No. 1. Accessible at: http://thephilanthropist.ca/index.php/phil/article/view/17/17

- Laforest, Rachel. (2014). *Government-Nonprofit Relations in Times of Recession*. Kingston: Queen's Policy Studies.

- Obar, J.A. (2014). "An analysis of social media adoption and perceived affordances by advocacy groups looking to advance activism in Canada." *Canadian journal of communication, 39*. Available at SSRN: http://ssrn.com/abstract=2254742

- Seitel, Fraser P. (2013). *The Practice of Public Relations*. 12th Edition. New York: Prentice Hall.

ABOUT THE AUTHOR

**Christopher Holz, MA
Principal, Campbell Strategies**

Christopher Holz is a seasoned public affairs executive with over fifteen years experience working with government decision-makers and clients across several public policy areas. He has served clients in various sectors including energy, real estate and infrastructure development, financial services, retail, health care (the College of Physicians and Surgeons of Ontario, Shoppers Drug Mart, Rexall-PharmaPlus, Sick Kids Hospital, The Scarborough Hospital), and the non-profit sector (Habitat for Humanity Canada, Sheridan College, ShelterNet, the Peel Children's Centre) among others. Mr. Holz was recently ranked as "one of the top ten lobbyists at Queen's Park" according to *Queen's Park Briefing*, a Toronto Star Intelligence Unit publication.

Previously, Mr. Holz served as Senior Communications Advisor and speechwriter for the Ontario Minister of Energy and the Chair of the Cabinet, and later as Senior Policy Advisor to the Ontario Minister of Finance. Before joining the provincial government, he was Vice-President of another leading government relations and communications firm.

Mr. Holz completed his undergraduate and post-graduate degrees at the University of Toronto, which included research work for his thesis at the University of Bath (United Kingdom) and the Katholische Universitat Brabant (The Netherlands). He is also a graduate of the Ontario Legislature Internship Programme.

CHAPTER 8

TELEFUNDRAISING

DAN ABRAHAM

It's different for us.

Working as a fundraiser for charities and non-profits may not be a path to wealth and fame, but it does bring a certain amount of respect and admiration. Many would consider it a perk of the job. You've probably attended a social gathering, say a cocktail party, where people are discussing their occupation. The responses are fairly predictable:

- Athlete or astronaut? *Loved.*
- Dentist or Lawyer? *Met with some gentle ribbing and paycheque envy.*
- Accountant or Human Resources professional? *Yawn. Next…*

read more…

- Fundraiser for charities and non-profits? "Hey, that's great! I've always wanted to do work that helps make the world a better place. Kudos to you for doing it! Let me top up your drink."
- Telemarketer? Cold stares, looks of disgust, and partygoers slowly back away: as if a skunk, with a giant pimple on its nose just emerged from your jacket pocket or handbag.
- Telefundraiser for charities and non-profits? See "telemarketer" above.

It's different for us.

Sure, the reaction to the telemarketer above is exaggerated a little. But the fact remains that telemarketing has a bad reputation. Of course, there are bad apples out there: boiler rooms, scam artists, or just rude and pushy telepests pushing crap you don't want. But in our world - the telefundraising for charities and non-profits world, those bad apples are the exception not the rule. So, like many victims of stereotyping, people who work in the telemarketing field (including those that are politely raising money for legitimate charities) get painted with an awfully broad brush. This is a problem.

But it's not just a problem for people who work in the telefundraising field directly. It's a problem for all fundraisers. We all agree that fundraising programs are most effective when they are integrated and multi-channel. Many of you agree that telefundraising is an important channel with a role to play in an integrated fundraising program. If you don't agree with that, keep reading, this chapter might change your mind. But wherever you are on that spectrum, the negative stereotypes associated with telemarketing – and by extension telefundraising – are a problem for you. Why? Because that person backing away at the cocktail party might be on the board that approves your fundraising budget. And when they see the telefundraising budget line, it's like a pimple-nosed skunk jumped off the spreadsheet. Therefore, one of the main purposes of this chapter is to give you the information you need to dispel those stereotypes and convince that board member (or executive director or key team member) to approve your proposed budget.

The next section "Mythbusters" is designed to provide you, the fundraising professional, with some ready rebuttals to standard objections to telemarketing/telefundraising.

MYTHBUSTERS

Telemarketing? Gross. Everyone hates those annoying calls. Telemarketers are rude, pushy, and always call at dinner.

Wow. Those are harsh, unfair and untrue characterizations – especially for the vast majority of people raising funds by phone for worthy and legitimate charities. Time to set the record straight.

But first, full disclosure: I've been around call centres for more than 25 years, the vast majority of those in telefundraising and the last 20 with the same firm. I've done it all: caller, phone room supervisor, and manager. From there I moved to client service and have spent the last 15 years helping to design and execute the telefundraising programs of some of Canada's largest charities and non-profits. This work features close collaboration with development teams, direct mail agencies, database specialists and others engaged in building the best fundraising program possible for a charity. So I do have some experience! But I'm also a little biased: it'll be good for me if this chapter leads more charities to engage in telefundraising. Hence the disclosure. At the same time, I feel passionately about the causes we raise money for and want every good charity to have the best fundraising program possible so they can contribute to a better society. And I believe that telefundraising is an essential component of an effective integrated fundraising program.

Have I established my bona-fides? Good. Enough about me. Let's bust some myths:

MYTH 1: "Everyone hates these calls."

Incorrect. In fact, it's a massive generalization from a small vocal minority that feels that way. Reality is far more nuanced and starts with a question: is there a pre-existing relationship between the entity calling and the person being called? If the answer is yes, there's a good chance the call will be welcome. If the answer is no, next ask whether the person being called might have some interest in the subject. Again, the answer will inform how welcome the call may be.

Now let's consider this from a telefundraising perspective. Are you calling donors or prospects? Donors like your charity; that's why they give/gave you money in the first place and we've found that most donors don't mind being called by a charity they support -- provided the caller is polite, respectful of the donor's time, and well-informed about the work of the organization.

Also, almost every phone sold over the last 25 years has a little screen that shows what number is calling. This affords many donors the opportunity to decide whether a given moment is an acceptable time to answer a call from an unknown number. If a donor has call display, and most do, when they pick up the phone they are generally receptive to your call. The law provides a multiplier effect: telemarketers (including telefundraisers) must – by law -- display a valid phone number.

Further, if a donor asks to be removed from the charity's calling list, we must honour this – again by law. This further increases the odds that your calls are welcome – especially when calling loyal donors who have been called previously. Even on the first ever dial-through of a donor list, the do-not-call requests are usually a single-digit percentage and get significantly lower on subsequent phone programs. And, really, "hate" is an awfully strong word. In fact, most donors who dislike fundraising calls will politely express that opinion and the telefundraiser will mark the donor as "do not call" and thank them for their time and support. In a donor context, if by "everyone hates these calls" they actually meant "almost no-one hates these calls" they were right.

But these are your donors: the heartbeat of your organization. So maybe most of them don't mind being phoned by your charity and some actually like it. And, ultimately, the numbers don't lie: donor response rates by phone are higher than by any other donor channel and the majority of donors (about 80%) do answer the phone. But what about prospects?

Let's go back to whether the prospect might have interest in your organization. The answer to that question will inform how receptive she might be to a fundraising call.

- Some non-donors are close to the organization and can be considered similarly to donors: staff, volunteers, loyal event participants, and individuals who donate to affiliated organizations (like people who donate to their local chapter but not the national organization).

- The next rung down would be one-time event participants and people who have taken an action on your behalf or subscribe to your newsletter. These people all have an affiliation with your organization and react similarly to a phone call as a new donor.

- On the next rung down you'll find donors to like-minded organizations. If matched with some consideration, there are some very complimentary and responsive fits in the fairly small universe of telefundraising list trades.

- At the bottom of the ladder are the people you have no idea about. This has a name: cold calling. In my experience, cold calling is virtually non-existent as a viable fundraising approach amongst reputable charities and ethical call centres. This is also mostly true of rented lists. People on these cold lists are those most likely to be annoyed by your call but those you are least likely to call in the first place.

In short, a lot more care goes into determining appropriate telefundraising lists than the vast majority of "telemarketing" detractors have ever considered. The end result is a wide variety of approaches and strategies that minimize calls to unreceptive lists and outcomes that benefit the charity, the donor, and the call centre.

MYTH 2: "Telemarketers are rude and pushy."

This is another one of those "wide brush" characterizations that is more likely to apply to cold calling than donor-focused telefundraising. AFP has a set of ethical fundraising guidelines that apply to telefundraising and a quality agency adheres to these. The guidelines effectively put premiums on politeness, honesty, and respect for donors. There is no place for rude and pushy telefundraisers in an AFP-member call-centre.

On the flipside are high-volume commercial call centres that lack a specific fundraising mandate or ethical standards. They're cheap. They'll sell anything. And some dabble in fundraising: either for large one-time-gift focused charities that have elevated low-cost over other considerations or, sadly, for organizations that might look and sound like charities but are not registered and basically exist to put a few bucks in someone's pocket then disappear. But even legitimate commercial call centres working for legitimate cost-obsessed charities often employ a scorched earth "don't take no for an answer" approach that alienates donors and trades quick cash for the long-term charity/donor relationship.

Sustainable charities are not built on small donations from one-off alienated donors – they are built on long-term relationships with loyal donors. The charity works to build building trust and credibility – measured as donor retention – then to move donors up the giving pyramid from new donor to monthly donor to major donor to legacy giver. A good telefundraising partner wants to take this donor journey with you by identifying opportunities for the effective use of the phone in your integrated fundraising program and then executing those phone programs with you. This is how a sustainable telefundraising business is built. Our interests are aligned.

So how do you differentiate between ethical telefundraisers and scorched earth operators? You can start with whether they are an AFP member in good standing. You can request references from similar organizations. You can even often tell by good-old-common sense: if they are promising very low cost unsophisticated services that feature large quantities of low value donors and quick cash, you should be very skeptical and probably look elsewhere.

Another good gauge, once you are working with a telefundraising partner, is the volume and nature of the complaints you are receiving.

> **Q: If an AFP-affiliated call centre contacted 10,000 active donors how many donor complaints would you expect? 25? 15?**
>
> **A: If you guessed less than five you are correct.**

Typically a mid-sized program (approx. 10,000 contacts) will generate 2 or 3 complaints. About half are valid. So out of 10,000 donor contacts, one or two have a legitimate beef about the call they received.

If everyone hated being phoned, and telemarketers were all rude and pushy don't you think there would be more than two legitimate complaints logged from 10,000 contacts? Now, if you need two or more hands to count the complaints, that should be a huge red flag and you should consider changing suppliers. By the way, if you have more than two hands you should also think about supplementing your fundraising career with a part time gig as a juggler.

Now, how do we know that some complaints are valid while others are not? Every call is recorded in most call centres. Did the caller say what the donor claimed she said? Press play. Sometimes we find that the donor's version of events is spot-on: the caller made a clear mistake. In this case, a responsible telefundraising entity will take the complaint very seriously by ensuring the caller receives training or discipline, or both.

Sometimes the recording shows that the donor embellished, fabricated, or simply misunderstood the caller's actions and we determine no wrongdoing on the part of the caller. Either way, a reputable call centre should be willing to provide you with a copy of the recording so you can follow up with the donor appropriately and, ultimately, decide for yourself if the complaint was legitimate. If the call centre is unwilling or unable to provide recordings of complaints, see: red flags above.

MYTH 3: "Telemarketers always call at dinner."

There's no getting around this one. Guilty as charged. Let's face it: many stereotypes have a kernel of truth to them. This is ours. For telefundraising to be effective, we need to call people when they're home. Working people are most likely to be home from about 5:30 PM and we are allowed to call until 9:00 PM. Most people also have dinner sometime between 5:30 and 9:00. Ergo: sometimes we interrupt people during dinner. Look - you can't make an omelette without breaking some eggs.

So, there is a kernel of truth to every stereotype, but also a heavy dose of exaggeration and this is true of "they always call at dinner." Using our call centre for specifics, but bearing in mind that these are essentially industry standard hours, we are open from 10:30 AM to 9:00 PM on weekdays and 11am to 5:00 PM on weekends. So, of the 10.5 hours on weekdays, only about 1/3 are during traditional dinner time and none of our weekend hours are at dinner time. And while we might look at 5:30 to 9:00 PM as the "dinner window," few spend all evening eating dinner. In lieu of hard science, I'm going to say that dinner is, for most people, 1 hour.

Time to get mathy: dinner is one hour and we phone for more than 10 hours per day. 1 in 10 chance to interrupt someone during dinner. But we also phone 6 hours on weekend days where we won't interrupt a dinner because our day ends at 5:00 PM. So, based on the random distribution of dials, there is now a 1/16 chance of interrupting someone during dinner. Most donors on most programs will be reached within the first four attempts meaning there is a good chance we will contact a donor before interrupting their dinner. Once a donor is contacted, they are not attempted again (until the next program, often the following year). So, in summary:

- 1/16 chance to interrupt dinner on every "random" dial.
- Most donors reached within four attempts, so 12/16 chance of not interrupting a donor's dinner on a specific phone campaign.

If you attempt to contact every donor once per year, you will – statistically – interrupt their dinner once every four years.

Now, we do tend to schedule more hours on weeknights than weekdays or weekends. And weekdays outnumber weekends, so the actual probability to interrupt dinner is probably closer to 1/12. On the flipside, many donors have call display and will simply ignore all (unknown) calls during dinner and never be interrupted. Let's call these factor's a wash.

So, when that person at the cocktail party claims that you always call during dinner, if they mean that your charity interrupts their dinner once every four years, they are right.

MYTH 4: A telemarketer ran off with my wife, stole my truck, ran over my dog, and interrupted my barbecue.

Oops, sorry, that's not a telemarketing myth, it's a country-music song lyric. Please ignore, accept my apologies, and let's move on to the next section y'all.

THE ADVANTAGES OF TELEFUNDRAISING

Telefundraising has unique and valuable characteristics that make it an essential component of a robust integrated multi-channel fundraising program. In this section, we'll look at some of those characteristics and their related applications. Sometimes these attributes and applications will be compared to their counterparts in other fundraising channels.

I should note here that any comparison that shows telefundraising in a favourable light is not meant to disparage another channel. As creative and innovative fundraisers, we should always use the best tool – or combination of tools -- for the job. Let's open the telefundraising toolbox and see what we find.

Monthly donations

Everyone has one thing they're *really* good at: like a musician with perfect pitch or your uncle that can toss a jellybean 10 feet in the air and catch it in his mouth.

Telefundraising's "Jellybean Trick" is its ability to cost-effectively convert one-time-gift (OTG) donors to monthly donors. As fundraisers, I'm assuming most of you are already aware of the value of monthly donations. If you aren't yet, just know this about monthly donors: very low attrition, very low maintenance and fundraising costs, very high long-term value. Now, here are some facts about monthly donations in a telefundraising context:

- Monthly conversion refers to calling OTG donors and asking them to switch to a monthly gift that will be "automatically" debited from their credit card or chequing account.
- Most (about 75%) of the donors who agree to give monthly, provide all the information needed to set up the recurring gift over the phone (the rest require a follow-up letter, fulfillment coupon, and BRE).
- Donors with a last OTG gift between $20 and $499 within the last 24 months are those most likely to become monthly donors over the phone.
- The segment in that $20-$499 group with the greatest propensity to become monthly donors are OTG donors who made their *first* gift to the charity in the last 3-12 month period. These

new donors are typically approached with an appeal that blends a "welcome" call with a monthly conversion ask.

- Donors who decline to give monthly will be asked for a one-time gift as a fall-back. These OTG gifts provide a tremendous "value added" component to a monthly conversion effort. They help you achieve your donor retention targets and provide immediate cash flow.

in this chapter for the entire case study so just know this: the panel that received both a mailing and a phone call generated more *direct mail* donations and *direct mail* revenue than the panel that received the mailing only. That's right, phoning the mail list actually boosted the direct mail results. Of course, that panel also generated donations and revenue on the phone. Multi-channel synergy isn't just a catch-phrase you read in books about fundraising: sometimes it's true.

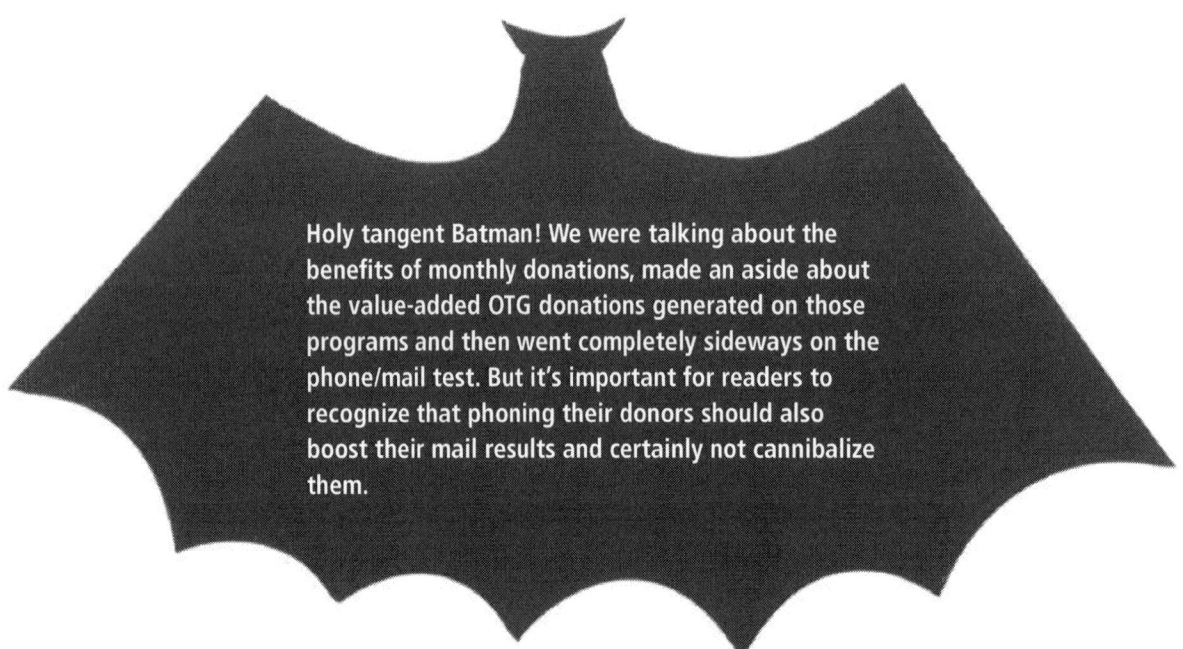

Holy tangent Batman! We were talking about the benefits of monthly donations, made an aside about the value-added OTG donations generated on those programs and then went completely sideways on the phone/mail test. But it's important for readers to recognize that phoning their donors should also boost their mail results and certainly not cannibalize them.

Monthly donations are realized in small increments over an extended period of time so the immediate cash from OTG gifts provide an excellent counter-balance from a budgeting perspective.

This is a good place to address another myth: that OTG gifts generated on telefundraising programs cannibalize donations that would have been made by mail. It's not true. Channel giving is not an either/or proposition.

This is more than just anecdotal observation. We ran a thorough scientific experiment for a large well-known Canadian non-profit -- in conjunction with their direct mail agency -- that *proved* this point. Essentially, we took their donor list and split it into three panels: one that was mailed only, one that was phoned only, and one that was both phoned and mailed. We wrote a case study on the findings. We don't have space

Now, less bats and more stats:

- Monthly donor attrition from telefundraising-acquired monthly donors is about 5% while Industry-wide OTG donor attrition can be as high as 50%.
- The *average* telefundraising-acquired monthly donor will stay on the monthly program for seven years.
- Monthly response rates typically range from 2% to 10% with outliers above and below.
- The main factor that informs where you'll land in that range is your sector. High profile health charities with large lists will tend to land at the lower end of the spectrum while small advocacy-focused organizations with highly engaged

donors will tend to land at the higher end. In between is everyone else.

- Other factors that will inform monthly response rate include: maturity level of list and fundraising program, size of list, strength of appeal, program timeline, experience and professionalism of telefundraisng supplier and – of course – overall fundraising strategy. With so many variables, one or more specific customized cost/revenue quotes that take all of the factors into consideration is a very good place to start if considering a monthly conversion phone program.

- On average, monthly conversion telefundraising programs break-even when you add the revenue generated by the first 12 monthly payments to the OTG revenue then subtract the cost of phoning. Due to sector and other variables mentioned above, this 12 month average include programs that break even anywhere from 3 to 24 months.

- When fundraising professionals discuss the phenomenal long-term ROI generated by monthly conversion phone programs it's because they will (on average) realize 84 months of revenue against costs covered by the first 12 months of revenue. Even when it takes 24 months to recoup costs, this is still a tremendous value proposition.

Those are some impressive numbers but the phone isn't the only fundraising channel that can obtain new monthly donors. True. You can, and should, find monthly donors by direct mail (DM) that share telefundraising's low attrition rate, though monthly response rates in DM pale in comparison to telefundraising, even with mailings that focus on monthly gifts.

So, what is it about telefundraising that makes it so effective at converting OTG donors to monthly donors? We don't know definitively, but we can speculate that, because it's a more "complicated" way to donate, some donors need guidance and someone to answer their questions before they can, or will, commit to an automatic debit. Of course, if needed, a caller can provide the gentle persuasive nudge to close the donation. Sometimes you just can't beat live human contact.

Here are two more monthly donation-oriented programs where the phone has proven to be the most effective medium:

- *Monthly upgrade.* Call existing monthly donors and ask them to slightly increase monthly support. Average increase is more than $5 per month and response rates typically range from 20-30%.

- *Monthly reactivation.* Attrition is low on phone and mail acquired monthly donors but it does happen. It happens for administrative reasons: credit card expires; is lost, stolen, or cancelled; chequing account moved to another bank, etc. It happens because a donor's financial situation changes. It almost never happens because the donor now dislikes your charity. 40-75% of very recently lapsed monthlies, expired/declined for administrative reasons, will renew their monthly gift. You will often see monthly response rates of 12-25% from your 1-2 year lapsed monthly file (all reasons). You will often see response rates of 5-10%, and programs that break even in twelve months or less, going back as far as ten years.

Ok, so telemarketing is great for monthly-oriented programs, while direct mail is less so, and we're crediting "live human contact" for this difference. So what about face-to-face fundraising, doesn't it feature "live human contact?" Yes it does. And face-to-face (f2f) is a very effective tool for building a monthly file. But face-to-face is almost exclusively an acquisition tool while phone programs are donor focused. Also, for a variety of reasons, monthly donor attrition on face-to-face monthlies is much higher than telefundraising and direct mail. Instead of 5%, f2f attrition rates can be as high as 50% (though often closer to 30-35%) But, ultimately, you shouldn't compare the channels apples-to-apples. Face-to-face is a great acquisition tool and telefundraising is a great donor conversion tool.

But what about building a monthly file through telephone acquisition? Keep reading.

TELEFUNDRAISING ACQUISITION FROM WEB-SOURCED LEADS

It's the 21st century: almost everyone uses the internet. And every charity has a website. Most charities' websites feature interactive elements such as calls to action, e-newsletter sign-ups, pledges, petitions, and more. Interested individuals, often with no prior relationship with your organization are finding your website, and signing up to take action or receive more information.

Historically, for a variety of reasons, these e-contacts would only be engaged by organizations' program/campaign/advocacy teams while development teams tended to focus on traditional lists for acquisition. But as the cost to acquire a donor has risen, development teams are creatively diversifying their list sources as they look for ways to cost-effectively acquire a new donor.

In telefundraising, this creativity has uncovered that web-sourced names have a strong propensity to donate by phone. The immediacy and interactive nature of the web has proven synergistic with the immediacy and interactive nature of the phone. Even better, web contacts will often make their first phone gift a monthly commitment.

We have ample evidence that the web/phone approach can work. But we've also seen very high variance on these programs: from crash-and-burn at the low end to better than a comparable *donor* program at the high end. So, to lower your variance, here are some factors that correlate with greater success:

- **Action.** People who take action on your behalf – such as sign a petition, sign a pledge, or subscribe to receive a newsletter are much more likely to donate than people who merely register to access information on your site.
- **Timeliness.** Web sourced names have a limited shelf life: best before 18 months and ideally contacted within 3-12 months since the last interaction.
- **Information.** We want to know what actions they've taken, how many actions they've taken, when the actions were taken, etc. This information allows a caller to make specific reference to the action, build rapport and make the appropriate case for giving.
- **Stewardship.** The first step when someone interacts with your website shouldn't be to call them for a donation. There should be: a welcome email; an update or two on issues of interest; an e-appeal; then the call.
- **Think local.** Names sourced from your own website and your own actions will usually outperform those found through 3rd party "activist portals." That said, 3rd party activist portals are a great way to augment your own names and find people who might not otherwise find you.
- **Segmentation.** Track results by things like number of actions, time since last action, and type of action and then use the results to optimize the current program and inform the next one.
- **Testing.** Start small, find what works, then roll it out.

So, that's it? Now I have all the info I need to convert web-acquired prospects to monthly donors? Not quite.

Before you optimize your strategy for generating the highest response rate possible, you need to make sure you *get contact info*. I've witnessed numerous great fundraising strategies for online-sourced names implode when the organization realizes that the only contact info they have for a donor is an email address. We can't phone email addresses. We can't find phone numbers from email addresses. We can't tell much of anything from many email addresses (who or what is wjhdjh@isp.com or scorpiongirl13@email.com or majordonor@whoami.ca). You need to collect at least *some* contact info in addition to email address. For example:

- Last name
- Postal code

With this info, we can find phone numbers for about 25% of the list.

- Full name
- Full mailing address

With this info, we can find phone numbers for about 56-60% of the list.

- Phone number

Nuff said.

Well, not quite "nuff." As much as I'd love to advise you to make phone number a required field, this can actually be counter-productive. People don't like filling out long forms and frankly, some people don't like giving out their phone number. The more info you require, the less likely the contact completes the form. There isn't a perfect balance, but the "sweet spot" seems to be full name and full mailing address. Never settle for less than last name and postal code.

One last great thing about these programs: the new donors you acquire through online channels are quite different demographically than what we typically see in a standard donor file. In short: they are (usually) younger. But they also have a tendency to make a monthly commitment as their first gift, and are reasonably comfortable providing their payment information over the phone. Ladies and gentlemen: the next generation of donors!

ADDITIONAL ADVANTAGES

Telefundraising has some other strengths and advantages. Here are a few quick ones:

- **Immediacy and fast turnaround.** A charity with a solid relationship with a telefundraising provider can have a fundraising list on the phones in just a day or two (though in a non-emergency 3-4 weeks is preferred) This is great when an unexpected event creates an urgent need for funds and organizational intervention. The phone is also a great tool for communicating urgency.
- **List cleanup.** There's great "value add" in the list cleanup that naturally occurs as part of every phone program: name and address changes, bad phone numbers found, deceased donors, language barriers, mail preferences, email address collection. These updates will typically be sent to the charity at the end of the campaign.
- **Donor feedback.** Another value add is the opportunity to gather intelligence and take the pulse of your file: a survey question; caller comments; post-campaign debrief with the telefundraising team; live monitoring of calls; or the strategic use of call recordings. Imagine standing over a donor's shoulder while they read your fundraising letter. With a call recording, you can effectively do this in telefundraising.
- **Lapsed (OTG) reactivation.** Direct Mail tends to be the driving force for this effort, due to lower costs, but telefundraising can play an important (and cost-effective) role too. Telefundraising will reliably renew 5-15% of the lapsed donors contacted, even though these individual haven't responded to a mailing for years (and in many cases they have received dozens of mailings in that time). There is a fundraising axiom that it's better to renew the support of a lapsed donor than find a new one. On that basis, before writing off a segment of lapsed donors because they've stopped responding to mail, put them on the phones and renew the support of 5% or more of the file.

SEGMENTATION, REAL-TIME FACTORS AND TESTING

One of the great things about a telefundraising program is that performance can be measured in real-time which allows for constant tweaks and adjustments to optimize performance. These performance optimizations might relate to pacing of calls, timing of calls, the composition of the calling team and more. A good telefundraising supplier should be looking at these metrics constantly and making adjustments to maximize your results.

Further, after designing intelligent list segmentation, you (the fundraising professional) can measure results-by-segment from the regular reports you receive from your telefundraising supplier. From there, as a sufficient sample size is built, you can start to manipulate the program to emphasize the strong segments and de-emphasize (or drop entirely) the weaker segments. This allows for a powerful level of control over real-time list composition and helps optimize your ROI and mitigate your risk. Also, the "real-time" learnings from your phone program can inform strategies across all channels.

The factors that provide such fine grain control of the micro-details of an individual telefundraising campaign have an important macro manifestation as well:

testing. In fact, along with monthly conversion, testing might be telefundaising's "Killer App." You might be thinking about adding a telefundraising component to your next annual plan but then in creeps the fear of the unknown. What if the industry standards don't apply to my charity and results underperform projections? Test. What if a board member has cold feet? Socks. I mean: Test.

Telefundraising is largely "pay as you go" with quite low upfront setup costs. The bulk of your costs will be accumulated either per calling hour or per contact. And when you tie this payment structure to all of the ways you can monitor, tweak, and optimize response, it creates a powerful platform for testing. Let's say you have 20,000 active OTG donors that you want to convert to monthly by phone. You'd like to assign the budget and dive in but you're nervous. Solution: test.

You can *plan* to call all 20,000 but can also start by simply *committing* to call 2,000 in a test. If performance targets are met, you can roll the calling out to the next 18,000. If they're not, you can simply stop the calling and move your budget to another phone program or to another channel altogether.

Of course, your test may show, via real-time segment analysis, that 10,000 of your OTG donors are viable monthly conversion prospects and 10,000 are not. So you rollout 8,000 more calls and reallocate the rest of your budget. There are as many variables as there are scenarios and it's not possible to discuss them all here. The bottom line is that you can significantly mitigate your risk in telefundraising in ways that are often not possible in other channels. Overall, it makes telefundraising a great channel for pilot projects, new message testing, or really any other application where dipping your toes in the water is preferable to diving into the deep end. Test. Test. TEST(ify).

> We've come a long way in this chapter. We laughed at all the great things you can do in the telefundraising channel. We cried at the horrible stereotypes and myths that unfairly sully the reputations of ethical telefundraisers. We really dug into those important areas so that every reader can make an *informed* decision regarding the possible fit of telefundraising and their charity. The rest of the chapter is information for those who do see a fit – and those who have taken the plunge already. Less in-depth, but still important, the next short sections will address whether you should outsource your telefundraising program, a quick review of telefundraising technology, and the Canadian regulatory environment. We're almost done. Let's get to it.

IN-HOUSE VS. OUTSOURCING

I've already put my bias on the record. I also spelled out the depth of my expertise. I hope you will trust the latter over your possible skepticism regarding the former when I tell you that – in the vast majority of cases – your organization will be better off outsourcing your telefundraising to a 3rd party supplier than going it alone with an in-house call centre. A properly functioning call centre operation is very labour intensive and features significant up-front and ongoing overhead costs.

You might think you can hire some callers, give them each a phone and a list of donors and reap the difference against the 3rd party costs. If only it was that easy. You also need experienced and qualified staff to hire, train and manage those callers. You need technical support to load lists into the dialer, generate reports, build segments and be available to manipulate those segments in real-time. You need processes for securely storing credit card numbers. You need hardware, software, space, and more.

Once you've made these significant investments, you have to phone your donors *all year round* in order to keep the operation going. This is a massive commitment to telefundraising so you have to be a very large organization with a very large telefundraising appetite to even consider this path.

The "year round" factor severely limits your ability to test -- and scale down or stop underperforming programs. It makes you less nimble and significantly increases your risk. You certainly can't just shut down every time a program performs poorly. If you do, you will lose all your staff and you'll quickly learn how difficult it is to find qualified quality replacements. People often think of telefundraising as an unskilled job. Not true. It is a difficult job that doesn't suit all temperaments or skillsets. There is a learning curve and ongoing training and performance management is essential. I could go on. Trust me when I tell you this is a very difficult business with a small margin for error. You don't want the headaches. This message has been reinforced to me on numerous occasions when I've been hired to audit an in-house call centre and uncovered what the development team considers an underwater albatross.

Let's not end this section on such a down note. There are times when it does make sense to phone in-house. Here are a few:

- **A small/specialized program**. Major donors. Planned giving. VIPs. Your 3rd party telefundraising partner would probably be able to assign a skilled senior caller to the project. But with large sums of money and important relationships at stake, you might feel more comfortable with a knowledgeable member of *you*r senior team conducting these calls.

- **Expired/declined credit cards**. Monthly donations by credit card will sometimes end when a card expires or is cancelled (usually because it's lost or stolen). In these cases, you want to call the donor quickly for new information. As the scale is usually very small, and time is of the essence, it often makes sense to have a staffer call these individuals. Further, as this is essentially an administrative call, very little fundraising experience/acumen is needed.

- **Small charity. Small list.** As long as the quantity is manageable (probably 500 donors or less), you can save money and learn what makes your donors tick by calling them internally.

- **You are a large university**. Many universities have in-house call centres. They have the dual purpose of raising money for the school and providing part-time employment to students. It's a nice symbiosis that really doesn't exist in many (if any) other sectors. In most other sectors, it's much harder to find suitable and willing calling staff.

You'll note that only the last example, involves an actual "call centre." There is definitely a time and place for calling donors in-house but times where building and maintaining your own call centre is required are few and far between.

TELEFUNDRAISING TECHNOLOGY

Let's talk about ancient times. Back when telefundraisers held handsets and *dialed* phones and scribbled call outcomes and donor comments on paper "lead sheets." Their desks didn't have computers on them but they did have ashtrays (*shudder*). Let's call these ancient days "The '80s." Like virtually every other facet of modern society, the telefundraising industry underwent a tremendous technological transformation from the end of the '80s to the end of the '90s. Back in the '80s, donors credit card numbers were scribbled on paper, and then held together with paperclips until couriered or even *faxed* to the charity (and like "Wake Me Up Before You Go-Go," let's agree to never speak of this '80s relic again).

Telefundraising was effective and profitable for charities in the '80s (and earlier) but it was crude and unsophisticated compared to the technological abilities we have today. Many of these abilities were covered in the "Advantages" section: from data-driven factors like real time reporting and segmentation analysis, to the ability to store terabytes of call recordings in something the size of a paperback. Modern telefundraising was born when personal computers reached affordable critical mass. But enough with the history lesson, here are a few more telefundraising tech terms you should know and understand:

Dialer. A dialer is a powerful server we load telephone numbers into that features hardware to efficiently dial those phone numbers and includes software to act as a caller interface. It has powerful database functionality to store donor information, segments, and codes. It also has many built-in reports that call centres use to manage productivity and performance and it contains all the information used to report on campaign metrics to charities. A dialer must be customizable so that the individual back-end requirements of the charity or their data house can be met by the supplier.

Predictive Dialer. Has all of the features of "dialer" above but also has the ability to dial ahead and weed out "junk" like no answers, answering machines, busy signals, etc. and only passes live donors to callers. It has voice-activated software that detects when a donor says "hello" and then sends the call to an available call centre agent. A predictive dialer is an incredible productivity tool. But it has a downside. Because the call is sent to agent after the donor says hello, there is an inherent lag (typically less than a second) between when the donor answers the phone and the caller starts talking. This is an annoyance, but even worse is the "dropped call." It's called a *predictive* dialer because it predicts how many calls to place per minute based on real-time data like size of list, time of day, callers on system, average call length, and more. Well, the prediction algorithms are not always correct (consider: just because it calculates an average call length doesn't mean that every call is precisely that length). When it's wrong, the donor says hello but hears only dead air because no agent is actually available. The donor generally says hello again then sighs and hangs up if no one comes on the line. This is a "dropped call" and pretty high on the list of things people dislike about telemarketing.

Please be heartened by the fact that "predictive mode" is optional on a predictive dialer. You can ask it to behave like a "person" and dial one number at a time which is called "preview dialing" (and which ensures no dropped calls) or you can "crank it up" for speed (predictive dialing). It's not uncommon for a call centre to use preview dialing for high-response rate current donor programs to ensure a high-quality donor experience and to use predictive dialing on large lapsed or prospecting lists where speed and productivity are necessary for cost-effectiveness.

The Web. We talked previously about the web as a source for telefundraising acquisition leads. But is that it? No, in fact the web has many call centre applications. And one important and emerging web application is using it to enter donations directly into a charity's existing web donation system from within a dialer environment. This innovation is great for security: the call centre no longer needs to store the donor's credit card number. It is also great for efficiency at both the call centre and charity levels as it cuts out numerous steps related to credit card storage (call centre), transfer (call centre to charity), and processing (charity). I'd estimate that about 20% of charities engaged in telefundraising are using a web portal for real-time donation processing and this percentage goes up every year.

THE CANADIAN REGULATORY ENVIRONMENT

Free beer! Now that I have your attention, let's talk briefly about the rules and regulations that govern the telefundraising industry in Canada. Fortunately, you can find most of them in one place: *Canadian Radio-television and Telecommunications Commission Unsolicited Telecommunications Rules.* (https://www.lnnte-dncl.gc.ca/nrt-ntr-eng)

Heretofore, we'll refer to these as the "CRTC Telemarketing Rules:" a broad and thorough set of rules and regulations that saw a major overhaul at the end of the last decade. The high profile element of that overhaul was the introduction of the National "Do Not Call List." Let's clear up something that has proven to be a point of confusion over the years:

> **Charities are exempt from the requirement to scrub calling lists against the National Do Not Call List. However, charities are not exempt from the rest of the CRTC Telemarketing Rules.**

To add to the confusion: charities are required, by law, to maintain their own internal do not call list. This list would be comprised of people that request not to be called or anyone who has asked for no solicitations (from any channel). In many cases, your do not call requests would be provided by the telefundraising company you hire to conduct your calls.

The telefundraising company also has to maintain its own "do not call" database, largely comprised of individuals who contact the call centre directly and ask to be added to their do not call list. Both the charity and the call centre are required, by law, to respect the wishes of their internal do not call requests even though the charity is exempt from the National Do Not Call List. Is your head spinning? Sorry. I guess all these "do not call" terms and free beer are a bad combo. Now, before we highlight some of the other topline rules, let's clear up one more point of confusion.

One of the CRTC's requirements is that all "Telemarketers" must register as a "Telemarketer" with the CRTC. If you are a charity hiring a 3rd party to conduct calls on your behalf, you probably assume that the 3rd party will take care of this registration. Incorrect. Per the CRTC:

> **Both the Call Centre and the client that hires the call centre to phone on their behalf are considered "Telemarketers" and BOTH must register as such with the CRTC.**

To add to the confusion, we all need to register via the National Do Not Call List section of the Telemarketing rules website, even if the charity is *exempt* from the National Do Not Call List. Sigh. I think I need a beer now.

But here's the good news: registering as a telemarketer only takes about 5 minutes, doesn't cost anything, and only needs to be done once annually.

Here are a few more topline telemarketing rules to be aware of:

- Permissible calling times are 9:00 AM to 9:30 PM on weekdays, and 10:00 AM to 6:00 PM on weekends.
- Disclosure rules require that a caller introduce herself by name (it can be a fictitious name), where she's calling from, and for whom she's calling on behalf.
- *Abandonment Rate* may not exceed 5% in any given month. Remember the "dropped calls" we discussed regarding predictive dialers? The CRTC expresses these in aggregate as "Abandonment Rate" and forbids more than 1 in 20 dropped calls over the course of a 30 day period. I'd like to point out here, before wrapping up this section, that the vast majority of the CRTC's telemarketing rules including many that were introduced in 2009, had already been considered best practices by ethical telefundraisers for decades.

CONCLUSION

So here we are at the end. If successful, the mythbusters section changed a few minds while the "telefundraising advantages" section provided some new ideas and strategies. In other words, some of us have been able to remove the Scarlet "T" from our shirts and you're going to confidently go to your board with a monthly conversion recommendation with all the knowledge you need to defend that decision.

You'll probably seek out a telefundraising supplier because running an in-house call centre is just not viable for the vast majority of charities. But either way you will register your organization as a "telemarketer" with the CRTC as required by law. You know that it will only take about five minutes to register with the CRTC and not cost anything. You also know, if you've been around telefundraising for a while, that the new rules imposed by the CRTC had been best-practices amongst ethical telefundraisers for years before the laws were even drafted.

I started this chapter by saying "It's different for us." I hope you now realize that in many ways we're all the same and, ultimately, we're all in this together.

ADDITIONAL REFERENCES

There isn't actually a wealth of material in the niche world of non-profit telefundraising. But here are a few titles and resources you might find worthwhile.

Books

- GREENFIELD, JAMES M. (2002). *Fundraising Fundamentals: A Guide to Annual Giving for Professionals and Volunteers.* AFP/Wiley Fund Development Series.

- PETERSON, KEN T. (1980). *How to Sell Successfully by Phone – Proven Techniques for Bigger Sales* The Dartnell Corporation. I'm recommending an "old school" telemarketing book so you can see how it was done back in "ancient times." Some is outdated. But some of these old chestnuts are just as effective today as they were when people actually bought encyclopedias over the phone.

- WALKUP, RENEE P. AND SANDRA MCKEE. (2009). *Selling to Anyone Over the Phone.* (This recent book includes many sales tips for telemarketing in the digital age. In many cases, the sales recommendations and tips can be applied to a telefundraising context.)

URLs

- HTTP://WWW.THEAGITATOR.NET/ This website features high quality content by and for fundraising professionals. Telefundraising articles and case studies are featured intermittently. The site also has a links section that is a wealth of additional resources. Annual subscription fee of $25 to $50 required for full access to archives.

- HTTP://WWW.CRTC.GC.CA/ENG/TRULES-REGLEST.HTM - *Canadian Radio-television and Telecommunications Commission Unsolicited Telecommunications Rules.*

- HTTPS://WWW.LNNTE-DNCL.GC.CA/IND/INSORG-REGORG-ENG - Register your charity as a telemarketer here.

ABOUT THE AUTHOR

Dan Abraham

Dan Abraham brings more than twenty years experience in telefundraising to his chapter for Excellence in Fundraising in Canada, Volume Two. Most of those years have been spent at Strategic Communications (Stratcom) where he currently serves as "Senior Director of Fundraising and Outreach." Over the last fifteen years, Dan has managed successful telefundraising campaigns for some of Canada's largest charities and non-profits.

Dan studied Journalism at Ryerson University where he specialized in magazine journalism and contributed to numerous student publications. Dan has taught direct response at Humber College, has led workshops on telefundraising for a wide range of audiences, and contributed to the CMA's Fundraiser's Handbook.

Dan lives in Toronto with his lovely partner Lisa, lovely daughter Jasmine, and dashing stepson Kieran. Dan plays and records music and is an avid record collector. Other hobbies include cycling, art, and football as well as a keen personal and professional interest in politics, environmental issues, and the events that shape the world.

CHAPTER 9

INTERNATIONAL FUNDRAISING

CATHY DAMINATO, MBA, ICD.D

At the root of what we do as fundraisers is the desire to help make the world a better place. In some cases our attention is focussed at the local level, adding to the social fabric of our communities by animating and enlivening the arts; ensuring hospitals have the diagnostic and treatment equipment needed to save and change lives; inspiring hope and opportunity through educating our youth; and providing housing, services and support to help lift the homeless and working poor out of the cycle of poverty. Others of us have a more global focus, being the first on scene when tragedy strikes; protecting children's rights to survive and thrive; providing clean water and the necessities of life for third world communities; protecting endangered species and habitat; and advocating for globally sustainable energy solutions to name a few.

read more...

This important work is accomplished by securing financial support from those members of our community with the ability and interest to support our causes. As wealth patterns shift around the world; as government funding declines while competition for charitable dollars intensifies at home; as opportunities to communicate and connect globally grow exponentially; and as recognition grows that world problems are ours to solve together, more and more of us are looking internationally to develop relationships and raise funds with new donors.

This chapter addresses fundraisers who are active in raising funds internationally or who aspire to do so with a focus on major gifts. It will help you decide if an international fundraising strategy is right for you and assess your institutional readiness to commit. Tips and tools are provided to help establish strategic focus. Lessons learned will be shared by fundraisers who have successfully ventured abroad.

GLOBAL GROWTH OF WEALTH

"There are always new places to go fishing. For any fisherman, there's always a new place, always a new horizon." –Jack Nicklaus

Understanding the remarkable shifts in the global economic growth and private wealth is critical to identifying and assessing fundraising opportunity. Global private financial wealth grew by 14.6% to $152 trillion in 2013 according to the Boston Consulting Group (BCG).[1] North America ($50 trillion) and Western Europe ($38 trillion) remained the wealthiest regions in 2013, with Asia-Pacific (excluding Japan) coming in third at $37 trillion.

The Asia-Pacific region (excluding Japan) represented the fastest-growing region worldwide. BCG noted that in 2008, Asia-Pacific had 50% less private wealth than North America. Since then it has closed that gap by half. Additionally, Asia-Pacific is expected to account for about 50% of total global wealth growth by the end of 2018. If their projections are accurate, Asia-Pacific will be the wealthiest region in the world

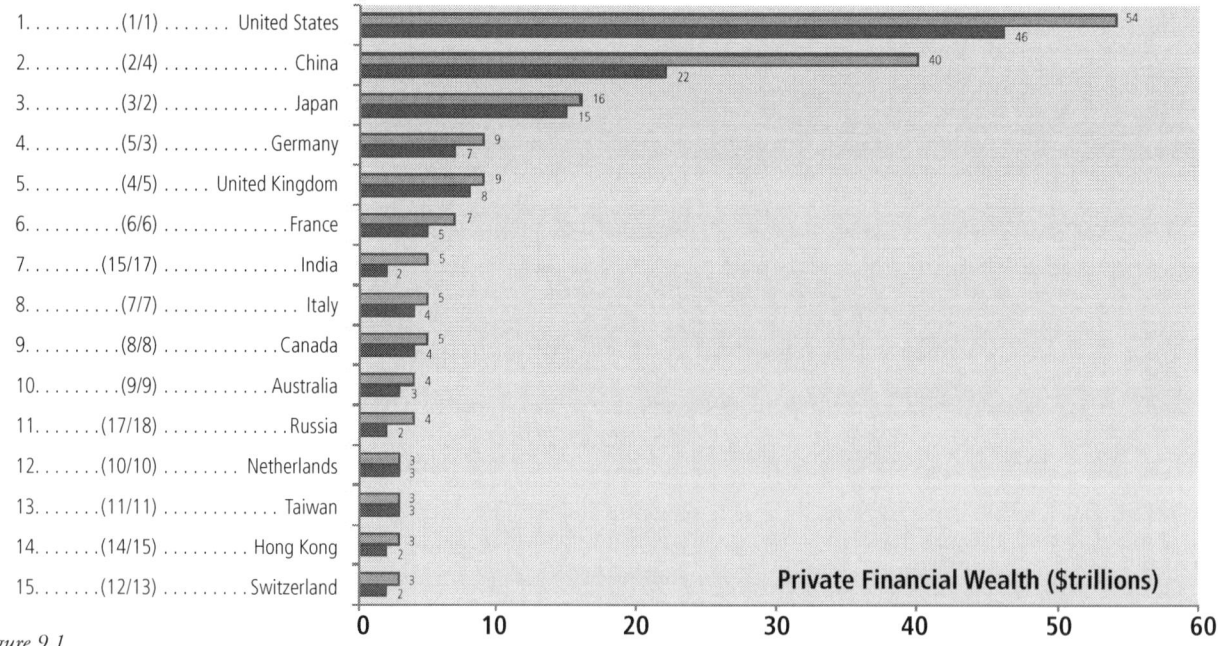

Figure 9.1

Projected Rank in 2018 (Rank in 2013/Rank in 2008)

1. . . . . (1/1) . . . . United States
2. . . . . (2/4) . . . . China
3. . . . . (3/2) . . . . Japan
4. . . . . (5/3) . . . . Germany
5. . . . . (4/5) . . . . . United Kingdom
6. . . . . (6/6) . . . . France
7. . . . . (15/17) . . . . India
8. . . . . (7/7) . . . . Italy
9. . . . . (8/8) . . . . Canada
10. . . . . (9/9) . . . . Australia
11. . . . . . . (17/18) . . . . Russia
12. . . . . . (10/10) . . . . Netherlands
13. . . . . . (11/11) . . . . Taiwan
14. . . . . . (14/15) . . . . Hong Kong
15. . . . . . (12/13) . . . . Switzerland

Private Financial Wealth ($trillions)

1 The Boston Consulting Group. (2014). *"Global Wealth 2014: Riding a Wave of Growth."* Retrieved June 2014, from bcg.perspectives by The Boston Consulting Group: https://www.bcgperspectives.com/content/articles/financial_institutions_business_unit_strategy_global_wealth_2014_riding_wave_growth/

($61 trillion), with North America falling to second place ($59 trillion).

The BCG report also clearly shows that 2013 was a good year for growth in the number of wealthy people around the world. As illustrated in Figure 9.2, the US accounted for the highest number of High Net Worth Individuals in 2013 (HNWI, those with investable assets of $1 million or more), followed by China and Japan. The robust wealth creation in China saw millionaire households rise from 1.5 million in 2012 to 2.4 million in 2013, surpassing Japan.

Qatar has the highest density of millionaires, 17.5%, followed by Switzerland, Singapore and Hong Kong. The report also showed that while the U.S. had the largest number of billionaires in 2013, the highest density of billionaire households was in Hong Kong (15.3 per million).

Looking to the future, North America will continue to be an important market for private philanthropy, but the new growth is in the Asia-Pacific region and other developing markets. HNWI in these markets are just starting to feel the effects of their visibility from a fundraising point of view, as opposed to their counterparts in North America, who tend to be well-known and intensely solicited. HNWI families are learning how to live with their new wealth, associated responsibilities and opportunities to effect change. From a prospecting perspective, this is certainly an area rife with opportunity for those organizations willing to invest the time and resources in building long-term, sustainable relationships.

INSTITUTIONAL READINESS

Knowing that there is a massive untapped philanthropic opportunity in developing economies such as China, Latin America, Eastern Europe and Russia, we need to assess whether it makes sense to plan a strategy to enter these emerging markets.

Figure 9.2 | The United States, China and Japan Had the Most Millionaires in 2013

Millionaire Households

Ultra-high-net-worth (UHNW) households
(more than $100 million in private financial wealth)

Number of millionaire households (thousands) 2013		Proportion of millionaire households (%) 2013		Number of UHNW households 2013		Proportion of UHNW households (per 100,00 households) 2013	
1. (1) United States	7,135	(1) Qatar	17.5	(1) United States	4,754	(1) Hong Kong	16.8
2. (2) China	2,378	(2) Switzerland	12.7	(2) United Kingdom	1,044	(2) Switzerland	11.3
3. (3) Japan	1,240	(3) Singapore	10.0	(4) China	983	(3) Austria	9.3
4. (4) United Kingdom	513	(4) Hong Kong	9.6	(3) Germany	881	(4) Norway	8.3
5. (6) Switzerland	435	(5) Kuwait	9.0	(5) Russia	536	(5) Singapore	7.4
6. (5) Germany	386	(6) Bahrain	5.9	(6) France	472	(6) Qatar	7.1
7. (7) Canada	384	(7) United States	5.9	(7) Canada	465	(7) Kuwait	4.5
8. (8) Taiwan	329	(8) Israel	4.6	(8) Hong Kong	417	(9) New Zealand	4.1
9. (9) Italy	281	(9) Taiwan	4.2	(9) Switzerland	388	(8) Belgium	4.1
10. (10) France	274	(10) Oman	3.7	(10) Italy	374	(12) United States	3.9
11. (11) Hong Kong	238	(11) Belgium	3.4	(11) Austria	344	(11) United Kingdom	3.9
12. (12) Netherlands	221	(12) UAE	3.3	(12) Turkey	288	(10) Israel	3.7
13. (13) Russia	213	(13) Saudi Arabia	3.1	(13) India	284	(16) Bahrain	3.7
14. (14) Australia	195	(14) Netherlands	3.0	(14) Australia	236	(15) Canada	3.5
15. (15) India	175	(15) Canada	2.9	(16) Brazil	227	(13) Ireland	3.4

Source: BCG Global Wealth Market Sizing Database, 2014
Notes: UAE is United Arab Emirates. Numbers in parentheses are 2012 rankings, determined on the basis of year-end 2013 exchange rates to exclude the effect of currency fluctuations.

Figure 9.2

Building on Bernard Ross' Five C's of new market entry for fundraising,[2] (Commitment, Competence, Competition, Context and Culture) I would propose Five C's as follows:

> **FIVE C'S OF NEW MARKET ENTRY FOR FUNDRAISING**
>
> 1. Case – do you have a case for support that maps to institutional priorities as well as international donors values and affiliations?
>
> 2. Commitment – do you have the financial resources to enter the market and sustain the effort and the support of your Board and CEO to do so?
>
> 3. Culture – do you have existing international relationships and an organizational culture that understands and embraces diversity?
>
> 4. Competition – who are your competitors and how does your brand compare?
>
> 5. Context – what are the local conditions that affect your ability to operate and export cash? Do you have the skills, knowledge and experience to make a successful entry?

1. Case

A campaign is a great time to seek clear decisions about institutional fundraising priorities, including international priorities. To understand if your priorities align with those of international prospects you need to understand their motivations for giving.

The *UBS-INSEAD Study on Family Philanthropy* in Asia provides insights on philanthropic motivations and challenges of Asian families in this rapidly growing economy. The study noted that while family philanthropic activities play a critical role in instilling family values, developing cohesion, expanding the roles of family members and developing capabilities around the world, these factors are even more relevant in Asia where the family continues to be an exceptionally strong locus for business and philanthropic activities.

Figure 9.3 shows 42% of the people and organizations surveyed noted the number one reason for engaging in philanthropy was "ensuring the continuity of family values or creating a lasting legacy."[3] The benefits to the family unit from philanthropic engagement include: teaching principles like compassion, courage and tolerance; fostering capacities for leadership, innovation and responsibility; and supporting family cohesion by providing

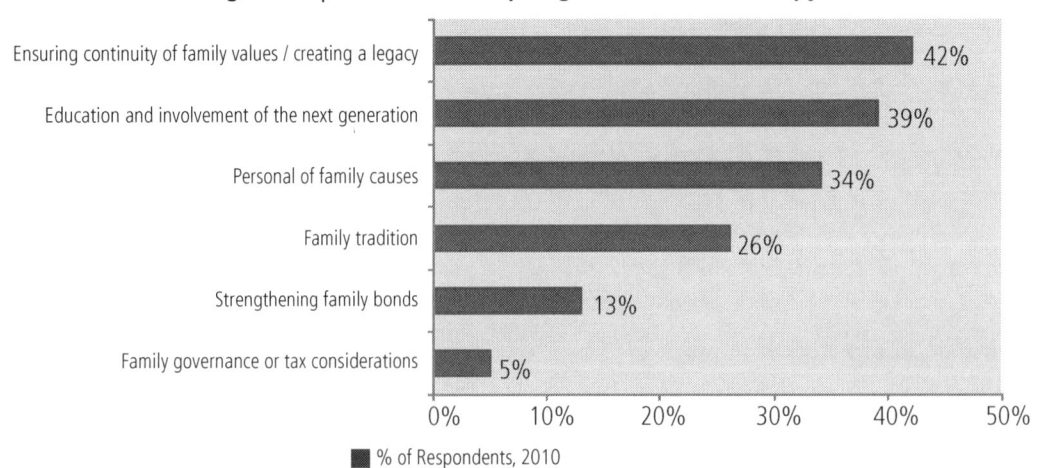

Figure 9.3 | Main Factors Inspiring Families' Philanthropy

- Ensuring continuity of family values / creating a legacy — 42%
- Education and involvement of the next generation — 39%
- Personal of family causes — 34%
- Family tradition — 26%
- Strengthening family bonds — 13%
- Family governance or tax considerations — 5%

■ % of Respondents, 2010

Figure 9.3

---

2 Ross, Bernard. The Management Centre in London, *Five C's of New Market Entry for Fundraising*.

3 Mahmood, Mahboob, and Santos, Filipe. (2011). *UBS-INSEAD Study on Family Philanthropy in Asia*. UBS Philanthropy Services and INSEAD.

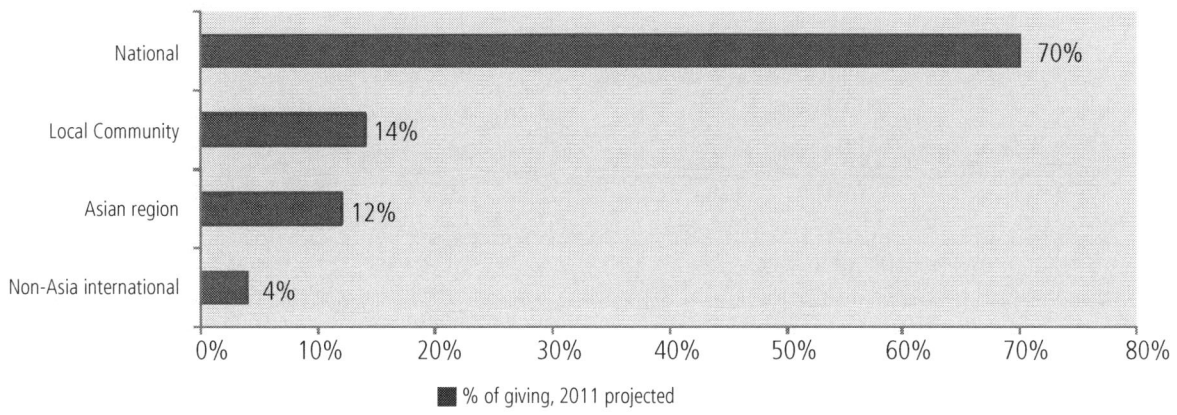

Figure 9.4

Figure 9.4

a common activity and goal for the family to pursue as a unit.

It is interesting to compare these findings with Canadian philanthropic motivations. Mallabone and Myers found the top five motivators for making a gift in Canada were: (i) belief in the vision and mission, (ii) helping those in need, (iii) giving back to the community, (iv) belief that the charity is accountable and that their (v) gift will make a difference.[4]

The UBS-INSEAD study also noted generational differences in family philanthropic activity.

- The older generation feels more responsible to the local community and is more influenced by tradition, while the younger generation is increasingly geared to national and international causes.

- The older generation focuses on sectors such as education, health and poverty, while the younger is more open to sectors such as the arts, civil rights and the environment.

- While the older generation tends to see giving as an end in itself, the younger generation tends to be more interested in measuring the impact of giving.

The strong preference in Asia to direct family philanthropy toward national-level causes can be seen in Figure 9.4. The UBS INSEAD study noted about 70% of giving was directed to such causes with a further 14% directed towards the local community. Of the 16% of

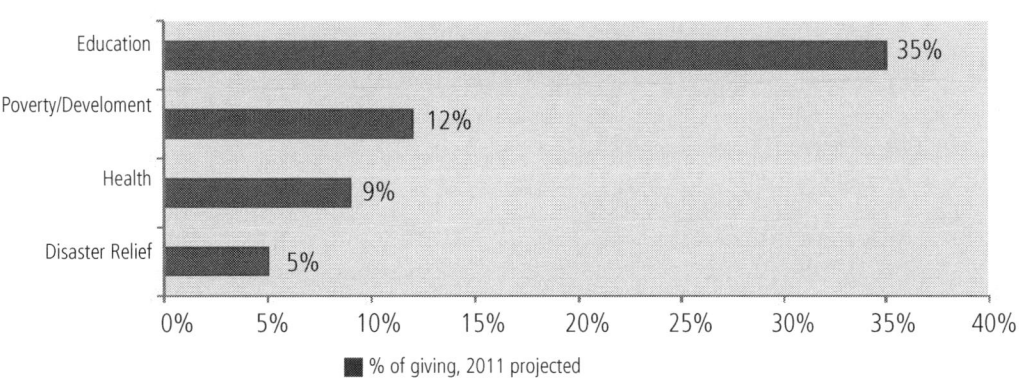

Figure 9.5

4   Mallabone, E.H. Guy, MA, CFRE and Myers, J.A. (Tony), PhD, CFRE, *The Motivations and Barriers to Philanthropic Giving by Entrepreneurs*, St. Mary's University, Minnesota, USA.

charitable giving directed internationally, 12% was focussed on the Asian region with only 4% directed towards non-Asian international causes. This highlights the importance of affiliation in driving family giving in Asia.

Figure 9.5 shows that education is the top cause for Asian family philanthropy accounting for 35% of giving. The study cited several reasons for this preference including deep cultural roots for educational support in Asia often tied to religious tradition and the belief that education is foundational to uplifting individuals and communities from poverty.[5]

In summary, the principal findings of the study were as follows:

i. Family giving across Asia is driven by affiliation (community, country, ethnicity, religion), sector (education, health, etc.), impact (social return on investment, problem solving) and pragmatism (personal, business, etc.).

ii. The affiliation factor is the principal driver of giving across most of Asia, with community, country and ethnicity being critical factors that determine the scope and direction of giving. (Figure 9.4)

iii. Within sectors, families across Asia predominantly contribute to educational causes. (Figure 9.5)

While the *UBS-INSEAD Study of Family Philanthropy* in Asia provides extraordinary insights into family values and practices, information is increasingly being published on philanthropy in other countries as well. A literature search can help identify useful information to plan your strategy.

Understanding the philanthropic motivations of families and the inter-generational differences is critical to building successful and sustainable philanthropic relationships in Asia and around the world. Building a strong Case for Support which speaks to these motivations is an essential step to engaging in international fundraising.

---

5 Mahmood, Mahbood, and Santos, Filipe. (2011). *UBS-INSEAD Study on Family Philanthropy in Asia*. UBS Philanthropy Services and INSEAD.

2. Commitment

As fundraising professionals, we are in the relationship business and face-to-face meetings are one of the most important ways we have to build and sustain mutually beneficial relationships. Working internationally, or even globally, requires a commitment that extends beyond executive missions where the President flies in once a year, waves the flag, hosts some meetings and flies off. To be successful, organizations need to find the most productive way to allocate limited financial and staff resources while managing competing priorities with a view to establishing trust, demonstrating a commitment for the long-term and building meaningful personal connections with donors and prospects.

Through the discussion of the case we have assessed organizational readiness from the perspective of strengths and priorities and how they match with international philanthropic interests. The next step is to assess the critical mass required for success.

EXAMPLE: TESTING YOUR CASE

At Simon Fraser University, once we had drafted what we felt was a clear and compelling case for Asian supporters translated into Mandarin, we decided to test it with alumni and key influencers in Asia and locally. Working with an independent consultant, we conducted nearly 30 face-to- face confidential interviews, both in Vancouver and abroad. The information gleaned from these interviews was invaluable, both from the perspective of further refining and presenting the case and for the development of a strategy to move forward. While testing your Case for Support with internal and external audiences is always important, it is especially important when dealing with cultures where you may not be as familiar with language, cultural practices and nuances. Even the style of the translation can have an impact on how the case is perceived.

From an educational institution's point of view, we look for alumni, parents, students and

Opportunity Map

	Top 5 Countries by Population		Activity to Date		Market Conditions
Country	Number of Constituents	Percent of Total Constituents	Percent with Good Addresses	Cumulative Giving (in US$)	GDP Growth
Canada	338	5.84	89	$3,724,008	0.40%
India	172	2.97	42	$400,998	7.09%
Korea	828	14.31	48	$175,000	2.22%
U.K.	307	5.3	73	$978,878	0.70%
Taiwan	623	10.77	56	$2,369,878	0.10%

Figure 9.6

volunteers to form the core of a philanthropic network. A hospital might consider grateful patients and families and volunteers. A robust pipeline of individuals, organizations, corporations, government officials and others who can positively influence your philanthropic goals is essential. Understanding how your brand is conceived in the geographic area relative to competitors is also important, as donors want to be associated with highly trusted and respected institutions and organizations.

Assuming you have institutional commitment to staff and fund the effort, and the critical mass of donors, prospects and volunteers for success, the next step is planning your market entry strategy. This will largely depend on budget and staff resources and requires commitment from the CEO and Board of Directors of your organization.

In his chapter "Map to the Global Village, International Prospect Research" from *Across Frontiers, New International Perspectives on Educational Fundraising*, Jay Frost offers a practical tool to help target areas of greatest opportunity for international fundraising.

His Opportunity Map[6] involves mapping your constituency by country, by activity to date and by market conditions as can be seen in the Chart provided (some sample data included).

Assessing your opportunity in this systematic fashion elevates your decision-making out of the realm of anecdote and enhances data driven decision-making that can be sustained over a period of years.

Barbara Miles, Vice-President Development and Alumni Engagement at the University of British Columbia, suggests this analysis can go even deeper with a focus on particular cities where the greatest opportunity for success exists. She states, "you cannot invest in international fundraising and alumni relations half-heartedly. You need to go back regularly year after year, and you must have the institutional buy-in and budgets to sustain the activity over the long term."

Another crucial consideration is whether to establish a satellite office to be closer to donors and prospects.

Donald Kirkwood, in his Chapter "Satellite Offices in International Fundraising" from *Across Frontiers, New International Perspectives on Educational Fundraising* notes the key factors to this decision are cost, scale, programmatic priorities and opportunity. While in many international cities, rental space and the associated overheads, administrative support and legal costs may seem prohibitive, there are savings on travel and accommodation. Kirkwood notes that institutions that opt

---

6   Frost, Jay; (2010). Map to the Global Village, International Prospect Research; *Across Frontiers: New International Perspectives on Educational Fundraising* (pp. 27-45). Washington: Council for advancement and Support of Education.

for the satellite office do not identify cost as the contributing decision to their decision, indicating other considerations trump costs.

Some institutions set up satellite offices when their constituent group reaches a certain scale, such as 10,000 alumni in the area. While fundraising is often central to the role of the satellite office, many institutions are careful to publicly emphasize other roles such as alumni relations, external relations, student recruitment and brand development.

With respect to program priority, there is no reason to proceed unless the city or region is already a declared institutional priority.

Finally, an institution's global philosophy and its relevance to the regional community are crucial factors in determining if a satellite office is to be established. The case must inspire philanthropic support from local constituents to encourage such an investment.

Kirkland concludes the decision to establish a satellite office is "more intuitive, subjective, pragmatic and opportunistic, than philosophical or even strategic."[7] Whatever your decision, ensure you position your institution for the long haul, with adequate resources and patience for a long-term return on investment.

At Simon Fraser University we too were struggling with the decision to establish a satellite office in Hong Kong. Our alumni chapter representatives were strongly encouraging us to do so. We decided to explore the issue with key alumni and influencers as part of our Asia study and were surprised by the response. While there was support for the establishment of an office in the future, the study told us there were other things we should be doing first that take precedence over this expensive investment. We are now working with alumni to raise our profile regionally through targeted programming. Additionally we intend to establish an International advisory committee reporting directly to the President. As the number of alumni in Hong Kong continues to grow, we are likely to establish an office in collaboration with External Affairs and Student Services.

3. Culture

As North America is quickly becoming more ethnically, culturally and socioeconomically diverse, as are the institutions we work for, we are becoming more effective at adopting conventional fundraising practices to appeal to specific populations in a manner more consistent with their culture and expectations.

Most of the major cities in Canada are multi-ethnic societies, affording fundraisers the opportunity to expand their knowledge and understanding of diversity and its impact on our society, and to develop their abilities to accommodate to the cultural styles, norms and preferences of donors and prospects in our communities. However, it takes concerted individual effort to truly expand your global horizons.

Gregory C. Unruh and Angela Cabrera, authors of "Join the Global Elite," *Harvard Business Review*, suggest building your global competencies through a three-step process:[8]

1. Acquire the knowledge, skills, and perspectives you need by both thinking (observe, study and open your mind to new experiences and cultures) and doing (forge relationships across national and cultural boundaries, start locally but travel, learn new languages, open your mind and heart).

2. Make use of your new global awareness by exploiting divergence (note differences among markets and use those observations to create value) convergence (note commonalities also to create value) and networks.

3. Become a global citizen, ensuring your work serves the world in positive ways.

While we need to improve the global competencies of administrators, and staff we

---

[7] Kirkland, Donald; (2010). "Satellite Offices in International Fundraising." *Across Frontiers: New International Perspectives on Educational Fundraising* (pp. 84). Washington: Council for Advancement and Support of Education.

[8] Unruh, Gregory C. and Cabrera, Angela Cabrera, (2013, May). Join the Global Elite, *Harvard Business Review*. Retrieved June 2014, from *Harvard Business Review*: http://hbr.org/2013/05/join-the-global-elite/ar/1

also need to strategically recruit fundraisers with a global perspective or ethnic background. Volunteers can also be extremely important in ensuring international fundraising success. Not only can they host events and open doors to individuals with affluence and influence we could not otherwise reach, they can advise on entry strategies into new markets. They have access to information that enables us to target our efforts in a productive way. They serve as conduits for prospects and donors who do not wish to share information with us directly. They can help build positive and support relationships with government officials. As knowledgeable ambassadors, they convey the relevance and importance of supporting the institution to the community. They can provide counsel and advice to your CEO on a regular basis.

Managing high level volunteers requires support from the highest levels of the institution and a commitment to regular meetings with the CEO. It requires an institutional culture that values volunteers as integral members of the community and provides resources to ensure volunteers are engaged and excited about the future of the organization.

Institutional competency in cultural diversity is essential to successful relationship building in new markets. Those institutions and organizations with diverse, open and accommodating internal cultures are more likely to translate those competencies to emerging markets with good effect.

4. Competition

Whenever you need to enter a new market you need to do an assessment of the competition and how your brand compares to theirs. The number of North American charities (particularly universities) that are committed to building their brand in Asia is high and many have set up satellite offices in Hong Kong and other parts of China.

Building your brand strategy to not only enhance your visibility and relevance to the broader community but to instil pride of association is key. While marketing collateral and efforts in international countries may need to be tweaked to reflect cultural differences, it should retain some relationship to the overall institutional brand.

When planning your strategy be realistic about expectations. Trying to compete head-to-head with much more established brands will require enormous resources and time. Instead, find a niche where your organization excels and build your brand from there. For example, a hospital may have a world-wide reputation for an innovative heart procedure, or a social services organization may have developed a local strategy to address homelessness that can be taken abroad. By focussing on these specific strengths you can enhance your reputation and build your brand over time.

While it is always challenging to quantify the impact of branding efforts on fundraising results, it is clear that without these investments, important connections will be more difficult to make, volunteers will be less invested in success, prospects will be more difficult to attract and fundraising results will suffer.

When assessing the competitive landscape look for opportunities to connect with competitors as collaborators. Together you can work on projects or societal issues of relevance to both institutions and the local community. Choosing the right competitor-collaborator can help elevate your brand by association. Access to established networks, government contacts and community and business leaders can also be facilitated with more established competitor-collaborators.

5. Context

While the "urge to give" is a universal human trait, many countries around the world have developed different ways of managing private philanthropy, from legal requirements, to tax regimes and the ability to export cash. In some countries, where wealth generation is more recent, there can be cultural inhibitions to public giving which needs to be managed.

While philanthropy has deep roots in many countries around the world, there has been dramatic change over the last few decades over how it is expressed in many countries.

China, for example has seen exponential growth in the non-profit sector over the past 20 years (from 4,446 in 1988 to 412,063 in 2008).[9]

At the same time there has been a growth in the number of charitable foundations. Reflecting China's dramatic economic and social development, these foundations tend to share five distinct features; top-down (government) support, a focus on disaster and poverty relief; massive public participation, a strong project drive and small size.[10]

These elements work well for annual giving programs. At the same time, as in North America, there is a growing gap in government funding and program needs necessitating the development of a major gifts culture as well.

In the Arab region, philanthropic activism is expanding largely due to massive new wealth from oil revenues. Features of philanthropy in this area include: active participation by members of reform-minded ruling families, the emergence of private-public partnerships; the emergence of community foundations that aggregate public contributions; and increasing prominence of women in philanthropy.[11]

Latin America offers significant potential for growth in philanthropic activity with relatively low per capita giving. Chile, Brazil and Mexico ranked 35, 91 and 76 on the World Giving Index 2013 which provides insight into the scope and nature of giving around the world.[12]

The United States and Canada ranked 1 and 2 by comparison.

India has taken a big leap in philanthropic engagement. The World Giving Index 2013 reported that more Indians donate money to charity in a month than anywhere else in the world. In 2011 this number measured at 163 million. In 2012 the number stands at 244 million, a dramatic increase suggesting India is flexing its philanthropic muscles.[13]

Wherever your strategy takes you, make sure you fully understand the history and context of philanthropy in each new market. Armed with this knowledge your chances for a successful entry will be dramatically improved.

Many fundraising professional associations such as CASE and AFP have resources for members on the subject of charitable gift laws, history of philanthropy and trends in the international context which are helpful in planning your international strategy.

CONCLUSIONS

While shifting global wealth patterns reveal an enormous opportunity for international fundraising it is important to note such efforts are highly complex, somewhat risky and generally slow to provide a return on investment. For those institutions and organizations where international and advancement strategy align; where a potentially robust pipeline and/or extraordinarily compelling case exist; where high level local volunteers can provide political and cultural knowledge and insights; and where robust financials can sustain a longer term return on investment, an international fundraising strategy makes sense.

Our role as fundraising professionals in this emerging opportunity will be to challenge convention and reach beyond the comfort of our own organizational culture, to be internationally engaged and to help shape and define the new models that will emerge in this exciting and rapidly changing world.

---

9   Xu, Dongli and Yang, Catherine, (2010). "China: New Directions in Philanthropy and Educational Fundraising." *Across Frontiers: New International Perspectives on Educational Fundraising* (p. 7). Washington: Council for Advancement and Support of Education.
10   Ibid.
11   Xu, Dongli and Yang, Catherine, (2010). "China: New Directions in Philanthropy and Educational Fundraising." *Across Frontiers: New International Perspectives on Educational Fundraising* (pp. 11-12). Washington: Council for Advancement and Support of Education.
12   Charities Aid Foundation. (2013). *World Giving Index 2013: A global view of giving trends.* (pp.26). Charities Aid Foundation 2013.

13   Charities Aid Foundation. (2013). *World Giving Index 2013: A global view of giving trends.* (pp. 5). Charities Aid Foundation 2013.

ACKNOWLEDGEMENTS

With deepest gratitude to the following individuals for sharing their international perspectives and experiences:

Blake Bromley, President, Benefic

Gretchen Dobson, Global Strategist

Ted Gerrard, President and CEO, SickKids Foundation

Barbara Miles, Vice-President, Development and Alumni Engagement, University of British Columbia

David Palmer, Vice-President, Advancement, University of Toronto

Marc Weinstein, Vice-Principal, Development and Alumni Relations, McGill University

TOP TWELVE TIPS TO BUILD A SUSTAINABLE INTERNATIONAL FUNDRAISING PROGRAM

1. Start small, build your program as you grow your internal competencies.
2. Do your research, understand the philanthropic history, motivations, political climate and context of the country you plan to visit.
3. Do your due diligence on prospective donors.
4. Ensure you have policies in place to protect your organization (i.e. removal of naming rights) in the event of legal or reputational issues.
5. Create a senior level international advisory committee to help guide and shape efforts, consult with the diaspora.
6. Test your case for relevance, appeal and appropriateness with potential prospects.
7. Build your competency as a global citizen.
8. Travel.
9. Hire fundraisers with expertise in specific geographic regions.
10. Listen, seek the meaning behind the words.
11. Take your time, build trust, it's all about relationships.
12. All fundraising is local – international donors usually want to see some benefit from giving internationally in their home community.

CASE STUDY 1: WHEN OPPORTUNITY KNOCKS

The inspiration to make a difference can come from unexpected sources. Our role as fundraising professionals is to recognize opportunity when it presents and act upon it.

Which is exactly what Ted Garrard, President and CEO of SickKids Foundation in Toronto, did when presented with the opportunity to address a serious global child health issue within six countries in the Caribbean.

Having successfully seen her young child treated for cancer at the Hospital for Sick Children in Toronto, the mother, originally from Barbados, asked what would have happened if her child had been treated in her home country.

The answer was disturbing. Statistics show that the survival rate of children with cancer in the Caribbean is less than 50% compared with a better than 80% survival rate in Canada. Grateful for her good fortune at having had her child treated in Canada, she wanted to do something to help improve child survival rates in her home country. She offered to fund a needs assessment ($150,000) through SickKids Foundation to see what could be done.

The assessment was completed over an 18-month period and noted deficiencies in four key areas; patient registries, training of health professionals, diagnostic and treatment equipment and access to experts through telemedicine.

A 5-year plan was developed to address the issues, and the Caribbean –SickKids Paediatric Cancer and Blood Disorders Project was born. The costs to complete the project were estimated to be $8 million, all of which needed to be fundraised.

The campaign targeted companies who did business in the Caribbean, families owning property in the Caribbean, local businesses in the area and the diaspora in the Greater Toronto area. In the first year they raised $7.2 million for this humanitarian effort.

Ted noted the secrets of the success of this campaign as follows:

1. Great project – this humanitarian project had a strong emotional appeal and was sanctioned under SickKids Global Child Health Program.

2. Existing relationships - Ted was able to capitalize on relationships he had established in the Caribbean through previous work at the University of Western Ontario.

3. SickKids reputation and expertise – gave the project credibility, opened doors.

4. Local champions - were identified to lead and publicly endorse the initiative.

5. High Commissions - for each country were engaged, often hosting events.

6. Local Media Partnerships - were established with both paid and earned media.

7. Satellite Foundations - were established to enable donors without assets in Canada to participate in local tax benefits.

8. Corporate support – opportunity to double up on commitments to existing pledges due to the strategic significance of the area and employee support.

CASE STUDY 1 (CONT.)

9. Individual Support – opportunity to have a different conversation with traditional SickKids donors, expanding their view beyond Canada.

This project was consistent with the vision and values of the Hospital for Sick Children in Toronto, fitting in the humanitarian focussed Global Child Health Program, and SickKids Foundation committed to making it happen. It had an exceptional case for support. It leveraged cultural connections with the Caribbean countries and the diaspora. It involved addressing issues of context through the establishment of satellite Foundations. As the capacity to address the issue locally was lacking, the leadership, expertise and resources of the Hospital for Sick Children and SickKids Foundation provided the platform for a win-win international initiative.

CASE STUDY 2:
UNDERSTANDING THE MEANING BEHIND THE WORDS

In a cross-cultural context, we sometimes miss the true intent of what a donor is trying to convey to us. Such was the case initiative to establish the first North American business school campus in Asia for the Ivey Business School of the University of Western Ontario.

David contacted alum Henry Cheng, then deputy head of the New World Development Company in Hong Kong, to discuss the opportunity. It was 1995, right before the scheduled 1997 handover of Hong Kong from Britain back to China. Anxiety for the future of Hong Kong was high. It was also a time when China was graduating a very limited supply of MBAs and business degree holders, despite the rapid proliferation of so-called "red-chip" companies. An innocent conversation with Mr. Cheng about the management needs of China's Red Army, one of the largest organizations in the world, was met with confusion at first. Only later, after repeated meetings and careful listening, did it become clear that Mr. Cheng saw his gift to Ivey delivering important and necessary value to China's emerging business landscape through management education, while helping reinforce Hong Kong's status as a business and financial gateway for Asia. It was a win-win for the Cheng family, for Hong Kong, and for the Ivey School.

Thanks to Mr. Cheng's generosity, Ivey opened its first international campus in Hong Kong in September 1997, just two months after the handover. Bearing the name of Mr. Cheng's father, the Cheng Yu Tung Management Institute has been a tremendous success, developing management expertise, cases, research, and programs, on Asian businesses and for Asian business leaders. It also stands as a meaningful example of how a donor's intent is sometimes revealed only over time, as the underlying context and motivations gradually become clear.

ADDITIONAL RESOURCES

- CAGNEY, P. (2013). The World Next Door. *Advancing Phlanthropy, Volume 20, Number 4* . Association of Fundraising Professionals.

- CHARITIES AID FOUNDATION. (2013). *World Giving Index 2013: A global view of giving trends.* Charities Aid Foundation 2013.

- DOBSON, G. (2011). *Being Global: Making the Case for International Alumni Relations.* Washington: Council for Advancement and Support of Education.

- DOBSON, G. C. (2013). *Setting the Agenda: Corporate and Foundation Support for Higher Education.*

- DOBSON, G., & KERR, R. A. (2013). *Strategic Steps to International Fundraising.* San Francisco, CA, USA.

- FROST, J. (2010). Map to the Global Village: International Prospect Research. In *Across Frontiers: New International Perspectives on Educational Fundraising* (pp. 27-45). Washington: Council for Advancement and Support of Education.

- KIRKWOOD, D. (2010). Satellite Offices in International Fundraising. In *Across Frontiers: New International Perspectives on Educational Fundraising* (pp. 73-85). Washington: Council for Advancement and Support of Education.

- MAHMOOD, M., & SANTOS, F. (2011). *UBS-INSEAD Study on Family Philanthropy in Asia.* UBS Philanthropy Services & INSEAD.

- RBC WEALTH MANAGEMENT. (2013). *Asia-Pacific Pushes Global HNWI Wealth to Record Levels.*

- RBC WEALTH MANAGEMENT. (2013). *HNWI Market Bounces Back, Pushing popluation and Wealth to Record Levels.*

- REICHENBACH, I. T. (2010). International Fundraising in a Campaign. In *Across Frontiers: New International Perspectives on Educational Fundraising* (pp. 14-59). Washington: Council for Advancement and Support of Education.

- SIDHU, L. (2010). Internationalizing the Annual Fund. In *Across Frontiers: New International Perspectives on Educational Fundraising* (pp. 61-72). Washington: Council for Advancement and Support of Education.

- THE BOSTON CONSULTING GROUP. (2014, JUNE). *Global Wealth 2014: Riding a Wave of Growth.* Retrieved June 2014, from bcg.perspectives by The Boston Consulting Group: https://www.bcgperspectives.com/content/articles/financial_institutions_business_unit_strategy_global_wealth_2014_riding_wave_growth/

- UNRUH, G. C., & CABRERA, Á. (2013, MAY). *Join the Global Elite.* Retrieved June 2014, from Harvard Business Review: http://hbr.org/2013/05/join-the-global-elite/ar/1

- UPSALL, D. (2013). Windows on the World of Fundraising: A glimpse at fundraising and philanthropy far and wide. *Advancing Philanthropy, Volume 20, Number 4* . Association of Fundraising Professionals.

- WAGNER, L. (2013). Vive la Diversité in Global Fundraising. *Advancing Philanthropy, Volume 20, Number 4* . Association of Fundraising Professionals.

- WOLFE, D. (2014). *Bring in Dollars from Abroad: International Fundraising Requires Intensive Planning, Community-Building.*

- XU, D., & YANG, C. (2010). China: New Directions in Philanthropy and Educational Fundraising. In *Across Frontiers: New International Perspectives on Educational Fundraising* (pp. 5-25). Washington: Council for Advancement and Support of Education.

ABOUT THE AUTHOR

Cathy Daminato, MBA, ICD.D

Cathy Daminato has devoted over 25 years of her life to fundraising and development in the education and health care sectors in Greater Vancouver. After completing her B.Sc. from Queens University and an MBA from the University of British Columbia, she held leadership roles at Douglas College, BCIT and Royal Columbian Hospital Foundation. In 2003, she became the first Vice-President of Advancement and Alumni Engagement at Simon Fraser University, tripling the fundraising activity, building endowments and raising significant funds for key capital projects. Most recently under Cathy's leadership SFU launched its largest fundraising effort to date, the $250 million Power of Engagement 50th Anniversary Campaign.

Cathy's leadership ability, strategic planning skills and marketing acumen have been critical to her success. She is more than willing to share her experiences and passion for philanthropy by giving her time to inspire and mentor others in the fundraising profession. She led the creation of a new fundraising management certificate program at BCIT, and served on various boards and committees of AFP nationally and internationally, including a term as Chair of the AFP Vancouver Chapter. She is currently a board member of the Canadian Council for the Advancement of Education.

CHAPTER 10

Charitable Gaming

TED GARRARD, MA

Charitable gaming in Canada, defined as gambling activities undertaken by charities and non-profit organizations, has become an important fundraising tool having generated billions of dollars to support charitable activities in communities since 1969 when charitable gaming was legalized in Canada.

read more…

Today, charitable gaming encompasses activities such as bingos, raffles, break-open tickets, and lotteries including mega charity lotteries, like the Princess Margaret Cancer Centre's Home Lottery, the Heart and Stroke Foundation Calendar Lottery or the B.C. Children's Hospital Choices Lottery, to name just three. While there is no record of the total number of charitable gaming licenses awarded across Canada we do know that in the case of charitable lotteries, 16,292 charity lottery licenses were granted in 2011 alone, and this number includes only the larger lotteries that require provincial rather than municipal licensing.[1]

For some charities, gaming represents a very significant source of fundraising revenue. For example, the Shock Trauma Air Rescue Service's (STARS) (which has sold out its lottery for the past 18 years), accounted for 45% of the organization's total net fundraising for the year ended December 31, 2012,[2] whereas SickKids Foundation's Dreams and Discoveries Lottery accounted for just 2.4% of total fundraising revenue for the year ended March 31, 2012.[3] Charitable gaming can be either a driving force for a charity's fundraising or one component of a more diversified platform of fundraising activities.

LEGAL AUTHORITY FOR CHARITABLE GAMING

The legal authority for charitable gaming rests in paragraph 207 (1)(b) of the *Criminal Code of Canada*. Paragraph 207(1)(b) of the *Criminal Code* provides that it is lawful:

> "...for a charitable or religious organization, pursuant to a license issued by the Lieutenant Governor in Council of a province or by such other person or authority in the province as may be specified by the Lieutenant Governor in Council thereof, to conduct and manage a lottery scheme in that province if the proceeds from the lottery are used for a charitable or religious object or purpose."[4]

There are several elements of this paragraph that are important.

First, a "charitable or religious" organization is the entity that may conduct and manage charitable gaming activities. According to Donald Bourgeois, author of *The Law of Charitable Gaming and Casinos*, it appears that the definition of "charitable" is the common law one since the phrase is not otherwise defined. Indeed, the courts have determined that the term "charitable" refers to "organizations which provide programs for the relief of poverty, the advancement of education, the advancement of religion, and other charitable purposes beneficial to the community."[5]

Second, the organization must obtain a "license" granting authorization to conduct charitable gaming activities such as bingos, raffles and lotteries. In most provinces, charitable gaming licensing is largely done at the provincial level although in Ontario most licensing has been delegated to municipalities, while in Nunavut and the Northwest Territories charitable gaming licenses have been delegated entirely to local municipalities.

Third, the organization/licensee must "conduct and manage" the charitable gaming activity. Control over the proceeds from charitable gaming is the responsibility of the licensee although this does not require the entire charitable activity to be operated by the licensee. Indeed, it has been recognized that the private sector may be involved in the supply of goods and services that are part of the overall charitable gaming activity. For example, it is not unusual for charity lotteries to employ outside consultants and other contractors to provide professional counsel, develop prizing packages, develop marketing creative and buy media on behalf of the charity.

The use of proceeds from charitable gaming is also defined in paragraph 207 (1)(b) and must be directed to a charitable or religious object or purpose.[6] An Ontario Order-in-Council provides a useful definition in the context of charitable lotteries, specifically:

> "...the gross proceeds from the lottery scheme shall be used for the charitable or religious objects or purposes providing a direct benefit to the residents of Ontario as set out by the licensee in the application for a license, less the cost of the

---

1 Greg Thomson and Ernie Cheng, (2013). "Charity Lotteries in Canada," *Charity Intelligence* Canada. p. 2.
2 2012 Governance and Financial Report, Shock Trauma Air Rescue Service, p. 14.
3 Financial Statements. (March 31, 2013) SickKids Foundation, p. 3.
4 Donald Bourgeois, "*Charitable Gaming: The Legal Context*," The Philanthropist, Volume 15, No. 4, p. 58.
5 Ibid., p. 58.
6 Ibid., p. 60.

prizes awarded and such reasonable and necessary expenses actually incurred in the management and conduct of the lottery, and such expenses shall be restricted to those set out in the terms and condition of the license."[7]

Groups in Alberta are eligible for charitable gaming licenses if they "actively deliver a charitable program or service that provides benefit to a significant segment of the community; the programs or services must be reasonably available to all members of the general public who qualify and wish to participate in that program or use the service."[8]

All provinces and territories take a similar approach, namely that the proceeds of charitable gaming must provide a direct benefit to the community, however each jurisdiction has different policies, guidelines and licensing application processes. Some provinces have regulations that mandate a minimum level of prize payout to prevent charitable gaming from being unfair to consumers. For example, the Alberta Gaming and Liquor Commission and Alcohol and Gaming Commission of Ontario requires that prizes be at least 20% of each licensed gaming activity, while the Province of Nova Scotia has no such requirement.[9]

While gambling is still illegal in Canada significant exceptions have been granted by the federal government to allow provincial governments and their Crown agencies the ability to conduct and manage it. Charitable and religious organizations have been extended similar, albeit more restrictive rights. You can access more information on each jurisdiction's regulations as follows:

Province/Territory	Agency Name	Website
Alberta	Alberta Gaming and Liquor Commission	www.aglc.ca
British Columbia	British Columbia Gaming Policy and Enforcement Branch	www.gaming.gov.bc.ca
Manitoba	Liquor and Gaming Authority of Manitoba	www.lgamanitoba.ca
New Brunswick	New Brunswick Lottery and Gaming Commission	www.gnb.ca
Newfoundland and Labrador	Service NL	www.servicenl.gov.nl.ca
Nova Scotia	Nova Scotia Alcohol and Gaming Division	www.novascotia.ca
Northwest Territories	Delegated to municipalities	Go to local municipal websites
Nunavut	Delegated to municipalities	Go to local municipal websites
Ontario	Alcohol and Gaming Commission of Ontario	www.agco.on.ca
Quebec	Regie des alcools, des courses et des jeux	www.racj.gouv.qc.ca
Prince Edward Island	PEI Department of Environment, Labour and Justice	www.gov.pe.ca
Saskatchewan	Saskatchewan Liquor and Gaming Authority	www.slga.gov.sk.ca
Yukon	Department of Community Services	www.community.gov.yk.ca

---

7 Ibid., p. 60.
8 Alberta Gaming and Liquor Commission, http://www.aglc.ca

9 Greg Thomson and Ernie Cheng, "Charity Lotteries in Canada," *Charity Intelligence*, November 2013, p. 7.

GOVERNMENT GAMING ACTIVITIES VS. CHARITABLE GAMING ACTIVITIES

Governments and charities are competitors in the gaming market. Each is trying to attract consumers to participate in their gaming activities and to generate as much net revenue as possible whether it is to fund the general operations of the provincial/territorial government or to fund the mission and objects of the charity.

There are, however, some important distinctions between government and charitable gaming. For example, there are certain gaming activities in Canada which have been deemed by provincial and territorial governments as not permissible for charities and non-profit groups to undertake. For example, "Charities cannot conduct any charitable gaming using slot machines or games operated on or through a video device or computer such as video lottery terminals."[10] These games are reserved for government-run lottery and gaming corporations only. Similarly, in the case of lotteries, a charitable lottery has to commit to awarding a certain number of prizes no matter how many tickets are sold, whereas government-run lotteries are able to fix their prizes to a defined percentage of tickets sold, meaning they will never run the risk of giving out more prizes than the revenue they collect from ticket sales.

Charitable gaming is also highly regulated and ironically the bulk of this regulation falls to provincial governments – who in turn are competing with charities for a share of the gaming pie.

SIZE, SCOPE AND BENEFITS TO CHARITABLE GAMING

The government-run gaming market in Canada has become enormous since the 1969 amendment to the Criminal Code. Combined revenues for the Atlantic Lottery Corporation, British Columbia Lottery Corporation, Loto-Quebec, Ontario Lottery and Gaming Corporation and Western Canada Lottery Corporation totaled some $15 billion in 2012 and generated net income of $5.5 billion.[11] By contrast, the charitable gaming market pales in size and is difficult to track and measure given that licensing can be done via hundreds of municipalities and given the fact that some provinces only track the largest events. Indeed, data reporting standards for charitable gaming activities aren't very transparent and vary considerably from province to province.[12] The Canada West Foundation estimated in 2005 that gross charitable gaming in Canada amounted to $1.4 billion or less than 10% of all gambling revenue in that year – both government and charitable.[13]

Looking at charitable lotteries, Charity Intelligence estimated that the total revenue from all charity lotteries in Canada amounted to $750 million in 2012 with net revenues of $200 million after accounting for prizes, marketing costs and lottery operations.[14] Contrast this with the July 6, 2012 and December 2013 Lotto Max lottery jackpots, each which reached $100 million![15]

When one considers that the total revenues that pass through Canadian charities (including governmental revenues) amount to $90 billion annually and that charitable donations by individual Canadians amounted to $8.3 billion in the 2010 tax year, it is clear that relative to the total revenue charities receive, and even to total individual donations made, charitable gaming revenue, estimated at $1.4 billion in 2005, is a relatively modest funding source.[16] So why are charities engaged in lotteries and other gaming activities when the net revenue from these activities is relatively small?

There are a number of answers to this question. First, there is a commonly held belief that people who participate in charitable gaming are unlikely to make donations to the charity in the first place. These "gamers," as they are called, represent a distinct segment of the population and are motivated by the opportunity to win something as opposed to making a gift to support a charity's mission. By engaging in gaming activities a charity has an opportunity to raise important revenue from these individuals.

---

10 Ibid., p. 61.
11 2013 Annual Reports, Atlantic Lottery Corporation, British Columbia Lottery Corporation, Loto-Quebec, Ontario Lottery and Gaming Corporation and Western Canada Lottery Corporation
12 Azmier, Jason J. "Gambling in Canada 2005," Canada West Foundation, June 2005, p. 3.
13 Ibid., p. 3.
14 Cheng, Ernie and Greg Thomson, "Charity Lotteries in Canada," *Charity Intelligence*, November 2013, p. 2.
15 Wikipedia, www.wikipedia.org/wiki/loto_max
16 Lasby, David. "Trends in Individual Giving 1984-2010," *Imagine Canada Research Bulletin*, December 2011, Vol. 15, No. 1, p. 1.

A second important factor is that the majority of gaming revenue is unrestricted in nature meaning that charities can use these unrestricted funds to support programs at their own discretion. Increasingly, charities are finding it difficult to attract unrestricted funding – lottery and charitable gaming provides a vehicle to do so.

A third reason is the opportunity that a charity has to build its brand and awareness of its work through the marketing and promotion that accompanies charitable gaming, particularly lotteries. This allows charities a secondary channel to build their profile without having to incur the added marketing expense as part of their charitable operations and further drive up their cost of fundraising.

There is also the opportunity for a charity to convert "gamers" to become regular donors to the charity or ask them to become donors through the lottery program. Indeed some "gamers" have shown they are very charitably minded too, perhaps having had an experience with the charity as a client, patient or volunteer. At Toronto's Hospital for Sick Children Foundation, reasonable success achieved converting lottery ticket purchasers to become one-time or monthly donors. Over the past 12 lotteries spanning a five-year period, more than 17,000 lottery purchasers have made a one-time donation with total contributions amounting to $752,000, or an average gift of $44. The percentage of purchasers who make one-time donations has continued to grow from a low of 2% of total ticket purchasers to more than 6% today. Almost 600 additional monthly donors were acquired through the lottery program and their cumulative giving over the five-year period totals $685,000. Moreover, very little attrition occurred in the monthly donors acquired through the lottery – they exhibit very strong loyalty. Unfortunately, there is no publicly available research in Canada that documents how successful charities have been in being able to convert gamers to become regular donors.

RISKS ASSOCIATED WITH CHARITABLE GAMING

While charities can derive financial and marketing benefit through charitable gaming it is also not for the faint of heart. There are several risks associated with the enterprise not least of which is the possibility that the charity may lose money.

1. **Slim margins**
   Many forms of charitable gaming operate with slim margins. Consider charitable lotteries as an example. In a November 2013 survey of 30 charity lotteries in *Canada Charity Intelligence* found that on average, 27% of each dollar of ticket revenue is retained by the charity with the remainder used to pay for prizes, marketing and operational expenses.[17] The same study found that at the high end some charities were able to generate a return of between 40-60% of sales while several had returns of less than 15%.[18]

   There are also many examples of charities that have actually *lost funds* through charitable gaming activities, which for some was a one-time experience they were able to weather. However, there have also been cases in which unprofitable gaming activities, particularly large lotteries, practically bankrupted a charity leaving them with severe financial deficits. For example, in 1997, lottery losses at the United Way of Peel Region resulted in a $3.3 million deficit for the organization requiring a bail out from the corporate sector to get the organization back on its feet. The Royal Columbian Hospital Foundation in New Westminster B.C. fell short in a lottery that offered three vacation homes in 2011, losing $3.3 million as well. That Foundation has not held a lottery since.[19]

2. **High marketing and operating costs**
   Many forms of charitable gaming have high marketing and operating costs. This is particularly true of charity lotteries. While provincial government lotteries run continuously around the year, charity lotteries do not. This requires the charity to invest in promotion to remind the public the lottery exists and what the deadlines are to buy tickets.

---

17   Cheng, Ernie and Greg Thomson. (2013). "Charity Lotteries in Canada." *Charity Intelligence*, p. 7.
18   Ibid., p. 5.
19   Ibid., p. 3.

The Criminal Code of Canada does not allow charities to operate any charitable gaming activities, including lotteries, "on or through a computer" meaning that charities are required to process and activate all sales manually and send customers their tickets by mail, adding to their lottery operating costs. The February 2014 federal budget proposes to amend the Criminal Code to permit charities to conduct some aspects of lotteries through computer technology including the use of e-commerce for purchasing, processing and issuing of lottery tickets. The budget also confirmed that it will engage in consultations with the provinces and territories on the proposed amendment to the Criminal Code so the actual timing of implementing these changes is unknown.

3. **Stability of gaming revenues**

   Another risk relates to the dependability or stability of charitable gaming revenues. In a 2000 study undertaken by the Canada West Foundation of Canadian Charities, 36% of respondents that utilize charitable gaming said that it was their most important source of revenue with another 24% indicating it was their second most important source of revenue.[20]

   A 2012 study undertaken by Deloitte on the charitable lottery market found that charitable lottery revenue accounted for 41.9% of Heart & Stroke Foundation's total fundraising activity net income, 36.2% for the Children's Hospital of Eastern Ontario and 23.8% for the Princess Margaret Hospital Foundation.[21] A high degree of dependency on charitable gaming revenue creates vulnerability for charities if, in a given year, they fail to meet their gaming targets. Indeed, in the Canada West Foundation survey only 12% of respondents thought that charitable gaming provided a "very stable" source of revenue.[22] Overall respondents were split, with 42% suggesting gambling revenue is stable and 42% feeling it is unstable.[23] The authors of the Canada West Foundation survey conclude that …"gambling is a very tenuous source of income (for charities). Factors beyond the control of the charitable sector limit the utility of gambling revenues in the development of long-term plans. Public dissatisfaction, political change and external competition each suggest that it would be imprudent for organizations to be too dependent on this revenue source."[24]

4. **Reduction of other charitable funding**

   Another risk is the fear that increased charitable gaming revenues may lead to reductions in other sources of charity funding including individual donations. The nature of the relationship between individual donations and charitable gaming is unclear. As noted above, conventional thinking has been that people that participate in charitable gaming are doing so primarily as "gamers" and would not otherwise be donors to the charity. On the other hand, as governments and charities publically tie gambling activities to worthwhile causes funded through gaming proceeds, charitable gaming may be seen as an alternate form of donation in the minds of some individuals. Moreover, as overall gaming revenue increases across the country, both by governments and charities, a relative decrease in disposable income of individual gamers must occur. This in turn diminishes the income pool from which to make charitable donations.

5. **Legal challenges**

   There is also the risk of something going wrong from a legal perspective, which can include everything from not obtaining the necessary licensing, to not fulfilling the prizing obligations, to fraudulent activities. Good planning and appropriate oversight to ensure compliance substantially reduces the risk. But it also requires charity Boards of Directors and staff to have a thorough understanding of the regulatory requirements related to charitable

---

20 Azmier, Jason J. and Robert Roach. (2000). "The Ethics of Charitable Gambling: A Survey," *Gambling in Canada Research Report No. 10*, Canada West Foundation, p. 10.
21 Deloitte Analysis of Ontario Charity Market, Report to SickKids Foundation, unpublished.
22 Azmier, Jason J. and Robert Roach. (2000). "The Ethics of Charitable Gambling: A Survey." *Gambling in Canada Research Report No. 10*, Canada West Foundation, p. 11.
23 Ibid., p. 11.
24 Ibid., p. 7.

gaming and effective mechanisms to monitor their charitable gaming activities.

6. **Societal issues**

Another risk to be considered is the role that charitable gaming may play in contributing to problem gambling and the impact of the behaviour of individuals with a gambling impulse disorder has upon themselves, their families and communities. A 2012 study prepared for the Ontario Problem Gambling Research Centre and the Ontario Ministry of Health and Long Term Care by Robert J. Williams, Rachel A. Volberg and Rhys Stevens found that the standard rate of problem gambling ranges from 0.8% in Ontario to 6.5% in New Brunswick with the average rate across all provinces of 2.4%.[25] Azmier in his 2000 Canada West Foundation study estimated that 3-5% of Canadians suffer from a gambling related disorder.[26]

Other studies have come to similar conclusions about charity lotteries, specifically that they are considered relatively low risk for gambling addictions.[27] Moreover, charity lotteries do not have the features consistent with common addictive traits (low-cost, high game/player interactivity and instant or quick feedback). Furthermore, the relative high cost of charity lottery ticket packages and the fact that buyers must wait several months between ticket purchase and final draw make it a lower risk form of problem gambling compared to other gaming activity. Notwithstanding these findings, charities do need to be mindful of this issue.

7. **Regressive taxation concerns**

There is also the concern that gambling, including charitable gaming, is a very regressive form of taxation with a greater proportion of gaming revenue, including charitable gaming, coming from lower income Canadians.[28] Regressive taxes are those that take a greater proportional share from the poor than from the wealthy with revenue that is lost by lower-income gamblers likely to have a greater impact on their ability to meet basic needs than that lost by wealthier gamblers. Karen Hayward writing in the Genuine Progress Index for Atlantic Canada notes that economists reached a consensus as early as the mid-1970's that gambling taxes were "overwhelmingly regressive," and twice as regressive as sales taxes.[29] Several studies have found that people in low-income brackets spend roughly the same absolute amount of money each year gambling as those in middle and upper-income brackets. However, the percentage of their income spent by low-income earners on gambling is higher than among those who are more affluent.[30] The implication of course is that revenue lost by lower-income gamblers is likely to have a greater impact on their ability to meet basic needs than that lost by wealthier gamblers.

THE ETHICS OF CHARITABLE GAMING

Problem gambling, regressive taxation, vulnerability and dependency on charitable gaming have called into question for many whether charitable gaming is an ethical activity for charities to engage in. As Bob Wyatt, Executive Director of the Muttart Foundation noted in a 2010 article in the Philanthropist, "...to the sector's discredit, few charities are raising the alarm about the extent to which gambling is financing "quality of life" issues across the country. I understand their reluctance, given their need to find money to deliver their programs. But it means that we aren't having the

---

25 Williams, Robert J., A. Volberg, and Rhys M.G. Stevens. (2012). *"The Population Prevalence of Problem Gambling: Methodological Influences, Standardized Rates, Jurisdictional Differences and Worldwide Trends."* Report Prepared for the Ontario Problem Gambling Centre & The Ontario Ministry of Health and Long Term Care, p. 42.

26 Azmier, Jason J. (2000). "Canadian Gambling Behaviours and Attitudes: Summary Report," *Gambling in Canada Research Report No. 8*, Canada West Foundation, p. 23.

27 Per Binde, *"What Are The Most Harmful Forms of Gambling? Analyzing Problem Gambling Prevalence Surveys*, Centre for Public Sector Research, CEFOS Working Paper 12, 2011, p. 18.

28 Azmier, Jason J. (2000). "Canadian Gambling Behaviours and Attitudes: Summary Report," *Gambling in Canada Research Report No. 8*, Canada West Foundation, p. 23.

29 Hayward, Karen. (2004). *"The Costs and Benefits of Gaming: A Literature Review with Emphasis on Nova Scotia,"* GPI Atlantic, p. 15.

30 Clotfelter, Charles T. and Philip J. Cook, (1990). "On the Economics of State Lotteries," *Journal of Economic Perspectives*, Volume 4, Number 4, p. 112.

debate about whether gambling should be the source of "quality of life" funding."[31]

The Canada West Foundation study, referenced above, found that charitable gaming does create an ethical issue for charities. Sixty-six per cent of the charity respondents to their survey did not report using charitable gaming between 1995-1999.[32] When asked why their organization did not use charitable gaming as a method, almost two-thirds of respondents said that ethical concerns were a primary factor.[33] Interestingly, this number dropped to 34% for non-religious charities and rose to 90% for religious organizations.[34] Board members are the most likely stakeholder group to voice concerns over ethical issues, however there were also high percentages of staff and volunteers that were concerned, suggesting that charities have a generally high level of awareness of the ethical trade-offs of charitable gaming.[35]

While there is little in the way on data about Canadians' attitudes toward gambling, what does exist suggest there is general support for it. Another Canada West Foundation Study, "*Canadian Gambling Behaviour and Attitudes: Summary Report,*" found that 63% of Canadians agreed that gambling is acceptable on the whole.[36] It is seen as reducing the overall tax burden, providing a source of entertainment, has economic development benefits, and funds worthwhile causes. In fact, when asked "who should primarily benefit from the proceeds of gambling," 43% of respondents in the Canada West Foundation study thought that charities should be the primary beneficiaries, more than twice the number of individuals that indicated that provincial governments should benefit (17%) and well beyond the support for all three levels of government combined (28%).[37]

Respondents were also asked the question of "what is the best way to fund charities in Canada?" Interestingly, respondent's views were split between individual donations (21%), corporate donations (20%) and charitable gaming (19%).[38]

The two Canada West Foundation surveys suggest that:
i) there is general support for gaming in Canada;
ii) that charities are seen as legitimate beneficiaries of gaming revenue;
iii) that gaming revenue is equally acceptable as individual or corporate donations, and
iv) that ethical concerns tend to be greatest from those stakeholders associated with the charities – board members, staff and other volunteers.

Unfortunately the Canada West Foundation studies, and most statistics on charitable gaming in this country are woefully out of date. Have public attitudes and charity concerns about charitable gaming changed? What is the true scope of charitable gaming activities in Canada? What impact is charitable gaming having on other forms of charitable giving? We really don't know, which underscores Mr. Wyatt's conclusion that there is no real debate occurring in this country on the merits of charitable gaming.

What is certain is that gaming involves both reward and risk to charities. The reward is the opportunity to generate substantial, mainly unrestricted revenue to support a charity's mission and to help further build the charity's awareness in the community. There are also risks – financial, legal, and ethical, that if realized can result in significant reputational damage for the charity if something goes wrong. Public and donor confidence can be shaken if a charity loses funds from its gaming activities. This risk is amplified if the charity has to subsidize any losses from the use of other donor funds or needs to curtail its programs or other funding commitments. In November 2013, CTV's investigative television program W5 aired a story that questioned the efficacy of charity lotteries following Charity Intelligence's examination of charity lotteries in Canada. Whether one agrees with some of the information presented by Charity Intelligence or W5, the fact is that public reports like this may impact the reputation of individual charities and the sector as a whole.

---

31 Bourgeois, Don and Bob Wyatt, (2010). "Charitable Gaming: Is it Worth the Gamble." *The Philanthropist*, Vol. 23, No. 3, p. 407.
32 Azmier, Jason J. and Robert Roach, (2000). "The Ethics of Charitable Gambling: A Survey." *Gambling in Canada Research Report No. 10*, Canada West Foundation, p. 9.
33 Ibid., p. 12
34 Ibid., p. 12
35 Ibid., p. 13
36 Azmier, Jason J. (2000) "Canadian Gambling Behaviours and Attitudes: Summary Report," *Gambling in Canada Research Report No. 8*, Canada West Foundation, p. 21.
37 Ibid., p.18.
38 Ibid., p.19

BUSINESS MODEL

If a charity engages in gaming it needs to understand that the model for this work is fundamentally different than the operation of other fundraising programs. Gaming activities, and in particular charity lotteries, is a business/social enterprise. Those who buy lottery, break-open or raffle tickets are customers, not donors, as they do not receive a charitable tax receipt. These programs operate on a self-funded basis with the cost of tickets paying for prizes, promotional activities and administration with net proceeds (profits) being returned to the charity (with the rare exception when a charity loses funds on gaming activity).

There is also specialized expertise required to operate these programs whether administered by the charity itself with dedicated staff or through the use of charitable gaming consultants. There is a whole science to establishing ticket prices, prizing, the odds of winning, and the timing and scope of promotional activity. Government regulation limits the amount of innovation that can be brought to bear in charitable gaming activities, although this is gradually changing as evidenced by the proposed changes to the Criminal Code to allow for certain e-commerce activities and in the Province of Ontario, the recent ability of charities to hold a 50/50 draw in conjunction with their charitable lotteries.

CONCLUSION

Gaming has become an important and generally accepted form of revenue generation for charities. There are both benefits and risks to the enterprise, which must be carefully weighed by the charity and its Board of Directors. The more dependent a charity is on charitable gaming revenue the more vulnerable the charity is, should gaming operations experience financial losses. Charitable gaming requires a high degree of sophistication, specialized expertise, sound planning, analysis and evaluation. Finally, the charitable sector as a whole would benefit from better and more current data on the size and scope of charitable gaming in the country, public attitudes to charitable gaming (and gambling as a whole), the role of problem gambling and other related ethical concerns.

Finally, as the CEO of a charity that does operate a charitable lottery I offer this advice:

- Ensure you understand all of the benefits and risks associated with charitable gaming.
- Fully engage your Board of Directors in ensuring they understand the benefits and risks.
- Understand the market in which you will conduct your gaming activities and the competitive environment, both government-run and other charitable gaming.
- Consider undertaking a feasibility study and market research to assess the local market's willingness to support your charitable gaming activities and the implications this might have to your other fundraising programs. If you are already operating gaming activities, invest in periodic market research to understand any shifts in the competitive landscape or changes in consumer behaviour.
- Understand the factors that motivate consumers to participate in your charity gaming activities – the relationship between cause, prizing, ticket pricing, odds of winning.
- Determine your charity's tolerance around its dependence on charitable gaming.
- Invest in the proper expertise to guide your charitable gaming activities, whether that be through your own staff, external consultants or a combination of both.
- Ensure you have a rigorous planning process, effective controls, effective monitoring and reporting systems, and evaluation systems.
- Ensure you have the capacity and necessary resources to market and promote your charitable gaming activities.
- Be prepared to test different variables in your gaming programs and evaluate their success (e.g. price points, prize offerings, marketing mix).
- Prepare a crisis communications plan in the event something goes wrong with your charity gaming programs.
- Understand how charitable gaming should be reported in your financial statements.
- Celebrate successes and learn from disappointments.

ADDITIONAL RESOURCES

Books, Articles and Reports

▶ AZMIER, JASON J. (2000). *Canadian Gambling Behaviour and Attitudes: Summary Report.* The Canada West Foundation.

▶ AZMIER, JASON J. (2005). *Gambling in Canada 2005: Statistics and Context.* The Canada West Foundation.

▶ AZMIER, JASON J. AND PAUL ROACH, (2000). *The Ethics of Charitable Gambling: A Survey.* Canada West Foundation.

▶ BOURGEOIS, DON. "Charitable Gaming: The Legal Context." *The Philanthropist,* Volume 15, No. 4.

▶ BOURGEOIS, DONALD. (1999). *The Law of Charitable Gaming and Casinos.* Toronto: Butterworth's.

▶ BOURGEOIS, DON AND BOB WYATT. (2010). "Charitable Gaming: Is it worth the Gamble." *The Philanthropist,* Volume 23.

▶ CHENG, ERNIE AND GREG THOMSON. (2003). "Charity Lotteries in Canada Charity." Intelligence Canada.

▶ CLOTFELTER, CHARLES AND PHILLIP COOK. (1990). "On the Economics of State Lotteries." *The Journal of Economic Perspectives,* Volume 4, Number 4.

ABOUT THE AUTHOR

Ted Garrard, MA

Ted Garrard is President & CEO of SickKids Foundation which supports one of the world's leading centres for pediatric care, research and learning – the Hospital for Sick Children. The Foundation raises more than $125 million annually, has endowments valued in excess of $900 million and is the largest non-governmental funder of children's health in Canada. Prior to joining the Foundation Ted served as Vice-President, External at The University of Western Ontario from 1996-2009, where he led campaigns that raised more than $600 million. He also spent 13 years at United Way of Toronto in a variety of roles including leading all fundraising operations. Ted is Chair of the Canadian Children's Hospital Foundation Executives, a director of Children's Miracle Network, past Chair of Imagine Canada, Past Chair of United Way of London-Middlesex, a past director of United Way/Centraide Canada, and a past director of the Canadian Council for Advancement in Education. He received the Association of Fundraising Professional's Outstanding Fundraising Executive Award in 1997, was named one of Canada's Top 40 Under 40 in 1998, and in 2014 was named Outstanding Communicator by the International Association of Business Communicators (IABC).

CHAPTER 11

SPONSORSHIP

BRENT BAROOTES, BA

When we think "sponsorship" in fundraising, we are sometimes not quite sure what we mean. Most of us would understand the difference between an annual campaign and a capital campaign, or a major gift and a planned gift, but when it comes to sponsorship, many of us think differently.

read more...

For some, sponsorship is putting up a logo and sending a letter of thanks. For others, it is just another word for a donation coming from a corporation, as opposed to an individual. For still others, it is an integrated marketing channel.

This chapter will provide you with a sponsorship reality check by:

- defining sponsorship versus philanthropy, grants, and underwriting;
- helping you determine how much annual revenue can be achieved;
- outlining what you must determine from your sponsorship prospects and understand how to obtain that information; and
- providing the essentials of building a custom sponsorship proposal.

TERMINOLOGY

From the beginning, it is important to understand the difference between philanthropy and sponsorship. So far this book has covered the history of fundraising, provided an understanding organizational culture, political fundraising, and much more. Now you will delve into some specific areas of fundraising that align or cross over with sponsorship; specifically cause related marketing, and to some extent, philanthropic naming, which will be differentiated in a moment. But first, what is sponsorship?

Sponsorship occurs when a cash or in-kind dollar amount is given by a business, brand, or company (not an individual, which is a donation) to a rights holder or sponsorship selling property including a charity, cause, non-profit, sport organization, municipality, government agency—anyone that sells sponsorship (be it for a golf tournament or naming a building) in exchange for the *commercial exploitation* of that rights holder or property.

I know the term "exploitation" sounds harsh, but it is not. It clearly defines that the sponsor will give the rights holder cash, and in exchange, they get marketing exposure and access to an audience for that same value. They give you $20,000, and you give them sponsorship marketing exposure worth $20,000. It is a business transaction in which each party receives a tangible benefit and the government (Canada Revenue Agency- CRA) deems it to be a fair exchange. This is different from a gift.

Gift vs Sponsorship

The CRA says a gift occurs when a company or individual gives money with no expectation of anything in return other than a tax receipt. In fact, you cannot legally give a donor tickets to your gala, a playing position in a golf tournament, or a banner hanging at an event if the value exceeds $75. Once the company receives a "benefit" in return, it is no longer a gift, but rather a business marketing or sponsorship transaction. The CRA does note that you can subtract any additional amount above the $75 from the charitable amount and be fine, but then it is not a gift nor a sponsorship, but rather just a purchase of goods or services.

To further illustrate this point: if a sponsor gives your organization $2500 and asks for a tax receipt, you cannot give it if they received benefits in return. For example, if you provide them with space for a banner at your event, four gala tickets, a speaking opportunity, an ad in the program, an article on the website and a chance to sample their product and the value of all those benefits came to $2000 you would have been providing them with "value" for $2000. But if they gave you $2500, then you could issue them a tax receipt for the $500 difference.

What about naming rights on buildings? If a building, room, or area is named for a person as opposed to a company, how is that different? In Chapter 15, Vincent Duckworth focuses specifically on philanthropic naming; those for individuals as opposed to companies. When a company (or a Foundation or association) names a room, building, or area (the "CP Rail Alumni Centre," for example), this is a sponsorship. No exceptions. When a company gets the exposure, then that is a sponsorship. They are receiving value in exchange for the money given. It should be noted that if the company does not "ask" for the recognition but rather is offered, it then can still be construed as a gift. The litmus test is to ask the company "what if we withdrew the naming rights, are you still OK with providing the gift?" If the response is yes, then it is a gift, if the donor changes their mind on the gift then it truly was about the recognition and not a gift but rather a sponsorship. Further along in this chapter, we will identify how you determine that value. This is important because sometimes the total contribution may be $500,000, but the "sponsorship marketing value" is only $300,000 as determined by an outside third party agency. Then the corporation or entity making the investment is eligible for a donation, charitable tax receipt for the balance, $200,000.

Cause Marketing vs Sponsorship

Cause marketing is also a form of corporate sponsorship. The company aligns itself with your cause to sell more of its "stuff." It is a business exchange. The company provides you with money in order to "exploit" your cause or brand. They feel that, if they are seen donating to you, they will sell more products. The critical thing here is to ensure that you get your fee up-front. You provide the cause and they provide the marketing! They must spend money to market the relationship. It cannot be only you doing the marketing. If the business doesn't do any marketing, then don't do it. If they don't pay you a set fee up-front, don't do it.

INTEGRATION OF SPONSORSHIP INTO FUND DEVELOPMENT

How does sponsorship fit into your overall fund development program?

Is there a conflict?

No!

Sponsorship works well with any integrated fund development program and traditional philanthropic campaign, be it annual, capital, or otherwise. If your major gift people are working with a company or major donor who owns or runs a company, there may be an opportunity for the company to be involved with you as well as the decision maker who makes a major gift. Likewise, if the sponsorship person in your organization is working with a company and the president or owner wants to make a gift, or there is an opportunity for staff to raise funds or make individual gifts, you can enhance a sponsorship program with a donor program. For example, Harvard Communications was a major sponsor of the Canada Games in Regina which was put on partially by the University of Regina. As a result of the sponsorship experience and other factors, the owner of Harvard Communications later gave a naming gift to the University because he was able to better appreciate the role of the university in the community.

Another example is the Enerflex sponsorship of the Enerflex Walk for MS in Alberta. The company became the title sponsor of the event, but employees also rose to the opportunity by individually raising money for the event. These two examples demonstrate how a corporate sponsorship can flow into donation opportunities down the road.

The **reality check** is that you must work with the prospect (donor or sponsor) to discover their needs and goals (philanthropy, driving business, or both) and then build the program that fits.

How much money can you generate?

This is the big question. In the business world and in the world of sponsorship marketing, the number of dollars you can receive is finite. It is important to remember that sponsorship is often called "the annual campaign at major gift levels." This is because the annual investment by a sponsor is often at the major gift level as opposed to the annual gift level, but they will give (invest) year after year if the value they receive is delivering results. There is a **reality check** here, though. You must first determine *what* you have to sell and then the related values.

ASSETS AND INVENTORY

In the sponsorship world, we use specific terminology just as in the philanthropic world. Let's define a few words.

Assets, or benefits, are what you and your organization have available to sell. The asset may be the naming right for a room or hallway; it may be the right for the sponsor to have their logo on your website; or it may be that the asset is the opportunity for the sponsor to have a walk-on part in your theatre company production.

When you assemble all your assets in a list, it is called an **inventory** of assets.

Finally, the dollar amount assigned to each asset in the inventory is called the **asset value**. The value is what the market says it is worth, just like the suggested manufacturers retail price on the window of a new car. It is the market value. The sponsor may not buy for that price. You may have to negotiate as you would for a car or house purchase. If you are the seller, you know what the market should bear when you conduct an accredited valuation of your assets.

Inventory development and valuation
Undertaking an asset inventory development and valuation is much like doing a feasibility study. This step is essential in any sponsorship program. A sponsorship inventory is a listing of all the assets or benefits that you have to sell. It provides you with a list of such assets so you know what you have to sell, and ultimately what each asset is worth. Then, when you go to build a proposal, you can offer the specific assets or benefits that will meet the needs of the prospect as well as build a package that is within the sponsor's budget.

You can do an asset inventory yourself or have a qualified agency do it for you. Your six steps to success in the development of a sponsorship program are:
1. Determine what you have to sell.
2. Determine market value of each and every asset.
3. From steps 1 and 2, determine what you can realistically achieve in annual sales and establish a sales process (where the responsibility of sales and fulfilment will lie).
4. Seek senior management / executive approval and then board approval.
5. Develop your sponsorship policy and get approval.
6. Hit the street and do discovery sessions, build proposals, close business, fulfil on what you promised, deliver fulfilment reports and then renew!

To build a comprehensive inventory of assets you need to look deep inside your organization and make a list of everything—yes *everything* you could sell. That means everything from logo exposure on your website and marketing materials to naming of programs and areas. You also need to include all assets associated with your social and digital marketing programs. In addition, your brand has value, so it should be included too. Will the sponsor be permitted to use your logo? Will they be allowed to use it all year; only at certain times of the year; overall with your organization, or only with a certain event or program? Don't worry about the sacred cows that your board will never let you sell or the fact that you have "never sold that before." Make a list of everything. Later on, you can determine if it will stay on the shelf or be removed.

While you are building your inventory of sponsorable assets, look beyond your fundraising events. Usually the assets that are most valuable to a sponsor are those aligned with the programs you operate for your users/clientele. In over 25 years of developing inventories, I have seldom seen an organization that cannot identity *at least 125* unique and individual assets and never has the list been below 75 items. It is often a **reality check** for organizations to see that their inventory of assets can be four or five times what they had originally identified at first blush.

Here is a sample of some assets that such an inventory may identify:
- Naming right of a building
- Naming right of a program
- Opportunity to speak at an event
- Opportunity to hang a banner at an event
- Venue signage
- Press conference inclusion
- Logo on web site
- Article about sponsor in newsletter
- Article about sponsor product in newsletter
- Article about sponsor on website
- Article about sponsor product on website
- Naming of a page on a website
- Presenting sponsor
- Official supplier
- Sponsor mentioned in Tweet
- Sponsor mentioned on a FaceBook post
- Opportunity to sample product
- Sponsor logo on your vehicle
- Sponsor logo on any advertising
- Sponsor logo on brochures
- Tickets to events
- Opportunity to meet celebrities associated to your organization
- And so on…

Once you have all the assets listed, you need to take the next step. This is to determine the real market value for each one. There are some old-fashioned ways that this has been done, but since you are reading this book, you are smart enough never to have used any of those methods!

Some people have used such methods as "I price it based on what I think I can get from the prospect." Others have used the method of "I will charge what my competition is charging," even if the quality of the events are not the same, but you think your golf tournament is as good as theirs! Finally, there is that "let me pick a number out of the sky and assign a value that I think it is worth."

Times have changed. Companies are looking for an audited, real market value for the assets they are buying. They want to know the real value, not what you *think* you can get from them as a sponsor. There are companies that do valuation of sponsorship assets for a living and these are the folks who can determine, as a third party outside your organization, what the value of each and every asset you have identified is worth. Those valuations identify the real market value of the assets you are offering. Better to be accurate from the start than ask for a number that is far from the real market value.

But how do you determine real market value yourself? How do you know that the value of a sponsor's logo on your web site can be calculated to the penny through the formula of "number of unique users to your website multiplied by about one third of a cent?" Here's an example:

The value of the sponsor's logo on your full page ad in the newspaper thanking everyone for participating in your event is worth, at most, 5% of the cash value of the ad. So, if the newspaper ad is worth $5,000, the real market value of the exposure to the sponsor is $250. Through industry accepted formulae and metrics, you can determine to the penny (not like we have them anymore in Canada) the value of the assets or proposal overall.

For more details on how many common assets are valued, please see **Appendix 1 - Inventory Asset Valuation Formulas Matrix** at the end of this chapter.

UNQUALIFIED VS. QUALIFIED PROSPECTS

Now that you fully understand the meaning of sponsorship versus philanthropy, and you know how to build your own inventory of sponsorable assets *and* you know how to use valuation formulae to determine real market value - you are ready to start talking sponsorship!

Without knowing what you have to sell and its value, you really cannot begin talking with prospects successfully. When prospecting, it is important to remember that, just because a bank made billions of dollars last year does not make it the right sponsor for your organization. To maximize revenue for your organization, you must determine the difference between unqualified prospects and qualified prospects. Qualified prospects are those companies that:

1. align with your mission;
2. have the money to invest; and
3. will benefit from the association.

To begin with, it's important to look for prospects that align with the organization's mission. If you have a policy of not being associated with alcohol, there is no sense adding a beer company to your prospect list. If you are a Christian faith-based organization, the company must recognize that and be willing to align with your faith.

Once you have determined if alignment is there, you will need to determine if the prospect has money to invest. If they have limited budgets or do not market themselves, they are more likely an unqualified prospect. An excellent way to determine capacity to invest, is to note who is advertising in newspapers; magazines; and on radio and TV. You know that they have money to spend on marketing because they are already spending. All you need to do is show them how, if they spend with your organization as a sponsor, they will receive a better return on their investment than if they spend the same amount with the local newspaper or radio station.

That leads to the final ways to determine an unqualified prospect from a qualified prospect. This is also the critical element that separates a sponsorship prospect from a philanthropic prospect. You have to determine if you have something the company needs—if you own (your sponsorable assets) something that a prospect needs, wants, or will help them be more successful in their business.

For example, if you can deliver a senior audience aged 60+ and the prospect is a nursing home, then that nursing home may benefit from being associated with you. Or, if you run an event that attracts thousands of participants from over 1,000km away, then an airline might be a prospect as people have to get to your city. Or, if you are a dance organization skewed toward females, with most of your dancers aged 10-16, you may want to prospect companies that produce or sell products to girls aged 10-16. You also need to know that, at this age, girls cannot get to dance on their own, and there are competitions, etc. Their parents (probably aged 40-55) with good household incomes (because participating in dance is not cheap) are an audience you can probably deliver.

Many brands and companies are seeking access to these types of customers so don't be fooled. Many charitable organizations think that their mission is the viewpoint from which they should build their prospect list. The **reality check** here is that it is the audience you deliver that is essential, not your mission.

AUDIENCE VS MISSION

Your mission must align with the prospect, but it is not the driving force. Let me explain.

If we were the national soccer association, we might first think of SportChek as a prospect. Sure, they sell sporting equipment and seek to reach soccer players as well as their parents. But what if you were to think about a donut/coffee shop as a prospect? The initial thought may be "no." Donuts are unhealthy and kids don't drink coffee. But if you look more deeply, it is not about the product the donut shop sells. It is about the audience it seeks to reach. It wants to reach families on the run, families with small children, and build a relationship with them. The donut shop wants the soccer parents to buy their child a donut as a treat after the game, grab a coffee for themselves, sit, relax, and chat about the game. If they do this, often the parents come to spend more time (perhaps in the morning on the way to work) at that donut shop because they have become used to going there.

Also, the families will feel an affinity with the donut/coffee shop because it "makes soccer happen" for their child. At the same time, the little soccer player becomes exposed to and learns that this donut shop has great treats. It is where "we always went after soccer games." They too will develop a brand affinity for this donut shop. So, perhaps Tim Horton's doesn't look like a fit to begin with, but when we look at what Tim's is trying to achieve, it is a perfect fit. Thus, we have "Timbits Soccer," "Timbits Hockey," and so on.

Building on this same example, few would think that a women's clothing store would be a soccer prospect. But when you look at it, the women's clothing store that is fashion conscious and appeals to women aged 25-54 is a perfect fit with soccer. The parent most closely associated with soccer is the "soccer mom." What a match! Hence, Winners invested in soccer even though it doesn't sell cleats, soccer balls, jerseys, or soccer shorts.

GETTING THE MEETING

Once we have determined who the prospect is, we next need to determine how to get the meeting. The great thing about sponsorship is that the money can come from multiple departments in a company. Unlike a philanthropic gift that comes from the CSR or Community Investment (donations) department, sponsorship revenue can come from the CSR, donations, sales, marketing, or Human Resources departments. All of them invest in sponsorship marketing. This means you have a great chance to make inroads with a prospect.

Like any prospecting process, find a champion. That champion may be someone from your donor list who works at the company, your friend from the book club, or the fellow you play hockey with or sit next to in church. The goal is to find a champion who believes in you or your organization's mission and will help you access the right people.

Remember a big **reality check** here. You are not approaching the company to ask for money for your organization. You are not asking for a donation. You are meeting to see how you can help them, not how they can help you. This will be the biggest paradigm shift between philanthropic giving and sponsorship. You are meeting with them to find out more about their business and how you can help them. You have assets. You have an audience. You have value. You are there to provide an opportunity for them to reach and position themselves with your audience. You are there to provide them with a marketing channel. In turn, they want your assets and opportunities, and will pay to get them. You are there to help them, not for them to help you. And when you help them, they pay you cash money. That is the cash that runs your organization!

When you remember that you have something they want, you are in the driver's seat. If they don't want to pay fair market value (which you have already determined in your sponsorship inventory asset valuation) for what you have to offer, move on and visit their competition. Don't undervalue and sell your assets for less than they are worth.

PROSPECT DISCOVERY

Your first several meetings with the prospect are all about learning about them. You should never ask for money on the first or second visit. You are there to learn. Find out more about their business. Find out what they really sell (Kodak sold memories, not cameras, film, or processing); determine where they spend their marketing dollars today (radio, social media, TV, etc.) and how much. Learn about their corporate culture, goals, and objectives. What other sponsorships do they invest in, and why? How are those successful, or not?

In the first several meetings, you are just asking questions. Once you have all the answers you need (such as budget, goals and objectives, timelines, etc.), you can build a proposal. Don't build or present a proposal until you have all the questions answered.

Here is what you are trying to determine:

- If they do other sponsorships; ask what they do, why they do it and how they measure success with it?
- Try to determine their budgets
- How do they measure success overall and within specific programs?
- What are their business goals and objectives? Do they need to:
  - generate leads
  - drive store traffic
  - engage staff with the cause
  - bolster public image
  - generate new recruitment leads
  - build brand
- How do they presently:
  - Engage staff
  - Recruit staff
  - Market products
  - Support community
- What is their fiscal year?
- When do they go into budget planning?
- Who is their competition?
- What differentiates them from their competition?

Once you have all the information you need, you are ready to build a customized proposal.

The **reality check** here is to never to build a proposal until you know all the answers; are guaranteed a "yes" as an answer to the amount of money you have agreed upon, and have determined what assets they will receive in exchange.

This is different from philanthropic fundraising with major gifts where the "ask" is often part of the discussion. With sponsorship, a business transaction in exchange of goods (exposure) for cash, you need to have all the answers *before* writing the proposal. Once you have the answers, then you can write the proposal and close it immediately. There should be no further objections once you present the proposal — it should be a formality in preparation for sign off.

CUSTOM PROPOSAL DEVELOPMENT

Reality check! Gold, silver, and bronze stock packages died with the dinosaurs.

The number one complaint from sponsors in the annual *Canadian Sponsorship Landscape Study* is that organizations selling sponsorship bring stock proposals versus customized proposals. They key to success is presenting a customized sponsorship proposal. We see those gold, silver, and bronze packages too often. If the gold is $25,000, the silver is $15,000, and the bronze is $5,000, what do we present when the sponsor says, "I have $10,000 to spend"? Do we present the $5,000 and leave money on the table, or the silver and have the sponsor say, "Sorry, I only have $10,000, so I cannot buy your $15,000 opportunity."

Here is another example to consider. A 25-28 year old woman walks into a car dealership. She has a three- and five-year-old with her. What does the salesperson immediately show her? Yes, the minivan. What does she do? She walks out. If the salesperson had taken the time to talk with her and ask about her needs, budget, etc., he would have discovered those were not her children, but rather a niece and nephew she was sitting for the day. She had $120,000 cash to spend on a Viper, but the sale was lost because the salesperson sold what he thought the prospect wanted instead of asking the questions that matter.

It is the same way we would cultivate a major gift donor; determine their desires and what makes them happy about your organization, then make the "right ask for the right amount at the right time to the right person by the right person." To be successful, sponsorship must use the same approach.

Remember, sponsorship is like an annual campaign at major gift levels. Too often, we learn from sponsors that they don't want a table at our gala, but we put it in anyway, either because "that is what is in the silver package" or "we need to fill the room." If they don't want the gala tickets, they won't send people and your room won't be full anyway! Perhaps they want an extra banner, that walk-on part in the play, or the right to sample product. You need to custom-build each proposal to ensure that the sponsor gets what they need, not what you want to give them.

If the discovery sessions are done correctly, you will know their business goals and objectives, the culture of their organization, and how much they have allocated to invest with you. You go back and look at your inventory of assets and choose the specific ones that will help them achieve their goal. You determine if it is in the budget range. Then, you prepare the proposal offering them the assets they need at the right investment level.

When you build a customized proposal, it is about the prospect, not your organization.

Typically, I see sponsorship proposals that might be ten pages. Nine pages are about the organization—how many children they have saved from the street, that their building was opened by the Queen, that they have been around for 80 years and that they have fundraising costs of only 2%, and so on. It seems that most sponsorship proposals are all about *you*! That needs to change.

Whether the typical proposal is 10 pages, 50 pages, or 5 pages, you only get one page about you. That's right …. only one page about you! What the prospect really cares about is how many more burgers you can sell for them, how you can make their employees feel better about the company, how you can help provide a much-needed PR boost, or what you audience you can deliver for sampling a new product. The prospect cares about themselves and what you can do for them. They really don't care about you or your organization. If they were buying a newspaper ad, they would not care who opened the building, or how many printing presses or employees they have. They would care about how their investment in that newspaper ad will deliver great ROI for them. The same goes for you. Custom-build a proposal that focuses on them and not you. Give them the assets they need to succeed. Then close the deal!

CLOSING THE DEAL

One of the most often forgotten stages of sponsorship is the "after-sale." In the world of sponsorship, there are two key elements to ensure take place after the deal is signed. One is fulfilment. This is a sponsorship word for stewardship.

Fulfilment is critical. This is where you as an organization need to deliver on all you promised. The speaking engagement for the sponsor… you need to make it happen. The tickets you promised must be delivered. The logo on your web site needs to appear on schedule. Delivering the opportunity to provide a coupon to all your donors or including an article in your newsletter are all critical to fulfillment. Failure to deliver on these things means the program won't work. The goals of the sponsor will not be achieved. This, in turn, means no potential renewal.

Fulfilment is more than a thank you letter and a lunch. It is staying in touch throughout the year, leading up to and after the event to learn what is new with your sponsor's company—what has changed and how you need to adjust their program to succeed all the time. Sponsorship is truly about relationships. The **reality check** is that it is not about pitching a package and waiting 11 months to go back and ask again. Real sponsorships with real results and long-term major gift level dollars are the result of a relationship between you and the sponsor.

Part of that relationship development is assisting your sponsor to *activate* on their investment with you. Activation refers to the money the sponsor spends above and beyond what they have invested with you to make the program work for both you and them. Sometimes, this is two or three times more than they are investing with you. If they spend $10,000 on a sponsorship, they should probably spend an additional $20-$30,000 to make the sponsorship work. This is sometimes hard for a charity, sport organization, non-profit, or membership association to understand. Many of us think (at least in the philanthropy world) that you need to get all that money, say $40,000, and it needs to come to you so you can fulfil your mission. In a philanthropic ask, that would be true. In a sponsorship situation, it is not. The "activation" dollars they spend are what fuel the program to be successful.

EXAMPLE 1 -

Let's use cause marketing as an example. If they agree to pay you a fee of ten cents for each stuffed bear they sell, but the bear manufacturer does not spend marketing money to promote the availability of the bear and the fact that a percentage of every sale goes to your cause, no one will know about it and neither of you will make any money.

EXAMPLE 2 -

A realtor recently sponsored a community block party. He bought a sponsorship. It gave him the rights to be the exclusive realtor sponsor at the block party. That meant no other realtor would be a sponsor and he would get all the exposure. There would be other sponsors, such as a grocery store and a landscaper, but no other realtors. In his sponsorship agreement, he also was granted the right to produce four large banners to hang at the site. He received the right to print and distribute pamphlets, conduct a door prize enter-to-win contest, and sample product, if he wished. For all these rights, he paid $1,000. Then he had to produce the banner and pamphlets, which cost him about $1,100. He then bought a bouncy castle for big kids to play on. He called it the Joe Realtor Kids Zone with signage. This cost about $1,700. He had an enter-to-win contest for the bouncy castle. Kids were encouraged to get their parents to enter-to-win (providing their names, telephone numbers, addresses, and email to qualify). One of those lucky kids would take the bouncy castle home at the end of the block party. He bought bottled water with his name and contact information printed on it so people could either enjoy it while at the block party or take some home. That was about another $200. He had staff on site to run the play area and hand out pamphlets. That was another $500. So, beyond his $1,000 investment with the community association, he invested another $3,500. That is three and-a-half times what he spent with the rights holder or seller—the community association. If he had not spent the additional $3,500, the sponsorship would have been a waste of money. So, what do you know? He listed and sold two homes in that community in the next three months. He had never had a listing in that neighborhood before. Each sold for over $1 million. At a 2.5% commission rate, he earned $50,000. I think his total $4,500 investment ($3,500 in activation and $1,000 in rights fees) paid off. Later that year, he listed three more properties, all of which sold as well.

Part of your role in the relationship is to help the sponsor spend and implement activation dollars. Often, that is a brainstorming exercise (like the community association did with the kids' bouncy castle idea) or helping to activate by providing volunteers as staff for the partner at the event. The additional dollars spent do not always have to be incremental. It could mean adding your logo to all their staff's business cards with the line "Proud to support ABC Organization," or they may already have a media buy in place and include you in the creative messaging. The **reality check** here is, if they don't spend this additional money, they won't be successful. If they are not successful, they will not return as a sponsor.

CONCLUSION

I hope that this chapter has allowed you to better understand sponsorship and the role it can play in your organization as part of your overall revenue diversification. As you have seen, it is a "different beast" in comparison to traditional philanthropic fundraising, but an excellent partner in what you are already doing when it is done correctly and professionally. When sponsorship is not done right, the revenue is low—it is not sustainable over the long-term and it produces no win-win scenario.

Here are the *Six Steps to Sponsorship Success*:
1. Know there is a difference between sponsorship and philanthropy.
2. Determine what you actually have to sell—create a comprehensive sponsorship asset inventory.
3. Establish the real market value of each asset so that you can determine accurately how much money you should be generating in annual sponsorship revenue, be able to custom build sponsorship proposals for prospects, and attach a real market value and investment ask.
4. Conduct discovery sessions. Build a true and meaningful relationship with the prospect. Determine their needs, goals, issues, culture, and budget before starting to build a proposal to present.
5. Custom build your sponsorship proposals—no gold, silver, and bronze packages. No pitching a package until you have all the answers, including a "yes" to what they will receive in assets and how much they will invest to acquire them.
6. Once the deal is closed, ensure that you fulfil on what you promised to deliver and work with the sponsor to activate on their investment.

ADDITIONAL RESOURCES

Books
- BAROOTES, BRENT AND JANET GADESKI. (2014). *Reality Check – Straight Talk About Sponsorship Marketing*. Civil Sector Publishing, Hilborn Group - http://hilborn-civilsectorpress.com/

URLs
- WWW.PARTNERSHIPGROUP.CA – This Canadian website hosts a list of industry definitions as well as white papers on discovery sessions, prospecting, industry trending, inventory asset valuation and more.

- WWW.POWERSPONSORSHIP.COM – Australian website hosted by author and industry leader Kim Skildum Reid and includes case studies, white papers and books.

- WWW.SPONSORSHIP.CA - The Sponsorship Report.

- WWW.SPONSORSHIPCONGRESS.CA - Western Sponsorship Congress.

- WWW.SPONSORSHIP.COM – American website that hosts articles, case studies and more.

APPENDIX 1 - INVENTORY ASSET VALUATION FORMULAS MATRIX

Sampling Opportunity Valuation

	Sample Value	Sampling Opportunity Value
Is the sampling product being handed out to a non-focused audience or without face to face interaction?	$0.05/sample	Number of people sampled x sample value
Is the sampling product being handed out to a targeted audience, with face-to-face interaction?	$0.20/sample	Number of people sampled x sample value

Tickets and Hospitality Valuation

	Ticket Value	Ticket and Hospitality Opportunity Value
The tickets have a face value and are for a venue that delivers greater than 70% capacity	Face Value	Ticket face value x number of tickets
The tickets have a face value and are for a venue that delivers less than 70% capacity	Face value	Ticket face value x capacity percentage x number of tickets
The tickets have no face value	(Value of the general benefits received at the event ÷ the number of guests)	Ticket calculated value x number of tickets
The tickets are VIP passes or accreditation	Regular ticket price plus 10% - 500% mark-up	Premium ticket price x number of tickets

Sponsor ID in Non-Measured Media Valuation

Property Publications	Mention Value	Media Mention Opportunity Value
Is the logo/ID located on a "sponsor page" with other sponsors inside the publication?	$0.00325/logo or mention	Mention value x number of publications printed
Is the logo/ID featured on it's own on the cover or back of the publication?	$0.025 - $0.065/logo or mention	Mention value x number of publications printed
Is the mention an advertisement in the publication?	Rate card values or $0.00325 - $0.065/ mention or advertisement	Mention value x number of publications printed
Tickets		
Is the logo/ID located with other sponsor logos/IDs?	$0.00325/ticket	Mention value x number of tickets printed
Is the logo/ID featured with few other logos or on its own?	$0.00325 - $0.04/ticket	Mention value x number of tickets printed
Is the logo/ID associated with a ticket back coupon opportunity?	$0.04 - $0.065/ticket	Mention value x number of tickets printed
Is the ticket for an event that would be considered a collector's item?	$0.04 - $0.065/ticket	Mention value x number of tickets printed

Websites

Description	Mention Value	Media Mention Opportunity Value
Logo Recognition on Front Page	$0.00325/unique user	Affected by the number of unique users, positioning, ownership stake (i.e. level of exclusivity, etc.)
Logo Link to Sponsor Site		Same as above - where is the logo located within the site - prominent?
Name Inclusion in editorial content	$0.0025 - $0.13/ unique user	Has there been pre-promotion of this piece, level of publicity.
Content Inclusion in information content/article		Looking here for more than a name mention but actual mention of product or values or services or endorsement in content or editorial on the web site.
Editorial Profile on web site		What the rate or range formula is for when the sponsor is the topic of an editorial or content, so an article about them and it must be affected by the number of unique users
Logo on specific page	$0.001 - $0.025/ unique user	Affected by the number of unique users and the hits on that general page
Internal Blog post internal (written by an employee or hired writer)	$0.050 - $1.00 / blog posted per year by someone with no ties to the property	Blog post made by the property themselves - demonstrates that they are an active and not stagnant user of social media and web. This would be lower than an external post. This rate is a blended measure of number of blogs annually and # of followers.
	$0.00325 - $0.065/ number of followers	
External Blog post	$0.050 - $1.00 / blog posted per year by someone with no ties to the property	Here we can say a post by an outside entity (hence interaction) is worth $X and then if they average 200 outside blog posts per year we know the value of those. This allows us to say "hey they get lots of interaction hence they are valuable". This rate is a blended measure of number of blogs annually and # of followers.
	$0.00325 - $0.065/ number of followers	
Home Page Banner ad	Rate card values or $0.00650 - $0.10/ unique user	Rate card rate for banner ad on the home page of a web site and it must be affected by the number of unique users.

Websites (cont.)

Description	Mention Value	Media Mention Opportunity Value
Specific Page Banner ad	Rate card values or $0.00650 - $0.10/ unique user	Rate card rate is for banner ad on a specific page of a web site - affected by the number of unique users
Home Page Pop Up ad	Rate card values or $0.00325 - $0.065/ unique user	Pop up ad that appears on a specific page of a web site - affected by the number of unique users
Specific Page Pop Up ad	Rate card values or $0.001 - $0.025/ unique user	Pop up ad that appears on the home page of a web site - affected by the number of unique users but lower range than above
Right to host live (and/or on-demand) stream on sponsor web site and/or social media channels.	$0.00325 - $0.065 x unique user	(For example, Rogers live streams Buskerfest festival via Rogers)
Rights to use sponsor images and video (before, during, after)	$0.00325 - $0.065 x number of followers	For set duration of no longer than six month pre or post event
Category exclusivity to property web site	$.0025 - $0.13 x unique user	

Geolocation Check-ins (Foursquare/Gowalla

Description	Mention Value	Media Mention Opportunity Value
Value of a friend	$0.00325 - $0.065/number of friends	As per others, the value of each follower or friend the property has on the medium
Value of number of badges	$0.025 - $0.065/# of badges existing for the property	Geolocation check in bonuses such as badges for visiting certain multiple locations of an industry like a "mall" or "hotel"
Value of number of Mayorships	$0.025 - $0.065/# of Mayorships existing for the property	The value to being the "King of the Castle" for a location such as Joe's Barber Shop or Roy Thompson Hall
Value of number of check ins	$0.005 - $0.065/check ins the property has	The value that is allocated to each check in for the property

Twitter Community

Description	Mention Value	Media Mention Opportunity Value
Number of followers value	$0.00325 - $0.065/ number of followers	Value per follower, range level to be determined by Klout score
Value of Tweet	$0.00325 - $0.065/ number of followers	
Value of a re-tweet	$0.065- $1.30/number of re-tweets on average per year	Increased value of each re-tweet because we know that follower is engaged enough and sees value to forward to network
Value of a mention	$0.0025 - $0.13/ number of followers	Value of a sponsor mention in a a tweet
Value of a Retweet mention	$0.0025 - $0.13/ number of followers	Value of a sponsor mention in a re-tweet, a re-tweet is when someone else shares the exact same message you have posted to Twitter and mentions your Twitter account
Sponsor name incorporated into property's official hashtag	$0.065- $1.30/number of tweets on average per year	Value is being associated with the hashtag for sponsor
Promotion of sponsor hashtags via event collateral	$0.00325 - $0.065/ quantity of collateral	Additional promotional value
Sponsor tweets, Instagram posts, etc. visible to attendees via on-site video boards	$0.00325 - $0.065 x number of attendees	Value of a sponsor mention in a tweet, or post, etc.

Mobile Related

Description	Mention Value	Media Mention Opportunity Value
Sponsor ads, features, links, etc. on property mobile site	$0.00325 - $0.065 x number of views	Branding on the elements
Category exclusivity to property mobile site	Rate card values or $0.00325 - $0.065 x number of views per year	Differentiated
Property to promote sponsor offer(s) and/or distribute mobile coupons to its digital media subscribers and/or to attendees checking in via smartphones	$0.00325 - $0.065 x number of followers x # posts	Reach through mobile couponing and re-couponing (forwarding of coupons)

App Related

Description	Mention Value	Media Mention Opportunity Value
Sponsor ID, ads, links and/or features in property's official app	$0.00325 - $0.065 x number of followers x # posts	
Category exclusivity to official app	$.0025 - $0.13 x unique user	
Right to create property's official app	$.0025 - $0.13 x unique user	

ABOUT THE AUTHOR

Brent Barootes, BA

Brent Barootes is President and CEO of the Partnership Group – Sponsorship Specialists™, an Alberta- based national sponsorship consulting firm. In the past 25 years Brent has worked directly or indirectly with many Canadian brands, corporations, small and medium businesses as well as charities, non-profits, professional and amateur sports teams, to develop, audit, enhance, design, and build effective sponsorship programs for them.

As a past Director of Development with the Canadian Breast Cancer Foundation as well as having worked with many small and large charities and non-profits, Brent truly understands how these organizations can generate additional revenue from a well-run corporate sponsorship program. Having delivered success in both the philanthropic world and the corporate sponsorship world Brent is the ideal candidate to be providing expertise in what corporate sponsorship is all about and how it differs from philanthropy.

Brent is engaged to annually deliver more that 45 speaking engagements from luncheon keynotes to half and full-day workshops. His expertise includes sponsorship valuations and audits, corporate measuring and investment in sponsorship for realized ROI, inventory/benefit asset development, asset valuation, sponsorship activation programs, package development, and mentoring of staff and volunteers engaging in sponsorship.

CHAPTER 12

FUNDRAISING CREATIVE

JOHN VANDUZER, BA (HONS)

A young black boy, one-and-a-half or maybe two years old, lies alone in a third-world hospital bed. There are no covers, just a blanket underneath his small body. The boy's too-small shirt covers only his chest; his belly, rounded and slightly distended, shines slightly, reflecting the dim, afternoon light. A large ill-fitted diaper overlaps the bulky mound of bandages that swell his thigh to three or four times its normal size. His left leg, gone, was amputated above the knee and the stump of it points at you, almost daring you to react.

To say something.

To *DO* something.

Anything!

Anything to undo what's just been done.

read more...

His head tilted slightly to one side, the boy appears both to be staring off into space and to be watching something – or someone – at the foot of his bed.

The large, grainy black and white photo reveals nine mostly white adults crowding around the boy's bed. You don't see much of them; indeed only their hands and forearms appear. Every one of them is making the same sign – the same gesture if you will – there's no mistaking the ubiquitous Facebook thumbs-up "Like" symbol.

At first glance, it appears that people are in the room with the boy, gathered around his bed. But by mimicking "Like" signs, with their hands balled up in a fist, their thumbs all sticking up, they look ridiculous. Dismissive. Almost cruel given what the boy has just been through. And where are his parents; why aren't they there? Were they injured, too? Or are they dead? What does the future hold for any or all of them? Surely the hands were photographed against a green screen in some fancy New York studio and superimposed over this real, caught-in-the-moment, brief second in time, documentary-style photo of the young child.

In tiny, reversed-out text, looking like it was written in old typewriter (complete with raised and imperfect letters) is the headline, "Liking isn't helping." And then stuck, almost as an afterthought in the bottom right-hand corner, is the remainder of the short message: *"Be a volunteer. Change a life. crisisrelief.org."* An equally small logo, *"Crisis Relief Singapore"* balances the text.

But back to the boy; it's impossible to stop looking at him.

His expression is mixed: equal measures worry and wonder. He both looks as if he wants help, but, at the very same time, doesn't expect that help will ever arrive. At least not now. Not to him, anyway.

Will it? Will help arrive? Or will the reader simply turn the page and read about the "17 ways to please your man?" It depends.

In a world of donor fatigue, reduced budgets and charities that all look and act the same, increasingly the difference between making the case and making people even notice you're making the case in the first place, is creative.

Your mission, vision and values may be amazing. You may be making a very real difference. Your need may be real and the differences you make, may be transforming hundreds and impacting thousands. But in the 24/7, distraction-oriented, media-saturated world we live in none of that – and I mean NONE OF THAT – matters in the slightest if people don't notice you.

Don't connect with you.

Don't come to care about you and what you do.

And don't donate to you.

Assuming yours is an admirable, well-run charity brimming with altruism, good deeds and even more good intentions, the only thing separating you from your current financial situation and your fundraising objectives is better fundraising creative.

And to be sure – to be certain you don't miss the point – just as "liking" isn't helping, neither is creative fundraising actually creative unless it creates a convincing argument as to why people should give. Approvals and awards are nice but not if the creative doesn't create more cash and fill your coffers.

80,000+ Canadian charities all want what you want: *money*. On the other hand, 34.5 million Canadians all want what they want which is to keep most of their money and give only a small bit of it away.

More than anything else, the single most important connecting point between charities and prospects is creative. Creative in ads like the one just described for Crisis Relief Singapore. Creative in direct mail, annual and capital appeals. Creative that invites participation: fundraising walks, tours and talks. Whatever.

> *Before a donor gives you a dollar she has to give a damn.*

Problem is, most creative isn't creative. It's invisible. Forgettable. Easy to miss or ignore. I'll let you prove it to yourself: what are the last three appeals you received from charities other than your own? You can't do it, can you? Why? It's because nothing they did connected or resonated with you. They didn't stand out. So you chucked them out.

But although it's easy to ignore other charities' appeals, there's no ignoring the fact that better creative will result in better fundraising. And better fundraising creative STARTS with a better creative brief.

> **EVALUATING YOUR CREATIVE BRIEF**
>
> Once written, the best way to evaluate if your creative brief is good or great is to ask yourself…
>
> - Is there a clear understanding of what the brand represents?
> - Is there a clear business strategy?
> - Is the target audience perceptively described?
> - Does the insight grab you?
> - Does the proposition tell you the answer or pass on the problem?
> - Is there a clear benefit to the donor to give?
> - Does it have an idea in it?
> - Is it "ownable?"
> - Could you work with it if it was written for you instead of by you?
> - Will it create the type of appeal or campaign that you think will encourage people to give?
> - Is this a great brief?
> - Does it encourage/inspire great creative?
> - Upon receiving the creative (ad, DM letter, etc.) would you donate?

To learn how to get noticed, here are four truisms that every fundraiser should champion when it comes to developing or evaluating fundraising creative.

1. **Have a Dickens of a time**

    From Charles Dickens' first novel, *The Pickwick Papers,* Mr. Pickwick's acquaintance, Mr. Jack Hopkins, the young surgeon, thought a surgical operation was successful if it was skillfully done. Mr. Pickwick, on the other hand, thought it was successful if the patient got well.

    Within the creative industry, it's easy to fool ourselves that we're doing well if we admire our work simply on the basis of its aesthetics. Skillful work may attract attention but the real value in creative comes in making it pay.

    Fundraisers' primary responsibility is to raise funds. The more the better! While we may think of ourselves as artists, we are first and foremost creative professionals tasked with helping charities raise the most money.

    If Mr. Pickwick were a modern day fundraiser, I believe he would argue that donor loyalty is stupid because such a statement suggests that donors owe something to their charity rather than the other way around. Donors aren't loyal like dogs and neither should they be. In fact, they are cats – free to do as they please, when they please and only if it pleases them. Loyalty isn't a donor issue, it's one which is borne solely by a charity and such loyalty is best manifested in the creative.

    The role of the creative is to breathe new life into an old problem (impoverished children, inadequate resources, the list goes on) so that people want to remedy the situation with their time, talent and treasure.

    Instead of playing it "safe" we need to be more daring.

2. **WANTED: Intelligent daring**

    Most fundraising appeals fall far short of their potential because they're derivative and uninspiring. They suffer from a lack of imagination and from "group think" (where a committee drafts or evaluates the RFP or weighs in on the creative once proposed, wringing every tasty bit out so that the result is the creative equivalent of Pablum.

    Instead, what's needed is what Leo Burnett, one of the grand daddies of advertising, called an attitude of *"intelligent daring."*

    After learning as much as they can about a charity's mission, vision and values and the specifics of the appeal in question, the creative must be allowed *(and expected)* to let the facts soak in and percolate. Deciding on both what to say and how best to say it takes time, and a good campaign will include a unique combination of reason, emotion and hunch spilling out with uninhibited warmth and candor while still remaining one hundred percent true.

Firmly rooted in reality, the campaign will skillfully and carefully guide the prospect into a dream state that is possible with his or her gift and those of other equally generous donors.

The best creatives bring intelligent daring to every task but such a trait does not allow for recklessness or abandonment of sheer talent, patience and perseverance. To be original is not to invent something new insofar as it is to discover something new in some age-old and by now commonplace problem. That's the talent and patience part.

But that's not all.

One must also persevere. In a letter he wrote to a peer, nineteenth century French novelist Gustave Flaubert famously wrote, "Whatever you want to say, there is only one word that will express it, one verb to make it move, one adjective to qualify it. You must seek that word, that verb and that adjective, and never be satisfied with approximations, never resort to tricks, even clever ones, or to verbal pirouettes to escape the difficulty."[1]

Of many rushed and/or low budget projects it's often said that the client got what they deserved. Maybe so. But such an assessment is never one that can be made of creatives who embody intelligent daring. Professionals with such a trait never compromise, never give in or give up and are never satisfied.

Here's one such example.

It's from a classified ad placed in the London Times on December 29, 1913 by Sir Ernest Shackleton who was seeking to recruit men to accompany him on an expedition to the South Pole: "Men wanted for hazardous journey.

Low wages, bitter cold, long hours of complete darkness. Safe return doubtful. Honour and recognition in event of success."[2]

Perhaps because it was a classified ad, or maybe because Shackleton was a no-nonsense kind of guy, but the text exemplifies an economy of words and a directness of purpose which is without equal even in today's "Twitterverse." Such an extreme focus and such an economy of words is sadly lacking in most charities' creative today. Far from offering intelligent daring, most creative is mindless "me-too" with one charity's message being indistinguishable from the next.

3. **Action!**
Intelligent daring inspires action! The best writing makes pictures in the mind and the best pictures write words in the heart of your prospect. Together, words that draw pictures and images that write words provide a compelling one-two punch that knocks out your prospect and compels her to give.

University of British Columbia neurologist Donald B. Caine says much the same thing when he observes, "emotion leads to action while reason leads to conclusions."[3]

An appeal that has logic without emotion will fail just as surely as an "ask" with emotion but no logic. An appeal that aims for the heart but misses the head, or hits the head and misses the heart won't work. As fundraisers, we are ultimately in the "action business" and so we often gravitate to the emotional side of the equation. But beware:

---

1   http://grammar.about.com/od/advicefromthepros/a/Writers-On-Writing-Ten-Tips-For-Finding-The-Right-Words.htm
2   http://www.antarctic-circle.org/advert.htm
3   http://en.wikipedia.org/wiki/Donald_Calne; http://www.finestquotes.com/author_quotes-author-Donald%20Calne-page-0.htm

prospects – especially new ones or those sitting on the fence – need a rational excuse to justify their emotional decisions.

> *Head + Heart = Success*
>
> *Head – Heart (or Heart – Head) = Failure*

Imagine that on your way to work today, you passed by a child who was shivering from the winter wind and snow. What would you do?

First posted on February 19, 2014, using a hidden camera, Norwegian-based SOS Children's Villages recorded what happened when everyday people passed by a shivering 11-year-old boy who was alone at an Oslo bus stop in the freezing cold. Entitled "Would you help a freezing child?" this so-called social experiment was all about heart. https://www.youtube.com/watch?v=92-QkW-pacB8

Or was it?

The fact is that a child is *(a)* alone and *(b)* freezing. Logic dictates that help is needed, and needed now!

As the youngster tries to warm himself, 22 of the 25 people who come to wait at the bus stop offer him their jacket, scarf or gloves and try to help him find his teacher. Ironically, the video that quickly went viral and has been viewed over 13 million times, was actually an appeal, one that drew viewers' attention to the millions of Syrian children who were facing a harsh winter without warm clothes or safe shelter.

The video about people responding with care and compassion to one boy demonstrates that we care about vulnerable children wherever they may be. Heart, yes. But brains, too, with a poignant example that it's in our nature to care.

We need more creative like that; creative that creates action!

4. **Are we there yet? Knowing when it's perfect**

Years ago when I worked at J. Walter Thompson, (then Canada's largest ad agency) I learned that the president of the firm thought nothing of inviting himself over for dinner to the homes of his management team. Curious about this, I dared to ask him why he did it. "Because I want to see for myself if my people really believe what they say," he answered with unusual candor. "You see, we produce copy (his all-encompassing term for commercials, ads, and point-of-purchase promotions) that sells products and I want to know if our top staff are "sold" on it or not. We make our money by selling Ford automobiles, Pepsi-Cola and any number of other fine brands and you can be sure that I get upset if there's a Chevy in their driveway and Coke in their fridge. To be sure, they don't have to have every brand we promote, but I expect to see many if not most of them in their cupboards, fridges and garages."

"You check?!" I asked, bug-eyed.

"Damn sure, I check," he replied with a chuckle. "And why not? First off, most of what we sell are commodities which means they are "me too" products in highly competitive categories. There's not much real difference between Pepsi and Coke so why not stock Pepsi since, at the very least, it helps pay your salary? But secondly, and more importantly, because our brands are so similar to other competing labels, I need to know everything I can about our products so I can find that single point of differentiation – that unique selling proposition if you will – that catapults our sales over those of the competition. Great creative comes as the result of superior product knowledge combined with a brilliant creative strategy born out of that single point of differentiation." The same is true of charities.

I would argue that an appeal is only complete when the people who know it best and have worked on it longest have made a gift on the basis of the appeal itself. If not, the appeal's not done. It's not perfect. It's not ready to go. That's right, it's only perfect when YOU give as a result of the creative.

CREATIVE LESSONS: A DOZEN REASONS TO THINK DIFFERENTLY

When old approaches don't *(or won't)* work new ideas are needed; *it's called creative, after all!* So create and be creative when doing so! Here are a few examples of how creative zigged when everyone else was zagging.

1. **What the bus bully video shows about raising money**
   When a video (http://www.youtube.com/watch?v=l93wAqnPQwk) went viral in 2012 that showed Karen Klein, a senior citizen bus monitor, being bullied and abused by grade 7 boys, the reaction was immediate and indignant. Within days, more than a million people saw the video. Within a week $650,000 was raised on her behalf so she wouldn't ever have to work again.

   Lesson: *I believe people supported Karen NOT because this was an exceptional case but because it was an exceptionally explicit video. The video proved to be a remarkable demonstration of what we knew in our hearts remains an everyday occurrence. We want it to stop. Money is an expression of our outrage; it's our vote for change.*

   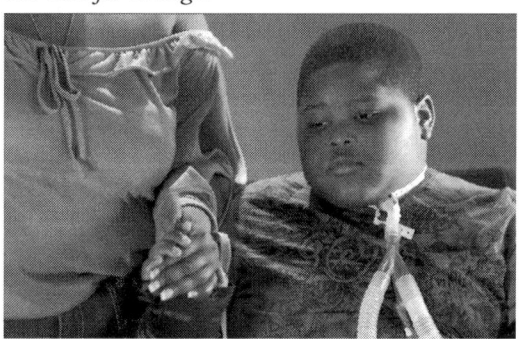

2. **Dnt Txt N Drv**
   Don't just tell me to stop texting. Convince me. German legend Werner Herzog created a 35 minute movie that compels you to save a second. And, in doing so, save a life. Go to: itcanwait.com and hit 'play' or, if it's not there, Google "From One Second to the Next." http://www.wernerherzog.com/index.php?id=128
   Lesson: *Just as it's been proven that long copy outpulls short copy in direct mail, a long video can do better than a short one if done well enough that it keeps people's attention throughout.*

3. **Guardian: Friend or foe?**
   Proving that target marketing in a mass media publication is possible, the UK's Guardian newspaper once again proved itself adept at garnering worldwide attention for next to no money. Even (and maybe, particularly) in merry old England, people either love or hate the monarchy. "Keep Calm and Click On," the Guardian's website seemed to say. As a royal watcher waiting for news of the birth of the future heir to the throne you simply clicked "Royalist?" in the upper right corner of the website and, not surprisingly, there was "muchness" about the duchess, her labour, and later, her baby boy. But for those who find the royals to be "a royal pain," you simply had to click "Republican" and any and all references to the baby and the bedlam surrounding the boy were gone faster than you could say cheerio.

   Bloody brilliant!

   Lesson: *Sometimes all it takes is some simple programming on a website to make all the difference. Now, if only the SPCA would take this idea and design their site to show cat videos to cat lovers, and pictures of pooches to those who would sooner cough up a fur ball than see a cat playing Chopin on the piano.*

4. **Tell it like it is**
   Geoffrey Canada, CEO and president of the Harlem Children's Zone delivered an unusual commencement address on May 17, 2012 at the University of Pennsylvania, during which he implored the graduating class to bring their talents and join his "losing team" in the war on poverty, violence and the lack of education. "Do you know why I offer you this opportunity to play on the losing side?" he asked. "Because in the end we are going to win. Because we are right."

The Harlem Children's Zone serves thousands of Central Harlem children from the time they are born through college, and is considered a model of positive community empowerment across the States. "If we continue to have neighbourhoods that the affluent are dying to get into, and the poor live in neighborhoods where they are just dying, we will have lost the promise of America. So you see, I know an enlightened, educated group of men and women [like yourselves] would not tolerate their country drifting towards this calamity. So in the end we will win."

Two lessons for the price of one: *First, use any and EVERY opportunity to share your message. Dr. Catherine Zahn, President and CEO of Centre for Addiction and Mental Health (CAMH) created quite an impact when she called her Toronto Ted Talk "We are all mentally ill" back in 2010. Years later, it's still going viral.*

Second, don't always talk about your successes; it's okay to focus on your failures if – and this is a big IF – if you can provide a convincing argument that by joining your "losing" team, the prospect can help make it a "winner."
(http://www.youtube.com/watch?v=cTF1ytiR9gE)

5. **Get "abreast" of the latest movie news** With a film degree and a collection in the thousands, I'm crazy about movies. And if those movies can be used to create awareness for a good cause, hey, so much the better. That's why I was so excited when I heard about Breast Fest, a short-film festival that targets breast cancer.

Lesson: *The festival is an excellent opportunity to not only spread the word about breast cancer through an engaging medium, but also for breast cancer survivors or those with the disease to meet and hear about people like themselves.
(I especially like that the supporters are ranked not with Platinum, Gold, Silver and Bronze levels, but 'D cup', 'C cup,' 'B cup,' down to 'A cup.')*
www.breastfest.ca

6. **Years later, a mind is STILL a terrible thing to waste**
At wishart, we're nuts about the history of advertising and one of the best in the history of charitable advertising is the United Negro College Fund. To creative and fundraising professionals alike and anyone looking to see how it's done, the UNCF deserves another look. As the United Negro College Fund website says *(www.uncf.org)*, forty years ago it was unthinkable that an African American could go to college. How the times have changed. And changed they have, with the generous support of the UNCF, which was established 40 years ago and now offers over 400 scholarships for young African American students who otherwise might not be able to go to college. In addition, they also support over 60,000 African American students across 39 member colleges.

One of the ads that started it all wasn't even an ad; it was a letter written on UNCF letterhead and placed on every seat of a commuter train leaving Grand Central Station for the affluent suburbs surrounding New York City. It began: *'When this train emerges from the tunnel at 108th Street this evening, look out of the window.'* What the privileged commuters saw was the black slums of Harlem. $26,000 poured in the next day, June 25, 1968.

Lesson: *Paint pictures with words. Allow your prospect to colour between the lines.*

7. **FreeRice.com**
   This is an on-line vocabulary game that donates your winnings to the less fortunate. Each time you identify the correct definition to a word from a list of four options, you feed someone ten grains of rice. The grains add up and when you're done the site donates the equivalent amount of real rice to a starving family through the United Nations World Food Program. You play, they eat. And because sponsors pay for the banner ads it doesn't cost you a penny.

   Lesson: *Using websites and social media, create a reason for people to interact with your charity on a daily basis and encourage their friends to do the same.*

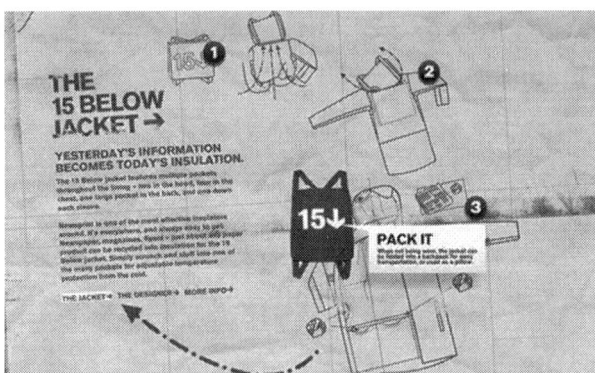

8. **A really cool idea!**
   Back in 2007, TAXI—an ad agency lauded for its work for WestJet, Telus and Koodoo Mobile—celebrated 15 years of success. Rather than have a birthday bash or run ads in trade journals extolling their virtues, to mark the occasion, they wanted a big idea – one that would give back to the community. The brief was sent out, and executive creative director, Steve Mykolyn, came back with The 15 Below Project. Its first initiative – a jacket for the homeless. The jacket would be breathable, waterproof, lightweight, and the lining would be made up of pockets throughout. And these pockets would be able to be stuffed with newspaper to provide adjustable levels of insulation from the cold. "We've survived 15 years, now we're going to help others survive the night," said Mykolyn, who enlisted long-time friend and designer, Lida Baday, to create the jacket.

   Adding weight to the 15-year theme, as well as lending the project a name, is the Cold Weather Alert many cities issue when the temperature drops to -15ºC. On behalf of clients and staff, three thousand 15 Below jackets have been donated to people living on the streets throughout Canada and the U.S. Go to: *http://15belowproject.org*.

   Lesson: *Any reason can be a reason to celebrate. A few times a year have a brainstorming session which generates ideas for your major corporate donors to help them create new and exciting ways to raise their profile and raise money on behalf of your charity.*

9. **Celebrity…**
   A) Tapping into today's celebrity culture
   What began as having restaurants ask for $1 donations for tap water in 2007, (the still very brilliant charity: water, www.charitywater.org) was done one better by UNICEF. In order to increase its funds towards the Tap Project, the UNICEF-created Celebrity Tap, which consists of packing water from the faucets of celebrities' homes, into fancy bottles. For every $5 donated through the Tap Project website, participants enter for a chance to win a case of the luxury celebrity tap water. The money raised from any donation related to Celebrity Tap is used to provide children with clean and safe water around the world. Aside from providing water from their own home, celebrities participating in this project volunteered their time for commercials and advertising campaigns to promote the UNICEF Tap Project.

   Lesson: *Tap into the celebrity culture.*

10. **Celebrity…**
    B) What's wrong with us?
    It's November 14th, 2013. In the Philippines,

10,000 people are dead and another 100,000 people are homeless, but all we're talking about is troubled Toronto mayor Rob Ford. Why? And why did no charity – much less those trying to raise money for the Philippine relief – jolt us from our idiocy?

Lesson: *Be topical. Capitalize on trends, news and what's happening in the here and now.*

11. **Celebrity…**
    C) Remember this worthy fundraiser on Remembrance Day
    To commemorate the 100th anniversary of Princess Patricia's Canadian Light Infantry, BC songwriting sensations, Bryan Adams and Jim Vallance penned a beautiful charity single, "Ric-A-Dam-Doo," commissioned by the Regiment's Colonel-in-Chief, the Right Honourable Adrienne Clarkson and available for sale through iTunes.

Lesson: *Where possible, compel celebrities to create something of value that literally gets your message out and generates income at the same time.*

12. **Celebrity…**
    D) Farewell, digital world (It's all for a Cause.)
    Everybody wants their 15 minutes of fame. Nowadays, it's easier than ever before, with social networking sites like Twitter and Facebook letting you broadcast all the interesting stuff you need to say across the internet for the world to read and take interest in. But as any aspiring internet celebrities will tell you, it's hard to get noticed in a culture of funny cat pictures and videos of people running into walls. How are charitable organizations supposed to break into this internet culture?

Sometimes in this world of increasing connectivity, the best way to be heard is to be quiet. This seems to be the main idea behind Alicia Keys' fundraising campaign titled "Buy Life." Celebrities went silent on Twitter and Facebook on World AIDS Day, until fans donated $1 million to "buy their lives back." You can donate money to the ongoing campaign, or take an oath of digital death yourself at *www.buylife.org*.

Lesson: *Zig when others are zagging. Do the opposite of what others are doing regardless of whether celebrities are involved. Case in point: A fundraising dinner I attended years ago attracted 100 people who each paid $100 to eat dinner. But there was a catch: it was a "hunger awareness meal" that demonstrated how most people eat. After drawing lots, fifteen "first world diners" got roast beef served to them by people in tuxedos. Another 20 people got served a "second world" dinner of borscht soup and a bun. The remaining 65 people – representing sixty five percent of the world's population –*
had to line up for a "third world dinner" of rice and water. The dinner cost very little to host, it made a huge profit, and thirty years after I first attended such an event I remember two things: the emptiness I felt in my stomach after I ate the rice, and the look of guilt (and even anguish) the few first world diners had as they reluctantly picked at their food.

CREATIVE BRIEFS

85,962[4] Canadian charities are competing for the attention of every single one of your donors. 85,962 charities are sending your donors countless letters, emails and text messages. They're tweeting and posting and running ads on TV, radio and in print. They're promoting galas and "athons" and walks and benefit concerts. They're doing all that and more.

So how are you to thrive, much less survive in such a competitive marketplace?

It's my view that the surest most cost-effective way to stand out from this soccer stadium-sized crowd is to be creative. And to have fabulous creative. And the surest, most cost-effective way to ensure your creative attracts attention, is to FIRST create a creative brief that demands attention and provides the inspiration that will inspire people to give. To be sure, a creative brief does not sit outside the creative process; rather it is the inspiration for and the beginning of the creative process.

When, in my younger days as an account executive, I would write a creative brief, such an undertaking would take up to six months. *(Ahh, the luxury of multi-million dollar budgets for Ford, Pepsi and P&G.)*

Fast forward to today, and only a very few not-for-profit clients or agencies inform their creatives with a cogent brief other than we need "x" by Tuesday or else. That's a threat, not a brief. Sadly – *no stupidly* – it doesn't get much better than this. The secret sauce in most creative isn't a saucy creative writer or designer, it's the creative brief. This document is the difference between a home run and a strike out.

Nowadays, good creative briefs are an exception rather than the rule. They're often too general, too cumbersome, and lacking in either insight or originality. *(Much like the creative which follows)*. Over the last quarter century in this sector, I have found that good communication all too often happens in spite of the creative brief, rather than because of the creative brief. In an increasingly competitive marketplace and with faster and faster deadlines, people can't skip this step and still expect results.

So what exactly IS a creative brief?

Functioning as the bridge between smart strategic thinking and great communication, a creative brief acts as the causal link between your cause and the effect of the appeal.

Keeping with the bridge analogy, the bigger the project, the stronger (but not necessarily bigger) the brief needs to be. One of ten or more direct mail appeals a year? The brief needs to focus on a specific project and motivation for giving. A rope bridge, if you like. A capital campaign which seeks to raise tens or even hundreds of millions of dollars? The brief needs to have the tensile strength to withstand 3-7 years of anything and everything.

Perhaps it goes without saying, but the key to a creative brief is that it be brief. Two to three pages for a big capital campaign. Max. Or short enough to fit on a napkin for a straightforward appeal.

Essentially, the key purpose of a creative brief is to distill information. A funnel comes to mind, but I prefer coffee. Take everything you know and grind it as if it were coffee beans. Place the contents in a coffeemaker and add (free-flowing ideas) like water. Writing the brief is like pushing the "on" button. In the heat of the moment only the best thinking filters through and produces a brief which is as flavourful, invigorating and inspiring as a hot cup of coffee on a cold winter morning. Too many ideas and not enough content produces a brief which is weak and thin. Too few ideas and too much content and you get a brief which is strong and bitter.

Not only does a creative brief function as something of a bridge, let me add that a good creative brief serves as both a foundation and a framework for your creative. Ideally, it contains a well-informed and clearly articulated summary of the key factors that can or will inspire the greatest number of recipients to give the greatest amount of money to you – or more accurately through you – in order to achieve the shared desired outcome.

I offer two very different sample briefs in the hope that they will inspire you to build your own bridge, something unique to the chasm you need to cross.

A. Traditional creative brief

Organizations are forever saying they're "customer-centered," and fundraisers say they're "donor centric," so prove it with an innovative creative brief built entirely around the prospect.

---

4   http://www.cra-arc.gc.ca/ebci/haip/srch/advancedsearchresult-eng.action?n=&b=&q=&s=registered&d=&e=+&c=&v=+&o=&z=&g=+&t=+&y=+&p=1

With the prospect at the centre, ask the following questions:

1. Who is our prospect?
Motivations, likes/dislikes, relationship to our charity, patterns of giving.

2. What does she care about?
And what does our appeal have in common with that? What's the big idea that will get her to open her purse to you? The closer your "whats" are, the closer you are to getting her gift. What is the unique selling proposition (USP), the single most relevant and differentiating idea that will spur the prospect to make a gift? What is the question in the mind of the prospect that we must answer before she pulls out her cheque book?

3. How can he help?
How will his donation make a difference/have an impact/lead to transformation?

4. Where should she give?
Most appeals include a BRE and response mechanism. Eblasts include a link to the donation page on a website. Some donors prefer to phone in their gift and some like to drop it off in person. Insure your appeal provides multiple options.

5. Why should they give?
Why should he sponsor 1, 2 or 3 children? And why now? Why should he give you one (more) nickel or hour of his time? Why are you most deserving of his next charitable gift? Why aren't they doing what you want them to do already?

6. When should he donate?
Sure, every appeal has a deadline but why is the gift needed now? Why not in two months or two years? Prove the need is timely (and not just because you have to make your budget forecast).

B. Non-traditional creative brief: Keep asking "Why?"
Answer the question that people ask most: why? Keep asking "why" until all the questions a prospect could have, have been answered.

- Why should major donors give you even more when they've already given so much?
- Why would a regular donor act irregularly and support this appeal?
- Why would a recent donor give when she only just gave?
- Why would a lapsed donor ever want to support you again (maybe they're not lapsed, maybe they're gone. And maybe they just gave and then gave up)?
- Why would you give if you were in any of the above categories?
- Why haven't you tried something else? (A cheaper solution? Avoiding the problem altogether?)
- Why me?
- Why *now?!*

HOW TO WRITE AN INSPIRING BRIEF

Remember that ad I mentioned in the introduction, the one with the boy with the amputated leg? Although I have no way of knowing what was written originally, here is the brief that *could* have inspired and produced the remarkable creative:

> *We are a small, Christian disaster relief organization based in Singapore. Compared to Red Cross or Médecins Sans Frontières we're virtual nobodies, little nobodies who nonetheless make a big impact in the lives of those we serve with love and mercy. When disaster strikes, we pay particular attention to the disadvantaged, women and children.*
>
> *We want money – sure, who doesn't – but we need volunteers most of all. Crisis Relief Singapore is a volunteer-based organization and we are in urgent need of volunteers who can contribute their time, talent and treasure in equal measure.*
>
> *The campaign must align with the organization's strategic objectives that are to raise awareness and provide opportunities for volunteers to serve in crisis relief. Yes, we are committed to train volunteers and*

prepare them for this work, but that's not something that needs to be communicated. Strip away everything that's superfluous; the ad must be super-extra-concentrated to have impact.

Key to our mission is "to meet felt needs and extend unconditional hope and love in crisis-hit locations."

We believe people have a God-given need to help others and the campaign should motivate like-minded people to act on this desire rather than simply sit back and either cheer from the sidelines or say, "what can I do?" and then do nothing.

The call to action is a simple URL (crisisrelief.org) where prospects can learn more. That's it. No print equivalent of the "donate now" button. Pleeze!

We have hundreds of excellent photos, photos that tell story after story after story of how volunteers have changed lives for the better. Even better, in most cases the volunteers aren't pictured; whoever sees the ad can imagine him or herself at the scene offering much-needed assistance.

We look forward to seeing emotionally-charged, high-impact, arresting creative that jolts well-meaning people out of their complacency and into action. Of course, if you produce an idea that compels you and two others to join us in the field, present it to us without delay (morning, noon or night). In fact, that's how we will judge the ad – if it convinces you to volunteer we're certain it'll do the same for others.

No, I didn't volunteer to join them on a medical mission trip but I did the next three best things:

I prayed for them. *Fervently!*

I just used their creative as a best-case example of how to do what we do (something I hope will inspire someone else to volunteer in my stead while I continue to go on mission trips to serve people in the Dominican Republic); and,

I made a donation.

Yes, I made a donation to a far-off charity I'd never heard of before without the slightest concern about whether I was going to be rewarded with a tax receipt. Why? Their creative was so compelling, their message so simple, and their cause so real, I had to give.

I had to help in any and every way I could!

That's the power of creative: the impact it makes increasingly represents the difference between "survive" and "thrive" in today's highly competitive charitable sector. It's the difference between fulfilling one's charitable mission and vision, or not. It's the difference between being a "have" and "have not" charity. Finally, it's the single best way to get ahead and not be found on the side of the road dead.

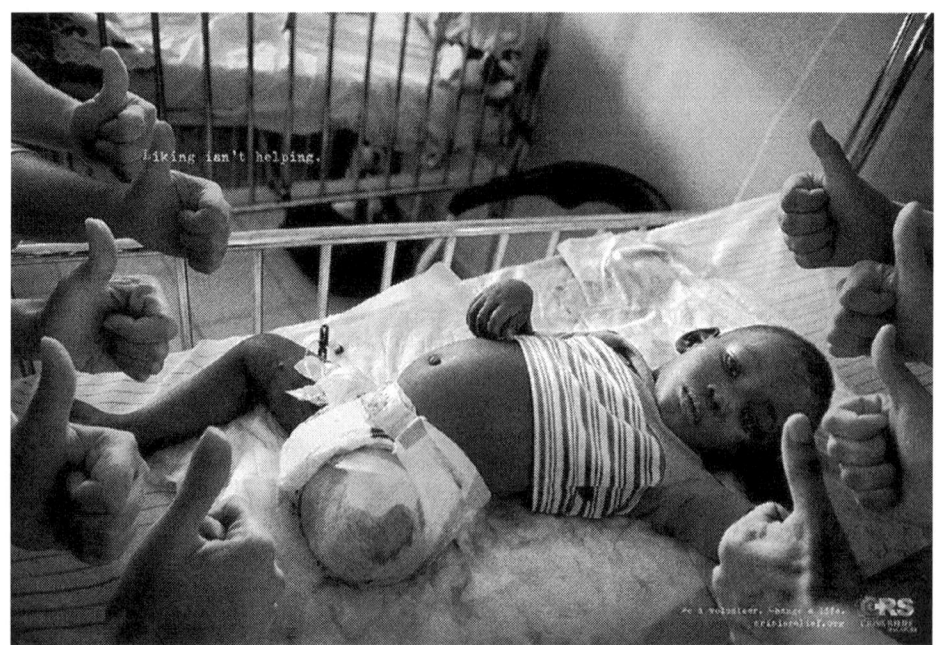

CREATIVE:
PUBLICIS,
SINGAPORE

ADDITIONAL RESOURCES

- Beckwith, Harry. (1997). *Selling the Invisible: A Field Guide to Modern Marketing.* USA, Warner Books.

- Caples, John. (1983). *How to Make your Advertising Make Money*, Englewood Cliffs, New Jersey, Prentice-Hall, Inc.

- Ogilvy, David. (1983). *Ogilvy On Advertising.* United Kingdom, Multimedia Publications (UK) Ltd.

- Ries, Al and Laura Ries. (1998). *22 Immutable Laws of Branding.* USA, HarperBusiness.

- Ries, Al and Jack Trout. (1981). *Positioning: The Battle for Your Mind.* Toronto, McGraw-Hill Book Company.

- Updegraff, Robert R. (1916). *Obvious Adams: The story of a Successful Businessman.* USA, The Updegraff Press.

URLs

- WWW.APPLIEDARTSMAG.COM
  Canada's Visual Communications Magazine

- WWW.COMMARTS.COM
  Communication Arts magazine's website

- WWW.GOOD.IS
  Creative Solutions for Living Well + Doing Good

- WWW.LUERZERSARCHIVE.NET
  Archive of advertising graphic design for print, television, product packaging, commercial illustration and other subject areas

- WWW.SOFII.ORG
  Showcase of Fundraising Innovation and Inspiration

- WWW.WISHART.NET
  WISHART: Creating the Greater Good

ABOUT THE AUTHOR

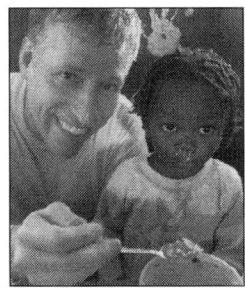

John VanDuzer, BAH

John is a graduate of Queen's University and was the recipient of that school's highest honour, the prestigious Tricolour Award. Since then he has worked at three of the country's largest ad agencies serving multi-million dollar clients you might have heard of: Ford, Pepsi, and Procter & Gamble. Throwing caution to the wind and trading in a six-figure salary for one a lot closer to $6,000, John founded WISHART.NET a quarter century ago and has been working tirelessly to create the greater good ever since.

John is one of the most accomplished and award-winning creatives in Canada, having won well over 200 awards. He credits his success not just to his staff and clients, but to his wife and four kids who are forever asking, "are we there yet?" Ever searching for new and better ideas, John is always thinking.

Canadian charities which are thinking about raising significantly more money invariably come to wishart; it has helped them raise more than one BILLION dollars in just the past ten years.

As a Christian, John has been helping people reconcile their faith and their finances, and the product of this calling is **Loonie: Crazy Talk about Faith and Finances** a book which was published earlier this year to great acclaim.

CHAPTER 13

COMMUNICATION AND MAJOR GIFTS

ANNE (COYLE) MELANSON, BPR, CFRE

The need for organizations and fundraising professionals to focus on growing their major gifts portfolio results from two irrefutable facts.

1. Charities must increasingly rely on major gifts to fulfill their social promise.

2. Major gifts can (and do) represent a disproportionate amount of most charities' bottom line revenue.

Communicating well with major gift donors means capturing their interest and inspiring their generosity in support of a worthwhile cause. Understanding what these donors want, their perspective and how you can better communicate with them is an important foundational step toward maximizing your organization's major gift potential.

read more…

While visiting Toronto in 2011, the CEO of a major charity paid an impromptu visit to a well-known Canadian philanthropist who had recently made a donation. They had never met before, but this would prove to be a fateful meeting.

The CEO was genuinely grateful for the donor's generosity and felt the need to say "thank you" personally. The discussion was cordial at first, and then warm, and evolved naturally to the subject of the charity's longer-term hopes and dreams. The CEO's passion for the opportunities ahead of them was clear. The donor understood the need.

"It keeps me awake some nights, wondering where we will find the funding," said the CEO as an aside. "I would be very grateful if you have any suggestions on where I can look for the support we need."

Two days later when the CEO returned home, there was an email from the donor in their inbox. "I've found your donor for you. It's me."

The resulting major gift (a real life example, in case you are wondering) became the largest single donation in the charity's history. It illustrates artful execution of the four elements of effective major donor communication:

- Audience: often your organization's best potential major donors are past donors who have contributed previously at smaller levels, and/or potential donors with a shared interest in your project or organizational goals.
- Content: communicating your mission, vision, gratitude and aspirations with passion and authenticity is paramount.
- Channel: making the effort to tailor your communication opportunity appropriately to the audience makes a profound difference (in this example, the communications opportunity was ideal…a bi-lateral dialogue in a face-to-face meeting).
- Feedback: focusing the communications subject matter to the donor's area of interest should be your top priority in every communication opportunity.

Success in major gift fundraising depends on purposeful, effective and impactful donor communication. At every stage of the donor cycle — from identification and qualification through cultivation, solicitation and stewardship — inspiring major acts of giving requires the artful application of communications best practices. This applies both in one-way communications activities, and two-way donor conversations.

Fads in communications techniques and rapidly changing communications platforms and channels abound. These can convolute charities' communications programs and over-complicate the task for fundraisers seeking to capture the attention and interest of potential major donors. Well-meaning charitable leaders and friends concerned with major gift revenue generation will ask questions like, "why don't we have a stronger presence on Facebook and social media to help get the word out to potential major donors?" New media are wonderful avenues for raising awareness for a cause, but these communications channels are frequently too indirect to rely on when communicating for major gifts.

It can be challenging to figure out where to start in designing and executing a communications program that will help attract major gifts. For organizations with more evolved and robust donor communications programs, it can be difficult to pinpoint those communication activities and resource investments that actually make a difference in furthering major gift work. For small and under-resourced charities, the challenge comes in determining which activities will lead to the desired communications outcomes, when time and resources are stretched.

In this chapter I provide insights and data from the sector, share the wisdom of other experts in the field, and outline a few lessons learned in the trenches over the course of 25 years of leading and advising capital campaigns and major gift programs. I will cover some best practices; giving TIPS! on devising your major gift communications plan, putting knowledge into practice, and identifying ways that you can set your charity's communications apart from the crowd.

THE MAJOR GIFT IMPERATIVE

The ability of your organization or institution to deliver on its mandate depends on major gifts.

Now more than ever, charities of all kinds and sizes are increasingly focusing their time and attention on their ability to attract major gifts.

Sometimes the pressure for major gift success comes from governing Boards concerned with bottom line financial results. Opportunities to have a greater or deeper social impact, or to accelerate the organization's mission delivery, will fuel the appetite for major gifts. Or perhaps an organization is simply ready to evolve from its typical fundraising mix of special event and annual fund revenue generators to the next natural step in fundraising growth.

Regardless of the internal impetus, from a statistical perspective it should come as no surprise that charities are paying more attention to their major gift potential and activities. In Canada today, more than four of every five dollars contributed to a charity comes from only 25% of the charity's donor base.[1] Major gifts can represent a significant source of bottom line revenue that many organizations need to deliver on their social promise.

UNDERSTANDING MAJOR DONORS

1. *Why donors give major gifts*

In 2000, fundraising experts Guy Mallabone and Tony Myers undertook an in-depth public opinion survey to determine motivators for Canadian charitable giving. The study[2] found that the motivational factor of *"belief/trust"* was the number one motivational factor inspiring people to make a major gift, followed closely by *"demonstrating results,"* *"I can make a difference,"* and *"I have a connection with the charity."*

A 2010 survey by Statistics Canada[3] supports and supplements the findings of Mallabone and Myers. In it, Canadians were asked a wide range of questions about their charitable giving, including their motivators for giving: 90% of donors cited feeling *compassion for people in need* as their reason for giving, followed closely by *personal belief in the cause*, and *the desire to contribute to their community*. Only about 60% of respondents indicated that being personally affected by the cause the organization supports was the reason for their philanthropy.

While neither survey specifically targeted major gift donors, both studies provide a valuable glimpse into the psyche of donors.

> **TIP!**
>
> Donors want to believe in and trust the organization they support, and will contribute because they feel compassion for the people served by the charity and/or its aims. These insights should inform what we communicate to donors.

Not all major gifts come from individuals. Canada's corporate and foundation sectors are major contributors to charities, accounting for about 15% of (all) charitable gifts contributed to Canadian charities.[4] Corporate motivations for making major gift investments can be vastly different than the motivations of individual donors. Regional and local business, as well as social service clubs and organizations, also make major gifts to charities.

While it can be difficult to find publicly available information about individual donors, it is often easier to research corporations, companies, foundations and social service organizations online.

> **TIP!**
>
> Taking the time to investigate a donor's stated philanthropic priorities and past giving behaviours, will help you to tailor communications to their area of interest.

As well, researching major donor prospects that fall into the corporate, company, foundation and service organization category is an important step in identifying the person or persons within those organizations to whom you should target communications efforts.

---

1 McLintock, Norah. (2004). *Understanding Canadian Donors: Using the National Survey of Giving, Volunteering and Participating to Build Your Fundraising Program.* Canadian Centre for Philanthropy, p. 9-16.
2 Mallabone, E.H. Guy and Tony J.A. Myers. *Motivating the MoneyGivers – Motivations and Barrier to Philanthropic Giving.* Masters Thesis, p.190, St. Mary's University, Minnesota, USA
3 Statistics Canada, *Canada Survey of Giving, Volunteering and Participating.* (Catalogue no. 11-008)– Chart, p. 33. Ottawa, Canada. 8 sons for

4 McClintock, Norah. (2004). *Understanding Canadian Donors: Using the National Survey of Giving, Volunteering and Participating to Build Your Fundraising Program.* Canadian Centre for Philanthropy, p.4.

2. What makes major donors different

Donors who give small monetary amounts to an organization typically trust "the brand" to effectively and efficiently spend their money in the area of greatest charitable need. In other words, the smaller the amount (in their eyes), the less inclined a donor is to require detailed specificity about its use.

Naturally, the reverse psychology holds true. The larger and more significant the gift amount requested, the more likely the donor is to require full disclosure on the use and application of funds, and whether and how the funds and their application achieved the promised outcomes. In short, major gift donors generally want and deserve to understand not only what you aim to achieve with their investment, but specifically how you will spend their donation to do so.

Beyond the specificity these donors seek, major donors often restrict their investments to programs, initiatives, and projects that align with their areas of priority interest. Understanding the areas of priority interest of a potential major donor helps the organization tailor the message accordingly.

Major gifts donors also need a more significant depth of information on the potential impact of their investment, both at the macro (ie, organizational) level, and the micro (ie individual) level. They want an understanding of the organization's big picture impact, like numbers served, financials, and other evaluative metrics. This supports the rational and intellectual aspects of their major gift decision-making. As well, they benefit from anecdotal allegories and stories of individuals and communities transformed or improved by their investment. This human element of the Case for Support is the story telling of real people's lives improved through philanthropy. It appeals to the emotional side of a donor's decision making process.

What major donors don't want

Here are the three most frequent complaints heard from major donors about the way charities communicate with them:

- *"I've made a major contribution but you still treat me like I'm a number."* If an alumnus of your university has just made a major gift, and a month later receives a standard, impersonal form letter from you asking for a gift to the annual fund, they will feel like you didn't even notice their major contribution.

- *"The only time I hear from you is when you want money."* Small-shop and over-taxed fundraising departments in particular are prone to falling into this trap. If you consider the vantage point of the donor, you will understand their cynicism. No donor wants to feel like an ATM machine.

- *"You spend too much on flashy communications efforts. You share too much information on things I'm not interested in."* Some organizations go overboard with their donor communications. Over-the-top direct mail and e-mail campaigns, elaborate print collaterals, lavish events and aggressive direct contact programs designed to "engage" donors in the mission of the organization often backfire. Donors will question how wisely your organization spends donated funds, at the same time they are wondering if you are pursuing them for the next big gift…and why.

It is important that you and your organization design a communications protocol that is balanced and that considers the content needs of your audience. Later this chapter will identify some ways to design and implement a tactical communications plan.

3. The importance of making the ask

Major gifts happen because someone asks someone for a major gift. Regardless of type, donors make major gifts because they are asked to do so.

You can design the most brilliant donor and stakeholder communications program in the world, win an award for its clever ideas, and execute if flawlessly. Absent a direct ask for support, your communications program alone is unlikely to yield the major gift support you seek. A volunteer, CEO, program staffer or professional fundraiser typically needs to put forward the specific request for major support either in verbal or written form (and often in both).

Twenty years ago a colleague of mine quipped "the best cultivation is an ask." An "ask" meeting gives you the rare opportunity to share your passion, vision and plans, and to elicit direct feedback on the program or initiative you are proposing for major gift support. Even when a major donor declines your request, you will have learned important information about the appropriateness of the amount of the request, timing, your next opportunity, where the donor's interests lie, and what type and level of financial investment they may be able to provide in the future.

TO SUM UP

Like all donors, those who make major gifts want to have trust in the charities they support; confident that their major investment will improve the quality of life for those in need and believing that their investment will deliver real results.

At a deeper level, individuals, corporations, foundations, companies and service organizations give major gifts for varying reasons. Understanding those motivations is an important step in customizing communication activities for major gifts.

Donors who give major gifts typically do so because they have a particular interest in a mission, goal, program, demographic or priority. Examining and understanding those interests will both help you to identify your target audience for major gift communications activities, and it will help you calibrate the content of your communications.

Because of the financial magnitude of their investment, donors who make major gifts often want more information, transparency, and details from the charity before (and sometimes after) making the gift. For the donor, making the decision often involves both intellectual and emotional components. Balancing factual and emotive components in the content for your major donor audience is an effective approach.

A communications protocol with your major donor audience should avoid heavy reliance on process-driven and boiler-plate communications that appear impersonal. As well, ignoring donors "between asks" or overwhelming them with too much communication activity are risky behaviours. Consciously and planfully choose communication content, frequency, and channels carefully, based on the audience's viewpoint. Feedback you gather from one-on-one interactions with members of your major donor audience (including solicitation meetings) can and should inform future communication with them, and with others as well.

With over 80,000 registered charities in Canada, major donors have an abundance of options for their charitable giving. They are inundated with messaging in broadcast and social media, and often are contacted directly and regularly by a host of worthwhile causes. Having your organization's case heard in this noisy environment takes strategic thinking and smart, targeted communications activities. It requires a desire to get a donor's attention *for what is likely to interest them*. It's also helpful to have genuine empathy for the fact that they are often pulled in multiple directions, by so many great causes who need their support.

DEVELOPING YOUR PLAN

1. *Who is your audience?*

Surprisingly, many organizations — from small community-based social charities to large universities with advanced fundraising programs — often find that pinpointing their major gift audience is challenging. While the question "who comprises our major gift audience?" seems simple in the abstract, it can be complicated to answer it in the real and very fluid world of organizational fundraising.

The good news (and the bad) is that each organization defines its major gifts audience in a different way, and so there really are no universal rules. You have latitude to define your major gift audience in a way that is useful. Answer the following questions to define your major gift audience and populate a list for major gift communications:

- What is the (minimum) future gift potential?
- What is the cumulative past giving history to us?
- What past and potential donors are most likely to have interest in our mission or special initiatives?
- Are there "key influencers" for major gifts that we should keep informed?
- How many individuals and organizations can we communicate with effectively in executing this plan?

Beyond these basic definitions, the process of identifying your audience requires more thorough work in order to be useful.

It's one thing to examine any past donor's financial contributions to your organization. It's entirely another to consider the nuances of past giving behaviour, and to evaluate future giving potential. Identifying your major gifts audience by gift level, type, loyalty, project/program giving and future potential is an important step in drilling down to a list of major gift prospects who will constitute your audience.

As well, many wise organizations include those who have given in-kind or volunteer support to your organization in the past. Loyalty is a key indicator of willingness to provide major support in the future. Often the only impediment to a past donor making a major gift today is current financial ability.

TIP!

Look carefully at previous long-term in-kind and volunteer supporters, and evaluate realistically whether there may be significant future major gift potential, before excluding them.

And finally, you must evaluate the relative effectiveness of including potential major donors who have never before contributed to your organization. While it can be tempting to include in your audience "all those we hope will contribute," this is rarely a useful approach. Donors recognize the generic "spray and pray" approach to communications. Thorough research and/or your anecdotal knowledge must lead you to a valid conclusion that the prospective donor will have a legitimate interest in the message you wish to relay.

2. *What is your content?*

Charities that develop high-impact content for major gift communications activities adhere to the following best practices:

- *Relevance* — focusing the crux of the content on the area of greatest likely interest to the donor audience;
- *Balance* — effectively weighing big picture, organizational impact, and fact-based information (that appeals to intellect) with effective and accurate storytelling about people, lives, communities, or need (that appeals to emotion);
- *Perspective* — framing stories and facts from the vantage point of what is important to the reader or audience, rather than the organization, and
- *Clarity* — presenting content in a manner that is easy to understand, and appealing to the audience.

Giving too much information is the most common error. Organizations often tell a story in five pages, when five *paragraphs* will do. Volunteers and staffers will share several illustrative examples with an audience from the podium, when one will make a more memorable impression. Piling on too much information about the organization's history, work, people, and plans forces the audience to dive into the haystack in search of the needle. Most members of your audience have neither the time nor the interest.

Instead, think about your organization's story and fundraising Case for Support as a topographic map that is viewed from an aerial perspective. Your job is to move a magnifying glass to the area that most interests and inspires your audience... amplifying the detail and showing them the interconnectivity to the larger story. And above all, keep it interesting!

In fundraising communications, content is often relayed in written form. This means that fundraisers and communications professionals need to be strong writers and good story-tellers in order to be prepare high-impact content. **Figure 13.1** offers tips on story-telling, and **Figure 13.2** provides practical suggestions to help in writing well.

3. *What are your available channels?*

The list of communications channels available to, and in use by, Canadian charities is too lengthy to itemize here. Commonly employed channels include direct mail, print and electronic newsletters and magazines, websites, Facebook, customized correspondence, public speeches and media interviews, traditional advertising, meetings, telephone conversations, invitations, publicity events, and on and on. The options are almost infinite.

The simplest way to get a handle on your available channels for major gift communications is to sit down and itemize all those opportunities you and your organization have to interact with your audience members. This approach supports a best practice "moves

> **STORYTELLING**
>
> - Frame your story from the perspective or experience of the beneficiary -- the person(s) whose life will be changed by the gift.
>
> - Focus on impact and outcomes.
>
> - Back up your claims with irrefutable facts.
>
> - Don't gild the lily. If there have been significant challenges in the past, be candid about the experience, and about what was learned. If there still are challenges, say so.
>
> - Be authentic. Avoid hyperbole, adverbs and adjectives. Let the facts tell the story. Allow the reader to deduce and decide. Write like a journalist.

Figure 13.1

management"[5] approach to major gifts (covered in *Excellence in Fundraising in Canada, Volume 1*).

While time-consuming, it is tremendously helpful to develop a detailed matrix of communications activities that your organization does (or can) undertake. Itemize everything from invitations to events to mass communications exposure for each member of your major gift audience. This will give a valuable birds-eye view of how (and what), in totality, you are communicating to them. It provides an important snapshot through the lens of the audience.

Larger organizations often employ multiple and more diverse channels. Different departments and personnel will contact members of your major donor audience, sometimes without your knowledge. While it is important to be aware of the nature of these communications and factor them into your audience-centric plan, no fundraiser should have the exclusive right to major donor communication. Program staff and others within your organization are frequently the most effective messengers with major donors. When a donor or

> **TIPS FOR GREAT WRITING**
>
> - At the outset, distill your entire story to three key points, and elaborate from there. State these key points in your introduction, and summarize in your conclusion.
>
> - Use simple, straightforward language and avoid jargon to make your content easy to digest and understand.
>
> - Use short, pithy sentences, with verbs in the active tense and as few adjectives and adverbs as possible.
>
> - Break up run-on sentences by using grammatical tools (like putting explanations in parentheses); correct usage of semi-colons for related concepts, and by calling attention to important ideas – like this one – with dash separators.
>
> - Alternate sentence length within standard-length paragraphs. For readability, use a maximum of four or five sentences per paragraph as follows: two short, one (or two) medium, and one long sentence with multiple commas.
>
> - Alternate paragraph length. No paragraph should claim more than 20% of the real estate of the page on which it resides. Try occasional use of one-sentence paragraphs to call attention to particularly important statements.
>
> - Use loads of white space. Big margins and lots of white space between paragraphs invite the eye to the paragraph and make them easier to digest.
>
> - Integrate lists and bullets. They provide structure and bring simplicity.
>
> - Use infographics! Some complex ideas, statistics, and relationships are best communicated visually.
>
> - Above all, be clear. Before you write, think. It's tough to write well unless you have a clear idea of exactly what you want to communicate.

Figure 13.2

---

5 "Moves" are the actions an organization takes to bring in donors, establish relationships, and renew contributions. David Dunlop, the Cornell University senior development officer who developed the concept of moves management, described the idea as "changing people's attitudes so they want to give." (from Wikipedia, "Moves Management.")

potential donor only hears from the fundraisers, that sends a strong signal and gives a slanted impression.

Ultimately the most effective plan balances general communication activities with customized ones. Your major donor audience needs to hear from the organization through broad efforts like newsletters, annual reports, mailings and media. But there is no replacement for old fashioned, customized, high-touch activities that are specific to an "audience of one."

In today's technology-driven age, taking the time to author and send a personal letter or report; making a phone call to update a donor; meeting them over a cup of coffee, or inviting them to spend time on-site at your organization, remain among the most impactful communications channels available to any Canadian charity focusing on major gifts.

4. *How will you get and use feedback?*

Mechanisms for audience feedback should be part of your communications plan. Major donor audiences need to have the opportunity to be heard, and what they have to say will help you improve results.

i. *Surveys*
Many organizations employ surveys (telephone, online or written) designed to elicit information from donors about "how we are doing" and "what you need from us." The very act of asking for an opinion implies that the organization has genuine interest in what the donor has to say. While surveys can be useful, they do have some inherent risks when applied universally to a major donor audience.

By design, surveys restrict the subject matter to the agenda of the organization. Respondents are asked to offer opinions on issues defined by the organization, rather than to offer commentary on those issues they themselves consider top priorities.

As well, surveys may be appropriate for long-standing volunteers and donors (ie, those that know your organization well), but are not appropriate for others....like the chief program officer of a major foundation that recently invested in a special project at your charity.

And finally, the reality is that some people get annoyed when you ask them to take the time to complete a survey.

> **TIP!**
>
> Before embarking on any kind of survey of your major gift audience, take the time to carefully tailor the survey content, and judiciously edit the list of recipients to include only the safest recipient names.

Ensure that major gift audience participants are thanked (personally, not electronically); that outcomes of the survey are communicated to them; and that important resulting feedback from the survey is actually implemented by the organization.

ii. *Conversations*
When it comes to eliciting feedback, there is simply no replacement for person-to-person interaction.

Every day your organization engages in conversation with members of your major donor audience. Staff, volunteers, board members, and friends are (sometimes unwittingly) talking with potential major donors and gathering feedback on your behalf.

The informal nature of these interactions means that important feedback may not be getting back to you. Most often the reason is that your organization's key ambassadors are unaware of how importance the individual or organization is to your major gift program.

Those closest to your organization's mission need to be aware of who is on your major gift prospect list. Strategic fundraisers will brief Board members and trusted staff and volunteers, enlisting their help in having bi-lateral conversations (impromptu or planned) designed to gain feedback on projects, programs, and priorities. This can and should become part of a comprehensive communications plan for major gifts.

Seasoned fundraisers and non-profit executives understand the importance of reaching out directly to members of their major gift audience, not just to report on events and progress, but to also ask for advice and feedback. The time to do this is at the stage when plans and priorities for the organization are being developed, not after-the-fact. Many organizations overlook the extraordinary opportunity they have to share their vision and plans with a potential major funder, and ask for input, *before* the plans have been finalized. Eliciting and acting on valuable stakeholder feedback builds buy-in for the initiative and earns credibility with major donors.

iii. *Opting (in and out)*
When it comes to mass print, electronic and automated telephone communications activities, all audience members should be afforded the courtesy of opting out (or in) at their discretion.

All general written and electronic communication materials designed to steward and cultivate interest should incorporate a simple means for recipients to opt out if they choose. As well, they should incorporate a simple mechanism for a recipient to opt in to additional material they are interested in receiving.

When recipients opt out of things like mailings, newsletters, e-zines and e-blasts, fundraisers sometimes interpret this as a serious negative and mistakenly place a "do not contact" flag on their file. This is often not the case. Reasons audience members opt out can include the desire to help the charity reduce mailing and production costs; to streamline their email inbox; or to reduce the number of telephone calls they receive.

If the individual in question is a member of your major gift audience, you should consider sending them a brief hand written note by mail acknowledging their wish and letting them know you will communicate with them in other ways in the future. For those that opt-in, you can drop a personal note thanking them for their interest in receiving further information and letting them know how and when they will receive it.

TO SUM UP

Developing an effective communication plan for major gift communications for your organization means both speaking and listening. A strong plan brings strategy and discipline to what your organization says, to whom, and how. As well, it incorporates meaningful opportunities to learn from feedback.

The first step in designing a plan is defining the audience for major gift communications. While every organization defines its major gift audience differently, it should minimally include potential major gift donors and donors who have given at major levels in the past. The audience can and should include major donors with a likely interest in the organization's mission and work. Loyal volunteers, long-standing smaller donors, and key friends can also be valuable for inclusion when defining the audience for major gift communication.

Organizations need to avoid overwhelming their audience with too much or irrelevant information when developing communications content. Calibrating content with the area of greatest likely interest of the audience is important. Good communications content balances information about big picture organizational impact with real life, authentic stories about lives changed. Clear presentation of the information increases effectiveness because it makes content easy for the audience to understand and digest. Well-written communication and effective storytelling are characteristics of great content.

Taking the time to inventory channels available to your organization will help to operationalize communication activities. Viewing all interactions that your organization has with members of its major donor audience gives an important, audience-centric vantage point on overall communication effectiveness. Communications channels can range from print and electronic publications, to personal interactions with audience members, and multiple options in between. A matrix of communications with your major donor audience will support "moves management" efforts with major donors and prospects. Being aware of other interactions your organization has with your major donor audience, outside of your department, will help you to utilize all communications channels to best effect. Beyond mass communication channels, a strong plan employs direct, personal communication techniques aimed at an "audience of one."

No comprehensive communication program for major gifts is complete without the use of effective mechanisms for feedback. While traditional donor surveys are one available option, they should be used carefully and strategically with any major gift audience. Two-way conversations are the most useful way to elicit feedback from your audience. Other trusted members of your organization — including Board members, staff, and volunteers — should be aware of the composition of your major gift audience, so that they too can be involved in the feedback-gathering process. The period *before* plans are set in stone is an opportune time to elicit important feedback directly from members of your major gift audience. Acknowledging and acting on worthwhile feedback is an important courtesy to extend to those who provide it.

Donors make major gifts as the means to philanthropic ends. Their interests, circumstances, and preferences run the gamut. Our responsibility as professionals is to take the time to understand their interests and tailor communications to both engage their interest, and inspire their generosity. That is the fundamental philosophy behind every effective major gift communication plan.

EXPERT ADVICE FROM THE FIELD

Fraser Green is one of Canada's leading experts fundraising and has authored and co-authored books including *3D Philanthropy* and *Iceberg Philanthropy*. Whether you are communicating one-to-one or one-to-many, Fraser endorses a simple but effective five-step philosophy of donor communication:

- Communication is a two-way exchange.
- Storytelling is the most powerful way to impart information.
- Listening to feedback guides your strategy, and makes donors feel valued.
- Your charity isn't the hero, your donor is.
- Asking great questions is one of your most important market research skills.

Nada Ristich is Director, Corporate Donations with BMO Financial Group. When it comes to applying to her organization for major support, she says, "Two-way communication is key." Wherever possible, Ristich urges organizations to initiate a discussion with potential funders first, long before preparing and submitting an extensive proposal for funding. "A good proposal," she says, "is good for both organizations." After a major gift has been committed, she encourages charities to keep the lines of communication open. "For a multi-year commitment we'll often agree to keep in touch annually, and we'll ask for a short- and long-term report on how the project is going, the impact of the gift, and so on," she says, adding, "if there are problems with where the program is going, then come to us, and we'll see how we can resolve it together."

Malcolm Burrows is Head of Philanthropic Advisory Services at Scotia Private Client Group. Over the years he has worked with, and counselled, countless individual philanthropists who make major gifts. He says - "Effective communication with major gift donors requires a balanced approach. First, charities need to be consistent and regular in their communication. Have a system. Define what needs to be communicated, when, and to whom. Be rigorous in delivery. Donors appreciate being in the 'loop' and charities need to make a point of being top of mind through a variety of media. The second element is more subtle and just as important. Major gift donors may demand regular information on your cause and its effectiveness, but what they remember and emotionally value is the meaningful moments, beautiful gestures and authentic human connections. They won't ask for these moments, but they are the magic that cements the relationship with your charity. It requires sensitivity and spontaneity to create these moments. Make sure they are part of your plan."

CONCLUSION

In *Excellence in Fundraising In Canada, Volume One*, Editor Guy Mallabone summed up a fundamental truth about major gift fundraising: "People give their money to things in their life that they are closest to. This includes themselves, their children, parents, school, community, the disease that took their parents' lives, etc. If you believe this…then our job as major gift fundraisers becomes focused on one key thing… bringing people closer to your organization."[6]

While the tools of the communications trade may be evolving, and lots of folks have opinions about how to best communicate in ways that nurture major gifts, the most important thing to remember is that at the heart of every major gift resides a donor motivated by the same desires they have always had:

- To be valued.
- To trust in your organization.
- To have confidence.
- To share with your organization a genuine belief in a cause.
- To effect a positive change in the world.

Organizational communications activities are not the only elements of good relationship management with major and potential major donors. But they are important ingredients that you need to be successful.

If you focus on the potential donor — who they are, how to reach them, what aspects of your organizational story will interest them most, and what they are signaling back to you — you will already be on the way to successful communications for major gifts.

Designing your major gift communication program around your audience with great content; employing effective channels and integrating valuable donor feedback, will elevate your charity's major gift fundraising results to the next level.

---

10 THINGS TO REMEMBER

1. Tomorrow's major donors are probably already giving to you.

2. Design tactical communications activities for a list of individuals/ organizations that you can reasonably manage.

3. Good donor communication is a two-way street.

4. Don't be shy about contacting donors directly with important information they will be interested in.

5. Calibrate your communications content to major donors (and potential donors) so that only 25% is the "organizational story" and 75% focuses on their area of interest.

6. Communicate directly with people based on how they communicate most often with you (email, phone, letters, texting, in person, etc.).

7. Conduct a communications 360 of who is communicating what and when, to whom.

8. Use the word "you" as often as possible in your communication.

9. Be candid and transparent.

10. Make sure your major donors and prospects have your direct contact coordinates.

---

6   Mallabone, Guy. (2011). *Excellence in Fundraising in Canada (Volume One)*, Chapter 9, Major Gifts.

ADDITIONAL RESOURCES

Books and Articles

▶ Burk, Penelope. (2003). *Donor-Centered Fundraising.* Toronto, ON: Burk & Associates Ltd.

▶ Joyaux, Simone P. (2011). *Strategic Fund Development: Building Profitable Relationships That Last.* Hoboken, NJ: John Wiley & Sons.

▶ Lagasse, Paul. "Dear, Near and Clear: How improving your organization's donor relations can help you provide more resources to more constituents more effectively and more often." *Advancing Philanthropy.* (November/December, 2010): 26.

▶ McClintock, Norah. (2004)."Understanding Canadian Donors: Using the National Survey of Giving, Volunteering and Participating to Build Your Fundraising Program." Canadian Centre for Philanthropy.

▶ Turcotte, Martin. "Charitable Giving by Canadians." *Canadian Social Trends.* Component of Statistics Canada Catalogue no 11-008-X (April 16, 2012).

ABOUT THE AUTHOR

Anne (Coyle) Melanson, BPR, CFRE

Anne is the President and CEO of Bloom Non Profit Consulting Group Inc. She earned her Bachelor of Public Relations Degree in 1988 from Mount Saint Vincent University and has held the CFRE designation since 2008.

Anne has been a professional fundraiser and an enthusiastic champion of Canadian charities for 25 years. Her areas of special expertise are major gifts programs, capital campaigns, and fundraising communications. She has held senior fundraising positions with Ketchum Canada (now KCI), Acadia University, and Saint Mary's University.

She has supported the fundraising profession as a volunteer and leader within AFP locally, nationally, and internationally. Anne was a nominee for AFP's Outstanding Fundraising Executive in 2003 and was named a "Woman of Excellence" by the Progress Club in 2010.

Anne is a sought-after coach and presenter, and has served clients in the charitable sector regionally, nationally and internationally with fundraising goals totaling more than $150 million. When not a fundraiser, she derives her greatest joys in life from her husband, two sons, a pair of Labrador retrievers, and a motorcycle.

CHAPTER 14

FUNDRAISING AND SOCIAL MEDIA

JAMES HOWE, BA, DIP. ED.

Social media is a game-changer in how social profits communicate with their donors and other supporters. If you'd like to use it for "social fundraising" it's important to understand the fundamentals of using social media and how to shift your mindset from your tried and true forms of communication.

read more…

This chapter deliberately avoids getting too specific on how to use or implement social media. Not only does a wealth of constantly updated information sources exist for this rapidly changing field, but *what you do* and *how you do it* also depends upon the culture and expectations of your organization and the considerations specific to your sector. A fundraising department in a large hospital in Quebec differs from a small environmental organization in British Columbia.

As fundraising happens with such a diverse range of situations, this chapter provides high-level advice that is appropriate for the common denominator of this range of situations and the many forms of social media such as:

- Have a personal experience with social media.
- Be genuine.
- Be social. Engage people.
- Integrate social media into how you work and live.
- Commit to what is required to be present on a social media platform.
- It's all about the long game.
- Value social media so that it is a priority for your time.
- Think about the fit of social media to your audience, staff and organization.
- Add value.
- Identify and connect with influencers to help you reach a wider network.

HOW MIKE FARWELL RAISES FUNDS WITH SOCIAL MEDIA

Mike Farwell may very well be the face of the future of social media fundraising for charities. He is not a fundraiser nor has he ever worked for a charity. Yet annually he raises thousands of dollars for Cystic Fibrosis Canada through his use of social media.

Farwell is not simply sitting behind his computer or staring at his phone and repeatedly asking for money. He sets a financial goal and establishes an attention-grabbing challenge. Then he leverages his relationships through social media to achieve them. One year he promised to skydive for the first time if he reached his financial goal. In 2014, he offered himself to do any type of work; from painting swimming pools to being a soda jerk on the condition that his wages go to Cystic Fibrosis.

Although Farwell is a Waterloo Region media personality, his fundraising is a personal effort and communicated almost entirely through his own social media presence. Without him, Cystic Fibrosis in Waterloo Region would not have the same profile nor achieve the same results for its annual fundraising efforts.

Mike Farwell is an *influencer*. He is active year-round on Twitter and Facebook. His content shows that he is interested in his community and cares about making it better but 11 months of the year he rarely talks about cystic fibrosis. In May however, he makes it his prime focus. He shares his compelling personal story to gain support from his social media connections to pursue a cure. His unique challenges gives him content to post and inspires others to give and share forward.

Farwell shows how social media allows someone committed to a cause to help a charity strive for its vision and deliver on its mission.

What is important for non-profit fundraisers to take away from Mike Farwell's story is that using social media is not all about having your organization use it directly to ask for financial gifts. What is more important is to use social media to connect people to your cause and over time enhance their commitment to it. That relationship-building process assists you to identify influencers who can use their own networks to benefit your work.

Influencers are all around you. Having a public profile such as being a media personality can help but social media gives everyone the tools to become an influencer and help your charity strive for its vision and deliver on your mission.

SOCIAL MEDIA USES FUNDRAISERS' BEST PRACTICES

When you stop to think about it, there is not much new about social media for fundraisers. Building relationships, identifying influencers and enhancing people's commitment to your cause are all things that fundraisers are already doing.

The biggest difference is in terms of scale. Social media allows you to reach many more people more frequently. Better yet, used effectively it has a multiplier effect that shares your key messages forward to new audiences from a trusted source—their friends, families and others they know well. That trust factor is why word of mouth has always been the most effective marketing tool. So think of social media as word of mouth marketing on a massive, exponential scale.

HOW TO USE SOCIAL MEDIA

The nature of social media is that it is constantly changing.

At one point, Facebook was the best place to reach teens. In less than a year, they left their parents behind and moved to Twitter. Now you might be more likely to find them on Instagram or Snapchat. But, a fast-growing demographic on Facebook is now seniors so you can connect with new group on a familiar platform.

Before 2014, if you mastered Facebook's "secret sauce"—a mixture of interesting content, frequency and engagement—you could reach people who liked your page without spending a cent. Since then, it's increasingly difficult to reach a large number of people without paying to sponsor (i.e. advertise) your content.

Even seemingly straight forward information such as how to set up a Youtube channel, or advice on the ways that images work better on Facebook than Twitter is constantly changing. Even if you managed to master that sort of knowledge, count on the fact that tomorrow something would change that requires you to learn new steps, or adapt your approach to sharing content.

That is the flexible nature of digital media and its rapid pace of change. So this chapter shares fundamentals of using social media rather than trying to walk you through how to use it.

Look for the most up-to-date information on how to maximize use of a social media, on related blogs, videos, webinars, workshops. There is a lot of information created especially for non-profits or you will find that most information is easily applied to a variety of organizations. There are also a number of consultants and coaches that can teach you how to use social media, including how to integrate it into your overall communications strategy.

Another great learning opportunity are low cost, professional development events provided by groups like:

- Netsquared / Net Tuesday – An initiative of TechSoup, these groups offer regular opportunities to connect and learn about non-profit use of technology and are available in Peterborough, Victoria, Surrey, Saskatoon, Toronto, Montreal and Vancouver. http://www.netsquared.org/unauthenticated#.U7Bvicog8kk. http://www.techsoupcanada.ca/node/2575

- Social Media Breakfast - for anyone interested in learning to improve their social media use in Calgary (https://twitter.com/smbyyc), Edmonton, Waterloo Region and Montreal.

- Third Tuesday - public relations oriented professional development organized on Meetup by Joe Thornley of Thornley Fallis in Ottawa, Toronto, Montreal and Calgary (http://www.meetup.com/third-tuesday-calgary)

A NEW MINDSET FOR COMMUNICATIONS

The biggest shift that is necessary to use social media is to leave behind the mindset of traditional methods of communicating to your audience. Whether it is use of a brochure, an annual report or even a website, we have relied mainly on one-way communication (also known as broadcasting). You put information out there and tried to get it into the right hands, but never anticipated directly hearing back from your audience and having a public conversation.

Social media means intentionally using two-way communication. You want to be having a conversation. While it may be a dialogue with only one person, it is public and others are paying attention. You may also be chatting with many individuals in a group conversation.

SOCIAL MEDIA IS ABOUT BUILDING RELATIONSHIPS

"Not everything your organization does in social media will have a direct causal relationship to donations or earned revenue. Much of social media's value lies in its ability to help you learn and improve, understand the attitudes and opinions of your stakeholders, and ultimately build relationships."[1]

As a fundraiser when you meet someone new, are the first words out of your mouth asking for a gift?

Not likely - unless you are okay with getting a lot of negative answers with the occasional small gift to get you to go away.

You get to know someone first as a person, and then gradually get a sense of what is important to them, also giving them a chance to get to know you and your organization. After you have a relationship established, you're more likely to make your ask and be successful. The larger the potential gift, the longer this process can take.

The same philosophy holds true for social media. Do not constantly use social media to ask people for money—or even to help you raise money. Take some time to get to know them, build a relationship and enhance their commitment to your cause.

Just ask planned giving and networking expert Paul Nazareth. He recognized how LinkedIn provided him a platform to demonstrate his subject matter expertise and an opportunity to build his network of contacts and enhance his relationships. He then learned he could apply his LinkedIn experience to other social media such as Twitter.

Social media is like a coffee shop

Think of whatever form of social media you are using as a coffee shop. If you never go to the same coffee shop regularly or you go to the same one but infrequently or at unpredictable times, you're unlikely to get to know anyone.

Go to the same coffee shop at the same time every day and you will start to see familiar faces and engage in some small talk. Over time, some of those conversations become more substantial and you start to get to know each other. Then a friendship may blossom and you'll be invested in each other's wellbeing.

Your behavior at the coffee shop provides the context for that relationship to blossom. How you use social media can open the same potential. For example, you need to know what the expectations are for the form of social media you are using and meet them. Twitter (twitter.com) for example requires a more frequent presence than Pinterest (pinterest.com).

Relationships build community

Knitting is often a solitary activity yet there is a vibrant community of knitters online. Their use of social media connects them with others sharing the same interest. They get to know each other as individuals but as they connect with enough individuals, they start to become a group and meet new people through common relationships. Slowly, they knit themselves together to form a community.

Social media allows for these types of connections to be made with people who otherwise would be unlikely to cross paths, even if they live in close proximity. It opens up possibilities for people to connect through common interests.

At this point, there likely are already communities online related to your cause. Find them and participate in them. Using the search function on the social media being used is likely enough to get you started. There are tools such as a hashtag (#) that the community is using. Hashtags are used on Twitter, Instagram and now Facebook. They help to collect all posts on a specific subject whether or not you follow those using it. For example, #vaw is used for talking about violence against women and can be used to search for all tweets related to that subject. Just be careful to respect the existing community and try to fit in.

As relationships with your organization and a sense of community deepen, it becomes easier to take them offline such as extending an invitation to participate in your next walk or golf tournament. And, you already know that the degree of commitment to the cause affects how much each individual raises or gives.

Effective use of social media requires the same patience and tactics as offline fundraising; place the emphasis upon building relationships and a sense of community. This takes time and allows you to develop a greater level of commitment by educating people about what you do, why you do it and how you and they together can make a difference.

---
1   Kanter, Beth and Paine, Katie Delahaye. (2012). *Measuring the Networked Nonprofit*. San Francisco, CA: Jossey-Bass A Wiley Imprint. p. 60.

CASE STUDY: PAYING IT FORWARD WITH 12 DAYS FOR GOOD

A Kitchener-Waterloo charity runs an annual social media based campaign in December that does not ask for money - but that makes a difference in the agency's fundraising results.

House of Friendship started the 12 Days for Good campaign in 2012 as a way to say thank you for the support it receives from the community each year and to pay that good fortune forward. It was inspired by decades of volunteers helping the agency run a holiday Christmas Hamper program that is supported by the Kitchener Conestoga Rotary Club's Annual Turkey Drive.

The Turkey Drive and Christmas Hamper program succeed using traditional fundraising techniques. Rather than trying to raise more funds in December for itself, House of Friendship wanted to use its good fortune and growing social media presence to inspire more good acts to be shared across their community.

"We looked for a way to make the good work we do in the community highly visible, yet in a way that was consistent with our core values," says Development Director, Christine Rier. "That includes sharing the good of our sister agencies because as strong as we are as a charity that only gets us so far. For a very healthy community, everyone needs to be strong."

This communications campaign shares the agency's approach to community-building through 12 daily themes during the Christmas Hamper program and Turkey Drive. The campaign is led by 12 "Do Gooders" who are local people or organizations that are normally active on social media as community builders.

The result of 12 Days for Good is a noticeable spike in social media activity, especially "Likes" for its Facebook page and "followers" on Twitter. While there is no ask, Rier says, "I find that the more we focus on communicating who we are, what we do, what we believe and our dream for the future, the better the results we see for our fundraising."

Website: 12daysforgood.com
VIDEO: 12 Days for Good: An interview with Christine Rier from the House of Friendship
http://youtu.be/XhVabMHUgsM

STAFFING SOCIAL MEDIA

Most organizations start using social media with existing staff resources, though some make it a volunteer opportunity.

Normally (except for the smallest social profits or grassroots organizations) having a staff member handling this duty is recommended. This person should be high enough up the org chart to know the organizational culture and priorities and be able to communicate without always seeking approval. Finding the time is a matter of shifting priorities (see Fundamental #7).

The best fit is with a communications staff member. If your agency doesn't have any, your growing use of social media can likely help build the case for allocating resources to hire a part-time or full-time communications person who has the expertise to share your stories and strategically reach your key audiences.

FUNDAMENTALS OF EFFECTIVE SOCIAL MEDIA

1. *Your personal experience with social media informs your professional use.*
   If you've never been on Reddit (FAQ at reddit.com/wiki/faq), you're unlikely to perform well in a Reddit AMA (Ask Me Anything) where you offer yourself up to answer questions from other users. So even if that is where the people you want to reach are found, it is not the place to start.

   Before you use any form of social media, have a personal experience with it first. That is as easy as signing up for a personal account, use the account to explore both your personal and professional interests and make a point of experiencing how to use it socially to connect with other people. You will also get a sense of what organizations are doing well in this social space and what does not work.

   Once you understand as an individual how social media, such as the blogging platform Tumblr, operates and what the expectations are, then you will know how to stand out for the right reasons instead of being invisible or sticking out for the wrong reasons.

2. *Be genuine. Talk like a person talking to people.*
Forget the official organizational voice that is used in brochures and newsletters. You are talking to people, so talk like a person. Use a casual, conversational voice. Listen and then respond in a timely fashion.

Be you. Be the person who works for your charity and be how you relate to people that you meet in that role. On the one hand, it is important to keep your brand in mind so that you deliver on your organization's promise to people. On the other hand, avoid interpreting your brand in a restrictive way that takes the person out of social media.

The Stratford Festival is a great example of the genuine use of social media as a person (stratfordfestival.ca/contactus/contactus.aspx?id=7616). Yes, they need to sell lots of tickets and also seek financial gifts but that is not the impression left by experiencing its social media. You know that there is a person on the other end and they get results even if they say something simple in a post like, "What a great day it is today!"

Watch: Lisa Middleton, former director of marketing for the Stratford Shakespeare Festival, at Tweetstock6: youtu.be/aiFpixiCWWA.

3. *Be social.*
If you walk into a reception and say something to a group of people talking to each other or throw a news release on a table and walk away, you may not make an impression upon them—or at least not a good one. There's etiquette about working your way into the conversation such as responding to what someone said or you say something to elicit a response, pay attention to it and respond appropriately.

Since social media is a *conversation*, similar etiquette is appropriate. If someone leaves a comment on your blog post for example, be sure that you acknowledge it and respond to it quickly.

Avoid just posting information or ideas and leaving. Stick around or come back soon to hear what others are saying. Then respond and see if they have something more to say. Also be sure to take the initiative to respond to what others are posting and answer questions.

4. *Think of social media as a behaviour.*
Odd as it may be to think of a set of tools as a behaviour, that is what separates dabbling in social media from effectively using it.

Look back at the introduction of e-mail and how using it became a behaviour. People already had enough to do at work. They did not have time for this new communication tool. Then it became important enough that they couldn't ignore it so they checked their e-mail at set times of their day. Over time, checking e-mail became an established behaviour. Gradually, people started leaving their e-mail program open so they knew when an e-mail arrived and could respond quickly if needed and now with smart phones, many people don't leave their desk (even to go the washroom) without taking their e-mail with them.

The same holds true with social media. You need to weave its use into how you work. Doing so can be as easy as working social media into your daily/weekly routines. Tools like Tweetdeck.com or Hootsuite.com provide dashboards that you can keep open to frequently and easily monitor multiple social media accounts. Apps on your smart phone make social media easy to check when you have a spare moment and also have alerts for when your attention is needed.

When you weave social media into how you work, you are naturally initiating and enhancing relationships and interacting with the information being shared. That is a sign that you are present as a participant in that space and not just a visitor.

5. *There is a difference between having an account and using it.*
If you have a Facebook page but rarely (if ever) post to it or even have long periods of inactivity, you are not using it. Even when you

do post something, the algorithm Facebook uses to determine who sees it is not likely to identify many people who have a strong relationship with your page. Having the Facebook logo on your annual report might look good but you are not going to get any results unless you are using it in a way that gets attention and allows you to build relationships and community.

While the expectations differ between social media, they all have certain levels of use that are required to be considered active.

So rather than trying to be on three or more social media sites and not actively using any of them, determine which one(s) are most important (see Fundamental #8 to learn more about how to choose your social media) and dedicate to using it effectively. Drop or add social media based upon your experience or capacity.

6. *There are no quick wins in social media. It's all about the long game.*
Yes, your video *might* go viral and social media increases the chances that it goes viral. But *most* videos, blog posts and tweets do not go viral and that is ok.

Relationships take time. Even when love occurs on first sight, developing and maintaining a relationship takes time.

Since social media is about building relationships that means it usually takes a while—possibly a long time—before it pays off. Money does not start arriving because you now use social media or even improved your use of it. You may need to show your expertise in solving the root causes of poverty and hunger over many years before you find enough people willing to donate enough to fund your research.

Blog posts are a great way to show that your organization's depth of knowledge in its field or your own personal knowledge in an area of work. The type and quality of content from others, that you share on LinkedIn or Twitter, also contributes to being considered a thought leader.

7. *Finding time is a question of priorities.*
Not enough time for social media? Not likely unless you value it less than what gets your time and resources.

Finding time for social media is just like finding time for anything else. It is a question of priorities. If you value it and it is important enough, you find the time. That may mean doing things differently, shifting duties from one position to another or stopping what is not a good use of time anymore.

For example, is the print newsletter that goes out quarterly and uses a lot of staff time the best way to use that resource? Is it worth the cost of printing and mailing too? Maybe the quarterly print newsletter is worthwhile but should the Financial Development Director be putting on the postage? Or should that be an administrative staff member, a volunteer or better yet a mailing house?

The point is that we all have things that we do because "that is how it is done," or what is expected. It is worthwhile to stop and figure out if that is the best use of resources, including time.

8. *Choose which social media fits best with you and your organization?*
The big question is which social media should your social profit be using. The answer depends upon what is the best fit for your organization and the audience you are trying to reach. It also depends upon who is responsible for social media and how much time they have available. Don't feel like you need to be on Facebook because "everyone else is" or that you have to jump on the next hot social media.

Ideally, you want to be where the people you want to reach are found. Not sure or want to confirm your thinking about where your audience is at? Ask them. Use an online survey tool, paper surveys, or ask people in person when they arrive for a program or service—whatever works best for you.

If, for example, you want to reach a professional audience, you want to be sure that you have a "Company Page" on LinkedIn. This page gives you a LinkedIn presence that is connected to current and former staff's personal profiles. It can also be useful to reach others working in your field and partnering agencies. Posting updates on your LinkedIn page can help you to connect with potential donors, board members and even possible new staff.

However, it also helps if the social media selected fits with the staff that are using it. Choosing to use a LinkedIn company page is not likely the best choice if the person responsible is not comfortable using LinkedIn, perhaps from not having any personal experience of it yet. Similarly, Facebook may be the place to start if that falls inside your staff's comfort zone more than Twitter or Snapchat.

Another factor to consider is how much time is available, and how much time is necessary to have a presence on a social media. A blog post (a blog includes a collection of online posts that are normally open to comments) a week is typically the minimum desired to be "active" yet a post can take one to three hours to write. A LinkedIn page generally requires less attention than its Facebook equivalent. Both Facebook and LinkedIn have a lower frequency expectation than Twitter.

Frequency of use expectations by social media

Social Media	Minimum	Desirable	Maximum	Advice
Facebook (Posts on Page)	1 per day	3	Normally no more than 1 per hour	Use Facebook page Insights to know when the largest number of people who like your page are online. Schedule posts for these times but monitor for responses.
Twitter (including tweets, retweets and responses)	3 per day (1 tweet, 1 response, 1 retweet)	6 - 10	Tough to tweet too much.	As your followers grow, you are best to tweet more frequently, including repetition of information shared to increase chances of catching someone while they are online. Schedule tweets for when your followers are online if you are able to respond to what others say and ask.
Blog	1x each week	1x each day	1x each day (unless additional posts are time sensitive and unexpected)	
LinkedIn Company Page	1x each week	1x each day	1x each day to all followers or each target segment.	Use the option to target posts to segments of your followers.
Other social media				Desirable frequency always depends upon norms of users in that space. Observe what other organizations are doing who are using that social media well.

Once you decide upon what social media you can commit to using, get started. Give yourself permission to start small especially if your organization does not have any full-time communications staff. You can always add more later on.

If it is important to be on more social media than your current resources can manage, maybe that makes it an organizational priority to acquire those resources.

Share content that is interesting or useful. Add value.
Be assured that if something is of interest to your agency, there are people online talking about it already.

Some charities are concerned that they have little to share or that they will quickly become annoyingly repetitive. If that sounds familiar, do not worry. You have stories and expertise all around you. Sometimes it is so commonplace to the staff that experience it all the time that it is easy to forget that the subject matter can be new and fascinating to someone with a different experience. Brainstorming is a great technique to build up a bank of content. Set a high, but realistic goal, like 100 blog post topics or 50 photo opportunities showing your mission in action.

Some charities are fortunate to recognize that they have more to share than they have capacity to share. If that sounds familiar, you have a great chance to be strategic in sharing your content. Consider using a social media planning calendar to schedule what you will post where and when. Set a monthly and/or weekly theme to give your planning some structure.

Noting special days for your organization or relevant to your audience can also be helpful. (See the Additional Resources at the end of this chapter for links to examples.)

Keep in mind that what you share needs to have value to your audience or else they will not care enough about it to engage with you. For example saying, "There's a great crowd today to hear our guest speaker Guy Mallabone," may solicit the response of "so what?" Whereas, sharing gems from Guy's speech give people some substance to think about or that may inspire giving.

CASE STUDY: HO HO HO! MERRY SOCIAL FUNDRAISING!

Started with a single tweet and promoted with a hashtag, HoHoTO is known as the party Twitter started. It is also a large annual fundraiser on behalf of Toronto's Daily Bread Food Bank.

When first held in 2008, the event was pulled together in 48 hours thanks to the power of social media, exceeding it's ambitious $10,000 goal. By 2010, it aimed to raise $80,000—or more than double what it raised its first two years. Still going strong in 2013, the event now has 100+ sponsors, 50+ volunteers, $10,000 in donated prizes and attracts more than 600 people.

HoHoTO has proven to be an extraordinary example of the power of self-organizing online communities. Toronto'a technology, digital marketing and social media communities come together, through their Twitter streams and Gmail accounts, to create what has become one of the biggest and most exciting seasonal gatherings in Toronto.

All of this is remarkable, but that's not really why we all come together each year to do this. We do this because sadly there is a need. People in our community need our help.
hohoto.ca/2010/10/28/hohoto-2010-bigger-and-better/

Social media has evolved a lot since this industry of digital early adopters created a successful fundraising event in 48 hours. Yet it still provides insights for organizations looking to tap into social fundraising:

1. People organize events because they know about your cause and care enough to help.
2. Connected influencers active on social media can enhance your efforts and possibly even create something out of nothing.
3. A connected community of active influencers can achieve even greater success and develop a sustainable fundraising event.
4. Without the first point, you are unlikely to break through the noise and grab the attention of influencers or the online communities they participate in.

Website: www.hohoTO.ca
VIDEO: hohoto.ca/2013/12/18/watch-a-short-video-about-the-hohoto-love/

Be generous: Share. Respond. Comment.
Think of this point as "Do unto others as you would have them do unto you." The vast majority of people who see your content will not interact with it. So a comment on a blog post or a retweet of your post on Twitter is often rare enough to be worth celebrating.

Keep that in mind as you come across content shared by other organizations. Sharing it forward to your community or commenting on it will be appreciated. Do so whether through your personal account or an organizational one.

Even better, be proactive and take the initiative to interact with others talking about what is important to your organization. That shows you are interested and may help connect you with a current or future influencer.

MEASURING YOUR SOCIAL MEDIA SUCCESS

> *"...effective measurement always measures the progress toward the mission, not just the size of the bank account."* [2]

A benefit of digital media, (which includes social media) is the ability to measure your success since it comes with lots of statistics. Having easy access to these numbers is a great gift to communicators but you need to proceed with caution. *Digital media* includes all forms of online communication. *Social media* includes those communications tools that focus on the ability for people to interact with other people—often in real time. So a website or an e-newsletter service, for example, are digital media but not social media.

Quality is more important than quantity. Be careful not to value numbers just because they are big. What's more important are numbers that show whether you are achieving your objectives.

For example, when looking at social media stats avoid defining success by the number of likes on your Facebook page or how many followers your Twitter account have. Both have their place when considered within a greater context but looking at them in isolation isn't useful and tends to be a vanity metric.

What's more valuable is how engaged is your community in these and other social spaces? Is it improving over time? Are you inspiring action? And most importantly; is your use of social media helping your organization to reach benchmarks that show you are achieving greater success in delivering your mission?

Some social media such as Facebook and LinkedIn come with their own free statistics to help you learn what your community is doing.

One way to determine if you are inspiring action is to measure activity on your website (with or without a blog). The free Google Analytics provides a wealth of comprehensive data but you may be served well enough by the stats provided by the easier to use free Jetpack plugin for Wordpress sites.

Determining social media's impact on operations means comparing results from a previous year when social media was not a factor or when social media was used differently. By doing so you can make a reasonable deduction that what you are doing new that is making the difference. For example, if social media is a key component of this year's awareness campaign, it can be credited as contributing to any resulting increase in requests to speak on that issue.

If you prefer, you can isolate the social media effect by monitoring what happens when it is the only way you are actively sharing your call to action.

How measurement can make social fundraising more effective

As a fundraiser, you may be thinking, "That's great if social media helps my organization make progress on its mission but I still need to hit my financial development targets."

That's why it is critical that as a fundraiser you care about measuring digital media and ensuring that you are looking at quality information rather than being pleased with quantity.

An excellent resource is *Measuring the Networked Nonprofit*[3] by non-profit technology icon Beth Kanter and measurement maven K.D. Paine. There's a whole chapter on how to use social media to turn your stakeholders into fundraisers, with advice on how to enjoy success with social fundraising.

---

[2] Kanter, Beth and Paine, Katie Delahaye. (2012). Measuring the Networked Nonprofit. San Francisco, CA: Jossey-Bass A Wiley Imprint. p. 110.

[3] Kanter, Beth and Paine, Katie Delahaye. (2012). *Measuring the Networked Nonprofit.* San Francisco, CA: Jossey-Bass A Wiley Imprint.

Analyzing the data available to you can help you make strategic improvement in your use of digital media. For example, when running a fundraising campaign on social media, you can track:

- Percentage increase in number of donors
- Percentage increases in higher levels of engagement
- Percentage increase in the size of the network

Tracking this data weekly and communicating via dashboards helps determine what social media activity is making a difference and what isn't helping.

NEXT STEPS

So what now? How do you get started or take your social media use to the next level? There are many potential next steps such as:

- Developing a social media strategy and/or policy
- Establishing guidelines for external users posting on your social media
- Determining who does what and determining internal processes
- Setting up an editorial calendar

The upside is that there is a wealth of material available that is up-to-date and easily available online. Likely you can even find packages that are specific to your sector or situation. If not, see if a sister organization or one that is similar can share what they have.

CASE STUDY: GIVING DAYS, A PROACTIVE APPROACH TO SOCIAL GIVING

With all the hype and very real potential of social fundraising, charities are trying to figure out how to cash in—without waiting to be the beneficiary of online influencers or communities deciding to support them.

This search for a proactive way to initiate a successful social giving campaign has found a promising opportunity in "Giving Days." These days are when a large number of charities, normally working within a common geographic area, encourage online giving through social media. They have been known to raise millions of dollars.

The best known is Giving Tuesday which started in the United States on the Tuesday after American Thanksgiving. It was promoted as a sort of antidote to the consumerism of Black Friday and Cyber Monday during Thanksgiving weekend.

Giving Tuesday was adopted as part of a national initiative by many Canadian charities in 2013. The first ever Giving Tuesday in Canada exceeded all expectations. More than 1,300 charities, foundations, groups, businesses and brands came together to participate. Together, these organizations launched an unprecedented campaign for giving, engaging millions of Canadians. Many organizations reported that their campaigns exceeded the targets and overall giving statistics for Canada were very impressive. Several online and mobile donations processors reported significant dollar increases for Giving Tuesday as compared to the same Tuesday in 2012.[4] Media coverage was also strong from coast to coast with major coverage online, in print and on television and radio.

Common strategies for success on Giving Days are to use social media ambassadors and to have a matching donor. As this technique is used more frequently, more is being learned about how to be successful so be sure to check out online fundraising blogs for the latest.

Website: givingtuesday.ca
VIDEOS: www.youtube.com/user/GivingTuesdayCa

Or you can learn from and adapt from other social profits who are sharing forward their "internal" advice on implementing or enhancing use of digital and social media. A couple of examples:

- A 90-page "survival guide" created by YMCA Canada (ymca.ca/en/what's-new/digital-engagement-survival-guide-.aspx) to assist its member associations
- The Toolkit for Ontario Public Health Units (http://www.publichealthontario.ca/fr/LearningAndDevelopment/Events/Pages/toolkit_planning_implementing_evaluating_social_media_Ontario_PHUs.aspx).

There are also collections of social media policies, and guidelines and tools that help to generate them.

Other great sources for know-how and ongoing professional development are associations like NTEN (nten.org) which is dedicated to helping non-profits maximize their use of technology by using it to fundraise and communicate.

CONCLUSION: RESULTS FLOW FROM EFFECTIVE SOCIAL MEDIA USE

Mike Farwell aimed to raise $5,000 for Cystic Fibrosis in 2014 through his #Farwell4Hire challenge. When he quickly exceeded it, he raised his goal to $10,000. By the end of May, he raised $20,590 and Waterloo Region raised more money than any other in Canada.

Before social media, Farwell would have had great difficulty raising that amount all by himself. Even with social media, he needs to be active year-round on his chosen platforms, be building relationships and be sharing content with value rather than continuously asking people for money. As a result, Farwell has built online communities that care about his personal cause. His efforts from previous years have also built a foundation for future success.

Mike Farwell's story demonstrates a number of lessons for successful social fundraising:

1. Get the fundamentals of effective social media right.
2. Build relationships.
3. Develop online communities.
4. Identify influencers. If your organization can connect with people (especially influencers like Mike Farwell) over the long-run, results will follow. You will see your social media use pay off in significant ways including enhancing your number of supporters and the strength of their commitment.
5. Improve your ability to deliver your mission and strive for your vision.

Do these things and you can reap the benefits of social fundraising.

One final piece of advice. While you can read about social media as much as you want, you learn it best by doing, so get started!

---

4 Retrieved June, 2014 from givingtuesday.ca/blog/2013/12/05/givingtuesday-highlights/#.U4zNx_k7um5

ADDITIONAL RESOURCES

Books

- Kanter, Beth and Katie Delahaye Paine. (2012). *Measuring the Networked Nonprofit: Using Data to Change the World.* San Francisco, CA: Jossey-Bass A Wiley Imprint.

- Kanter, Beth and Alison Fine. (2010). *The Networked Nonprofit: Connecting with Social Media to Drive Change.* San Francisco, CA: Jossey-Bass A Wiley Imprint.

Online articles and blog posts

- Kanter, Beth. "#GivingTuesday: How Sharing Best Practices Is Building A Global Philanthropic Movement," bethkanter.org/givingtuesday-dec3/#sthash.8VVceK7l.dpuf .

- Kerr, Clair. "How Does Your Organization Define "Success" in Social Media Fundraising?" http://www.afpnet.org/ResourceCenter/ArticleDetail.cfm?ItemNumber=20295.

- "How to Hold the Perfect reddit AMA (Ask Me Anything)" groupsrc.com/how-to-hold-the-the-perfect-reddit-ama-ask-me-anything/.

- Mansfield, Heather. "Mobile and social media are powerful fundraising tools: An excerpt from Mobile for Good." issuu.com/ntenorg/docs/nten_change_june2014_final/35?e=11383070/8364413.

- Schwartz, Nancy with John Haydon. "Nonprofit Facebook ROI—Yay or Nay?" (2014). (gettingattention.org/2014/04/nonprofit-facebook-roi/.

URLs

- bethkanter.org - Beth Kanter's Blog: For all things nonprofit & digital media including social media

- communicateandhowe.com/2014/03/04/social_media_planning_calendar/ - Here's a social media planning calendar, Communicate & Howe! (March 2014).

- communicateandhowe.com – Communicate & Howe! A look at how to meet the integrated communications needs of nonprofits with a focus on using social media

- johnhaydon.com – Advice for non-profits on using Facebook and other digital marketing communications tools.

- kdpaine.blogs.com – How to measure social media and other key communications tools.

- http://www.lightboxcollaborative.com/2014-editorial-calendar - Become Your Own Publishing Powerhouse with LightBox Collaborative's 2014 Editorial Calendar, Lightbox Collaborative (December 2013).

- nonprofitmarcommunity.com/ - Managed by Torontonian Marlene Oliveira, this site includes posts on social media within a non-profit communications context.

- nten.org - See its blog and other options under "Learn" for all things non-profit and technology related including social media.

- http://www.publichealthontario.ca/fr/LearningAndDevelopment/Events/Pages/Toolkit_Planning_Implementing_Evaluating_Social_Media_Ontario_PHUs.aspx - Social Media Toolkit for Ontario Public Health Units (Released, April 1, 2014).

- techsoupcanada.ca/en/taxonomy/term/282 – posts related to community and social media.

- YMCA.CA/EN/WHAT'S-NEW/DIGITAL-ENGAGEMENT-SURVIVAL-GUIDE-.ASPX - YMCA Digital Engagement Survival Guide.

Case Studies

- CRUSE, AMY. ED. "Twestival - grassroots fundraising from volunteers." (sofii.org/node/601).

- LEUKEMIA & LYMPHOMA SOCIETY OF CANADA, HOOTSUITE. (www.slideshare.net/hootsuite/lss-casestudy).

ABOUT THE AUTHOR

James Howe, BA, Dip. Ed.

James Howe possesses a proven track record of success over 20 years as a creative, innovative communications professional. He uses integrated marketing communications to help charities and non-profits deliver their mission and strive for their vision.

James is the Chief Idea Guy at his full-service communications firm, Communicate & Howe! (communicateandhowe.com). He's led awareness campaigns for Women's Crisis Services of Waterloo Region and worked on annual reports and other communications material for clients such as the Kitchener-Waterloo Humane Society and World Accord. Previously, he was director of communications for the YMCAs of Cambridge & Kitchener-Waterloo and communicated for Toronto's Daily Bread Food Bank.

He regularly speaks to at conferences and events such as participating in two panels at the 2014 Non-profit Technology Conference in Washington D.C. His blog is ranked among the "Top 150 Non-profit Blogs."

CHAPTER 15

PHILANTHROPIC NAMING

VINCENT E DUCKWORTH, BSC, CFRE

Boards of directors, fundraising volunteers, and fundraisers are all asking for philanthropic and sponsorship naming plans to become an integral part of the fundraising planning process. The traditional foundational documents for a successful fundraising program have been a Case for Support and a fund development plan. This dynamic duo now has a sidekick: The philanthropic naming plan.

read more…

Naming public spaces to recognize the contributions of individuals is not new. In Europe and North America, many of the most important cathedrals and public squares are named for individuals (and in many cases, their associated giving).

In Canada, two of our most widely recognized philanthropic namings are those associated with McGill University and McMaster University. Both of these universities were founded through significant acts of philanthropy and were subsequently named to honour those gifts.

What is new is that philanthropic naming has become mainstream. It is no longer the purview of a small number of community leaders.

This chapter, for the first time, presents this relatively new area of knowledge broadly to the professional fundraising community in Canada. This chapter will help you understand the context for philanthropic naming and how to incorporate philanthropic naming policy and valuation into your fundraising practice.

We encourage you will share this chapter with your board and your organizational leadership to help them understand philanthropic naming and we encourage you, as a professional fundraiser, to use this chapter as a springboard to develop a philanthropic naming plan for your organization.

PHILANTHROPIC NAMING TODAY

A question often asked about philanthropic naming is: Why do we do it? The short answer is because it represents the ultimate form of enduring recognition and acknowledgement for our most committed donors.

The longer answer is because, many donors are looking for this type of recognition, our governing boards (who not only represent our communities but who, themselves, are often significant donors to our causes) expect this type of planning and, finally, we do it because it adds a significant professional tool to our fundraising toolbox.

Donors interest

There are many reasons why donors are interested in philanthropic naming. Three of the most common are:
1. To be remembered
2. To honour others
3. To be associated with something they care about

These are easy to understand. Most of us want to be remembered. We all have people in our lives that we want to recognize and we want the world to know what we care (and cared) about.

Good questions to ask donors who may be interested in making a naming gift:

- Is the naming meant to honour them personally?
- Is the naming meant to honour someone else who is important to him or her?

When working on a naming gift, we already have a sense that the donor cares about our organization. What we also need to discover is whether there are aspects of our organization that specifically resonate with the donor.

For example, if the gift is to a performing arts organization, is it the performance space (e.g. the stage and seating area), the public space (e.g. the main lobby), or the performers' space (e.g. the dressing rooms) that are important to the donor?

What about motivation?

Donors *are* interested in philanthropic naming. This interest *does not*, however, translate to mean that the recognition associated with philanthropic naming is a primary motivation when they are considering making a gift. Research conducted by Mallabone and Myers found that "direct benefits" (including philanthropic naming) was a relatively low priority as a primary motivator for making a gift.[1]

The primary motivation for making a gift remains belief in the mission and vision of an organization. We caution you to resist the urge to "lead" with philanthropic naming. Its best and most appropriate use is when the donor brings it up specifically or when they have made a gift where a philanthropic naming would be an appropriate form of recognition for their gift.

Board expectations

Boards of directors have increasingly sophisticated expectations of the planning and execution of fundraising activity. In addition to wanting to see a Case for Support and a campaign plan, boards now expect to

---
1 Mallabone, Guy & Tony Myers. (2000). *Motivators and Barriers to Philanthropic Giving by Entrepreneurs.* Saint Mary's University of Minnesota.

see a philanthropic and sponsorship naming plan as an early part of fundraising strategy. Philanthropic naming policy is also becoming one of the "big 3" polices that boards debate and create; (1) gift acceptance; (2) stewardship; and, (3) naming.

Boards want to know that their organization's naming opportunities and valuations are:

- Of sufficient quantity to provide a range of recognition and acknowledgement opportunities for donors;
- Of sufficient quantity to provide the fundraising team (and hence, the fundraising program) with enough opportunities to recognize all of the naming gifts that will make up the fundraising goal; and
- Of a quality that is in harmony with the organization's mission and vision.

Good boards are also engaged in the fundraising activity of the organization. As fundraising volunteers, they want to have an understanding of the naming opportunities and to be able to speak to the rationale behind why they were selected and how the valuations were developed.

SOLICITATION PLANNING

Working with prospective donors who are likely to be interested and capable of making philanthropic naming gifts requires significant experience, planning and execution. For these prospective donors, philanthropic naming has a significant role in your solicitation plan or, more specifically, the stewardship and recognition plans for your prospective donor.

Solicitation plans include, among other things, information on the interests of the prospective donor. They should also include personalized information on the recognition and stewardship aspects associated with the target gift level.

Key questions to answer in your solicitation plan include:

- **Are there naming opportunities, at the right gift level, that align with the interests of the donor?** I once worked with a donor who had made a $1 million commitment to a health charity I was assisting. She was particularly interested in pediatric cardiology. We knew this before we solicited the gift (it was part of our solicitation plan). With this knowledge, we were able to visit her and suggest three distinct philanthropic naming opportunities linked to her interests at the $1 million level. She was impressed.

- **How does the donor want to be formally recognized with the naming?** For example, would they like to have their name, their family name, or another name used in the formal recognition associated with the naming? Exploring and landing the answer or basket of answers to this question is critical to developing a strong proposal for the prospective donor.

MYTHS AND PHILANTHROPIC NAMING

MYTH:
We can't give our donor a charitable tax receipt if we recognize them with a philanthropic naming.

Some people believe that recognition in the form of a philanthropic naming invalidates the opportunity for the donor to receive a charitable tax receipt. This is, most often, not correct. Unlike sponsorship naming which is a commercial transaction involving a contractual and mutual exchange of value (see Brent Barootes' excellent definition of sponsorship in Chapter 11), philanthropic naming does *not* involve a mutual exchange of value, and therefore the gift is typically eligible for a charitable tax receipt.

The value of a philanthropic gift can be, and often is, 20 times or more the value that would be ascribed to a space if evaluated using sponsorship methodologies. Philanthropic naming also does not involve a legal contract. Non-binding gift agreements, however, are common and encouraged. Philanthropic naming is an important extension of existing philanthropic recognition and stewardship practices and should be used as such. Where the risk of the gift not being deemed entirely charitable arises is when an organization uses philanthropic naming as the lead activity in a solicitation process. For example, beginning a solicitation with a prospective donor by giving them a list of naming opportunities to "choose" from would be considered leading with philanthropic naming.

MYTH:
Naming spaces and programs for gifts and sponsorships will erode mission and brand.

Not if done with diligence and care. In fact, when done purposefully and thoughtfully, philanthropic and sponsorship naming can significantly enhance your reputation and your brand, and hence, your mission.

Aligning your organization with the right prospective donor is a critical aspect to naming. Shared values are crucial as is the reputation of the donor and their associates. Good practice is to have this aspect of philanthropic naming as the first statement in your naming policies (see section on naming policies later in this chapter).

It is also important to recognize that having every program and space named is not the goal. A reasonable number of selective, strategic, and significant philanthropic namings completed by the end of a successful fundraising campaign will achieve much more for your reputation than naming every space in your inventory. Significant namings tell the community that you are both important and worth investing in.

MYTH:
Philanthropic naming is only for "ultra-big" gifts.

It is easy to understand why you might associate philanthropic naming with only very large gifts. Often, it is these gifts and their associated namings that get the most media attention.

Philanthropic naming is not only for "ultra-big" gifts. In fact, it is critical for a successful campaign that philanthropic naming opportunities be available across a wide range of gift levels. What is important is that the size of the gift be "significant." While the definition of a significant gift can be very different from organization to organization, it is not unusual for the values of naming gifts to range from $5,000 (think naming of a dormitory room) to $5 million (or higher) in any given philanthropic naming inventory.

Having philanthropic naming opportunities that are only available to a few elite donors is a mistake.

Fundraising today is an inclusive activity and naming values for the full range of significant gifts tells the community that you are an inclusive organization.

Information on how to develop philanthropic naming opportunities across a wide range of giving levels is discussed in the "Developing your inventory section" of this chapter.

MYTH:
Philanthropic naming is only useful for new capital projects.

It is true that developing a philanthropic naming inventory is more straightforward with a defined fundraising goal. However, existing buildings and spaces also have value and this value can be determined through a variety of methods including using known replacement costs or imputed costs based on similar spaces.

Notwithstanding, for this edition of *Excellence in Fundraising in Canada*, we will be focused on developing philanthropic naming inventory for new capital projects.

MYTH:
Philanthropic naming is only useful for "bricks and mortar."

Philanthropic naming is often associated with the naming of a physical space but it is widely used to name non-physical aspects as well. Examples of this include the naming of programs, schools, and endowments. It is interesting to note that some of the largest philanthropic naming gifts in Canada have been associated with aspects of an organization that are either non-physical or transcend the physical. Most notably, in recent years, have been the philanthropic naming of Schools of Business, Medicine and Engineering.

More information on the naming of schools and programs can be found in the "Naming programs and schools" section of this chapter.

PHILANTHROPIC NAMING PLAN

Like a campaign plan or a Case for Support, a philanthropic naming plan is a critical element for fundraising planning. A philanthropic naming plan helps provide guidance to your organization on how and when to accept a philanthropic naming opportunity.

Being asked to develop a philanthropic naming plan can be a daunting prospect. Where do you start? What resources do you need? Asking the right questions and developing the right answers will turn what appears to be an insurmountable task into an achievable plan.

A philanthropic naming plan is comprised, minimally, of the following two components:

1. **Naming Policies** – A board approved set of statements that guide your organization's acceptance and treatment of philanthropic naming gifts and explain how your organization will work with donors over the life of their naming gift.
2. **Naming Opportunities (the "Inventory")** – A listing of institutional assets, each with its own gift value, which are available to be named for philanthropic gifts.

In developing your Philanthropic Naming Plan, consideration should be giving to the following two questions:

1. **What is your fundraising goal?**
   In Canada, funding for public capital projects typically comes from three main sources:
   i. Public sources (government)
   ii. Private sources (individual and corporate funding)
   iii. Institutional sources (the organization's own revenue generation, debt financing, etc.)

   For new capital projects, it is critical to the development of a philanthropic naming plan that you understand how much funding is coming from each of these sources. How much from each will be a strong determining factor in the approach you will take in developing the values for your naming plan.

2. **What are your naming policies?**
   The most important component of a philanthropic naming plan is the naming policy. Naming policies are those board-approved statements, guidelines and procedures related to naming that protect the rights and reputation of both the organization and the donor.

Naming policies need to contain, at a minimum, the following four elements:

   i. *Statements that indicate the need for current and ongoing alignment between the values of the donor and the values of your organization.* These statements need to indicate that the organization has the right, at any time and at its own discretion, to remove the name of the donor from a named element should the future values of the donor deviate from those of the organization.

   ii. *Statements that indicate what spaces, programs, or facilities are available to be named and those that are not available to be named.* These statements should include procedures related to specifying special naming categories (for example, the naming of an academic program) as well as the processes required to name a space when no financial gift is involved (honourific naming).

   iii. *Statements that indicate how long the philanthropic naming will remain in place.* Philanthropic naming is typically a long-duration activity. Terms in excess of 20 years, "for the life of the building" and even in perpetuity are not uncommon. It should be noted that, regardless of whether a gift is from an individual or a corporation, if the gift is philanthropic, the duration of the naming should be the same. This is why it is important to determine if the naming is a philanthropic or a sponsorship naming. The duration of a sponsorship naming is determined by the sponsorship contract and is typically shorter in duration with the contributions spread out equally over the term of the sponsorship.

   iv. *Statements that indicate the approval processes for various naming levels and categories.* For example, it is common (and recommended) for the naming of exterior spaces and for gifts above a certain threshold to require board approval prior to the acceptance of a philanthropic naming gift. For all other philanthropic naming approvals, senior management are typically given this authority.

> ### TIP #1: DOCUMENT YOUR WORK
>
> Developing a philanthropic naming plan is more than just pulling together a spreadsheet. Equally important is being able to present your thinking to others including your Board of Directors, your colleagues and, of course, donors.
>
> To ensure that you are able to share, you will want to document your journey. Throughout the process, it will be important that you:
>
> - Retain your source material
>
> - Document your methodology (order of steps, interim results, outcomes, changes you made along the way including why, etc.)
>
> Before presenting your plan to your colleagues and, especially, to your approval bodies, you will want to gather these materials, findings and process steps into one cohesive written document.

DEVELOPING YOUR INVENTORY

Details matter. How well an organization keeps track of these details is often the difference between success and failure in fundraising. The details that matter in philanthropic naming is the list of naming opportunities, their proper names, where they are located, and their values. This listing is commonly referred to as a *naming inventory*.

Throughout the next section of this chapter, we will be using the example of a new capital project as the basis for the development of a philanthropic naming plan. As previously mentioned, philanthropic naming plans are also used for existing physical assets as well as non-physical assets.

This next section highlights the steps needed to prepare your naming inventory for valuation. It presumes that you are focused on a new capital project, that you already know how much of the capital cost needs to be raised from private sector fundraising, and that you have access to building plans.

There are three key steps to consider when developing your inventory:

1. **Working with building plans.**

    The functional design of a capital project is a critical tool for developing a naming inventory. Functional designs include floor plans, site plans and a host of information important to understanding the overall scope and ultimate use of a project.

    Of most use to you is information that speaks to:

    • Where are the spaces located?

    • How big are the spaces?

    • What are the spaces going to be used for?

    It is important to first gain an understanding of where each space is located, how they are situated relative to each other and their overall role in the building's design. Access to the architect or building designer will greatly improve your understanding of a project.

    Knowing the size of a space is important. Knowing where the entryways, elevators, multi-volume spaces and landscape elements are and understanding how the individual spaces work together and the overall "flow" of a building will make your plan transcendent.

    Beyond knowing the size and the location of each space, it is also important that you gain an understanding of the intended use for each space. Is it a classroom? An office? A storage space? A performance hall?

    As part of this exercise, information on the intended capacity (e.g. 12-seat boardroom, 36-seat classroom, etc.), circulation traffic and space access protocols (e.g. key-card access only, public space, etc.) should also be gathered.

2. **Organizing your information.**

    Once you have gathered all of this information it's time to get organized. One of the easiest ways to do this is to enter the information into a spreadsheet. With the information you have already gathered, you can begin to populate this spreadsheet.

    You will want to include a functional description for each space as well as the size and location for each space. A sample structure is shown in Figure 15.1.

represent the entire institute. As these spaces are identified, they should be added to the inventory (e.g. naming of the first floor, naming of the entire building, etc.) as separate line items.

It is good practice to list the sizes of these special spaces as the sum of the sizes of their constituent components. For example, if there are three classrooms located beside each other, each of which have sizes of 250, the addition to the inventory might read: Classroom Suite #1 with a total size of 750.

This also applies to listings associated with

\multicolumn{10}{c}{Basic Philanthropic Naming Inventory Worksheet}
NID	Description	Utility Category	Location	Size	Base Value	Utility Index	Location Index	Intermediate Value	Final Value
	Information you have				Information you add				

Figure 15.1

Once you have all of the explicit inventory items recorded in the spreadsheet, it is time to add the "special" spaces to the inventory. Special spaces are additional elements that are typically aggregations of co-located spaces but they also can include full-volume (more than one floor) atriums, mezzanines, etc.

Examples of things to look for include:

- Spaces with similar functionality located beside each other (e.g. three laboratories beside each other on the second floor of the building).
- The entire floor or wing of a building.
- The entire building itself.

Spaces do not have to be physically contiguous to qualify as a special space. For example, a research institute may include a number of spaces in a building that, individually, are not located beside each other but together

entire floors and the entire building. For spaces that represent a volume of space (like an atrium that extends through the full volume of a five-story building without having five actual floor plates), a common approach is to represent the size of this space as if the floor plates did exist. If the atrium cited had a main floor size of 600, its special space size would be 3000 (5 x 600).

3. **Simplify.**

    Up to this stage, you have been working with information that you have been given. A necessary and important next step is to add category information to the inventory. Adding category information begins the process of grouping like spaces together so they can be ranked as a group as opposed to individual inventory elements. Every inventory has a natural set of categories. For the purposes of philanthropic naming, these categories are based on the use of the space in question. For example, when working with an inventory for an education space, your categories might include:

- Classrooms
- Laboratories
- Study spaces
- Social spaces
- Public spaces
- Meeting spaces

You can imagine other category groupings depending on the nature of the project being evaluated. For example, a theatre company might have spaces like presentation spaces, performer spaces, etc. Once you have assigned a category to each element, you will be ready to begin the valuation process.

TIP #2: BE SMART ABOUT CATEGORIES

The goal of assigning categories is to group a large number of inventory elements into a significantly smaller number of category groupings. Generally, the number of categories you develop should be less than 20 and ideally, ten or less.

VALUATION

Valuation is the critical aspect of a philanthropic naming inventory. This is where you go through the process of determining and assigning a gift value to each inventory element. These gift level values will form the basis from which you will be discussing recognition opportunities with donors.

Philanthropic naming values, often, *are not* shared publicly. Instead, they are used as an *internal* guideline for fundraisers, leaders, and governance bodies when discussing naming recognition for specific gifts. Assigning gift level values to your philanthropic naming inventory is a six-step process:

1. **Calculating the base value of inventory elements**

    To determine the base value of an element, the fundraising value per unit of size (base rate) needs to be determined. Two pieces of information are required to determine the base rate for your project:

    i. Fundraising cost base

    ii. Total size of all naming space (you already know this)

    Because the objective of developing a philanthropic naming value is to provide recognition for private sector funders to a project, it is recommended that the fundraising cost base be the private sector fundraising goal.

    The process to determine the base rate (C) is as follows. The dollar amount of the private sector fundraising goal (A) is divided by the total size of naming space (B). Figure 15.2 shows an example of this base rate calculation using a private sector fundraising goal of $25 million and a total naming space size of 100,000 sq. ft.

A	Private Sector Fundraising Goal	$25,000,000
B	Total Space Size of All Naming Opportunities	100,000
C	Base Rate (A/B) $/sq.ft.	$250

Figure 15.2

To determine the base value (E) of a physical space element in the inventory, this base rate (C) is then multiplied by the size of the space (D). The resulting dollar amount is the base value of the space.

Figure 15.3 shows an example of this base value calculation.

	C	D	E
Description	Base Rate, $/sq. ft.	Size, sq. ft.	Base Value (D x C)
Performance Hall	$250	4000	$1,000,000

Figure 15.3

The underlying principle for this calculation is that if every unit of space available for naming were "sold," the entire fundraising goal would be met.

Figure 15.4 shows a sample listing of spaces with the base values calculated.

NID	Description	Base Rate (C)	Size, sq. ft. (D)	Base Value (E)
001	Performance Hall	$250	4000	**$1,000,000**
002	Reception Lobby	$250	800	**$200,000**
003	Classroom	$250	500	**$125,000**
004	Walkway	$250	150	**$37,500**

Figure 15.4

"Selling" every space is rarely practical and almost never desirable. It is rarely practical because, up to this stage, the philanthropic naming inventory has been developed based on the assumption that every space has an equal chance of being named.

This rarely occurs in practice because fundraising campaigns are much more complex and donor interests much more varied than can be predicted in advance. To offset this, philanthropic naming inventories have much more inventory capacity than is needed to recognize all naming gifts in a campaign. How much more is discussed later in this chapter.

Also, selling every space is almost never desirable because our communities expect that a reasonable amount of philanthropic naming needs to occur to support the *stewardship* needs of a fundraising campaign. What they do not expect (nor do they support) is an organization losing its identity due to having too much space named. Having every space in a facility named tends to erode the organizational brand. At its worst, such an outcome is typified by a sentiment that "Organization X is all about the money."

2. **Premiums and discounts**

Not all inventory elements are created equal. You can imagine a number of factors that may make a difference to whether one space is more valuable than another. For example, with sponsorship naming (the cousin of philanthropic naming), one of the most important factors is the number of interactions with or in close proximity to the space. For philanthropic naming, this factor plays a role but is much less explicit than in sponsorship naming.

For philanthropic naming, the two most important factors that can increase or decrease the value of a space are **utility** and **location**.

For the purposes of determining philanthropic naming value, these factors are most commonly expressed as percentage values (index values) that range from 0% to 200%. Figure 15.5, highlights typical ranges for utility and location indices.

Discount Values	0.25
	0.50
	0.75
Neutral Value	1.00
Premium Values	1.25
	1.50
	1.75
	2.00

Figure 15.5

3. **Calculating intermediate naming values**

   Once you have calculated the base value of all inventory elements, and have determined the premiums or discounts to be applied to these elements, you are ready to calculate the *Intermediate Naming Value*. This is done by applying the use and location premiums or discounts to the base value.

   In conducting this application, there are two key concepts to keep in mind:

   a) **Utility**: *Spaces with higher "utility" have high value.*

   - Public spaces are worth more than private spaces.
   - Student/patient/customer/patron spaces worth more than researcher/clinician/staff spaces.
   - Laboratory/program spaces are worth more than office spaces.

   b) **Location**: *Spaces with higher traffic and public exposure have high value*

   - Locations accessible to the public are worth more than private or secure spaces.
   - Lower floors are generally worth more.
   - Spaces adjacent/visible from high traffic locations are worth more.

Utility index

The intended or current use of a space is the utility of the space. You have already identified your utility categories — they are the very same as those previously identified as space grouping categories.

The utility ranking of a space is very organization-specific. For example, the relative importance of a classroom space can range from quite low to very high depending on the mission of the organization space. For a performing arts facility, classroom space would often be less important than performance space. Conversely, for an educational facility, the reverse would likely be true.

To develop a slate of utility index values, the list of space categories first needs to be ranked in order of importance from highest to lowest. It is not uncommon for more than one space category to be equally ranked. However, it is good practice to ensure that there is enough variation in the rankings to be able to develop a range of utility index values.

A practical approach to developing a ranked listing is to first have your fundraising staff develop their own ranked category list. In addition to and independent from this ranking, bring together a small group of stakeholders and ask them to rank the space category list from most important to least important (1 - 10 for example).

Good diversity within the stakeholder group is important to the validity of the overall ranking process. For an educational institution, this group might include:

- Administrators
- Students
- Faculty
- Marketing staff
- Donors
- Alumni

With the results of your internal and stakeholder group's ranking, you are now ready to produce the utility index.

Remember:

- Index values <u>below 1</u> will decrease (apply a discount to) the value of the space in question.
- Index values <u>equal to 1</u> are neutral and won't affect the value of the space.
- Index values <u>above 1</u> will increase (apply a premium to) the value of the space.

> **TIP #3: DON'T AVERAGE RANKING RESULTS**
>
> After seeking input from stakeholders on the relative values of each utility category, resist the urge to average the results to establish the overall ranking. Instead, the stakeholder group's input should be used to validate and improve the initial ranking undertaken by the fund development professionals. You are looking for trends, not absolutes.

It is good practice to have index values that span the range from above 0% up to 200%. Index values above 200% are difficult to justify and inappropriately skew the data.

Figure 15.6 shows an example of a ranked category list and the resulting likely utility index values for an educational institution.

Sample Ranking (1 being the highest, 5 being the lowest)	Utility Category	Likely Utility Index Values
1	Classroom	2.00
2	Laboratory	1.75
3	Public Space	1.50
4	Social Space	1.50
5	Study Space	1.00
6	Meeting Space	0.50

Figure 15.6

Location Index

The location index is a set of values that either decrease (apply a discount to) or increase (apply a premium to) the base values depending on the location of the space. Location is loosely related to the interaction component found with sponsorship valuation.

The interaction component for buildings is often referred to as "circulation." Spaces with high circulation see more human "traffic" than those spaces with lower circulation. As a result, spaces with higher circulation (i.e. lobbies, main entrances, atriums etc.) often have higher location index values than those spaces located further away from the main entrance (levels above or below level 1).

Special attention needs to be placed on spaces located near connections to other buildings (+15 walkways for example) and other locations where relatively high circulation can occur (levels with food service for example).

In addition to circulation, access is a determining factor in the relative value of a location. Spaces that require key-card access usually have a lower location index value than those with public access.

To produce the location index, start with a listing of each level in the facility. As an example, for a building with four at or above-grade floors and a basement, this list would contain five rows (Levels 0 - 4).

Using information such as the location of the main entrance, where the elevators and stairs are located, whether there are connections to other buildings and the general access characteristics of the building, produce a ranked list of each of the five levels. Using this ranking, a set of location index values can be developed.

Figure 15.7 shows an example of typical location index values for a facility that has the following characteristics: Five levels, Level 0 and Level 3 are card-access only, the entrance is on Level 1, there is a +15 connection on Level 2.

Location	Typical Location Index Values
Level 0 (basement)	0.50
Level 1 (main floor)	1.50
Level 2 (+15 access)	1.50
Level 3 (card access only)	0.25
Level 4 (public access)	1.00

Figure 15.7

4. **Special spaces and program elements**
   With the base values assigned, the utility and location indices can then be applied to each element to provide an intermediate naming value. This intermediate value is not the final naming value, but you are now more than half-way there.

The intermediate naming value is calculated by taking the utility and location index values and applying them to the base value. The net result is a naming value that has been either decreased or increased in value to take into account both its utility and its location.

Figure 15.8 shows an example of the calculation.

5. **Testing values against the standards-of-giving chart**

   A philanthropic naming plan is only as good as how well it reflects well-recognized patterns in giving.

   The best benchmark for these patterns of giving is the standards-of-giving chart or giving table. This table is widely recognized as representing the number and relative size of gifts in most major gift campaigns.[2] These tables typically show a small number of large gifts and a large number of smaller gifts with an increase in the number of donors and a corresponding decrease in the giving level from the top of the chart to the bottom of the table.

   Because the standards-of-giving chart represents the reality of major gift giving so accurately, it is also an excellent tool to evaluate the naming inventory. If the number of opportunities and the value of these opportunities is a close match to the standard-of-giving chart, your naming inventory has passed its first important reality test.

   To put your naming inventory into a giving table format, simply order the giving levels from largest to smallest and then put the number of elements associated with each level beside each corresponding giving level. An example of a philanthropic naming inventory presented as a standard giving chart is shown in Figure 15.9.

> **TIP #4:**
> **USE MS EXCEL TO BUILD YOUR STANDARD GIVING CHART FROM YOUR NAMING INVENTORY**
>
> If you are using MS Excel, producing a standards-of-giving chart from your naming inventory is as simple as using the pivot table feature in the software. For added understanding of the interrelationships in your naming inventory, add in columns to represent cumulative giving and cumulative number of opportunities (including columns to calculate the percentages in each). The adage that 80% - 90% of your gifts will come from 10% to 20% of your donors will be clearly highlighted in a well-valued naming inventory.

Your naming inventory may not match up perfectly with the standards-of-giving chart at first (this is why you use this test). Using your knowledge of how the standards-of-giving chart should look, you can make the adjustments to various valuations to bring your inventory in line with these standards.

It is during this stage that you will also want to determine the total value of all of your inventory elements. The total value of your inventory should be between two and four times greater than your private sector fundraising goal. Having more inventory than you need is important for the following reasons:

- Philanthropic naming inventories are stewardship tools. The ability to offer more than one recognition option to naming donors shows that you are a donor-centered organization.

- Not every space will be named … nor should it be. Having a total inventory value at a significant multiple of the private sector fundraising goal ensures that enough naming gifts can be secured to complete the campaign without having to name every space.

---

2   Dove, Kent E. (2001). Conducting a Successful Fundraising Program. Chapter Eight: Constructing and Using the Standards-of-Giving Chart. John Wiley & Sons, Inc.

duckworth on PHILANTHROPIC NAMING

NID	Description	Utility Category	Location	Base Rate	Size, sq. ft.	E Base Value	F Utility Index	G Location Index	Intermediate Naming Value (E x F x G)	Relative Value Change from Base Value
001	Study Lounge #1	Study Space	Level 0	$250	150	$37,500	1.00	0.50	$18,750	?
002	Reception Lobby	Public Space	Level 1	$250	1012	$253,000	1.50	1.50	$569,250	?
003	Cafeteria	Social Space	Level 2	$250	2250	$562,500	1.50	1.50	$1,265,625	?
004	Classroom #1	Classroom	Level 2	$250	759	$189,750	2.00	1.50	$569,250	?
005	Classroom #2	Classroom	Level 2	$250	759	$189,750	2.00	1.50	$569,250	?
006	Classroom Suite	Special Space	Level 2	$250	1518	$379,500	2.00	1.50	$1,138,500	?
007	Meeting Room	Meeting Space	Level 2	$250	150	$37,500	0.50	1.50	$28,125	?
008	Naming of Level 2	Special Space	Level 2	$250	3725	$931,250	1.00	1.50	$1,396,875	?
009	Research Laboratory	Laboratory	Level 3	$250	1844	$461,000	1.50	0.25	$172,875	?
010	Chemistry Laboratory #1	Laboratory	Level 4	$250	806	$201,500	1.50	1.00	$302,250	?
011	Chemistry Laboratory #2	Laboratory	Level 4	$250	806	$201,500	1.50	1.00	$302,250	?
012	Chemistry Laboratory Suite	Special Space	Level 4	$250	1612	$403,000	1.50	1.00	$604,500	?
013	Naming of Level 4	Special Space	Level 4	$250	1832	$458,000	1.00	1.00	$458,000	NC
014	Study Lounge #2	Study Space	Level 4	$250	220	$55,000	1.00	1.00	$55,000	NC

Figure 15.8

Sample Philanthropic Naming Inventory		
Description	Intermediate Naming Value	Naming Gift Level
Naming of the Surgical Wing	$1,111,254	$1,000,000
Patient Waiting Area	$497,000	$500,000
Large Surgical Suite #1	$196,500	$250,000
Large Surgical Suite #2	$196,500	$250,000
Small Surgical Suite #1	$106,777	$100,000
Small Surgical Suite #2	$106,777	$100,000
Small Surgical Suite #3	$106,777	$100,000
Patient Consult Room #1	$42,340	$50,000
Patient Consult Room #2	$42,340	$50,000
Patient Consult Room #3	$42,340	$50,000
Patient Consult Room #4	$42,340	$50,000
Patient Consult Room #5	$42,340	$50,000
Totals	12	$2,550,000

Figure 15.9

6. **External validation**
   You are almost done. The last step is one when your experience and the experience of your peers should be formally brought into the process.

Philanthropic Naming Inventory in Standard Giving Chart Format		
Standard Giving Levels	Number of Opportunities	Total Number at Giving Level
$1,000,000	1	$1,000,000
$500,000	1	$500,000
$250,000	2	$500,000
$100,000	3	$300,000
$50,000	5	$250,000
Totals	12	$2,550,000

Philanthropic naming, as a core fund development methodology, has gained significant ground in Canada in the last ten years. With this maturing, many organizations have successfully named spaces that are likely very similar to yours. A market scan, first locally, then regionally and, in some cases nationally, will help you substantiate the final values of your inventory elements.

It is important to know the benchmarks (or, in some cases, if these benchmarks *even exist*) but it is just as important to understand what your organization is attempting to do (or should be attempting to do) through its philanthropic naming. If your organization aspires to position itself higher in the marketplace (in terms of reputation), these benchmarks will likely only serve as a starting point for your valuation.

Congratulations! You now have a philanthropic naming inventory with values that you can now call *final naming values*.

DEEPER TOPICS IN NAMING

A) Naming entire buildings

An important (and very visible) philanthropic naming is the naming of an entire building for a donor. In Canada, the generally accepted standard for new buildings whose capital cost is greater than $10 million and whose private sector fundraising goal is between 30% and 40% of this is to consider naming the entire facility for a philanthropic gift of 50% or more of the private sector fundraising goal.

For example, for a building whose capital cost is $100 million and whose fundraising goal is $30 million (the remaining $70 million is coming from government funding), the value to name the entire building is likely close to $15 million (50% of $30 million.)

For buildings whose capital cost is less than $10 million, the private sector fundraising goal is not an important factor. In these cases, it is not uncommon to establish a floor value of one-third of the total capital cost. For example, for a building whose capital cost is $6 million, the value to name the entire building is likely close to $2 million (one-third of $6 million).

B) Moving beyond the physical: Naming programs and schools

Philanthropic naming is not limited to physical space. Programs, institutes, schools and other non-physical entities are often strong candidates for philanthropic naming.

Programs are generally better suited to sponsorship naming (annualized value based primarily on interaction components, typically with a fixed term of ten years or less). To consider a program for philanthropic naming (enduring value based primarily on intrinsic components, typically with long terms of twenty years or more), the program must be one that is going to be around for a long time. Excellent examples of programs in this category include the naming of Departments or Schools in higher education.

There is no standard methodology in the marketplace to determine the philanthropic value of programs like these but there are excellent benchmarks. Figure 15.10 shows a sampling of schools philanthropically named in Canada over the last 20 years.

Looking deeper into these benchmarks, there are some interesting characteristics that you can use to

School Naming	University	Donor	Gift Size
Ingram School of Nursing	McGill University	Richard S. Ingram	$9 million
Marcel A. Desautels Faculty of Music	University of Manitoba	Marcel A. Desautels	$20 million
Michael G. DeGroote School of Medicine	McMaster University	Michael G. DeGroote	$105 million
N. Murray Edwards School of Business	University of Saskatchewan	N. Murray Edwards	$11 million
Rotman School of Management	University of Toronto	Sandra and Joseph Rotman	$15 million
Sauder School of Business	University of British Columbia	William A. Sauder	$20 million
Schulich School of Engineering	University of Calgary	Seymour Schulich	$25 million

Figure 15.10

set a "floor" value to philanthropic naming of your programs. Many of these namings share the following characteristics:

- Often, the philanthropic naming value is a significant multiple of the operating budget associated with the named program. In many cases, these gifts are close to three times the value of the operating budget of the associated program.

- Often, a significant fraction (up to two-thirds) of the gift is in the form of an endowment with the remainder being non-endowed. If two-thirds of a program gift is in the form of an endowment and one-third of the gift is available immediately, the named program effectively doubles its budget in the first year of the gift and will see 10% of its budget as endowment proceeds in perpetuity. Put in tangible terms, to philanthropically name a program with an operating budget of $10 million, the minimum naming gift should be $30 million with $20 million put into an endowment and $10 million available to the program immediately. For every year thereafter, this program would have the use of 5% of the endowment or $1 million.

CONCLUSION

The philanthropic naming plan joins the Case for Support, the campaign plan, and the development plan as one of the important documents required for successful fundraising. At a minimum, a philanthropic naming plan includes a listing of naming opportunities and a set of naming policies.

Philanthropic naming plans are often used to value existing physical assets, non-physical assets like programs and schools, and new capital projects.

To develop a listing of naming opportunities for new capital projects that includes valuations that are reasonable and explainable, a rational approach to developing these valuations is required. This approach involves establishing a *base rate* for each unit of namable space and then applying a premium or a discount to each space based on its *utility* and its *location*.

These values need to be tested using the *standards-of-giving chart* and existing *market benchmarks* as guides.

Philanthropic naming is suited as a *recognition and stewardship tool* and, in general, *should not* be used to "lead" solicitation activities with a prospective donor.

ADDITIONAL RESOURCES

Books
- Burton, Terry. (2008). *Naming Rights, Legacy Gifts & Corporate Money.* John Wiley & Sons, Inc.

- Dove, Kent E. (2001). *Conducting a Successful Fundraising Program.* John Wiley & Sons, Inc.

URLs
- http://www.crescendofundraising.ca/samplenamingpolicy.pdf - *Sample Naming Policy*

ABOUT THE AUTHOR

Vincent Duckworth, BSc, CFRE

Vincent Duckworth has been a fundraising professional for 20 years. He began his career in fundraising when joined the University of Alberta as the Faculty of Engineering's first director of development in 1995. He is one of the very few professional fundraisers in Canada who also has a degree in engineering. While at the University of Alberta, he played a important role in their first major fundraising campaign.

Vincent went on to lead the NAIT campaign, a $14 million comprehensive fundraising effort. Over a two-year period, he and his team raised $24 million at average pace of $1 million per month. When he returned to the University of Alberta in 2002, this time in Medicine and Dentistry, he led the effort to raise the funds for two new health research buildings.

In 2007, Vincent founded a fundraising consultancy in Calgary, Crescendo Fundraising Inc.

He has led or advised the fundraising teams for many of Canada's transformational facility projects. He is internationally recognized as an expert on campaign design, strategy and major gift performance, he is also the leading Canadian authority on philanthropic naming.

Vincent and his partner, Christine Fraser, have three children and they live in Calgary.

CHAPTER 16

Entrepreneurial Fundraising

KATHRYN BABCOCK, MPA, CFRE

"The progress of the world will call for the best that all of us have to give."
- Mary Macleod Bethune

Entrepreneurial fundraising is about raising money in a way that challenges the status quo. Fueled by passion, it is a mindset that seeks out opportunity, embraces risk, and acts with courage in the service of changing the world.

read more…

We live in a time of almost unlimited fundraising opportunities. This exists alongside a race-against-the-clock urgency that these opportunities be pursued with full entrepreneurial fervour.

However much it is that we currently raise, the status quo still finds the world troubled by poverty, violence, sickness, oppression and environmental degradation. We need to raise more. We need to harness entrepreneurial thinking to catapult our fundraising efforts.

> *Entrepreneurship: "the pursuit of opportunity without regard to resources currently controlled."* [1]

By this definition almost every charity in the world was born entrepreneurial – with a vision that outstripped the human and financial resources that were currently on hand. Whether a charity was established two months ago or 200 years ago, it started with the identification of an opportunity to make the world better. As fundraisers we are the servants of this opportunity - we are the conductors of the financial resources that make this vision of a better world possible.

There are an ever-increasing number of social entrepreneurs and charities looking for new solutions to address intractable problems. Social entrepreneurs are defined as "individuals with innovative solutions to society's most pressing social problems." [2]

These individuals are characterized as "ambitious and persistent, tackling major social issues and offering new ideas for wide-scale change." [3] It is a great thing that new solutions are in hand, or are at least at the stage of being readily imagined. How dreadful it would be if we had no idea how to make things better. But we do. Our organizations are being called to step-up to have greater impact; to articulate new visions that well outstrip the resources currently controlled. As the experts in finding the resources for this work, we need to keep pace and step-up to our entrepreneurial best.

Our job as fundraisers is to relentlessly pursue opportunities with the boldness born of the vision we serve. To that end, this chapter offers five key concepts to cultivate your "inner fundraising entrepreneur."

CONCEPT #1: WE "SELL" A PRODUCT FOR WHICH THERE IS UNLIMITED DEMAND

As fundraisers we are ultimately in the business of *happiness* – we are the conduit for increasing the happiness of the less-advantaged and making the people, who come on board to do so, feel really happy!

We "sell" happiness in two ways:

1. By making the case that the charitable donation will ultimately result in increased happiness for the end recipient—whether it is by providing clean water, building a community centre, providing free jazz lessons to inner-city schools, providing shelter for an abused woman, finding a cure for childhood leukemia or protecting endangered species.
2. By increasing the happiness of the donor through their experience of having made the donation. This comes both through the self-actualization of the donor making the gift (their feelings of being part of something greater than themselves, and the experience of being altruistic) and their experience of our gratitude as the charity who has received their gift.

Generosity is the road to happiness. As fundraisers, we have the map and just the right vehicle to suggest!

Human beings are biologically wired to move toward that which makes us feel good. There is a myriad of research that links generosity with happiness (you may want to send a copy of *How of Happiness*[4] by Sonja Lyubomirsky to donors before asking for a large gift.

Howard Stevenson—who not only is considered the "Godfather of entrepreneurial studies at Harvard Business School,"[5] but has also helped to raise $1billion—says it this way: "I believe that there are four things that make us feel successful in life: achievement, significance, legacy, and happiness. Philanthropy is an opportunity to satisfy each of these key motivations."[6]

---

1   Eric Shurenberg. http://www.inc.com/eric-schurenberg/the-best-definition-of-entepreneurship.html . Cites the widely-regarded definition Harvard Business School professor Howard Stevenson, D.B.A., first coined in 1975.
2   Ashoka Innovators for the Public. https://www.ashoka.org/social_entrepreneur
3   Ibid.

4   Sonya Lyubomirsky. (2007). *How of Happiness: A New Approach to getting the life you want.* Penguin Group.
5   Thomas R. Eisenmann. (2013). *Entrepreneurship: A Working Definition.* Retrieved from http://blogs.hbr.org/2013/01/what-is-entrepreneurship/Jan
6   Shirley M Spence and Howard H. Stevenson. (2011). *Getting to Giving: Fundraising the Entrepreneurial Way.* Publisher: Timberline. pp242-243.

As fundraisers we are a conduit to bringing joy into the world. If you think of Maslow's hierarchy of needs – we are filling the bottom of the pyramid (providing for the physiological and security needs of recipients) by filling the top (self-actualization of the donors). A new twist on "top down fundraising."

TIPS!

- **Review your Case for Support to ensure that it brings to life the happiness that your charity is in the business of creating.** For example, if you are working on behalf of children with disabilities – describe the joy the child experiences when they take their first steps and the emotional experience of the parents watching them do so. Or if you are building a well in a developing country, bring to life the relief of women no longer having to walk 20 miles to find water and their joy in knowing the water is clean and will only be a source of life to their children (rather than possible disease). You can test out the case with prospective donors. Ask the question: Does the happiness that we are bringing to our clients come through in our messaging? Keep revising it until it does!

- **Review your donor recognition and stewardship program to ensure you are delivering as much happiness as possible at each point of contact.** Ask yourself: How is this event, or recognition piece giving the donor a sense of legacy, achievement or significance? When in doubt – ask your donors if they are happy!

While it is true that as fundraisers much of what we sell is intangible, this also holds true for lots of companies. For example: car companies sell people cars that not only will functionally take them from point A to point B but will make them feel that they are people of a certain status, or people who value the safety of their children, or have a spirit of adventure. It is the intangibles in which the functional is wrapped that people are really buying. Our product is *impact* wrapped in the priceless intangibles of donors feeling a sense of achievement, significance, legacy, and ultimately happiness.

There is an unlimited demand for happiness. The world is our oyster!

CONCEPT #2: BOLDNESS MOVES MOUNTAINS

"Boldness has genius, power and magic in it."
–Johann Wolfgang von Goethe

The vision of your organization needs to be compelling enough to dwarf any trepidation. You need to be convinced that your charity is doing something of paramount importance (ideally the most important thing you can possibly imagine). The motivation for someone to give is the same as your motivation to ask: so that the donor can be part of creating a compelling change in the world.

In Jim Collins' extraordinary book, *Good to Great and the Social Sectors*, he quotes a social sector leader: "I am motivated first and always for the greatness of our work, not myself."[7] In other words, you must be convinced of the greatness of the work that your fundraising effort will support and translate this into your Case for Support.

"Conquer cancer in our lifetime," is a wonderful example of a bold vision - a vision that is fueling a $1 billion fundraising platform for Princess Margaret Hospital, a leading cancer hospital located in Toronto. The money raised is earmarked in specific ways but it is all in the service of this extraordinary vision. This vision is greater than the scope of their organization but it captures the purpose of their work and inspires people to fund it. This vision gives people the chance to conquer cancer in their lifetime. Who would say no to that?

Once we have a persuasive and passionate Case for Support, and have researched the prospect, we need to be bold in our ask. This does not mean that there is always an absence of fear – sometimes there is a lot on the line and rejection can be intimidating - but as fundraisers we have agreed to step out of our comfort zone in the service of a vision greater than ourselves.

---

7 Jim Collins. (2005). *Good To Great and the Social Sectors*. p 11.

And then as we step out with boldness, the words of Audre Lorde come to life: *"When I dare to be powerful, to use my strength in the service of my vision, it becomes less and less important if I am afraid."* [8]

TIP!

- Before you approach a donor ask: What would I ask for if I knew that success was guaranteed?

CONCEPT #3: OPPORTUNITIES ABOUND

The ability to identify and pursue opportunities is central to the definition of entrepreneurship and foundational to our success as fundraisers.

Opportunities can be categorized in *three* ways:

1. **Opportunities *within* resources currently controlled.**

The following resources are currently under the control of your organization, and they represent the "lowest hanging fruit" and the best place to start. These resources include:
- all donors (individual, government, corporate and foundation)
- volunteers
- employees
- events
- suppliers

In mining for opportunities with current supporters, look for points of leverage. Let's walk through two examples.

Example #1: A charity had a longstanding breakfast event for which they sold tickets and sponsorship. After several years they started to leverage the event by using it as a platform for making an individual donation ask of those in attendance. There was initial reluctance to do this because the view was that the audience had already donated by purchasing a ticket and they were afraid of alienating the audience – but they took a risk. This had a great response and they further leveraged the opportunity to secure a donor each year to match donations. Furthermore, at a recent event they had a prominent donor stand up and promise to match the donations made in the room that morning – with no cap! What was once an event that raised $200K suddenly jumped to raising $1 million.

Example #2: A company made a corporate gift to a charity. In addition, they gave their employees an opportunity to make a donation to the charity via payroll deduction. The charity was one of five other charities that were on the payroll deduction list. To leverage the opportunity, and encourage uptake on the payroll option, the charity approached an individual donor to increase their donation to match all of the payroll deduction donations made by employees. This increased the level of engagement of the donor to the charity and provided great incentive for the employees of the company to make a donation. The corporate partner also appreciated the entrepreneurial approach and the way in which it breathed life into their employee giving program.

These are just two configurations of a hundred possibilities – the commonality is an "opportunity mindset" brought to bear in the analysis of what is possible and what your charity has to offer.

In each category of resource there are new opportunities:

- Your corporate donors have an employee base that consists of potential individual donors;
- Individual donors (and volunteers) have connections to potential corporate donors. Mine your relationship database to collect the information as a basis for approach, and make sure you are capturing as much information about a donor as possible;
- Events are an opportunity to cultivate both individual and corporate donors.

---

8 Audre Lorde. (1997). "The Cancer Journals, Special Edition." Aunt Lute Books, San Francisco, CA. p. 13.

• Let's walk through an example from a corporate resource. Your charity has a corporate donor who makes an annual charitable gift. You are both in the business of making (raising) money – how can you help each other? Consider these questions in light of the strength of your relationship and the business type.

What else can they do?
- Sponsor an event?
- Match donations made through your direct mail campaign?
- Make a per tweet donation on a given day?
- Provide gift cards as a thank you to donors?
- Provide tickets or a box at sporting events to recognize individual donors or to host clients of the organization?
- Provide services or products to reduce the costs to your charity (i.e. do your printing, provide translation, web development, human resource training)?
- Ask their employees to donate?
- Create lunch and learn opportunities for employees to learn about what you are doing?
- Reach out to their suppliers to ask them for a donation?
- Make introductions to other companies?
- Give you proceeds from a golf tournament?
- Host a workplace fundraiser?
- Mention your charity when they run radio ads for their products?
- Donate ad space in their publication or as part of their company's print media buy?
- Sponsor your newsletter?
- Provide meeting space, office equipment or furniture?
- Be the lead gift on your capital campaign?
- Provide volunteers for events?
- Provide senior volunteers for the Board or fundraising committees?
- Encourage their PR or ad agencies to work with you to build your profile?
- Give you silent auction items?

What else can you do?
- Create volunteer opportunities for their employees?
- Provide profile in your communication vehicles?
- Nominate them for corporate citizenship awards?
- Provide sampling opportunities?
- Give out their branded mugs at your events?
- Provide your donors/members a coupon for their product?
- Have special updates with your CEO?
- Give special access at your events?
- Provide them compelling material for their internal and external communication vehicles?
- Take out an ad in a local paper to recognize them (via donated media space of course)?
- Facilitate introductions to your stakeholders?
- Make presentations to their employees?
- Put their name on a building, program or as part of an event title?
- Create a donor wall in your reception area?

This list is not exhaustive and through the relationship-building process both you and the donor will cultivate ways of supporting each other. The purpose of the exercise is to spark thinking about how to grow support from current donors. It is often easier to get additional support from existing donors than to find new ones. (Questions for each category of resources can be found at *www.babcockandcompany.com*)

2. **Pursuit of opportunities *outside* of resources currently controlled.**

In tandem with mining internal opportunities we need to capitalize on opportunities in the broader context:
- 84% of Canadians 15+ make charitable donations.[9] This makes it a cultural norm to give – so momentum is in our favour. What

---

9 Statistics Canada: *Charitable Giving by Canadians*. Retrieved from http://www.statcan.gc.ca/pub/11-008-x/2012001/article/11637-eng.htm

percentage of Canadians currently give to your charity? What percentage would you like this to be? What could inspire them to do so?

- Religiously active donors give three times as much as other Canadians.[10] Is there an opportunity to cultivate this group within your charity? (Some possible alignments could include themes of social justice and peace.) Can you meet with your donors who are religiously active to get their advice on how to translate your Case for Support in a way that would resonate within that community?

- There are 422,000 millionaires in Canada.[11] How many do you think you could persuade to support your cause?

- There is a 1 trillion dollar transfer of wealth coming over the next 20 years through inheritance - the largest intergenerational transfer of wealth in Canadian history. If we could redirect 20% of that "off the top" via planned giving of aging Canadians, it would represent a $200 billion lift to charities. Does planned giving represent an opportunity for your charity?

- Women have more resources at their disposal than at any time in history and they outlive their husbands by an average of five years! Does your charity have a strategy to reach women as donors? Can this strategy work jointly with companies that want to reach women as customers?

- As of 2010 there were 2.8 million Canadian citizens living abroad[12] (plus an unknown number of former citizens and descendents of citizens). This is almost 10% of all Canadian citizens and represents a larger population than live in six provinces! Is there a reason your work would be compelling for them to support? If so, a good place to start to find your prospects is through Canadian Clubs and Associations listed at *www.international.gc.ca* or on *www.canuckabroad.com*

10 ibid.
11 Huffington Post. Retrieved from http://www.huffingtonpost.ca/2013/05/11/richest-countries-cities-world_n_3254976.html
12 Asia Pacific Foundation of Canada – Canadians Abroad Project 2010. http://www.asiapacific.ca/sites/default/files/filefield/UsandThem.pdf

While it is true that there is significant competition among charities for donations, collectively we have captured only a fraction of the market. Charitable giving in Canada represents 0.1% of household assets. Canadians have household assets of $8.1 trillion– so the $10.6 billion made in charitable donations represents approx. 0.12% of assets – (one tenth of one percent) – the market has not even begun to be saturated![13] To repeat: opportunities abound.

3. **Opportunity knocks.**

For opportunity to knock it needs to know your address! The most exuberant gifts are often from donors who seek out the charity based on its reputation. This requires great skill both in raising the profile of the organization and then in the stewarding of the initial interest. The opportunities are earned – in the first instance by having an excellent track record and an inspiring vision, and in the second by cultivating the opportunity.

Examples:

- A donor who had heard about the work of a charity sent in an unsolicited donation for $25,000 and the charity, as a result of 10 years of careful and heartfelt stewardship, was the recipient of a more than $15 million bequest from the donor's estate.

- A company called to see if they could donate product; this represented the first step in a ten-year multi-million dollar partnership.

- A foundation approached a charity and offered to make a donation to support social justice work in two provinces, if the charity could get the governments in those provinces to match the donation. With that leverage, the charity was able to facilitate the match and the gift came to fruition; consequently, as you read this, life- saving work that otherwise wouldn't be happening, is happening!

You are the answer to a donor's need for legacy, achievement, profile – let yourself be found! There are many ways to do this – at a minimum you need a website, but really the sky is the limit and can include PSA's, a social media campaign, and getting in front

13 RBC report (2012). http://www.rbc.com/economics/economic-reports/pdf/other-reports/hhfinances.pdf

of advisors who are helping clients to direct their gifts or planned gifts (check out *www.leavealegacy.ca*)

One important caveat: not all opportunities should be pursued. The point is not to be chasing 100 different opportunities but to cultivate a mindset that is open to opportunity and quickly capitalize on the ones with the greatest possible return. The company calling to make a $5,000 donation could present an opportunity for a $1 million gift over time. Or they could present a drain on your organization because they only ever will give you $5,000 and they want stewardship at the level of a $100,000 donor. The $5,000 could be the "thin edge of the wedge" or the "beginning of the end." We need to do our homework; be open to possibilities; be courageous in their pursuit; and if we make a mistake, to be willing to walk away. At all times we need to be nimble. Our skill as fundraisers is to actively cultivate opportunities while having a laser focus on both short- and long-term return on investment.

CONCEPT #4
MONEY IS OUR PRIMARY PERFORMANCE METRIC

"Yesterday's home runs don't win today's games."
– Babe Ruth

Although the successes of the organizations we work for are ultimately measured by the societal impact they make possible – as fundraisers, we are measured by the amount of money we raise, pure and simple. We need to get as good as we can possibly get at doing just that, by building our skill as fundraisers and building our knowledge of the fundraising tools at our disposal.

As fundraisers we are the part of the charitable ratio that nobody likes … the part that deals with the cost of fundraising!

> **TIP!**
> - Look at your most successful donor relationships and ask: How did these relationships come to be, and how can we replicate that process?
> - What untapped opportunities are there within these current relationships?

Although there is a lot of great work being done to educate donors about how necessary fundraising and administration is to create social impact (Imagine Canada has a wonderful new narrative[14] on the subject) – the fact remains that we have a fixed number of hours in the day. We need to get as good as possible at using our time to generate the best rate of revenue return for our charities.

We have to be continually asking the questions: How can we do this better? More efficiently? And with greater impact?

Keys to raising the most money possible:

A) Master an understanding of all the funding tools at your disposal.

You can only decide if a certain activity is offering the best return on investment if you are familiar with all the tools. The "finance don't fundraise"[15] concept was coined by Nell Edgington who talks about creating a financial model for the social change that you want to create which articulates how much money you need, over what period of time, how it will come in and what activities are required. It is different than a typical fundraising plan in that it includes the building of capacity and sustainability of your organization using all the financial levers that are available – and to be on top of all of the revenue opportunities – not just the philanthropic ones.

The following is a top level breakdown of funding vehicles. For the ones that you are

---

14 Imagine Canada http://imaginecanadadev.devcloud.acquia-sites.com/resources-and-tools/narrative (2014)
15 Nell Edgington, www.socialvelocity.net http://www.socialvelocity.net/financing-not-fundraising-a-social-velocity-blog-series/

already using – find the other charities that are doing this amazingly well and see what you can learn. For those that might be new and are quickly developing (i.e. crowdfunding and social finance) get to know them; they each have key success factors – and assess their applicability to your charity.

Vehicles at a Glance

i. Donations
- Individual broad base (direct mail, crowd funding, telethons, telephone solicitation, street solicitation, social media, third party events)
- Individual targeted (through annual, capital or endowment campaign)
- Foundations (public and private)
- Corporations (cause marketing, sponsorship, community investment, employee giving, third party events)
- Special Events (galas, golf tournaments, pledge based)

ii. Earned Income
- Membership fees
- User/Program/Registration fees
- Admission/performance
- Tuition
- Advertising

iii. Investment Income
- Interest from an endowment fund

iv. Social Finance
- Social Impact Bonds
- Impact Investing
- Social Purpose Enterprise (earned income)
- Debt financing

Social finance is a burgeoning field in Canada. It is defined as "an approach to mobilizing private capital that delivers a social dividend and an economic return to achieve social and environmental goals. It creates opportunities for investors to finance projects that benefit society and for community organizations to access new sources of funds."[16]

Chapter 18 addresses social finance in masterful detail. As it is a fast-moving and complex field of opportunity, here are additional resources to help you navigate:

- Social Finance Overview - *http://impactinvesting.marsdd.com*
- Assessment tool to see if your charity could benefit from social finance tools - *http://www.innoweave.ca/en/modules /social-finance*.
- To assess if social enterprise might be right for your charity, check out: *http://www.socialenterprisecanada.ca/en/toolkits/devtoolkit/nav/AssessReadiness.html*

B) Take responsibility for reaching your fundraising target

When we step-up and take 100% responsibility for fundraising goals it unleashes creativity and unearths opportunities. There will always be good reasons why we miss a target: i.e. we didn't set the goal; the economy is in a downturn; an event was rained out; a company goes bankrupt, etc. But whatever the reason, there are fundraisers who *in spite* of all those factors (and more) are meeting their goals.

Instead of asking "how can I raise this amount of money?" Ask the question: If I HAD to raise this amount of money what would I do? It is a subtle but powerful distinction.

There are often lives riding on the outcome of our efforts – we need to commit to doing whatever it takes (within professional guidelines of course!). High stakes and unequivocal commitment unleash amazing possibilities.

C) Be at the top of your game

"You must either modify your dreams or magnify your skills." – Jim Rohn

---

16 Employment and Social Development Canada. http://www.edsc.gc.ca/eng/consultations/social_finance/index.shtml

The most important competition is against the best version of ourselves; the world needs the best that we have to offer.

Identify what are you are good at and then consider what would be better than good - what would "superb" look like? Identify what you do poorly and consider what "better" would look like. There is considerable research that suggests it is a much better investment of time and energy to take what we are good at and become great at it - rather than focusing on what we do poorly and become mediocre at it – but many of us are in smaller organizations where we need to be as good as we can be on all fronts.

To spark insight into where to focus training efforts ask yourself:

- If I had to double the amount I raised next year how would I go about it?
- What additional skills would help me raise this amount of money?

For example, do you need help in building the case, persuasion, public speaking, data mining, prospecting, stewardship or management? If you are stuck ask your supervisor, CEO or colleague for feedback on what they think your greatest strength and weakness is – get training on both so that you can be superb on the first and not a liability to your organization on the second!

For every competency gap there are an abundance of training opportunities. Identify the gap, hunt down the resources, and if they are not free of charge, bring the resources to the table; we are fundraisers – getting things for free is what we do!

For instance, one fundraiser recognized that she needed more management training in order to help her team rise to their fundraising potential. Her organization had only a tiny budget for professional development, so:

- She asked someone external to her organization to mentor her.
- She negotiated a pro bono partnership with a training organization which not only provided superb training opportunities for her but also for the entire organization.
- She identified an (out of town) university management course, and made the case to the organization that it would result in her team raising more money. She also noted that if they paid for the tuition she would pay for travel and accommodation. They agreed!

Study the best fundraisers and read books written not only by expert fundraisers but also experts in the skill areas that comprise fundraising (marketing, sales, presentations, persuasion, prospecting, direct response and management).

D) Focus

"Start today, not tomorrow.
If anything, you should have started yesterday."
– Emil Motycka

Block time each day to focus on new opportunities. Protect the time and do it daily – preferably first thing in the morning. This is partly about time management but mostly about figuring out what is the most critical thing for you to be focused on in order to exceed your fundraising targets.

There are two excellent books which underscore the power of priority and focus:

- *Essentialism: the Disciplined Pursuit of Less* by Greg McKeown
- *The One Thing* by Gary Keller & Jay Papasan.

Keller & Papasan also have great tools on their website to help you focus your efforts and to secure the best ROI for your time *http://www.the1thing.com/resources*.

> **TIP!**
>
> - Ask yourself what one thing could you do each day that would ensure you exceed your annual fundraising targets?

CONCEPT #5: CULTIVATE AN ENTREPRENEURIAL SPIRIT

"If everything seems under control, you're just not going fast enough." – Mario Andretti

Every area of fundraising can benefit from cultivating an entrepreneurial way of thinking and behaving:

A) Take (calculated) risks

"One doesn't discover new lands without consenting to lose sight of the shore." – Andre Gide

A successful entrepreneur recently told me in passing that "entrepreneurs are delusional by nature." I believe this is also characteristic of the intrepid fundraiser. We need to believe that our project is so compelling that everyone would want to support it! Our "delusional" optimism propels us to new heights, while our awareness of the inputs and processes required to reach our goals keeps us grounded. As per the definition of entrepreneurship, we are pursuing opportunities beyond the resources currently controlled but we, of course, need to understand the resources with which we are starting.

B) Redefine failure

"Most great people have attained their greatest success just one step beyond their greatest failure."
– Napoleon Hill

"I have not failed. I've just found 10,000 ways that won't work." – Thomas Edison

Entrepreneurs don't fail - they pivot! Entrepreneurs expect setbacks as part of their ascent. If we test the market and it doesn't work, we have a treasure trove of information from which to learn, redirect and launch again. Our fundraising "failures" are the building blocks for success at a much higher level. Failure teaches us what the gap is to success and how we need to adapt (by building our skills, changing our approach).

C) Be playful

"WE'RE RAISING MONEY FOR A LOCAL CHARITY. WOULD YOU CARE TO ADD $10,000 TO YOUR PURCHASE?"

Entrepreneurs have been likened to children in their exuberance: the proverbial kid in a candy store. Some of the best fundraising I have come across has playfulness to it.

One of the best planned giving appeals was in a newsletter that came out around Valentine's Day from the Ms. Foundation (a U.S. Women's Foundation) with the article caption: "Are you a secret admirer? Let us know if you have left us in your Will!" This is wonderful because it takes a subject that is sometimes sensitive and makes it fun. This would also be fun to pitch to a chocolate company to sponsor. (i.e. "Let us know that you have our charity in your Will and we will send you a heart shape box of chocolates.")

Another playful approach was shared with me by a fundraiser for a theology school at an Ivy League University. She told me that when they needed to raise funds for the theology school, they didn't go to their alumni (too many of them take vows of poverty!) so they went to the *business school* alumni who may have sold their souls somewhere along the way and wanted to buy them back through a donation to the Theology School.

The Canadian Women's Foundation created Canada's first "charitable IPO - Immediate Public Opportunity" (a takeoff on the Initial Public Offering) to invest in the "futures" of girls. Each "share" was $100 (a straight donation with a certificate as the thank you). This was modeled on a fundraiser in the US which had become famous because Warren Buffet bought the first share. As a women's charity, the Canadian Women's Foundation made a playful adaptation by approaching Doris Buffet (Warren's sister) to buy the first share. She happily agreed; the "IPO" was launched at the Toronto Stock Exchange with a young girl ringing the bell.

If we can evoke a feeling of delight in donors – they are more likely to return our calls!

TIPS!

- If your fundraising target is "a sure thing" – then increase it!

- If you are afraid to do something – do it immediately!

- If you have what you think is a great fundraising idea – try it!

- When you encounter a setback, reframe it as something that is bringing you closer to a game-changing breakthrough.

BONUS CONCEPT: ENTREPRENEURS ARE OUR GREATEST ALLY

One of the most under-leveraged resources are entrepreneurs themselves.

For the fundraising professional, entrepreneurs are our greatest allies because they themselves *are* fundraisers. Entrepreneurs have to persuade venture capitalists/investors (major donors) to give them money and then daily they need to persuade customers (donors) to do the same. They are often doing it on a shoe string budget, compelled by a vision. There is nobody better to understand the feeling of having a big vision and very limited resources, than an entrepreneur.

Fortunately for us there are an estimated 1 million entrepreneurs in Canada, 50,000 of whom are classified as high growth enterprises[17] (code for their being a relentless entrepreneur somewhere in the mix).

Entrepreneurs' brains are focused on money and getting more of it – and so are ours. It is the same thinking process – we are on the same team!

In addition to the money that they or their respective businesses might donate to our cause, they are invaluable to our charities as strategists and in my experience if you engage them on strategy, their resources will follow.

A charity wanted to grow their pledge-based event from 1,000 participants to 100,000 participants within five years, with the goal of raising $20 million. The charity had low brand visibility, a very limited marketing budget and was competing against highly resourced/high profile events. But what they had was a breakthrough concept and a compelling vision of what that 100,000 participants would make possible.

Through their networks they approached a highly successful entrepreneur and asked her to lead them in a brainstorming session on how to grow from 1,000 to 100,000. They provided a brief in her "language" i.e. what she would do if she wanted to grow from 1,000 customers to 100,000 customers and move from sales of $500,000 to $20 million (on a shoe string budget, with low brand recognition). The entrepreneur met with the fundraising team and over the course of 1.5 hours, shook things up and provided great insight! She knew exactly what to do because she had just taken a great idea, and on a miniscule budget, made it into a

---

17 Start Up Canada. http://www.startupcan.ca/about/why-it-matters

multi-million dollar business. In the process of facilitating the session, she became inspired and offered to help the charity realize its vision of 100,000 participants. In a way… she just donated $20 million!

Another way of engaging entrepreneurs is to ask if you can meet with them to test your Case for Support. Entrepreneurs are masters in the art of persuasion. They can provide great feedback and once they are convinced of your cause, then you indeed have a persuasive Case for Support (and in all likelihood a new donor!)

And, of course, if you want to create or expand a social enterprise, get the advice of the most successful entrepreneurs that you know.

There are lots of ways to connect with entrepreneurs, including mining your networks, connecting with your local chamber of commerce or business improvement area, or combing the top 100 entrepreneur lists. The fastest way to enable you to reach the most entrepreneurs is through an amazing resource called Clarity FM which lets you access 30,000 business experts – most of whom are entrepreneurs. Go to *https://clarity.fm/how-it-works* pick who you want to talk to, arrange a call and pay a small amount per minute (it ranges depending on who it is and many of them contribute their fees to charity). You can talk to them for five minutes or five hours! An hour might cost $100 – and you are getting amazing entrepreneurs to answer any questions you have. Here are a few to try:

- If you were sitting in my shoes, at my charity and this was your scenario, what would you do?
- Does this Case for Support compel you? How would you change it up?

The opportunities to tap into the intellectual capital of entrepreneurs are virtually endless. Our greatest allies are just a click away!

CONCLUSION

Tory Burch, a renowned entrepreneur, captured the essence of entrepreneurial fundraising in a recent speech where she said:

"Being an entrepreneur is a state of mind. It's about seeing connections others can't, seizing opportunities others won't, and forging new directions that others haven't." [18]

Nothing less than the healing of the world rests on our collective ability as fundraisers to cultivate this way of working.

FINAL TIPS

- Ensure the *vision* of your charity dwarfs any trepidation you have about asking for donations.

- Before you approach a donor ask: What would I ask for if I knew that success was guaranteed?

- Cultivate an opportunity mindset that continually scans internally and externally for ways to raise more money.

- Take risks and then take responsibility.

- Actively engage entrepreneurs.

- Become the very best fundraiser you can be – the world needs nothing less.

---

18 Tory Burch commencement address at Babson College. (2014). http://www.babson.edu/news-events/events/commencement/2014-recap/pages/burch-tory.aspx

ADDITIONAL RESOURCES

Books

- COLLINS, JIM. (2005). *Good to Great and the Social Sectors.*

- KELLER, GARY AND JAY PAPASAN. (2013). *The One Thing.* Bard Press.

- LYUBOMIRSKY, SONYA. (2007). *The How of Happiness: A new approach to getting the life you want.* Penguin Group.

- MALLABONE, E.H. GUY AND TONY J.A. MYERS. "Motivation and Barriers to Philanthropic Giving by Entrepreneurs," Master's Thesis. St. Mary's University, Minnesota USA.

- MCKEOWN, GREG. (2014). *Essentialism: The Disciplined Pursuit of Less.* Crown Business.

- STEVENSON, HOWARD. (2011). *Getting to Giving: Fundraising the Entrepreneurial Way.* Timberline.

URLs

- HTTP://WWW.ESDC.GC.CA/ENG/CONSULTATIONS/SOCIAL_FINANCE/REPORT/INDEX.SHTML - Social Finance Report: Employment and social development Canada

- HTTP://KCIPHILANTHROPY.COM/DOWNLOAD_TRENDS/2013_2/INDEX.HTML - Social Finance Overview by KCI

- WWW.SOCIALVELOCITY.NET

- HTTP://WWW.STATCAN.GC.CA/PUB/11-008-X/2012001/ARTICLE/11637-ENG.HTM - Charitable Giving in Canada

- HTTP://WWW.TECHSOUPCANADA.CA/EN/COMMUNITY/BLOG/WHICH-CROWDFUNDING-PLATFORM-IS-BEST-FOR-YOUR-NONPROFIT - Online Guide to Canadian crowdfunding platforms

- HTTP://WWW.TECHSOUPCANADA.CA/EN/COMMUNITY/BLOG/WHAT-NONPROFITS-NEED-TO-KNOW-ABOUT-CROWDFUNDING

ABOUT THE AUTHOR

Kathryn Babcock, MPA, CFRE

A specialist in both grassroots fundraising and multi-million dollar corporate partnerships, Kathryn has honed an entrepreneurial approach that leverages assets and opportunities.

Through cultivating an entrepreneurial fundraising mindset, Kathryn helped catapult the Canadian Women's Foundation to become of one of the largest women's foundations in the world. This included the creation of Canada's first charitable IPO, a multi-million dollar women moving women campaign, and a national media and retail partnership.

As principal of Babcock & Company, Kathryn specializes in helping charities to raise more money through breakthrough ideation that gets results.

CHAPTER 17

GRANTWRITING

ROB PEACOCK, MA, CFRE

Grantwriting is the process of requesting financial support through written proposals submitted to foundations and other organizations seeking to fund charities in achieving shared goals.

From the basic definition above, grantwriting would appear to be a straightforward process. Yet, many Canadian charities might admit that their grantwriting program is among the most misunderstood and under-utilized areas of their fundraising portfolio.

read more…

If fundraising is both an art and a science, grantwriting is its "written art." Like other methods of fundraising, grantwriting success is built on the foundation of direct and indirect relationships with prospective donors. As with major gifts or direct marketing appeals, the successful grant solicitation must clearly articulate the need for support, the impact of donor investment, and the particular strengths of the project being proposed. It must also provide donors the opportunity to support a mission or project that aligns with their own philanthropic goals.

This chapter provides an overview of the grantwriting function – including its unique role and benefits within a fundraising program, common facts and myths, the anatomy of a winning proposal, and tips and best practices to inspire grantwriting success.

ASSESSING YOUR ORGANIZATIONAL READINESS

Any charitable organization, from small to regional to national in scope, should explore the possibility of implementing a grantwriting program within its fundraising portfolio. There are several appealing reasons to do so.

A grantwriting program builds the prospect pipeline by opening doors to foundations and other granting bodies to create new revenue streams. For cost-conscious charities, a grantwriting program is a low-cost opportunity to diversify and grow a fundraising portfolio.

However, while grantwriting is certainly inexpensive when compared to other types of fundraising programs, successful grantwriting requires a specialized skill set: the ability to write proposals that are clear, succinct, compelling, thorough, and directly address the unique funding criteria of the prospective donor. As such, not every organization is always ready to execute this type of process at every given opportunity.

Fundraising departments often rationalize this dilemma as a human resources issue –

"We lack fundraising staff with direct experience and expertise in grantwriting."

or

"Our staff are so over-extended with other responsibilities that they can't devote the time that a successful grantwriting program requires."

However, as important as these two obstacles are to preventing effective grantwriting, so too is the charity's overall *organizational readiness* to support and sustain a grantwriting program:

- Does the organizational mission/vision articulate a strategic direction with an operating plan in place?
- Does the organization have a solid budget with policies and systems in place?
- Does the organization have clearly defined organizational priorities or projects for which it requires funding? Are these initiatives clearly scoped and defined, and is the link with the organization's mission/vision clearly defined?
- Is management prepared to conduct program evaluation based on the grant, and equipped to support the project with human resources and technology?
- Does the charity have the staff capacity to enable delivery of the goals and objectives sought?

As a rule of thumb, more time is spent on the actual program planning for the grant than the actual writing and packaging of the proposal. Moreover, the charity with excellent program planning will find that their grant proposal is that much easier to fine-tune and complete.

No grantwriting program will be successful, regardless of the quality of talent put in place, if the organization has not clearly defined its purpose, funding needs, strategies and budget. This is of course true with other fundraising programs as well. But, no other fundraising area exposes poor organizational planning more than grantwriting, where the facts are laid bare within the proposal.

HIRING HELP

Grantwriters require a unique skill set to be successful. In small charities, the grantwriting function is likely handled by a fundraiser who is responsible for many other areas of resource development. Large charities may retain a number of full-time staff specifically focused on grantwriting. For many charities in between, the challenge is to identify whether the best results will be achieved through current resources, or cobbling together whatever resources are available to hire staff or project workers on a full- or part-time basis.

Given their specific skill sets and responsibilities, grantwriting is one area of the resource development portfolio that is often outsourced to freelancers. The greatest challenge for many Canadian charities is that quality grantwriters are in high demand.

The traditional method of print and online job postings is not always an effective method for recruiting freelance or staff grantwriters. By far the most useful of these in Canada are Charity Village (*www.charityvillage.ca*) and the *Association of Fundraising Professionals* chapter in your community. Larger employment sites such as Workopolis or Monster tend to yield a very large, but often unqualified pool of applicants. The best way to recruit freelance grantwriters is through word of mouth. LinkedIn is also a very useful tool for finding and connecting with potential freelancers.

Grantwriters may be retained on an hourly basis or at an agreed-upon rate per project. However, as with other types of fundraising, under no circumstances should charities agree to compensate the hired grantwriter based on a percentage of the total funds raised. Such compensation is considered unethical across the charitable sector, and is strongly discouraged by the Association of Fundraising Professionals.

QUALITIES AND SKILLS OF A GRANTWRITER: A CHECKLIST

Grantwriters must synthesize and interpret complex conceptual information to develop clear and compelling materials for donors who may know little of the organization or its needs. Successful grantwriters tend to have the following skills:

- Ability to write clearly and succinctly (a natural verbal fluency is invaluable);
- Strong reading comprehension and research skills;
- Able to break down complex concepts into clear, understandable "sound bites" that can be understood by non-experts;
- Write with a passionate understanding of the subject matter;
- Positions the ask to demonstrate the benefits of investment to the funder;
- Ability to manage multiple grant projects and deadlines;
- Strong interpersonal skills, the ability to work independently to drive projects to completion; and
- Not afraid to ask questions!

MYTHS AND FACTS

MYTH: *Grantwriting is a mysterious practice that should be undertaken only by professional writers with deep experience in grantwriting.*

FACT:
While grants should be considered as a possible revenue stream in every charity's world, there seems to be a degree of mystery and trepidation around the process itself. Grants are *not* free money; they involve a tremendous amount of preparation and planning to enhance the capability and capacity of a charity to make a difference. The grantmaking process is basically rational giving, with guidelines based on the funder's identified priorities.

While proficiency with the written word is a useful asset for successful grantwriting, it is not the most critical element of your proposal. Granting bodies do not award grants for verbal wordplay or virtuosity. Successful grantwriting begins with access to detailed organizational planning materials, providing the fundraiser with the organizational "raw data" required to complete the application. The application itself is then prepared and submitted adhering to the following basic principles:

- Ensure that the proposed initiative for which the proposal will request funding meets a philanthropic need that is currently unmet.
- Develop a clear plan for the strategy, implementation and evaluation of the initiative *before* drafting a single word of the proposal.
- Conduct thorough research to ensure the initiative will achieve the funder's philanthropic objectives – in addition to the charity's own!
- Build a relationship with the funder prior to submission – this can provide valuable insight into the evaluation process and areas of strengths/weaknesses in your proposal.

MYTH: *It is the grantwriter's responsibility as the architect of the grant proposal, to lead the programmatic development of the initiative for which funding will be sought.*

FACT:
Developing new programs or initiatives should be completed by the organization's program staff, who are the experts on the charity's mission, vision and operations. It is the experienced member on the development staff that will have the skills to help market the program to prospective funders – i.e., to prepare a proposal that articulates the vision of the program staff, identify potential funders who will be interested in the application, and prepare a proposal that clearly demonstrates alignment with their investing criteria.

MYTH: *Longer proposals are often more successful than short proposals.*

FACT:
Many people think that "longer-is-better" because it can contain more detailed information on the project and therefore have a greater opportunity to demonstrate alignment with the funder's objectives. In reality, this is a dangerous assumption to make. The proposal's format will vary depending on the funder, but invariably, grants contain similar components, with a sound plan to meet an important need and impact. The length of the proposal itself is not important if it succeeds in meeting the application criteria.

Generally speaking, there are three grant formats that are the most common. In some cases, the prospective funder will indicate what proposal style is preferred, or provide a standardized application form for the charity to complete. If no direction is given, the grantwriter may choose one of the following:

The **letter of intent** is generally two pages, and provides a very brief description of the project, asking the prospective funder whether a longer, more detailed proposal would be considered, subject to criteria eligibility. The letter of intent should:

- Include a summary of the proposed investment and its purpose up front.
- Highlight the philanthropic alignment between charity and funder.

- Provide a brief synthesis of supporting documentation.
- Make a request for actionable follow up (e.g., permission to submit a proposal).

The **letter proposal** is arguably the most popular, and is often three to five pages in total, with a specified funding request. This format is often more of an introduction of the proposed idea, used to determine potential funding interest. The letter proposal generally includes subtitled sections such as:

- Overview of the initiative and funding request.
- Detailed need for support and alignment with funder (with brief background information about the organization making the request).
- Greater detail on the initiative to be funded (including a summary of objectives, methodology, funding requirements and outcomes).
- Total amount to be requested over a defined period of time.
- Offer to submit a detailed full proposal at the funder's request.

The **full proposal** includes a covering letter with a summary, often anywhere from 5-25 pages, plus attachments. Most importantly, all proposals will contain a detailed budget outlining the proposed allocation of funds. The full proposal should include detailed sections for each of the following, up to several pages each:

- Executive Summary (outlining the request amount and term and summarizing the initiative to be funded)
- Organizational Information (including mission/vision, history and impact)
- Philanthropic Alignment with Funder
- Problem Statement (background)
- Objectives
- Strategy/Methodology
- Outcomes/Impact
- Evaluation
- Timeline
- Budget
- Sustainability (how the initiative will be sustained beyond the initial funding period)
- Appendices (e.g., strategic plan, operating plan, audited financial statements, lists of board directors and fundraising leadership, organization charts, etc.)

MYTH: *Grants are traditionally best suited for organizations seeking funds for capital support or special project funding.*

FACT:
Given the range of organizations that exist with varying needs, Canadian granting bodies may make investments in a number of areas:

Funds for capital support are often sought in the context of a capital campaign. These intensive efforts seek funding within a critical period of time, usually for construction and renovation of facilities, or the purchase of equipment or land.

Special project funding is often targeted to increase organizational capacity to better support and fulfil administrative and fundraising objectives.

Program or project funding is often used to start and/or expand programs, or launch a limited-time initiative.

Operating funding, often known as unrestricted revenue, is sought for ongoing costs associated with running the charity. Grantwriters will find that it is often easier to prepare program or capital grant applications than operating funding.

Endowments are sought to provide support for grants aimed at long-term investments that generate interest income over a number of years.

Some funders will entertain proposals seeking investment for any of the above purposes. In most cases, however, funders will clearly outline their investment interests.

RESEARCH: IDENTIFYING POTENTIAL FUNDING SOURCES

While there are many types of granting bodies to which grantwriters submit proposals, the most common are public and private foundations. According to Philanthropic Foundations Canada, of the 85,000 registered charities in Canada, approximately 10,000 of them are foundations (split nearly equally between private and public foundations), representing more than $4.5 billion in grants in 2012.

The key to a winning grant application is to identify and apply to potential funders whose stated philanthropic objectives directly align with the charitable organization. Finding those foundations may seem a daunting task – what's important is to know where to look.

For a fee, there are a small number of service providers who provide useful search engines to identify charities of potential interest, including background information on their granting history and philanthropic mandate. Two of the most popular are:

- Grant Connect (*www.grantconnect.ca*)
- Foundation Search (*www.foundationsearch.ca*).

As with much of what is found on the internet, the relevancy and currency of this information should always be verified.

Another method for identifying foundations that may be interested in supporting your grant application is to review the annual reports and donor recognition pages of competitive charities. These can provide useful clues to other foundations that have not been considered and the general parameters of their giving levels.

Many foundations have websites that hold much of the information that grantseekers require to determine if there's a match. In addition to reviewing funder websites, grantwriters should review CRA T3010 submissions for any public foundations that they may approach for a request. (CRA T3010 forms are available through the Canada Revenue Agency Charities Directorate at *www.cra-arc.gc.ca/charities*.)

RELATIONSHIPS: THE FOUNDATION FOR SUCCESS

Like all other types of fundraising, grantwriting is based on relationships. After establishing a fit with a potential funder through research, the relationship-building process becomes important for developing an understanding of the funder and ensuring that the grantwriter has all the latest information to submit an application with a high probability for success.

Too many grantwriters submit an application without taking the time to introduce themselves and ask any questions they may have *prior* to submission. It is not rude to contact a funder by phone or email! Rather, it demonstrates that care is being taken to prepare a proposal that is tailored to the funder's specific wishes. A few basic ways to approach a funder to help "open the door" include:

- Calling the funder directly to ask specific questions about their mandate, proposal formatting preferences, evaluation criteria and deadlines.

- Before calling a funder to pitch an idea, it is important to be prepared with highlights of the organizational program and questions that may be asked and answered within a 15-minute conversation. Clarification of any initial questions the grantseeker has will be helpful in making sure that the proposal contains the nuances that reflects acute knowledge of the funder – that one understands the funder's needs. Some funders may even be willing to provide some initial input on the specific concept to be put forward in the proposal.

- Sending a letter of inquiry to the funder in advance of a formal proposal. The letter of inquiry is one of the first steps to more formally build the relationship with the prospective funder. It provides background on the organization and the prospective initiative to be supported. Most importantly, it enables the grantseeker to think through the "proposal process" before developing a full proposal.

- Inviting the funder to the organization for a tour or a special event or arrange a meeting to seek the funder's advice.

Meeting a prospective funder face-to-face provides a tremendous occasion to manage expectations and solidify follow-up proposal content by covering some of the following topics:

- Establish credibility of the organization seeking the grant
- Need for the proposed project
- Demonstrated community interest in the initiative
- Proposed outcomes
- Costs, including other revenue sources for the initiative
- How the funder's objectives will be met through this grant

At the very least, it is always recommended to ask a prospective funder's permission to include them on the charity's mailing list for newsletters and key special events such as annual meetings, and/or to be sent periodic updates and briefs on organizational progress and success.

THE TOP TEN QUESTIONS THAT A SUCCESSFUL PROPOSAL MUST ADDRESS

What follows are "the big questions" asked of every grant proposal and which must be answered in the body of your application:

1. What is the mission and identity of the charity seeking the grant?
2. What is the initiative that requires funding?
3. What is the importance of the proposed initiative and the difference it will make?
4. What outcomes will be accomplished as a result of this grant, and during the period of the grant? How will the initiative be evaluated?
5. Why should the organization undertake the project and why should it be funded by the funder?
6. What is the cost of the project – and over what period of time?
7. What community need is being addressed and improved by the grant initiative?
8. How will the charity know if the grant initiative has succeeded?
9. Are there any other sources of funding available to help with the project costs?
10. How will the charity's program or service be funded for long-term sustainability?

ANATOMY OF A WINNING PROPOSAL

No two successful grant proposals look exactly like, but each will follow a similar framework with similar components. The framework and structure of these components may vary somewhat according to the wishes of the funder, and many funders provide their own guidelines for structuring proposals. It is critical that grantwriters structure their proposals *exactly* as requested by the funder; otherwise, the grantwriter risks having the proposal dismissed.

More and more funders today request that grantwriters complete a standardized application form. Strong application forms will generally follow the template above, providing the grantwriter with a built-in structure that may be helpful in keeping the proposal on track.

The following components are generally found within all grant proposal frameworks:

i.) **Problem statement**: Describes the unmet need to be addressed, and how the charity is the ideal organization to tackle this problem. Sometimes referred to as the "statement of need," the problem statement helps guide and prepare the actual problem that the charity will address and/or solve through the proposal.

Some basic guidelines for developing the problem statement include:

- Focus on the target audience the organization serves, and their specific needs (rather than the charity's needs);
- Clearly articulate the specific need being addressed, and how it relates to organizational mission and the funder's charitable mandate;
- Address how the problem will be solved with the proposed grant; and
- State how the charity will substantiate the need.

It is important not to overstate, but to focus on what the project will reasonably accomplish. If the initiative involves the participation of multiple organizations, explain in detail how the collaborative aspects of the proposal will be managed.

In a full proposal format, the problem statement should be no more than three to five pages and use clear data to support the assumptions. It will also be helpful to provide a comparative analysis (as and where possible).

Quotes from third-party experts provide excellent back-up information and lend authority to the validity and importance of the proposed grant.

It is also effective to include real-life stories from people who have benefitted from the type of initiative being proposed.

Finally, conveying a compelling sense of urgency will provide emphasis on why funding is needed *now*.

ii.) **Objectives**: Outlines the specific and measurable goals of the initiative and the benefits it will provide, and what outcomes will be achieved.

The next step in the process is to develop solid goals and define what accomplishments the initiative will achieve with funding. Generally speaking, the objectives show "how" an organization will know if it's meeting its goal. The goal itself is "what" the program aspires to achieve on behalf of the charity.

It is important to ensure that the grant proposal's objectives focus on outcomes and not the process itself. Outcomes spell results for charitable actions. In other words: what will be different – and how will it be measured? Focused outcomes provide greater flexibility for the organization to reach its intended results – whereas process sometimes bogs the charity down in achieving outcomes.

When writing outcome objectives, it often is helpful to clearly articulate the results to be accomplished:

- What key areas is the charity seeking to change, based on its problem statement?
- How will change be measured, and to what degree?
- Over what time period will change take place?

SMART planning helps considerably with this process: developing outcomes that are **S**pecific, **M**easurable, **A**chievable, **R**elevant and **T**imebound. Objectives that adhere to the principles of SMART are powerful indicators of success with funders and the organization itself.

As a reminder, it is important not to over-commit and under-deliver. The process for the charity needs to be manageable and clear.

Finally, use the grant proposal to demonstrate the positive impact of this initiative on the community and, more specifically, those whom the initiative directly benefits the most. Alternatively, it is often useful to convey the alternative situation – what would happen if the project was *not* funded?

iii.) **Methodology**: Lays out clearly and sequentially how the initiative will be carried out with funding.

The step takes the funder through the strategies that the charity is proposing to accomplish its objectives. Methods are detailed descriptions of the activities necessary to achieve results. Reference to research is often helpful in providing relevance and external validation to the process. Include areas such as which staff will implement the program, who it will serve and what activities will be carried out.

It is also helpful to clarify whether the models proposed are already in existence, or whether this initiative is a new and innovative approach to solving the problem. Making sure that proposed activities are implemented within a realistic timeframe is critical to funding success.

When writing the proposal, align the charity's methods to the program objectives, tie the resources required to the proposed methods, explain the rationale, build in phased activities that move sequentially to the desired results and communicate clearly so that the funder is able to comprehend everything that is proposed.

iv.) **Evaluation**: Outlines the process by which the charity and funder will assess the overall success of the initiative.

This step determines efficiency, effectiveness and impact of the proposal. The process should provide an objective report that documents the return on investment for funders. It identifies how change can be measured as a result of the proposal, and moreover, it helps the charity determine whether the program can be expanded for greater impact in the future – and what funding requirements exist to seek financial support.

The evaluation component addresses questions that the charity and funder will have:

- How will the charity/funder know if the initiative did what it was designed to do?
- What impact did the initiative have on the community?
- What did the organization learn from the experience it had?
- What didn't work, and why?

A good evaluation supports the proposal itself, tests the proposal's hypothesis and reassures the funder about the organization. Evaluation enables the organization to learn more about the strengths and weaknesses of the program. Finally, evaluation provides some benefit to the public, ultimately the greatest responsibility to both the charity and funder.

Essentially, this step ensures that the proposal has been written effectively. The ability to understand both the big picture and the individual pieces that make up the program requires dedicated thinking.

v.) **Future funding/sustainability**: Makes clear how the program will (or will not) become self-sustaining in the future (once the funding period is over).

This is the section where funders want to know how the charity will grow through the process of the grant period. In other words, how will the charity plan to pay for its future implementation? How will the charity continue to do good work after the grant period has been completed?

For many funders, the initiative's future funding sustainability is a key consideration in the decision to make an investment. It is important to remember that the funder's investment is seen as being catalytic. Very few funders will continue to support charities beyond its initial investment.

The sustainability section of the proposal must address the result for the intended communities impacted, but it must also provide the framework to show how the charity will continue the program and how the staff will make this plan happen.

vi.) **Budget**: Presents complete accounting for the funds requested in the grant, as well as relevant financial information for the grantseeking organization.

When applying for grants, there are typically two budgets that are required – the "program budget" that funds are sought for, and the organization's overall "operating budget" (usually contained within an appendix).

The program budget is the most important part of the grant proposal. It provides a description of how the program will be executed during the time period of the grant by depicting what the budget entails, how the money will make an impact and what skill sets the organization has to implement and manage the program.

Generally speaking, there are a few stages that are necessary for developing a program budget, including research, program documentation, program review during the grant review process, and overall budget justification.

Ensure that everything that is required by the funder has been provided with justification of any budget items that stand out or seem to be costlier than others.

vii.) **Summary**: Delivers a brief and persuasive closing bringing together the various components to summarize the proposal's highlights.

The proposal summary is a clear encapsulation of the strongest key elements within the grant application. When preparing a summary, look at the problem statements, observe the goals, understand the measurement and evaluation process, and address the long-term sustainability relative to the organizational budget.

The summary should contain the specific purpose of the grant, why the charity is qualified to carry out the initiative, the anticipated results, the total budget, and how much funding is requested by the organization.

A good place to start the grant proposal … is at the *end*. An important consideration for achieving success is the funder's proposal evaluation criteria, which provides clues to the proposal components of the greatest importance and where the grantwriter should focus attention. Beginning with a thorough examination of the evaluation process used to evaluate the project's success will give grantwriters important clues as to what to focus on within the grant proposal. Many funders make their internal evaluation criteria available on the website or will discuss it in a preliminary meeting prior to submitting a proposal.

> **TIP!**
>
> Some helpful examples of great grant success stories may be found on the Philanthropic Foundations Canada website at *pfc.ca/resources/great-grant-stories/*

BEST PRACTICES FOR FUNDRAISING GRANTS

Grantwriters should picture the reader when preparing the proposal – to convey excitement and a sense of mission, while achieving the funder's objectives. Ensure that there are compelling facts that highlight why the grant will matter and keep in mind that the investment must also help advance the funder's mission.

An organization's grant request will come from the identified problem or need and how the grant will help solve that problem, and why the project is important to the target audience it will impact.

As such, some of the following concepts will help guide the grantmaking process:

- Make the proposal visually attractive and strictly adhere to all grant guidelines as provided by the funder. In other words, "cutting and pasting" content from other proposals is rarely successful. Tailoring each proposal to the individual grant maker is critical.

- Use a clear, well-reasoned and thoughtful writing style with an emotional appeal. When writing grants, many folks seem to revert automatically to a stiff formal writing style, with plenty of jargon throughout. Jargon acts as a barrier to understanding; although grant proposals are formal documents, the language within them should not be. It is the balancing of facts and analysis with a compelling emotional angle that makes good proposals sing. Do not presume that the funder knows your subject as well as you do.

- Use data that is relevant and current to demonstrate the need and impact of the proposed project. Where possible, include both proprietary and independent research data. Credit any references that are used and avoid using research data more than three or four years old if possible. Remember, stats are most effective when used somewhat sparingly, and linked with an emotional connection.

- The window for grantwriting often operates within a six-month timeframe. Planning ahead will help with meeting funder deadlines as well as the research and writing process.

- Reporting guidelines exist for every foundation and are important to follow from a stewardship perspective. Ensure that all deadlines are met and that the appropriate information is assembled for a clear and concise presentation.

CONCLUSION

Grantwriting is not for the faint of heart – it is the art of positioning your organization's priorities using clear language to achieve a funder's philanthropic objectives, and not merely your own. What begins as a complex and chaotic process of gathering information and evaluating organizational priorities must end with a single document – one that is clear, logical, purposeful and yet emotionally compelling. It is a document that above all, must stand entirely on its own merits, without a personal presentation or a significant number of supporting documents. It must pull together the solutions for the challenge at hand and challenge the charity in the planning and preparation as well as compel the prospective benefactor in the response and reply. Strong writing is important, yet compassionate understanding is of essence in this important area of philanthropy.

Success in grantwriting is both challenging and rewarding. The decision to undertake grantwriting as part of your fundraising portfolio is not to be made lightly – it is a decision requiring a great deal of effort. Yet for any organization willing to seriously commit to the practice, grantwriting offers new and untapped revenue streams and opportunities for meaningful partnerships over the short- and long-term.

ADDITIONAL RESOURCES

Books

- Golden Brown, Larissa. (2001). *Demystifying Grant Seeking: What You Really Need to Do to Get Grants.* Jossey-Bass.

- Hall, Mary S. (2003). *Getting Funded: The Complete Guide to Writing Grant Proposals.* Continuing Education Press.

- Karsh, Ellen and Arlen Sue Fox. (2009). *The Only Grant-Writing Book You'll Ever Need: Top Grant Writers and Grant Givers Share Their Secrets.* Basic Books.

- O'Neal-McElrath, Tori. (2013). *Winning Grants Step by Step: The Complete Workbook for Planning, Developing and Writing Successful Proposals.* Jossey-Bass.

- Warwick, Mal. (2013). *How to Write Successful Fundraising Appeals.* Jossey-Bass.

- *Top Twelve Grantwriting Tips for Fundraising Success.* Corporate & Government Relations, University of Richmond.

URLs

- http://www.cfc-fcc.ca/about-cfs/find-a-community.cfm - Community Foundation Finder

- https://charityvillage.com/directories/funders/canadian-foundations.aspx - Charity Village – Canadian Foundations.

- www2.davidson.edu/academics/gc/gc_forms/Top Twelve Grant Writing Tips for Success.doc

- www.nsegap.ualberta.ca/en/Grant_Writing_Resources.aspx - University of Alberta

- www.pfc.ca - Philanthropic Foundations Canada

- http://pfc.ca/wp-content/uploads/pfc-grantmaking-guide-2012-full-en.pdf - *"Good Grantmaking – A Guide for Canadian Foundations."* Philanthropic Foundations Canada.

ABOUT THE AUTHOR

**Rob Peacock, MA CFRE
CEO, Peacock Philanthropic Counsel Inc.**

Rob Peacock is a Certified Fundraising Executive with over 28 years of fundraising experience from various philanthropic sectors — including health care, education, arts and social services.

Rob holds a Masters degree in Philanthropy and Development and was a faculty member of Humber College's Fundraising and Volunteer Management Program.

An active volunteer all his life, Rob is Past Chair of the International Development Committee of the Association of Fundraising Professionals as well as Past Chair of the Canada Council.

He currently serves on the Advisory Committee for the Masters in Philanthropy and Nonprofit Leadership at Carleton University, Canada's first Masters program in Philanthropy, and is the author of two books: *Face Time: Relationship Philanthropy, A Resource for Canadian Major Gift Fundraising* and *Engagement – A Resource for Canadian Volunteer Boards*.

CHAPTER 18

CHARITY IN BUSINESS

JOHN BAKER, BA AND JOHN PEPIN, MA

For many, the terms charity and business might seem somewhat contradictory. In the Canadian context, a charitable organization is one that benefits the public within the four pillars recognized by the income tax act – that is: (i) alleviation of poverty; (ii) the advancement of education; (iii) the advancement of religion; (iv) or other purpose that benefits the community. Business, on the other hand, is an organization that trade goods and services to consumers – with an implied motivation of profit.

Social enterprise combines the two above.

read more…

There exists, however, some convergence between charity and business that has led to new terms and concepts including:

Social entrepreneurship – building upon the definition of entrepreneurship provided in Chapter 16 on Entrepreneurial Fundraising (the pursuit of opportunity without regard to resources currently controlled); social entrepreneurship is the pursuit of social change (the opportunity) without regard to resources currently controlled. It should be noted that this is only the author's definition as there is no general agreement on specific definitions.

Earned income (and earned income activity) - Imagine Canada defines earned income as the sale of products, services, processes, expertise and intellectual property for monetary return.

Social enterprise – there is no common definition, however for the purposes of this chapter, social enterprises are "...businesses whose primary purpose is the common good. They use the methods and disciplines of business and the power of the marketplace to advance their social, environmental and human justice agendas."[1]

Venturesome[2] proposes three social enterprise models, defining them from a social impact perspective. These include:

i.) enterprise activity that focuses on maximizing profit, with the profits going to support social ends ("profit generator model");

ii.) enterprise activity with social impact, with a balancing of commercial activity with social mission ("trade-off model"), and

iii.) an enterprise activity that has a social impact generating financial returns that grow as the social impact grows ("lock-step model").

Social purpose business – used interchangeably with Social Enterprise.

Another aspect related to this convergence is social investment; defined as being the supply of finance and non-financial support with the objective of strengthening an organization's social, economic, environmental or cultural impact whilst potentially seeking a financial return on capital and/or community or organizational financial sustainability and viability. Venture philanthropy may be categorized as a form of social investment seeking a social return at the same time as attempting to achieve organizational and/or community sustainability and viability. Investing for financial gains alone would not fall within this definition.

Venture Philanthropy – often also referred to as "high engagement giving"- is continuously evolving in practice and definition. Venture philanthropy is defined as:

"Capital and human resources invested in charities and social enterprises by various types of investors in search of a social return on their investment; involving high-engagement over many years with fixed milestones and tangible returns and exits achieved by developing alternative, sustainable income."

This chapter will provide some background to this convergence and highlight best practices that will assist in navigating successfully the convergence of charities in business. As suggested in Chapter 16, this convergence is the natural extension of the entrepreneurial spirit inherent in the voluntary sector.

HISTORICAL AND CURRENT CONTEXT

In its most recent survey of the sector, Imagine Canada reports that somewhere between 55% and 77% of voluntary sector organizations engage in earned income activities. These earned income activities range from fee for service models to membership dues to a full range of market-based activities. The larger the organization (by budget size) the more likely the organization engages in some form of business activity and most are engaged in running more than one. While earned income is an important part of the revenue mix, it is not the dominant form of revenue for the voluntary sector.

Canadian voluntary sector organizations operating business and conducting business-like activity have been common for many years, going back well into the last century – Good Will Industries, Salvation Army and Girl Guides of Canada have been engaged in business-like activity for a very long time. While not a new form of revenue for voluntary sector organizations, reduced government funding, increased competition for

---
1 https://www.se-alliance.org/what-is-social-enterprise
2 *Three Models of Social Enterprises: Creating social impact through trading activities Parts 1 and 2.* (2008) www.vventuresome.org.

fundraising dollars/grants and a general increase in the numbers of voluntary sector organizations competing for revenue, there is an increasing interest in entrepreneurial activities.

It should be noted that in the UK, a number of charities have fully-owned subsidiaries (trading companies) with a small minority establishing a holding company (share capital) that creates profit generating mission-related businesses. This has led to some charities taking their intellectual capital and experience and re-packaging it and selling to a completely different marketplace such as the corporate sector.

The increase in interest in these types of entrepreneurial activities has encouraged the development of new terms and practices within the sector. Some of the terms that dominate discussion include:

- Social entrepreneurship
- Earned income
- Revenue diversification
- Social enterprise
- Social innovation
- Social purpose business
- Social return on investment
- Social finance
- Impact investment
- Social franchising

This chapter will also discuss some of these concepts and offer best practice observations for the fund raising professional who might advise a voluntary sector organization as they seek to embark upon, or grow entrepreneurial activities. And while definitions are an interesting point of discussion and debate, only a limited amount of this chapter will be dedicated to these definitions. The root concepts in this discussion (business, enterprise, entrepreneurship, innovations, return on investment, finance etc.) are somewhat well-understood and defined. The art lies in the application of these concepts to address social issues - whatever these social issues may be.

THE CASE FOR ENTREPRENEURSHIP IN VOLUNTARY SECTOR ORGANIZATIONS: WHAT IS SOCIAL ENTREPRENEURSHIP?

As the overarching concept, social entrepreneurship may include starting an earned income business, but this does not need to be the only definition. Entrepreneurship is really an attitude, rather than an activity. Social entrepreneurial organizations have a different style of leadership from traditional voluntary sector organizations. Social entrepreneurs are consumed by delivering the maximum social return on the investment, as measured by their community vision and specific mission, and they deliver this value through an attitude that sees market change as an opportunity.

Social entrepreneurs create, but not in order to blindly follow the latest "treat-of-the-week" trend. Creation is analyzed relative to criteria deeply integrated with an organization's strategic plan. Finally, while social entrepreneurs are consumed by their mission, they are not consumed by their ego, and they actively seek partners in their quest to improve their community.

So yes, social entrepreneurship often does include the creation of earned income ventures, but not all earned income is social entrepreneurship, and not all social entrepreneurs operate earned income ventures. This chapter talks a lot about issues facing earned income ventures, but we urge you to not consider these concepts in isolation. Social entrepreneurship is the application of entrepreneurial attitudes to voluntary sector organizations.

Studies in the UK have indicated that:

- Social enterprises are recession-busters
- Social enterprises are optimistic
- Social enterprises are profitable
- Social enterprises vary widely in scale
- Scale is important
- Profit reinvestment for social goals is a reality
- The scope of operations is mainly, but not universally, very local
- The public sector is a key customer

CHARACTERISTICS OF SOCIAL ENTREPRENEURS

Being entrepreneurial does not necessarily mean starting or owning a business, or even operating a commercial venture. As mentioned in the introduction, entrepreneurship is the pursuit of opportunity without regard for resources controlled. Entrepreneurship exists in very large and mature organizations, and it can also be absent in start-ups. It can be found in non-profits without any earned income, and it can be missing in for-profit companies. We like to define entrepreneurship as *an attitude towards change*. The following are elements of this attitude:

- *See change as the norm and as healthy.* Entrepreneurs thrive in a changing marketplace. They do not fear change – they embrace it.
- *Be responsive to and embrace change.* More to the point, an entrepreneur exploits change and is able to benefit from it. Entrepreneurial organizations respond to change by providing better solutions for their clients.
- *Always search for change.* Being able to respond to change requires that you discover it early, or lead the change. Entrepreneurs monitor their customers, suppliers and competitors for new developments, needs and solutions. Entrepreneurs also monitor other sectors and industries to get ideas.
- *Be client focused.* Ultimately change is about the client. The organizations most able to leverage change, whether in the for-profit or non-profit sector, are those who think about change from the perspective of their customers.
- *Shift resources from lower to higher areas of productivity.* An entrepreneur manages the use of resources carefully. If you offer a portfolio of products or programs, constantly evaluate which are the most effective either in terms of profit and/or in terms of mission effectiveness. Entrepreneurs are not afraid to stop poor performing programs and move resources to high performing ones.
- *Take calculated risks.* Contrary to popular belief, entrepreneurs do not seek risk. Entrepreneurs, especially social entrepreneurs, should act to reduce unnecessary risk. However, if the potential is strong, entrepreneurs are willing to take calculated risks to achieve extraordinary results.
- *Create something new.* Entrepreneurs push boundaries to create new solutions for their clients.
- *Strive for transparency.* In order to be effective at allocating resources, strive to be transparent in everything you do. To make entrepreneurial decisions, you need to have good information and controls.

BENEFITS OF SOCIAL ENTREPRENEURSHIP

A social entrepreneurial approach is the most effective way to stimulate innovation and income in the voluntary sector (e.g. social enterprises create unrestricted funds while fulfilling a charity's mission) and we provide reasons for this as follows. (Please keep in mind that this list is for the broad concept of social entrepreneurship, rather than the specific application of earned income ventures.)

- *Encourages the evaluation of resource effectiveness.* True social entrepreneurs are consumed by the concept of social return on investment, or perhaps even "mission return on investment." Social entrepreneurship means always considering whether resources are most efficiently allocated to addressing the social problem the organization is created to address. Nothing is sacred, except the vision/mission itself.
- *Reflects and responds to a dynamic market environment.* Social entrepreneurship recognizes that organizations are part of a system and a marketplace that is changing. Social entrepreneurs thrive as markets change.
- *Encourages innovative solutions.* Social entrepreneurial processes encourage new approaches to old problems; they describe a way to discover new initiatives and opportunities and screen these opportunities so that the most effective are pursued.
- *Reduces barriers.* Traditional organizations face and create many barriers. Entrepreneurial ap-

proaches reduce these barriers, especially barriers towards: Realizing financial value, creating new initiatives, partnering with others and rewarding success.

- *Leads to organizational sustainability.* Entrepreneurial approaches encourage organizational sustainability.

- *Encourages holistic approaches.* Social entrepreneurs look at root causes and systems – not just isolated issues. Although a social entrepreneur may directly only contribute to addressing one component of a social problem, they are acutely aware of their role in the system and partner with others to address solutions from a holistic perspective.

BENEFITS OF GENERATING EARNED INCOME

Most commonly when people speak of social entrepreneurship they are thinking earned income and more recently, social enterprise. While social entrepreneurship is the broader concept, commercial activity and earned income remain the dominant forms of the entrepreneurial attitude. As a subset of social entrepreneurship, generating earned income is distinct from fundraising. Consider the following benefits of integrating commercial activity into a voluntary sectors organizations revenue mix:

- *Diversifies funding sources.* An organization that is reliant on a few funders is vulnerable to changes in market conditions or "hot issues," particularly when funds primarily come from government or foundations. A diversified funding base provides insurance.

- *Funds overhead.* It can be difficult to fund the development of a strong management team and support tools, despite their importance to organizational effectiveness. Earned income is unrestricted income and can be used for administration.

- *Funds innovation.* An organization that generates its own funds can afford to experiment with riskier (but potentially revolutionary) approaches to social change.

- *Supports unpopular causes.* Earned income can fund the mission of an organization that does not have a strong donor constituency.

- *Creates an entrepreneurial spirit.* The rigor and spirit of building a business can also be applied to building strong social programs.

- *Enhances understanding of clients.* A business must be customer-centric to survive. Developing a business is a source of feedback about customer needs.

- *Tests social value.* A test of whether you have created value is asking someone to pay more than it cost you to create a product or service.

- *Adds skills and competencies to the organization.* Marketing, financial, managerial and research skills can also be applied to core social mission delivery and organizational development.

- *Enhances the profile of the organization.* Strong social businesses make news and attract the support of new funders and collaborators.

RISKS

There are risks to be managed though the process of setting up and developing a social enterprise. Generic risks from an organizational perspective include:

- Process risks - Dedicated resources/investment, support of the champion, and a systematic approach are essential.

- Experience - Developing a culture of business is important so commercial decisions are made using commercial criteria.

- External conditions – Competitive issues must be addressed.

- Core mission ethos and services must be protected throughout the process.

- Focus – Confusion of ends may occur, understanding and balancing the financial return with the social return should be considered.

- Legal – an inappropriate legal structure may work against achieving the ends of the social enterprise, so choose carefully.

BEST PRACTICES – CHARITY IN BUSINESS

1. **Strategic planning**

    Being entrepreneurial requires a deliberate effort from the Board, executives and staff of voluntary sector organizations. In many organizations, acting in a business-like fashion can threaten established organizational culture, norms and values. Preparation, with an emphasis on building a robust strategic plan, enables an organization to fully realize its potential while protecting and supporting its core culture and values. The strategic plan provides a framework for decision-making that guides the choices you make in developing and running your organization in an entrepreneurial fashion.

    There are numerous strategic planning processes used by voluntary sector organizations that will assist in building business activity. A good strategic plan should create an organizational direction that reflects the changing environment and the goals of the organization within that environment. At its core, the planning process should consider the link or purpose of entrepreneurial/business activity within the overall intent of the organization. Furthermore, the success of entrepreneurial activity is linking the strategic plan to the day-to-day activity of the organization through annual business plans that clearly state the annual objectives, resource implications and workflow relationships.

    Too often voluntary sector organizations are unable to answer the following questions:

    a) Where, specifically, is entrepreneurial/business activity contemplated and supported within the strategic plan?

    b) What is the specific purpose of the entrepreneurial/business activity as it relates to the mission of the organization?

    If an organization is unable to answer these simple strategic questions, entrepreneurial activity will be without a strategic sponsor – an orphaned and under-resourced activity within the broader organization.

2. **Good process**

    As a voluntary sector organization embraces entrepreneurial activity, it becomes important to use processes that are effective at selecting and developing ideas that are then supported by the organization. Effective process has the following characteristics:

    - *Simple.* A good process does not need to be complex. Indeed, experience has shown that complex rating systems rarely provide an answer that is different from a simple 1-3 scale.

    - *Not onerous.* If you want to encourage entrepreneurship, you cannot stifle it through onerous process. A process should be justifiable and fair, but it should also be quick. Generally, the level of due diligence required should increase as you become more comfortable with an opportunity. At the earliest stages, the bar should be set relatively low to allow an opportunity to be considered further. There will be an opportunity for more rigor after some priorities have been set.

    - *Fair and transparent.* Transparency prevents second-guessing and encourages commitment. Agree to the process and criteria up-front, then live by it.

    - *Continuous innovation comes at inconvenient times.* There should be a mechanism to consider ideas outside the formal process.

    - *Provides feedback.* The contributor of an idea should be able to find out its status and why it was accepted or rejected.

    - *Recognizes resources and limitations.* The process needs to be doable in your organization. The level of rigor should in part depend on the amount of time available.

- *Encourages creativity.* Out of the box thinking should be encouraged. Have a forum (such as brainstorming) for outrageous ideas.
- *Respects intuition, bound by logic.* There is a balance that needs to be maintained between intuition and logic. Intuition is incredibly powerful in the early stages of idea generation and screening. It needs to be respected. But at some point, the idea needs to be able to be justified through the logic of clear criteria.

3. **The idea**

   If you put a group of people familiar with an organization or its clients in a room for 30 minutes, they can easily generate dozens of ideas for initiatives that might be applicable. This is true whether looking for strategic initiatives, business ideas, or fundraising concepts. Yet the hard reality of entrepreneurship is that the majority of new ideas fail. Here are some pointers on how the most compelling new initiatives might be identified.

   The starting point of any business development process should be brainstorming and freewheeling. While there may already be a few ideas worthy of consideration, process is stronger when all ideas are put on the table first. Even if you are already pretty clear about what you want to do, brainstorming (and subsequent screening) provides a check. If an idea is really that strong, it will do well in the screening exercise. A good brainstorming and screening process protects the organization from second-guessing after a decision has been made. It gives confidence that the full range of alternatives was fairly considered.

   A good process will identify opportunities likely to be successful and that share the following characteristics:

- It is consistent with the social mission
- Meets a defined customer need with a specific competitive advantage
- Leverages the assets of the organization
- Can be developed into a credible business plan
- Risk can be managed and an exit plan can be defined
- Has growth opportunities
- Can be piloted on a small scale and does not have high fixed costs
- Once selected, long-term success of any opportunity is then dependent upon running the initiative with a strict eye on the business outcomes defined within the business plan (guidelines are available through numerous web sites noted at the end of this chapter).

Important elements of a business plan in addition to the content:

> **WHO IS THE PLAN FOR?**
>
> Choose to answer questions appropriate to meeting the purpose of the plan and for its audience. For example, the plan may be written for:
>
> - Oneself; to get a clear focus re. one's own thinking as well as for monitoring and controlling future progress.
> - The Team; to involve them, gain commitment.
> - External funders or investors; the plan provides a Case for Support and investment.
> - Internal funders; to persuade senior executives or the trustees to support you.
> - Shareholders, members or boards; to reinforce confidence in you and the plan.

EVALUATING A PLAN

When a management's business plan is assembled, there are a number of yardsticks that can be used to evaluate it. These include:

- Having a clearly articulated, strong business case

- Is there a market need? What is the extent of that market today and into the future (including an understanding of the industry and the specific market segment you are addressing)?

- Do you have a product to meet the market need? Who are the competition and how do you stack up against them? What is your unique selling point (USP)?

- How does the business work – the business strategy and the business model?

- Do you have the people to make it work in terms of the mission-related activities as a commercial-type enterprise?

- How do the finances stack up – profit and loss over a three to five year time frame, cash flow, investment needs and return on investment (social and financial)?

- Is the financial investment available to support the initial start-up costs and cash flow needs?

- Comparison of objectives and projected performance with other companies and social enterprises - Does the plan make sense in the light of what others have achieved in similar businesses?

- Profile of financial projections - Does the time to break even make sense? Are the margins realistic? Do the terms of business and working capital requirements tie up with each other?

- Sensitivity to and impact of variations in plan - What shocks and variations can the plan withstand before the business is in difficulty?

- If the business requires external capital does its profile fit with a recognizable source of capital?

- Parallel motivation and objectives as between potential investors and management - Do the management and potential investors agree on the issues of major importance? Would the potential investors understand the business, and will management and investors be able to communicate when things go wrong? Does the pattern of likely funding requirements fit with the profile of potential investor? Has management actually invested in the business demonstrating their own commitment to the plan?

- Has the management assembled a team that incorporates the experience to develop the business profitably in its chosen market? It must be clear that the management team will make the transition to good performance in the private company sector.

4. **Marketing**

   Some studies have claimed that the difference between business activities that succeed and fail is primarily one of implementation, rather than the product. In particular, sales and marketing are critical to developing a sustainable business model within voluntary sector organizations. These are unusual concepts for voluntary sector organizations that must be understood by voluntary sector organizations as they embrace entrepreneurial activity.

   The key marketing concepts include:

   - *Identify a target customer segment.* Be specific. What are the characteristics of your customer? How do you identify who they are? How big is this segment? What are their primary needs?

   - *Develop your position within the segment.* What need will you address within the segment? Why will your target customer gain from buying your product?

   - *Develop a product strategy.* How will you differentiate your product from others within the segment? What will be your competitive edge – price, quality, service accessibility?

   - *Develop a pricing strategy.* How will you price with reference to the prevailing market rate and to the value that you are creating for customers? What do you want your price to say about your product (cheapest, best quality, best value)? It is not about how much it took to make the product but rather what is the customer prepared to pay for the product. Too often voluntary sector organizations seek to compete on price.

   - *Develop a promotional strategy.* What is the best mechanism to raise awareness of your product within your segment? How will your target customer find out about your product? Options might include broad-based advertising, web-based advertising, referrals, trade shows or partnerships. Relying on mission to sell is not a promotional strategy.

   - *Develop a sales strategy.* What sales channels will you use to sell your product to your segment? How will your customers connect with your product and purchase it? Options might include a direct sales force, a distributor, other third parties, retail stores or e-commerce. Choose the channels that your segment is most likely to buy from. When possible, leverage others who are already talking to the target customer about the problem the product addresses.

5. **Human resource considerations**

   Human capital is the single most compelling challenge in entrepreneurial activity within the voluntary sector. Entrepreneurial skills and business competencies are specific to those engaged in business and (some argue) are difficult to learn within the voluntary sector. Sound human resource strategies that clearly identify skill and competency gaps within the business activity will guide the organization in filling the gaps. Hire those that have business sensibilities and knowledge – and then teach the social context/outcome. While the reverse is possible – it is far more difficult.

6. **Structuring the venture**

   Capital structure refers to the governance, legal form, and ownership of the business idea. Traditionally, the sector views the business activity from strictly not-for-profit or for-profit structure perspective and a strategic concern. Success in business activity might better consider these structures as tactical concerns – responding to the question – what capital structure bests serves the business intent/outcomes of the activity? This section explores several topics related to capital structure.

   A) **Some legal guidelines**

   There is usually a way to make it work. With appropriate legal advice, almost anything can be achieved from a business perspective. There is generally a way to structure a venture that is legal, transparent, ethical, and risk managed.

   Get advice from legal counsel. The issues, however, are complex and specialized. Without legal advice, an organization may set itself up for future problems. Almost any business can be run by a voluntary sector organization when properly structured, but a poor structure can jeopardize tax-exempt status or put the organization at significant financial risk.

The right time to get advice is after you know what you want to accomplish. Legal counsel works best when business objectives are clear, capital needs are identified, business operating parameters are developed and risks are identified. Until these questions are answered, legal advice will have limited utility.

There are some general legal principles that should be kept in mind as the venture is developed. These are generalizations only and should not replace legal advice.

- Commercial income generated by a non-profit/charity that is directly related to the mission is generally acceptable. Raising money is not the mission – what matters is the nature of the activity itself.
- If properly structured, the typical worst-case scenario for a commercial activity is to create a for-profit subsidiary and pay taxes on profit.
- Ownership and anything that looks like ownership is not generally possible in a non-profit structure. If ownership/shares offers are necessary for the success of the activity, a for-profit/share capital structure is the only viable form.
- Transparency and simplicity is generally a good strategy. There is no need to get complex in structure – it is better to be clear.

NOTE – *This analysis is not intended to be legal advice and any decisions on corporate structure should be made with the assistance of a qualified lawyer.*

B) **For-profit vs. non-profit**

Voluntary sector organizations, particularly those based on earned income, often struggle with the question of what legal structure is the most appropriate (for-profit, not-for-profit, charity or a hybrid). In many cases, there is not a regulatory requirement to be one or the other, and the question is more strategic. Legal structure is an operational decision, which is driven by the business plan. Form follows function, rather than the other way around. At the core of this decision is the type of capital that is required to fund the business plan of the organization.

Becoming a non-profit closes the door to the capital markets and market mechanisms for rewarding performance. Raising large amounts of capital can be much easier in a for-profit environment than through grantwriting and fundraising. For-profits also have the potential to sell a successful spin-off and immediately capture the financial value. Non-profits cannot be sold. On the other hand, being a for-profit makes the government a financial partner without a corresponding investment and few philanthropists will give money outright to a for-profit without the tax advantage of a donation status. Another consideration of a for-profit is that investors seeking a financial return may force the organization to compromise on its mission at times; however there are a number of mechanisms that may be used to maintain control over the enterprise and its mission and ethos including: clear decision-making rules in a shareholders agreement; the articles designed to make it difficult to change the objects and ethos of the social enterprise; Board representation; etc.

Reasons to spin-off a subsidiary

In many cases, there is not a regulatory requirement to spin-off commercial activity as a for-profit company. CRA permits some commercial activity in the non-profit structure. While not necessarily legally required, there are some good business reasons to consider creating a separate for-profit for your business:

- *Avoids management distraction.* The business can be run to maximize profit. The non-profit can be run to maximize social benefit. Neither management team is distracted from their primary purpose.
- *Reduces bureaucracy.* A small independent venture can be nimble and focused. A small program in a big charity can be forgotten.
- *Aligns talent, both at the management and Board levels.* Managing a charity requires a different skill set than managing a business. A separate

business can attract a Board of experts in the industry.

- *Achieves transparency and simplicity.* Donors or investors can support the organization that is the right fit for their needs. Regulators have a clear picture of each organization.
- *Shields the voluntary sector organization from business risk.* As the owner of a separate corporation, the non-profit can limit its potential loss to the initial investment it makes. Outside investors can be sought to further limit risk.
- *Enables investment in the business.* A for-profit has more options for raising investment capital since it can offer ownership.
- *May be sold to investors, employees or another company.* A separate business can be sold outright as an exit strategy.

A for-profit subsidiary is not appropriate for all business concepts. There are some downsides. The benefits should be weighed against the following:

- Some infrastructure will be duplicated, leading to extra expenses.
- Mission-related business activity may be tax-free if structured in the non-profit.
- A for-profit cannot directly accept charitable donations.
- Social focus may be lost. A for-profit has a fiduciary duty to shareholders.

Financing

Funding innovation does not need to rely solely on donations or cash reserves. This section explores non-traditional financing options, other than earned income, grants, events and contributions. Depending on the capital structure, access to other forms of funding may be:

- *Venture philanthropy.* Philanthropists are increasingly using the strategies of venture capitalists to make their donations more effective. A for-profit company can sell shares to venture capitalists, angels, employees, other charities, foundations, and association members or the donor base. Social venture capitalists evaluate their investments from a social and financial lens.
- *Distributor / Partner investment.* A business partner may make an investment to help the partnership succeed.
- *Licensing / Franchising.* Funds can be raised and the required investment reduced by selling intellectual property through licensing or franchising agreements.
- *Bank loans / Other debt.* Non-profits increasingly borrow money from banks and suppliers, or even issue bonds. This is appropriate for projects that have a predictable long-term cash flow structure.
- *Guarantee pledges.* Some innovative organizations will ask a supporter to pledge assets as security on a loan or as a down payment on a mortgage. The guarantee enables access to financing that the organization may otherwise not qualify to receive, and the donor can expect their assets to earn a market return before being returned.
- *Program-related investments* (PRIs) (CRA CG 014 dated 26 July 1012). A PRI is not an investment in the conventional financial sense. While PRIs may generate a financial return, they are not made for that reason. A PRI usually involves the return, or potential return, of capital (funds or property) within a set period of time, but this is not a requirement. A PRI may also yield additional revenue for the investor charity (such as interest), but the yield of additional revenue can be below market rates.
- *Corporate partnerships / Cause-related marketing.* Building strategic partnerships with companies can lead to financial and non-financial benefits. The best deals leverage the strategic plan of both partners to create unique value. Similarly, "affinity" deals work best when there is a strong strategic fit.
- *Planned giving / Legacy vehicles.* Some planned giving vehicles offer the donor cash flow before their death. Strategic use of planned giving can change the donor/recipient relationship.

7. Portfolio planning

It is important to develop a social enterprise trading portfolio investment plan for organizations that have more than one enterprise. This type of planning:

- Supports informed decision-making about strategic investment, reducing investment risks.
- Improves enterprise portfolio performance, creating greater enterprise value and returns.
- Provides a transformational vision supporting change and growth.
- Develops a clear enterprise portfolio growth action plan with a clear milestone-driven change management plan.
- Reinforces benchmarking and performance measurement.

A portfolio plan answers the following questions:

- Where are we now?
- Where do we want to be?
- What will it look like when we get there?
- What do we need to do?
- When do we need to do it?

It provides a process for keeping the enterprise portfolio vibrant, diversified and balanced; for planning and priority setting including criteria to:

- Evaluate existing enterprises re. which ones to grow/invest in; maintain and defend because they are profitable but further significant investment may not achieve greater returns; or wind down because they are no longer achieving acceptable social and financial returns.
- Identify cross marketing opportunities.
- Plan resource allocation (effort, finances, expertise, staffing) for new enterprises to add to the portfolio.
- Develop and implement exit strategies.
- Evaluate and prioritize new enterprise ideas (read on for an approach to encourage enterprise idea generation within an organization).

CURRENT AND FUTURE DEVELOPMENTS/TRENDS

In 2003, Imagine Canada reported through its *National Survey of Nonprofit and Voluntary Sector Organizations* that:

- Big organizations are getting bigger
- Larger organizations are more dependent on government funding
- Resources, although not declining, may remain inadequate
- Capacity problems may prevent many from fulfilling their mission

Recent developments, (including reduced government funding, increased competition for philanthropic dollars and a general increase in the number of organizations) are causing voluntary sector organizations to seek more business-like alternatives to addressing their issues.

Some argue that the Canadian expectation that government will step in where markets fail has caused Canada to lag others in developing the alternatives that will better support the voluntary sector. Certainly Canada lags United Kingdom and United States in specific innovations that may better support entrepreneurial and business activity in the voluntary and social enterprise sectors.

Emerging conversations include:

New legal forms

Some argue that there are insufficient legal forms (current legal forms include share capital companies, non-share capital companies, charities etc) in Canada to properly support the development of business activity with the voluntary sector. International examples of emerging legal forms include Limited Liability Low-profit Corporations (L3C USA) and Community Interest Corporations (CIC UK). Verifiable audit process like B Corps (USA and Canada) are also emerging.

Given the complex nature of federal and provincial responsibilities associated with business incorporation there are a number of regional conversations ongoing but none yet have moved to the development of any new legal forms.

For the most part, voluntary sector organizations "find a way" to achieve business outcomes that support their missions through existing legal forms.

Social return on investment (SROI)

Somewhat immature in Canada, there are some early pioneers in the practice of measuring SROI including Social Capital Partners in Toronto, Atira Property Management Service in Vancouver and Inner City Renovation/Community Ownership Solutions out of Winnipeg.

SROI is an attempt to quantify the social value being generated by an organization as a function of an investment made in that organization. The concept is intended to provide an evaluation strategy to determine which organizations and programs are delivering the "best" social returns. This approach is gaining popularity as competition for charitable dollars continues to increase and social organizations recognize the need to report on the social value of their work.

There is no common metric for all social outcomes but rather a diverse set of tools designed using a common set of principles:

- *Involve stakeholders.* Stakeholders should inform what gets measured and how this is measured and valued.
- *Understand what changes.* Articulate how change is created and evaluate this through evidence gathered, recognizing positive and negative changes as well as those that are intended and unintended.
- *Value the things that matter.* Use financial proxies in order that the value of the outcomes can be recognized.
- *Only include what is material.* Determine what information and evidence must be included in the accounts to give a true and fair picture, such that stakeholders can draw reasonable conclusions about impact.
- *Do not over-claim.* Organizations should only claim the value that they are responsible for creating.
- *Be transparent.* Demonstrate the basis on which the analysis may be considered accurate and honest and show that it will be reported to and discussed with stakeholders.
- *Verify the result.* Ensure appropriate independent verification of the account.

Social finance

Social finance is the emerging field encouraging the use of private capital for public good. The conversation is somewhat more mature in the United Kingdom – while the conversation has just begun in Canada.

Donor/ Social Investor	Pitch	Results
Donor A (Traditional philanthropist)	Case for Support approach using typical charity language. **Case for Support** • Mission – what you want to achieve • Introduction/overview summarizing the main points • The needs you are meeting • Use statistics, case studies, authoritative sources • Give a sense of urgency, importance and potential impact • How you will meet the needs – describe the project(s) • Why support the charity? • Organizational credibility, USP, accomplishments, impact, and other donors • Detailed budget • Who's involved – Board, staff, partners, donors	Tax efficient donation

Donor/ Social Investor	Pitch	Results
Donor B (Social investor donor)	Business Case approach using social investment language. Taking a social investment approach with no financial return to the donor/ social investor; the social investor seeking a societal return on their investment (outcome, impact, social return on investment). **Business Case** - Problem/market need - Your solution - Description of the service/enterprise, activity and business model - Unique Selling Point (USP)/competitive difference - Strategy and people to make it work - Finances - The ask: investment needed (money/resources) - Societal returns: financial return on investment (FROI)/Social return on investment (SROI) (triple bottom line) - Your organization – you are a winner (effectiveness/impact, financial stability, successes, other social investors)	Tax efficient donation
Donor C Similar to Donor B; however, the donor, a group of donors or corporations and their employees wish to get involved e.g. Venture Philanthropy type model. They establish or contribute to a fund(s) which are an in-house semi-independent fund co-managed by the social investors and the charity.	Business Case approach using social investment language outlining ways the social investor may engage. *Venture philanthropy* is defined as: Capital and human resources invested in charities by various types of investors in search of a societal return on their investment. Venture philanthropy involves a high engagement over many years with fixed milestones and tangible returns/impact and an exit achieved by developing alternative, sustainable income. As social investors, venture philanthropists seek the most efficient use of their money in achieving a desired social goal. Like venture capitalists, venture philanthropy investors seek to maximize their return by adding value beyond the monetary contribution through the contribution of expertise and strategic guidance.	Tax efficient donation and donor expertise applied over a number of years.

Donor/ Social Investor	Pitch	Results
Person D The social investor seeking a financial return for themselves along with achieving a societal impact.	Social investment is defined as the supply of finance and non-financial support with the objective of either strengthening an organization's social, health, environmental, economic or cultural impact (see Donor B and C above); or, achieving the above whilst creating a financial return for the social investor. Investing for financial gains alone would not fall within this definition. There are three basic categories of social investors: i. Wholesalers who fund intermediaries ii. Intermediaries: retail funders who invest in charities and social enterprises iii. Investees: charities/social enterprises who receive the investment	Tax efficient investment in the charity's social enterprise activities or into a social venture capital investment fund (i.e. the charity's intermediary fund).

Sponsored by the Government of Canada, recent consultations include the gathering of concepts that should be considered within the emerging field of Canadian social finance. The resulting government summary identifies some fifteen current programs worthy of further study. *www.esdc.gc.ca/eng/consultations/social_finance/report/index.shtml*

Concepts in social finance include tools such as *Social Impact Bonds*(SIB). The SIB is a bond offering generally backed by government where the financial returns offered is linked to those who invest in programs designed to address measurable social return – like recidivism, youth unemployment and homelessness. Private investment in the bond is encouraged by government guaranteeing a specific return contingent upon specific social returns being met. If targets are not met, no return on the investment is made.

Any number of provinces are also entering the consultation/pilot project phase of social finance development. *www.Socialfinance.ca* is the preferred reference for these developments.

Integrated fundraising campaign - combining a major donor/social investment

Voluntary sector organizations, when wishing to raise significant sums of money often embark on a major donor campaign – a traditional approach that uses a Case for Support to attract donations from high net worth individuals, corporations and trusts; usually in the form of tax efficient donations. Some institutions (like universities) may raise investment funds for specific commercial ventures. These two approaches are usually separate activities; generally not leveraging relationships with each other.

An integrated fundraising campaign brings the two together, combining traditional major donor approaches with social investment thereby making it an integrated campaign – the campaign funding/investing in investable propositions, that is - lists of items that the charity is raising funds for:

- Program/service quality enhancement, growth, and new service development to meet emerging or unmet needs; capital campaigns; research.

- Social enterprises new product development and growth; supporting external partners/key stakeholders.

- Creating an infrastructure that will support greater organizational effectiveness, efficiencies and growth.

This approach allows for the leveraging of relationships, cross marketing and up selling. In the simplest terms there are different approaches to different donors, depending on their perspective.

For example:

It is important to be investable-ready, creating a social entrepreneurial context and address organizational readiness issues.

CONCLUSION

While at risk of becoming the latest "flavour of the month," entrepreneurial activity within the Canadian voluntary sector appears to be accelerating. The concepts mentioned within this chapter are the subject of numerous regional and national studies and initiatives – and the subject matter can easily fill a volume of its own. Within the limits of this chapter, an attempt has been made to provide some context and a framework of best practice for the fundraising professional to consider – it is simply an introduction. The material is by no means exhaustive. There are consulting professionals and academics involved full-time in the study and application of these concepts. The essence remains the delicate balancing social and business outcomes.

Charities in business can provoke the extremes of debate – on the one hand some claim that the secret is for voluntary sector organizations to be more business-like. However, if only businesses were more socially-minded perhaps we could solve all the world's problems. The truth and the future lies somewhere between.

TIPS!

- Strategic planning is important; without it, business and entrepreneurial activity will struggle.
- Entrepreneurial activity will change the culture of an organization. Accept it and prepare for it.
- The discipline of multiyear planning that connects the strategic plan to the day-to-day life of the voluntary sector organization is essential.
- Use robust processes to develop and screen business ideas. It reduces risk.
- Recognize that good ideas can come from anywhere and at the most inconvenient times. Be ready with process.
- Marketing (customer) perspectives are key; charge for value-created in comparison to the competition.
- Hire business people that understand the industry or activity that you are pursuing.
- Form follows function. First understand the intent and plan for the business, then get legal advice.
- Seek to understand the social return involved in the business activity . What social outcome is produced at what price.
- Find new financing tools.
- Consider creating an integrated fundraising campaign.

ADDITIONAL RESOURCES

Books

- BORNSTEIN, DAVID. *How to Change the World: Social Entrepreneurs and the Power of New Ideas.* Oxford University Press.

- BOSCHEE, JERR. *The Social Enterprise Sourcebook – Profiles of Social Purpose Businesses Operated by Nonprofit Organizations.* Northland Institute.

- BOSCHEE, JERR. *Migrating from Innovation to Entrepreneurship: How Nonprofits are Moving toward Sustainability and Self-Sufficiency.* The Institute for Social Entrepreneurs.

- BRINCKERHOFF, PETER. *Social Entrepreneurship: The Art of Mission Based Innovation*; Wiley

- DEES, J. GREGORY; JED EMERSON AND PETER Economy. *Enterprising Nonprofits: A Toolkit for Social Entrepreneurs*; Wiley.

- DEES, J. GREGORY ET AL., *Strategic Tools for Social Entrepreneurs: Enhancing the Performance of Your Enterprising Nonprofit.* Wiley.

- LARSON, ROLFE. *Venture Forth! The Essential Guide to Starting a Moneymaking Business in Your Nonprofit Organization.* Amherst H. Wilder Foundation (Wilder Publishing Center).

- OSTER, MASSARSKY, BEINHACKER, *Generating and Sustaining Nonprofit Earned Income*; Jossey-Bass

- PEPIN, JOHN. *A Guide to Revenue Diversification for Directors of Non-Profit Organizations*; Canadian Society of Association Executives

- ROBINSON, ANDY. *Selling Social Change (Without Selling Out).* Chardon Press Series.

- SHORE, BILL. *The Cathedral Within.* Random House.

- STECKEL, SIMONS AND TANEN SIMONS. *Making Money While Making a Difference.* High Tide Press.

- STECKEL, RICHARD. *Filthy Rich: How to Turn Your Nonprofit Fantasies into Cold, Hard Cash.* Ten Speed Press.

URLs

- APERIO. WWW.APERIO.CA. The website includes a number of our own publications, templates, a current list of links and books, and case studies of social entrepreneurs.

- CANADIAN SOCIAL ECONOMY HUB – CENTRE CANADIEN D'ÉCONOMIE SOCIALE. WWW.SOCIALECONOMYHUB.CA . A portal for resources impacting the social economy in Canada.

- CANADIAN SOCIAL ENTREPRENEURSHIP FOUNDATION. WWW.CSEF.CA Supports social entrepreneurship in Canada.

- CENTER FOR SOCIAL INNOVATION. WWW.GSB.STANFORD.EDU/CSI. The publisher of the Stanford Social Innovation Review and also offers other resources of interest to the field.

- COMMUNITY WEALTH VENTURES. WWW.COMMUNITYWEALTH.COM. A directory of non-profit organizations with business ventures and has published a number of reports offering an overview of social enterprise in the United States, including essays, case studies, practical lessons, and survey results for organizations seeking to diversify their revenue streams.

- GOVERNMENT OF CANADA. WWW.ESDC.GC.CA/ENG/CONSULTATIONS/SOCIAL_FINANCE/REPORT/. Summarizes the recent federal consultations.

- NEW PROFIT INC. WWW.NEWPROFIT.ORG. A venture philanthropy firm committed to the practice of venture philanthropy and the evolution of a new market for social change. Its goal is to effect large-scale social change by applying venture capital practices to philanthropy.

- PETER F. DRUCKER CANADIAN FOUNDATION. WWW.INNOVATION-AWARD.CA. Celebrates and shares innovative practices found in non-profit organizations in Canada.

- SOCIAL EDGE. WWW.SOCIALEDGE.ORG. A resource for social entrepreneurs.

- SOCIAL ENTERPRISE CANADA. WWW.SOCIALENTERPRISECANADA.CA. The national network for social enterprises containing a full range of resources for enterprise activity within the voluntary sector.

- SOCIAL ENTERPRISE ALLIANCE. WWW.SE-ALLIANCE.ORG. A network of support connecting entrepreneurial non-profits with learning opportunities, technical assistance and resources to further their efforts.

- SOCIAL FINANCE CANADA. WWW.SOCIALFINACE.CA. A collection of resource material and conversations regarding current issues around social finance in Canada.

- SOCIAL RETURNS. WWW.SOCIALRETURNS.ORG. Provides educational and financial support for non-profit enterprise through its business plan competition. Social Returns was inspired by the Partnership for Nonprofit Ventures, which is no longer active, but still hosts a website with significant resources (www.ventures.yale.edu).

- THE ROBERTS ENTERPRISE DEVELOPMENT FUND. WWW.REDF.ORG A venture philanthropy firm focused on building job and training social enterprises in the San Francisco area. It has published several guides and reports for social entrepreneurs, and is considered the leading expert on Social Return on Investment (SROI).

Case Studies

- While there is no central resource for case studies of business activities within the voluntary sector in Canada, the most robust in North America is Centre for Advancement of Social Entrepreneurship *http://caseatduke.org/knowledge/casestudies/index.html*.

In Canada, there are a few resources that discuss the concepts mentioned within this Chapter.

- HTTP://INNOWEAVE.CA/EN/RESOURCES. Social Enterprise examples include St John's Bakery (Toronto), Have Culinary Training (Vancouver). Social finance case studies include Atira Property Management Services (Vancouver) and The Centre for Social Innovation (Toronto)

- HTTP://TRICOFOUNDATION.CA/WORDPRESS/CATEGORY/CANADIAN-SOCIAL-ENTERPRISES/ The sponsors of The Social Enterprize Award, Trico Foundation provides a lengthy list of Social Enterprise case studies.

Selected Associations

- ASSOCIATION OF FUNDRAISING PROFESSIONALS WWW.AFPNET.ORG Local chapters across Canada, including Association des professionnels en gestion philanthropique (QC). www.apgp.com

- CANADIAN COMMUNITY ECONOMIC DEVELOPMENT NETWORK – LE RÉSEAU CANADIEN DE DÉVELOPPEMENT ÉCONOMIQUE COMMUNAUTAIRE. www.ccednet-rcdec.ca

- CANADIAN SOCIAL ENTREPRENEURS NETWORK www.csen.ca

- CANADIAN SOCIETY OF ASSOCIATION EXECUTIVES – SOCIÉTÉ CANADIENNE DES DIRECTEURS D'ASSOCIATION www.csae.com

- CHANTIER DE L'ÉCONOMIE SOCIALE. www.chantier.qc.ca

- CONSEIL CANADIEN DE LA COOPÉRATION. www.ccc.coop

- FONDATION DE L'ENTREPRENEURSHIP. www.entrepreneurship.qc.ca

- IMAGINE CANADA. www.imagine.ca

- PAN CANADIAN COMMUNITY FUTURES NETWORK – RÉSEAU PANCANADIEN DES SOCIÉTÉ D'AIDE AU DÉVELOPPEMENT DES COLLECTIVITÉS. www.communityfutures.ca

- RÉSEAU DE DÉVELOPPEMENT ÉCONOMIQUE ET D'EMPLOYABILITÉ. www.rdee.ca

- VOLUNTARY GATEWAY – PORTAIL COMMUNAUTAIRE. www.voluntarygateway.ca

ABOUT THE AUTHORS

**John Baker, BA
CEO and Partner,
Aperio Group**

John has an extensive breadth of Executive and Chief Executive experience in the public, private and not-for-profit sectors and has a broad background in strategic and business planning. Prior to his work with Aperio, he was the Founding President of Proventus Inc., a for-profit spin off of a not-for-profit association, and prior to that the President and CEO of the Ontario Service Safety Alliance.

John is also a retired Naval Officer having elected early retirement after 21 years of service in the Canadian Navy. He has a BA in International Studies from the Royal Military College of Canada, has attended the Banff School of Management and The Aresty Institute of Executive Education - Wharton School, University of Pennsylvania. He is also a member of the faculty of the Schulich School of Business York University.

**John Pepin, MA
Chief Executive,
Philanthropy Impact,
Aperio Group**

Based in the UK for 15 years, John Pepin spent over 15 years as a chief executive of a variety of Canadian charities/ social enterprises/ associations; and he has 17 years experience as a social entrepreneurial consultant internationally. He has successful turnaround experience as an Interim chief executive of a charity in 2013.

His experience includes: strategic and business planning, governance, enterprise development and growth, research and evaluation, social investment, revenue generation/ fundraising, organisational turnaround and growth, change management, and collaboration; and as a facilitator, trainer, mentor, board trustee and board chair, and speaker; and he has published articles and has research experience in the areas of social enterprise, trade and professional association financial sustainability, governance, social investment funds, privatization and the third sector, venture philanthropy, and collaboration in the non-profit sector, and a book providing guidance on social enterprise.

He has experience in innovative service and program design, project and venture start-up and management, and business strategy consulting across multiple third sector verticals. He is passionate about social change, innovation and growth in organizational reach and impact; a strong all-rounder, bringing proven service design, commercial acumen, operational management, business strategy and partnership building expertise to create sustainable social ventures.

INDEX

A

Abraham, Dan *166, 167*
accountability *30, 36, 45, 113, 137*
ACFRE *11, 13, 23, 26, 49, 79, 80*
acquisition *102, 148, 159, 160, 164*
advertising *136, 200, 201, 217, 221, 222, 227, 234, 313*
affinity *17, 125, 202, 315*
AFP *4, 6, 23, 41, 42, 44, 60, 106, 131, 155, 156, 166, 183, 240*
Algonquin College *44*
alumni *77, 110, 132, 286*
annual fund *47, 96, 104, 129, 143, 231, 232, 244, 251, 286*
annual giving *61, 63, 97*
annual report *236, 245, 249, 256, 296*
assets *199*
Association of Fundraising Professionals *4, 23, 26, 41, 42, 44, 49, 56, 60, 77, 81, 106, 111, 132, 182, 293, 302, 322*
Association of Healthcare Philanthropy *111*
audit *114, 125, 149, 163, 213, 316*

B

Babcock, Kathryn *277, 289*
Baker, John *305, 323*
Barootes, Brent *197, 213, 261*
benchmarking *316*
benchmarks *77, 101, 105, 252, 272, 273, 274*
bequests *22, 76, 101, 102, 103*
BMO *123, 238*
Bow Valley College *44*
Burrows, Malcolm *238*

C

CAGP *44*
call centre *154, 155, 156, 162, 163, 164, 165*
Canada Revenue Agency *23, 41, 136, 138, 149, 150, 198, 296*
Canadian Association of Gift Planners *44, 76*
Canadian Centre for Philanthropy *22, 23, 36, 231, 240*
capacity *7, 8, 30, 32, 54, 73, 79, 97, 99, 111, 118, 125, 146, 150, 181, 193, 201, 207, 249, 251, 264, 267, 283, 292, 294, 295*
capital campaign *129, 136, 147, 197, 224, 230, 240, 281, 295, 319*
Carleton University *4, 44, 50, 110, 302*
case for support *149, 181*
cause marketing *205, 284*
certification *23, 26, 41, 45, 50*
Certified Fundraising Executive *23, 26, 302*
CFRE *4, 23, 36, 41, 45, 49, 53, 57, 76, 121, 130, 132, 173, 229, 240, 259, 275, 277, 289, 291*
charitable donations *17, 19, 22, 188, 190, 281, 282, 315*
charitable foundation *18, 22*
Charity Intelligence *186, 187, 188, 189, 192*
China *14, 178, 181, 182*
corporate foundations *74*
cost per dollar raised *44, 96, 98, 99, 101, 102*
Criminal Code of Canada *186, 190*
crowdsourcing *124*
CRTC *164, 165*
Cystic Fibrosis Canada *244*

D

Daminato, Cathy *183*
diaspora *25, 124, 125, 180, 181*
digital media *77, 118, 212, 245, 252, 253, 255*
direct mail *62, 63, 77, 99, 128, 154, 158, 159, 216, 220, 224, 232, 234, 281, 284*
direct response *99, 166, 285*
donor cycle *230*
donor fatigue *216*

E

endowment *21, 274, 284*
ethical fundraising *35, 155*
ethics *45, 81, 191*
External Equity *39*

F

Facebook *37, 128, 146, 216, 223, 230, 234, 244, 245, 246, 247, 248, 249, 250, 252, 255*
face-to-face *64, 159, 174, 207, 230, 296*
feasibility study *193, 200*
Fox, Terry *21*
freelancers *293*
fund development committee *62*

G

Garrard, Ted *180, 194*
Georgian College *44*
giving pyramid *156*
Giving Tuesday *253*
globalization *122*

Google *128, 220, 252*
Google Analytics *252*
government funding *14, 16, 21, 136, 137, 147, 273, 306, 316*
Government Relations *150, 151, 302*
grant *17, 21, 22, 35, 66, 72, 75, 136, 292, 293, 294, 295, 296, 297, 298, 299, 300*
grantwriter *293, 294, 296, 297, 300*
Greenfield, Deborah *121, 132*
Green, Fraser *238*

H

Hardy, Patricia *13, 26*
Heart & Stroke Foundation *190*
Holz, Christopher *135, 151*
Howe, James *243, 256*
Humber College *44, 166, 302*

I

Imagine Canada *23, 26, 54, 116, 138, 150, 188, 194, 283, 306, 316, 322*
Income Tax Act *138, 149*
influencer *244, 252*
integrated fundraising *5, 154, 156, 319, 320*
Internal Equity *39*
inventory *199, 200, 201, 203, 204, 206, 213, 237, 262, 264, 265, 266, 267, 268, 270, 272*

L

Latin America *127*
leadership *58, 59, 96, 97, 100, 105, 112, 113, 115, 117, 118, 130, 150, 181, 183, 260, 295, 307*
legacy donors *76*
legacy gift *76*
Legacy Giving *33*
LinkedIn *37, 106, 246, 249, 250, 252, 293*
lotteries *186, 188, 189, 190, 191, 192, 193*

M

major gift *32, 35, 43, 74, 78, 96, 97, 99, 103, 104, 112, 113, 118, 127, 130, 197, 199, 203, 204, 205, 229, 230, 231, 232, 233, 234, 235, 236, 237, 238, 239, 240, 270, 275, 292*
Mallabone, Guy *1, 4, 6, 8, 9, 113, 114, 231, 239, 251*
McConnell, Tim *29, 50*
McManus, Andrea *49, 111*
McMaster University *260, 273*

media *24, 37, 73, 77, 78, 124, 128, 130, 132, 136, 139, 140, 141, 142, 143, 145, 146, 147, 148, 149, 151, 180, 186, 203, 205, 209, 210, 216, 220, 222, 230, 233, 234, 236, 238, 243, 244, 245, 246, 247, 248, 249, 250, 251, 252, 253, 254, 255, 262, 281, 282, 284, 289*
Mehta, Krishan *121, 132*
Melanson (Coyle), Anne *229, 240*
millennial *117*
Mohawk College *44*
monthly giving *74, 77, 78*
Morris, Andrea *109, 118*
Morris, Kelly *109, 118*
moves management *235, 237*

N

naming *198, 199, 200, 259, 260, 261, 262, 263, 264, 265, 266, 267, 268, 269, 270, 272, 273, 274, 275*
naming inventory *262, 264, 266, 267, 270, 272*
National Philanthropy Day *23*
Nazareth, Paul *246*
newsletter *64, 65, 66, 67, 76, 77, 99, 155, 160, 200, 204, 249, 281, 286*
NSFRE *23*

O

online fundraising *253*

P

Peacock, Rob *291, 302*
Pepin, John *305, 323*
Perry, Gail *57, 80*
planned gifts *283*
planned giving *44, 59, 76, 79, 81, 96, 101, 104, 132, 246, 282, 286, 315*
Princess Margaret Hospital Foundation *190*
pro bono *285*
prospect research *74, 75*
prospects *35, 38, 58, 60, 62, 67, 68, 74, 75, 79, 101, 102, 104, 127, 130, 155, 160, 162, 198, 201, 206, 216, 219, 226, 231, 234, 237, 239, 282*
public foundations *296*

R

real estate *151, 235*
real market value *201, 206*
Reddit *247*

Regina Humane Society *58, 76*
Return on Investment *322*
Ristich, Nada *238*
rolling average *95*
Royal Bank of Canada *124*

S

signage *200, 205*
Simon Fraser University *183*
solicitation plan *261*
sponsorship *77, 127, 197, 198, 199, 200, 201, 202, 203, 204, 205, 206, 213, 259, 261, 262, 263, 267, 269, 273, 280, 284*
stakeholder *140, 142, 192, 232, 237, 268, 269*
statement of need *297*
stewardship *74, 77, 78, 99, 110, 111, 113, 115, 204, 230, 261, 267, 270, 274, 279, 282, 283, 285, 301*
Strong, Suzette *130*

T

T3010 *22, 296*
Tapestry Foundation *98, 99, 100*
tax credit *22*
telemarketing *77, 154, 155, 157, 159, 164, 165, 166*
The Fundraising Audit Handbook *4, 79, 114*
The Stratford Festival *248*
transparency *233, 308, 315*
Twitter *78, 80, 146, 211, 223, 244, 245, 246, 247, 249, 250, 251, 252*

U

underwriting *198*
unique selling proposition *219, 225*
University of British Columbia *107, 114, 179, 183, 218, 273*
University of Regina *199*
University of Toronto *19, 50, 132, 150, 151, 179, 273*
University of Waterloo *110*

V

valuation *200, 201, 203, 206, 213, 260, 264, 266, 269, 272*
Valuation *201, 266*
value proposition *24, 159*
VanDuzer, John *215, 227*
Vanier College *44, 50*
Van Sacker, Karen *43, 107*

Veneema, Pearl *72*
volunteer *35, 36, 37, 56, 58, 67, 103, 104, 105, 112, 115, 124, 129, 146, 189, 216, 225, 226, 232, 234, 240, 247, 249, 281, 302*

W

Weir, Leslie *23*
World Giving Index *178, 182*

Y

YouTube *110, 128, 219, 220, 221, 253*

Made in the USA
Charleston, SC
14 November 2014